The Battle for Jerusalem, June 5-7, 1967

AMONG LIONS

J. Robert Moskin

BALLANTINE BOOKS • NEW YORK

Library of Congress Catalog Card Number: 81-71671

ISBN 0-345-29673-7

This edition published by arrangement with Arbor House

Manufactured in the United States of America

First Ballantine Books Edition: May 1983

Fear no more the heat o' the sun,
Nor the furious winter's rages;
Thou thy worldly task hast done,
Home art gone, and ta'en thy wages.
Golden lads and girls all must,
As chimney-sweepers, come to dust.

SHAKESPEARE, *Cymbeline*

*My soul is among lions: and I lie
even among them that are set on fire,
even the sons of men, whose teeth
are spears and arrows, and their tongue
a sharp sword.*

PSALMS 57, VERSE 4

CONTENTS

Appendices

THE LIONS GATE

SHORTLY BEFORE TEN O'CLOCK ON WEDNESDAY MORNING, June 7, 1967, two half-tracks loaded with Israeli paratroopers smashed through the massive wooden doors of the Lions Gate into the walled Old City of Jerusalem. For nineteen years, the rulers of the Hashemite Kingdom of Jordan had allowed no Israeli into the Old City.

The half-tracks stopped at the foot of the Via Dolorosa, the steep alley up which, tradition says, Jesus walked to his Crucifixion. The battle-weary soldiers jumped down, moved swiftly leftward, returning scattered fire from Arabs on the rooftops. The paratroopers came to the Temple Mount.

On this flat hilltop, 1,893 years before, Titus' Roman legions had destroyed the Second Temple of the Jews. Now here, atop the Temple Mount, on the steps of the Muslims' Dome of the Rock, the colonel of the Israeli paratroop brigade and the captain of his lead company hugged each other. Neither could speak.

This book tells the story of the most important battle in urban warfare since the battle for Stalingrad in World War II. Stalingrad was a struggle that lasted months and was fought by hundreds of thousands of men and tanks; the battle for

Jerusalem, a generation later, took less than sixty hours and involved only a few thousand soldiers. But in both cases, the effects were enormous and lasting. Stalingrad made a Hitlerian Europe impossible. The battle for Jerusalem—in a city beloved by millions of Christians, Jews and Muslims—changed the face of the Middle East.

In 1948, the new-born State of Israel fought the neighboring Arab nations for Jerusalem. The Arabs won the heart of the city—the walled Old City and the Holy Places of Judaism, Christianity and Islam. The city was divided in two along an armed "Green Line." That battle in 1948—a defeat for the Israelis—has been glorified in many tellings. The short, bloody battle of 1967, when the Israelis won the city, has been almost totally neglected, although it set the stage for much of the turmoil in the Middle East ever since.

For thousands of years, peoples and faiths have clashed in Jerusalem. The city has been a revered symbol for those who follow each of the three monotheistic religions. The events of June 1967 form one more chapter, in our time, of that continuing struggle.

For three days, streets and homes became a battlefield. People fought or hid from battle in their own hometown. One Jordanian Bedouin brigade, supplemented by tanks, artillery and other infantry units, fought, in the end, against three brigades of Israeli reservists and was overwhelmed.

The battle can be quickly summarized. At 7:45 on Monday morning, June 5, 1967, Israel attacked Egypt, which was threatening its existence. By 11:20, Jordan began shelling Israeli Jerusalem; its civilians fled into basements and shelters. At 1:30, Jordan's army assaulted the Hill of Evil Counsel, the ridge south of the city on which stood the headquarters of the United Nations Truce Supervision Organization. The Israelis' Jerusalem Brigade counterattacked and drove the Jordanian army from the hill and from the nearby fortified Arab village of Sur Bahir.

Monday night, the Israelis' Harel Brigade of tanks and mechanized infantry crossed the Green Line into the hills north of the city and at dawn met and threw back the Patton tanks coming up from the Jordan Valley to defend Jordanian Jerusalem. At 2 A.M. Tuesday, the Israeli paratroop Fifty-fifth Brigade attacked across the border inside the city and fought the Jordanian infantry brigade just north of the walled Old City.

The fighting raged all through Tuesday. The paratroopers encircled the Old City on the north and the Jerusalem Brigade enveloped it on the south. That night, most of the Jordanian army withdrew from the city.

Wednesday morning, the paratroopers swept the now undefended ridge east of the city and penetrated the Old City through the Lions Gate, while the Jerusalem Brigade entered the Old City from the south. At 10 A.M., the paratroopers captured the Temple Mount, the ancient site of the Temple of the Jews and of the Muslims' sacred Dome of the Rock. By 2:30 P.M., organized fighting in the Old City was finished. After nineteen years of division, the city of Jerusalem was united. The Jews ruled the entire city for the first time in nearly two thousand years.

How the Israelis won the city and the Arabs lost it has never before been told definitively. This account is based on firsthand interviews with those who fought on both sides and many men and women of Jerusalem who survived the battle.

We live with the consequences of this unexpected Israeli conquest of Jerusalem and the West Bank. It led to the Yom Kippur War of 1973, the Camp David agreements of 1979 and the war in Lebanon in 1982. The ultimate fate of the Arabs of Palestine continues to be the subject of bitter and often violent dispute that threatens the peace of the world. All this recent history—stretching into our futures—hinges on the battle for Jerusalem in the spring of 1967. It is the story of this city and of this battle that is told here.

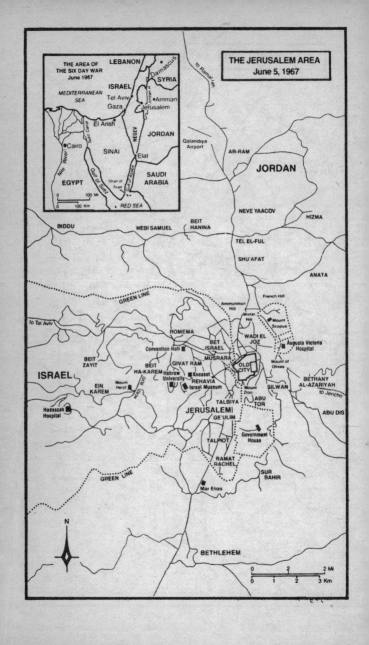

THE JERUSALEM AREA
June 5, 1967

THE AREA OF
THE SIX DAY WAR
June 1967

LEBANON

SYRIA
Damascus

ISRAEL

MEDITERRANEAN
SEA

Tel Aviv

Gaza

Jerusalem

Amman

El Arish

JORDAN

NEGEV

SINAI

EGYPT

Cairo

Nile River

Suez Canal

Gulf of Suez

Elat

Strait of Tiran

Gulf of Aqaba

SAUDI
ARABIA

RED SEA

0   100 Ml
0   100 Km

to Ramallah

Qalandiya
Airport

AR-RAM

JORDAN

NEVE YAACOV

HIZMA

BIDDU

NEBI SAMUEL

BEIT
HANINA

TEL EL-FUL

SHU'AFAT

ANATA

GREEN LINE

Ammunition
Hill

French Hill

Mivtar
Hill

Mount
Scopus

to Tel Aviv

ROMEMA

Convention Hall

BET
ISRAEL

MUSRARA

WADI EL
JOZ

Augusta Victoria
Hospital

BEIT
ZAYIT

BEIT
HA-KAREM

GIVAT RAM

Hebrew
University

Knesset

Israel Museum

REHAVIA

OLD
CITY

Mount of
Olives

ISRAEL

EIN
KAREM

Mount
Herzl

Herzl Blvd.

TALBIYA

Mount
Zion

SILWAN

BETHANY
AL-AZARIYAH

to Jericho

ABU DIS

Hadassah
Hospital

JERUSALEM

GE'ULIM

ABU
TOR

Government
House

TALPIOT

RAMAT
RACHEL

SUR
BAHIR

GREEN LINE

Mar Elias

N

BETHLEHEM

0   2 Mi
0   1   2   3 Km

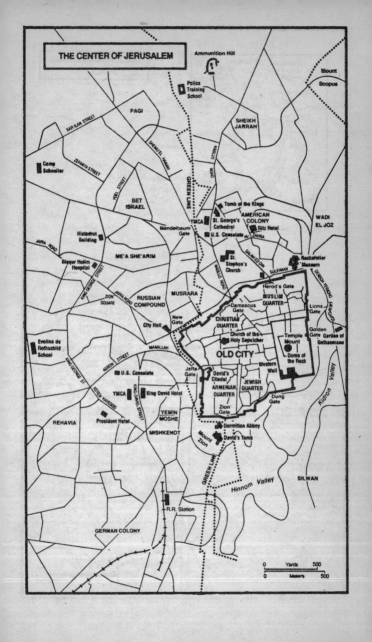

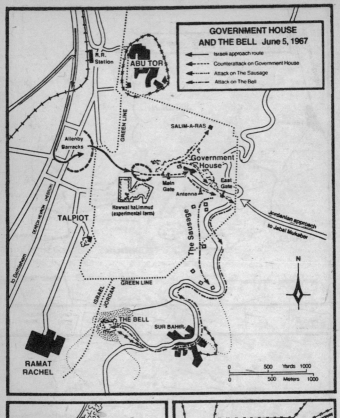

GOVERNMENT HOUSE AND THE BELL June 5, 1967

- ⬅ Israeli approach route
- ⬅ Counterattack on Government House
- ⬅ Attack on The Sausage
- ⬅ Attack on The Bell

R.R. Station

ABU TOR

GREEN LINE

SALIM-A-RAS

Allenby Barracks

Government House

Main Gate

East Gate

Antenna

Hawwat haLimmud (experimental farm)

TALPIOT

The Sausage

Jordanian approach to Jabal Mukaber

DERECH HEVRON (HEBRON)

to Bethlehem

GREEN LINE

ISRAEL
JORDAN

THE BELL

SUR BAHIR

N

RAMAT RACHEL

| 0 | 500 | Yards | 1000 |
| 0 | 500 | Meters | 1000 |

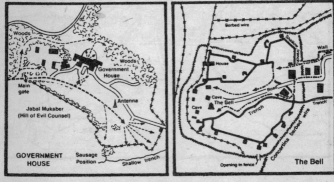

Woods

Woods

Government House

Main gate

Antenna

Jabal Mukaber (Hill of Evil Counsel)

Sausage Position

Shallow trench

GOVERNMENT HOUSE

Barbed wire

House

Shallow trench

Wall

Cave

The Bell

Road

Cave

Trench

Trench

Concertina barbed wire

Opening in fence

The Bell

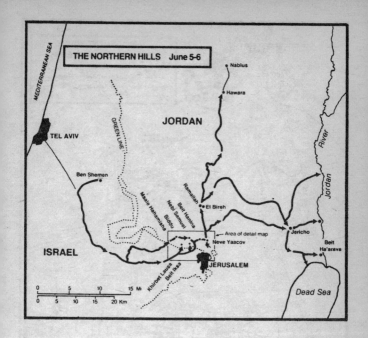

THE NORTHERN HILLS   June 5-6

MEDITERRANEAN SEA

TEL AVIV

Ben Shemen

GREEN LINE

JORDAN

Nablus

Hawara

Ramallah

El Bireh

Maale Hahamisha
Beit Hanina
Nebi Samuel
Biddu

Neve Yaacov

Area of detail map

Jericho

Jordan River

Beit Ha'arava

ISRAEL

Khirbet Lausa
Beit Iksa

JERUSALEM

Dead Sea

| 0 | 5 | 10 | 15 Mi |
| 0 | 5 | 10 | 15 | 20 Km |

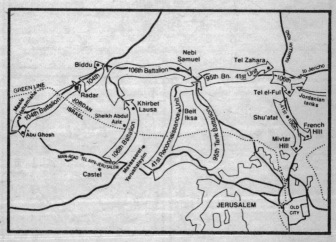

Biddu

Nebi Samuel

Tel Zahara

to Jericho

106th Battalion

95th Bn.

41st Unit

106th

RAMALLAH ROAD

104th

GREEN LINE

Radar

Khirbet Lausa

Tel el-Ful

Jordanian tanks

Maale Hahamisha

104th Battalion

JORDAN

Sheikh Abdul Aziz

Beit Iksa

41st Reconnaissance Unit

Shu'afat

41ST

106th

ISRAEL

95th Tank Battalion

French Hill

Abu Ghosh

106th Battalion

Mivtar Hill

MAIN ROAD

TEL AVIV–JERUSALEM

Motza
Mevasseret
Yerushalayim

Castel

JERUSALEM

OLD CITY

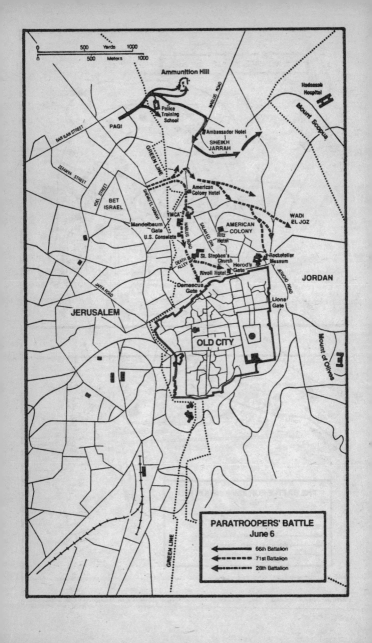

PARATROOPERS' BATTLE
June 6

← 66th Battalion
←- 71st Battalion
←·- 28th Battalion

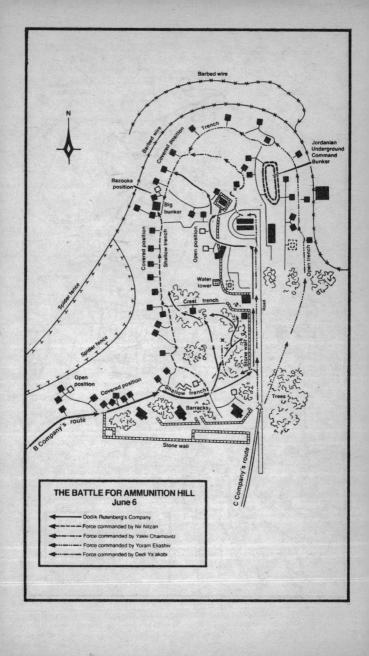

THE BATTLE FOR AMMUNITION HILL
June 6

Dodik Rutenberg's Company
Force commanded by Nir Nitzan
Force commanded by Yakki Chaimovitz
Force commanded by Yoram Eliashiv
Force commanded by Dedi Ya'akobi

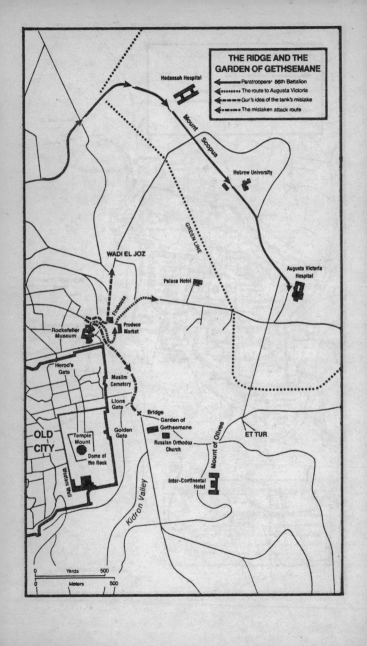

THE RIDGE AND THE
GARDEN OF GETHSEMANE

Paratroopers' 66th Battalion
The route to Augusta Victoria
Gur's idea of the tank's mistake
The mistaken attack route

Hadassah Hospital

Mount Scopus

Hebrew University

GREEN LINE

WADI EL JOZ

Palace Hotel

Augusta Victoria
Hospital

Rockefeller
Museum

Firehouse

Produce
Market

Herod's Gate

Muslim
Cemetery

Lions
Gate

Bridge

Garden of
Gethsemane

ET TUR

OLD
CITY

Temple
Mount

Golden
Gate

Russian Orthodox
Church

Mount of Olives

Dome of
the Rock

Inter-Continental
Hotel

Western Wall

Kidron Valley

0   Yards   500
0   Meters   500

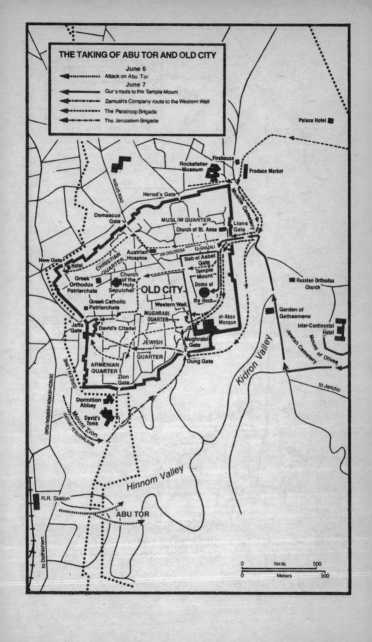

THE TAKING OF ABU TOR AND OLD CITY

June 6
→ Attack on Abu Tor

June 7
→ Gur's route to the Temple Mount
→ Zamush's Company route to the Western Wall
→ The Paratroop Brigade
→ The Jerusalem Brigade

Palace Hotel

Rockefeller Museum
Firehouse
Produce Market

Herod's Gate

Damascus Gate

MUSLIM QUARTER
Church of St. Anne
Lions Gate

New Gate

Austrian Hospice
VIA DOLOROSA
EL-GHAZALI
Bab el Asbat Gate

Hotel
CHRISTIAN QUARTER
Greek Orthodox Patriarchate
Church of the Holy Sepulcher
OLD CITY
Temple Mount
Dome of the Rock

Russian Orthodox Church

Greek Catholic Patriarchate
MUGHRABI QUARTER
Western Wall
al-Aksa Mosque

Garden of Gethsemane

Jaffa Gate
David's Citadel
JEWISH QUARTER
Mughrabi Gate

Inter-Continental Hotel

ARMENIAN QUARTER
Zion Gate
Dung Gate

Kidron Valley
Jewish Cemetery
Mount of Olives

to Jericho

Dormition Abbey
David's Tomb
Mount Zion

Hinnom Valley

R.R. Station

ABU TOR

to Bethlehem

| 0 | Yards | 500 |
| 0 | Meters | 500 |

CHRONOLOGY OF THE BATTLE FOR JERUSALEM

Monday—June 5, 1967

7:45 A.M.	Israeli air attack on Egyptian Air Force
11:00	Jordan officially enters war against Israel
11:20	Jordan begins shelling Israeli Jerusalem
1:30 P.M.	Jordan attacks Hill of Evil Counsel
3:05	Israel gives order to counterattack Government House compound
3:52	Jerusalem Brigade blows open door of Government House
4:30	Jerusalem Brigade seizes The Sausage position
5:00	Harel Brigade starts attack across the Green Line
6:30	Jerusalem Brigade assaults Sur Bahir
Evening	Israeli Cabinet decides to attack Jordanian Jerusalem

Tuesday—June 6, 1967

2:00 A.M.	Paratroop brigade crosses the Green Line in Jerusalem
6:00	Harel Brigade spearhead meets Jordanian tanks
6:55	66th Battalion paratroopers conquer Ammunition Hill
3:00 P.M.	Jerusalem Brigade attacks Abu Tor
7:30	Paratroop brigade starts abortive attack on Augusta Victoria
Evening	Israeli Cabinet decides to conquer the Old City
Night	Jordanian army withdraws from Jerusalem

Wednesday—June 7, 1967

5:00 A.M.	Israeli Cabinet agrees on plan to attack the Old City
7:30	Jerusalem Brigade enters Dung Gate of the Old City
8:30	Paratroop brigade attacks the Ridge
9:45	Paratroop brigade enters Lions Gate of the Old City
10:00	Paratroop brigade announces capture of Temple Mount
2:30 P.M.	Last organized fight in the Old City

GROUND FORCES IN THE BATTLE FOR JERUSALEM

Israeli

16th (Jerusalem) Infantry Brigade (Amitai)
62nd Battalion (first line) (Rothschild)
68th Battalion (first line) (Opher)
161st Battalion (first line) (Driezin)
163rd Battalion (first line) (Peikas)
90th Reconnaissance Company (Langotsky)

10th (Harel) Mechanized Brigade (Ben-Ari)
95th Tank Battalion (Dahav)
104th Armored Battalion (Ben-David)
106th Armored Battalion (Gal)
41st Reconnaissance Company (Eshkol)
110-mm Mortars Attached (Arad)

55th (Paratroopers) Brigade (Gur)
28th Battalion (Fradkin)
66th Battalion (Yaffe)
71st Battalion (Eilam)
Reconnaissance Unit Attached (Kapusta)

Jordanian

4th (King Talal) Infantry Brigade (Hazzáa)
2nd (Hussein) Battalion (Kreishan)
4th Battalion
8th Battalion

9th Field Artillery Regiment (Salah)
First Battery (Fayyadh)
Second Battery (Jawdat)
Third Battery (Hafez)

Imam Ali Infantry Brigade (Shihadeh)
Ussamah Bin Zeid Battalion (Badi Awad)

60th Armored Brigade (Bin Shaker)
5th Tank Battalion (Khlaif Awad)

Part I

THE DECISION

— Chapter 1 —

THE DREAMS OF MEN

WHAT HAPPENED IN THE CITY OF JERUSALEM BETWEEN MONDay and Wednesday, June 5–7, 1967, is already part of the mythic story of mankind. Its meaning is in the dreams and madness of men.

What else explains the agonized decision-making, the fumbling warfare, the terror and the courage of the human beings who tried to survive in the gun-sprayed city or killed the enemy—their neighbors? What else explains the thousand corpses lying in the hospital morgues or in the streets or buried hurriedly in green gardens?

This is the story of the battle for the holy city of Jerusalem in the spring of 1967 and of the people who fought and lived and died in it.

This story takes place in the nexus of the Western world. Jerusalem is the hallowed womb of religions, the splendrous golden hilltop city where for millennia men and women have searched for faith in God and reason for life. Here they have worked out the ethical rules by which they could live together—and have so often killed each other.

For at least three thousand years, this has been a holy city. It is a quiet hilltown intensely loved by and sacred to millions of Christians, Jews and Muslims. What happened here, in mysterious ways, arouses the entire Western world.

This unplanned battle took sixty hours. In those hours the world was changed; and then the huddled, terrified residents of the city leapt out of their shelters with a spasm of joy; or they lay dead or mutilated by forces that had exploded out of thousands of years of human history.

When the battle began, Jerusalem had been divided between Israel and Jordan for nineteen years—ripped through its middle by barbed wire, minefields and concrete barriers. No Berlin Wall shut off one side from the other; the border here was alive. Enemies lived within sight of each other, shouted at each other, shot each other.

Jerusalem was like an egg; with the golden-walled Old City at its core and surrounded by the newer quarters, Arab to the northeast and Jewish to the west. Right through the city ran the Green Line. East of this line was Jordan—the Old City and the Arab neighborhoods and still farther east of the Old City a protective high ridge from Mount Scopus to the Mount of Olives. West of the Green Line was the Jewish city that Israel had made its capital.

Before the battle, the Israelis felt their lives were at risk, threatened by the mobilized armies of Egypt. Israel urged Jordan to stay out of the fight; Jordan tried to take advantage of what it perceived to be Israel's weakness. Jordan's soldiers fought bravely; but in the end, Jordan lost her part of the city and the West Bank of the Jordan River. The Israelis won a triumph such as they had never known before. When the battle was finished, Jerusalem was reunited and at peace—and suddenly the Middle East's most emotional problem.

Sometimes in history, unexpected events make unpremeditated battle inevitable. This is one of those rare moments.

History is made up of dreams and legends and visions. They constitute the memory of man and the crucible in which he stirs his aspirations. When men's dreams conflict, they can cause hatred and violence. Men kill other men for the sake of ideas and memories.

Why repeatedly through history have men fought and died for Jerusalem—a city that has no particular material consequence, no natural resources, that produces none of the products and wealth of industrialized society, that offers neither entry nor passage to the markets of the modern world?

For its beauty perhaps, but for its spiritual meaning certainly. Enormous numbers of people find solace in Jerusalem. And still it has become the pit in which men have chosen to do battle since before history was written. In the spring of 1967, Jerusalem once more became the arena of man's compulsion to kill his fellow man for the sake of legends, dreams and visions.

Jews have conquered Jerusalem four times: David about

1000 B.C., the Maccabees in 152 B.C., and Bar Kochba in A.D. 132. The fourth time was in June 1967. It is too soon to know whose name will be attached to this latest conquest—or to know how long it will last. Jerusalem is the heart of the tiny keystone of the globe that clamps together three continents—a land bridge too important and strategic to insure permanency.

Repeatedly, momentous events have happened here. This is the legendary site of Abraham's interrupted sacrifice of his son Isaac. The City of David. The place of Calvary and Resurrection. The Rock from which, tradition says, Muhammad rose on his night journey. The goal of the Crusaders.

The fact that all three great monotheistic religions have roots in Jerusalem cannot be accidental. This beautiful place in the mystical Judean hills is conducive to meditation and inspires wonder at the meaning of life. One of the world's oldest cities, Jerusalem sits at the crossroads of ancient trade routes through the hills that form the bony spine between the Mediterranean coastal plain and the Jordan River Valley. Signs of human habitation have been found dating back at least four thousand years. As the archaeologists dig down, they expose to light layer upon layer of the civilizations that have swept over this city. The diggers have uncovered relics of the City of David, the First Temple that Solomon built on the threshing floor of Arauna and where he installed the Ark of the Lord, the Second Temple of 515 B.C., the Babylonians, Assyrians, Persians, the Herodian constructions of the time of Jesus, the remains of the Tenth Roman Legion, the Roman city of Aelia Capitolina, the Byzantines, the Muslims, the Crusaders, the Mamelukes, Sultan Suleiman the Magnificent who built the present Old City walls, the Turks, British and Jordanians. The city has survived them all. Through the ages it has attracted men like moths to some unexplainable light.

Jerusalem's history over the last millennium is simply told. The Muslims conquered the city in A.D. 638 and ruled it for more than a thousand years, except for the interruption when the Crusaders seized it in 1099. By one of the exquisite coincidences of history, the Crusaders marched on Jerusalem on Monday, June 6, and about noon on June 7 first sighted the Holy City from the peak of Nebi Samuel, which Muslims believe to be the site of the tomb of the prophet Samuel. The climax of this book takes place 868 years later—to the exact day.

The Crusader force of more than 1,200 knights and 12,000 foot soldiers successfully attacked the city's northern wall near Herod's Gate on the night of July 13–14. They killed tens of thousands of Muslims and burned to death all the Jews in their central synagogue.

Christian rule lasted less than a century. On October 2, 1187, the Muslims drove the Crusaders from the city. The Ayyubid Sultan Saladin—who was a Kurd and not an Arab—ruled the Muslim world from the Nile to Mesopotamia. He was humane toward non-Muslims and made a treaty with King Richard the Lion-Hearted of England in 1192 to allow pilgrims to visit the Holy Places freely.

The Crusaders regained sovereignty over the city briefly by treaty in 1229, but fifteen years later they allied themselves with Syria in a war against Egypt and were slaughtered by Egyptian mercenaries. For the next 673 years, Jerusalem was ruled by Muslims: the Syrian-based Ayyubids until 1260 and the Egyptian-based Mamelukes until 1517. After that it was a provincial town of the Ottoman Empire, although Jews made up a majority of its population from about 1880.[1]

Until the 1860s, Jerusalem, standing on two hills, was totally encased in stone walls two and a half miles around and enclosing an area one kilometer square. On every side but the north the walled city was also protected by steep ravines—the Valley of Hinnom or Gehenna and the Valley of Kidron or Jehoshaphat. The walls were pierced by seven gates; one, the Golden Gate, had been sealed up for three centuries, and an eighth (New Gate) was cut through near the northwest corner in 1887.

In the 1860s, inside the city walls lived some eighteen thousand people, half of whom were Jews. The city—divided into quarters for each major group: Muslim, Jewish, Armenian and Christian—was crowded and poor; the streets, narrow and winding. It was to this teeming, neglected hilltown—and to the swamps and deserts of Palestine—that Jews of Eastern Europe came in the second half of the nineteenth century to escape pogroms and persecution.

Almost no one lived outside the walls. In 1857, Sir Moses Montefiore of London built a windmill just west of the city;

and in 1860 with the help of Judah Touro of New Orleans, he built Mishkenot Sha'ananim to encourage Jews inside the walls to dare to live outside. During the next years, other suburbs grew outside the walls and the city expanded.

During World War I, the British General Edmund Allenby invaded Jerusalem on Sunday, December 9, 1917. Mayor Hussein Effendi al-Husseini, carrying a torn white sheet from the American Colony Hospital, surrendered the city. Mrs. Bertha Spafford Vester of the American Colony wrote, "A Christian army entered the Holy City for the first time in nearly a thousand years."

The British fought the Turks on Mount Scopus and north of the city as far as the village of Shu'afat. On December 11, General Allenby entered the Jaffa Gate on foot as a pilgrim; and a proclamation was read on the steps of the Citadel at the Tower of David in the Old City announcing that the Holy Places would be protected. In the picture made at the time, the Chief Rabbi of Jerusalem stood next to the Mufti. It was still possible. Mrs. Vester wrote joyously, "Palestine had a so-called Christian government for the first time since the Crusaders were driven out by Saladin. . . . We thought then we were witnessing the triumph of the last crusade. A Christian nation had conquered Palestine!"[2]

For three decades, the British ruled Jerusalem—after July 24, 1922, under a League of Nations Mandate. The international deliberations over the formation of the Mandate at San Remo, Italy, in April 1920—plus increased Jewish immigration—aroused the fury of Arab militants and ignited riots in Jerusalem. In the Old City, shops were looted and people killed. Jewish and Arab nationalism sparked repeated violence.

Jewish nationalism—Zionism—was based on a desire spurred by some Jewish leaders in Europe to bring together the Jews of the Diaspora—scattered abroad since the destruction of the Second Temple. Paradoxically, Zionism's purpose was both to find a refuge against the persecution and discrimination of many Christian and Muslim nations in which they lived and also to prevent the assimilation of Jews into the cultural and religious life of nations that did welcome them and grant them political emancipation.

After World War I, Arab nationalism was fanned by the occupation of much of the Arab world by the European Christian powers that replaced the Ottoman Empire, now deceased. With the influx into Palestine of Jews fleeing from Hitler, the threat of Jewish nationalism and Nazi propaganda heightened Arab nationalistic sentiments and encouraged efforts at unity among disparate Arab peoples and leaders. In the post-World War II disintegration of Western European colonialism, Arab nationalism sprang into full force.

The British in Palestine had also to deal with the disputatious Christian denominations jealous of their rights and privileges in the various Holy Places. The British authorities adopted the Status Quo of 1852, the arrangement by which the Ottoman Empire had regulated the quarreling Christians.[3]

World War II cracked European colonialism; and under the attacks of both Jewish and Arab antagonists and terrorists, the British, exhausted by World War II and the constant warring in Mandatory Palestine, announced in May 1947 that they were leaving.

The Jerusalem from which the British withdrew had grown to 165,000 people, of whom 100,000 were Jews, 40,000 Muslims and 25,000 Christians. Only 2,000 of the Jews remained in the Jewish Quarter inside the walls. The Jewish center of population had spread westward, and the expanding Arab population had stretched out to the north and south. The walled Old City had diminished in demographic and commercial importance; but it remained the city's spiritual and religious heart.

The United Nations General Assembly in New York on November 29, 1947, voted 33 to 13 to divide Palestine from the Mediterranean to the Jordan River between Jews and Arabs and declare Jerusalem a *corpus separatum*, a separate, internationalized city.

But that was not to be. The day after the UN adopted the resolution of partition, fighting began. The Arabs rejected partition. Jews called it the War of Independence; Christians, the "war against the partition of Palestine."[4] Jews and Arabs fought for Jerusalem, and by February 1948 the Arabs virtually cut off the city from the Jewish centers of strength on the coastal plain. The British marched out, ending their mandate at midnight on May 15, 1948; and the State of Israel was established.

Within hours, the armies of six Arab nations attacked Israel. The British-led Arab Legion of Transjordan, Egyptian forces and the local Palestinian Arabs fought Jerusalem's Jews. In a prolonged and bloody battle, neither side could conquer all of the city. Between them was finally drawn the "Green Line." The Jordanians held the Old City within the walls. The city was cut in halves, brutally sliced through streets and buildings. To divide a living city is as hideous as bisecting any living thing.

This division of Jerusalem was the result not so much of religious antagonisms as of nationalistic rivalries. The Jerusalem of David and Jesus and, in a sense, Muhammad could not be divided. It was unified by history and by faith. But the Jerusalem of Zionism and Arab nationalism was divided by force and was to be reunited by force.

In 1948, 1,700 Jewish residents were forced out of the Jewish Quarter of the Old City. Jews were shut outside the Old City gates, tantalizingly close to the Temple Mount's Western Wall, the object of their prayers around the world for nearly two millennia. The Israelis made the western sector of Jerusalem their political capital in 1950, although virtually none of the world recognized it as such. Most nations regarded the United Nations' *corpus separatum* as the city's last legal definition.

The Old City and the eastern sectors of Jerusalem became part of the British-created Hashemite Kingdom of Jordan. The Holy Places of Jerusalem, despite Paragraph 8 of the 1949 Armistice Agreement between Israel and Jordan, were closed to all Jews and to Muslim citizens of Israel. Some Christians in Israel were permitted to pass through the Mandelbaum Gate and visit the Church of the Holy Sepulcher, which had been consecrated in A.D. 335, and the other Holy Places in East Jerusalem at Christmas; and foreign Christians were permitted on Easter.[5]

The population of Jewish Jerusalem grew from 84,000 in November 1948 to 197,000 in 1967.[6] By the latter date, the overwhelming majority were families who orginated in Africa and Asia—the Arab world. Only a quarter were immigrants from Europe and America.

Their city was no longer a crossroads but a cul-de-sac surrounded on three sides by Jordan. Roads now ended in Jerusalem. And the city was isolated in other ways, being only marginal to the economy of the rest of Israel. It was a university city, a religious center, a governmental and bureaucratic city.

9

It had little industry, and many young people left for job opportunities in Tel Aviv. In those days, says one commentator, "Jerusalem had the quality of a tranquil, introverted provincial city."[7]

On the other side of the barbed wire, East Jerusalem prospered even less. It had 67,000 people, of whom 25,000 lived inside the Old City. Jordan's capital remained Amman, as it had since 1923, in the hills across the Jordan Valley. Amman's population increased from 61,000 in 1948 to 311,000 in 1967. Palestinian Arabs, and especially East Jerusalemites, felt a growing dissatisfaction with the Jordanian policy of building up Amman and neglecting Jerusalem.

The Jordanization of Jerusalem increased after the murder of King Abdallah of Jordan by a Palestinian Arab, reportedly hired by relatives of the former Grand Mufti of Jerusalem. Abdallah, who might have signed an agreement with Israel, was killed as he entered the al-Aksa Mosque on the Temple Mount on Friday, July 20, 1951, to pray. The assassin also fired at the sixteen-year-old Prince Hussein standing by his grandfather's side.[8]

When young Hussein ibn Talal became king in May 1953, the more radical Palestinian Arabs, who had been suppressed by Abdallah, attacked the Jordanian government's policies, especially its close ties with the British. Only after bloody riots and several coups was the young king able to gain the upper hand in 1957. These events discouraged farther any Hashemite interest in developing Jerusalem. Demonstrations broke out in the city and the army killed dozens of civilians.

The troubled division of Jerusalem lasted for nineteen years. Then in sixty embattled hours the Israeli army conquered the Arab half of the city and drove the Jordanian army back across the narrow, muddy Jordan River. The struggle for Jerusalem was returned to the diplomats, the politicians, the clergy and the terrorists.

The Israelis seized the Arab sector of the city because the Jordanians gave them the opportunity. The Israeli government, preparing to meet the threat from Egypt, tried to avoid a second-front battle against Jordan. If the Jordanians had not attacked, the Old City and the West Bank might still be in Jordanian hands today.

Only a twist of fortune, or God or Allah, the religious might say, provoked the Jordanians to attack and lose the city. It was certainly true that Israelis had dreams and contingency plans to regain the eastern half of the city and the revered Western Wall of the Temple enclosure. But few Jews expected to see Jerusalem reunited in their lifetime; and when the moment came, they were unready and unsure. Not even King Hussein claims that the Israelis lured the Jordanians to make the first move—and so drastically change history.

Whatever will be Jerusalem's future, the Israeli conquest was an historic moment—the first time in more than eighteen hundred years that the Jews ruled all of the City of Jerusalem and its ancient walled Old City. In the reunited city, all those who believed in its sanctity were free to worship at the places they regarded as holy. And Jersualem reunited became a focal point of danger for the Middle East and the world.

— Chapter 2 —

"WE'LL HAVE TO TAKE IT BACK"

U.S. AMBASSADOR WALWORTH BARBOUR SAT IN THE vaulted lobby of Jerusalem's King David Hotel and watched the military parade on television. A few of the hotel staff watched with him. Virtually all the guests had gone to see the excitement firsthand. The diplomatic corps was boycotting the parade; but Ambassador Barbour, heavy-set and popular, did show up at the president of Israel's reception.

It was Monday, May 15, 1967—precisely three weeks before the Six Day War—and the Jewish State was celebrating its nineteenth Independence Day. Only once in every nineteen years does the Gregorian calendar match the Hebrew calendar and does Israeli Independence Day—the 5th of Iyar—fall on May 15. This was the first time they coincided since the British Mandate ended and the State was established.

It was also the first time in half a dozen years that the Independence Day Parade was held in Jerusalem. The *Jerusalem Post* editorialized: "The parade is being held again, in part so that there shall be no shadow of misunderstanding—Jerusalem is Israel."[1]

That morning, the 90-piece Israel Defense Forces band blared into the jammed 18,000-seat Hebrew University stadium. Tens of thousands of Israelis lined the four-mile route as sixteen hundred men and women marched with light weapons, 81-mm mortars and antiaircraft guns. Because of the 1949 Armistice Agreement, there were no tanks, planes or heavy weapons. The Jordanians had protested the parade, but many Israelis ridiculed it as puny and feared it would be taken as a symbol of weakness.

The *New York Times* called it "a modest parade."[2] Former Prime Minister David Ben-Gurion stayed away because he had wanted a stronger show of force.

In the stadium's reviewing stand stood President Zalman Shazar, Prime Minister Levi Eshkol and Chief of Staff Yitzhak Rabin. An aide whispered to Rabin that Egyptian forces had been spotted marching through Cairo on their way to the Sinai Peninsula. Rabin repeated the message into Prime Minister Eshkol's ear.[3]

For many weeks, trouble had been brewing in the north. The Syrians claimed Israeli tractors were trying to cultivate disputed land between the two countries and shelled the tractors from the Golan Heights. The Israelis claimed the Syrians were bombarding their settlements, harassing fishermen and farmers near the border and sending over armed raiders. They also accused the Syrians of trying to control the headwaters of the vital Jordan River. Both sides retaliated. On April 7, Israeli planes shot down seven Syrian MIGs.

"That was, I believe, the beginning of the war," says F. T. Liu, the principal political advisor to the United Nations Truce Supervision Organization based in Jerusalem. Liu carried the main burden of the UN's effort to prevent an outbreak of war between Israel and Syria.

The Soviet Union stirred the pot by telling an Egyptian parliamentary delegation headed by Anwar el-Sadat that Israel intended to attack Syria.[4] President Gamal Abdel Nasser of Egypt decided he had to react to the Soviet reports that the Israelis were massing troops on the Syrian border and to the Syrians' nervous calls for help. Nasser was trying to orchestrate pan-Arab nationalism and coordinate Arab action against Israel and her Western supporters.

Anwar al-Khatib, then the forty-eight-year-old Jordanian Governor of Jerusalem, says: "Nasser's reaction was that he would come to the help of Syria if Syria was exposed to attack. So he started massing troops in the Sinai. Nasser was under the mistaken illusion that there was a threat against Syria. He was certain he was not ready for a fight—just for a show of strength.

"After the war I had a meeting with Prime Minister Levi Eshkol and he told me the following story: One night after midnight, he was awakened by the Soviet ambassador [Dimitri Chuvakhin], who delivered a message from Moscow that the Israelis should not attack Syria and should withdraw their forces from the Syrian borders. Eshkol replied to the ambassador: 'I am ready to go with you in my pajamas and robe to the borders, and we will not find a single tank there.'

"I think the story of the massing forces at Syria was invented to push Nasser into this trap. The Russians had their part in it. Nasser said frankly that he was trapped."

Jordan did its bit to keep on the pressure by boycotting three major American companies for trading with Israel: Ford, Coca-Cola and the Radio Corporation of America.[5]

On May 15, Israeli attention swiveled nervously from north to south. Nasser started moving one hundred thousand troops across the Suez Canal into the Sinai desert and to Sharm el-Sheikh at the entrance to the Gulf of Aqaba. He announced that he would attack Israel if it tried to topple the Syrian regime in Damascus.

That evening, while the Egyptian forces advanced, in Jerusalem's Convention Hall a huge noisy crowd gathered for the annual song festival sponsored by Kol Yisrael, the national broadcasting system. This year, at the request of Jerusalem's Mayor Teddy Kollek, Kol Yisrael had asked Naomi Shemer, a successful young songwriter, to compose a song about Jerusalem.

Naomi Shemer, an articulate, dark-haired poet in song, had been born in Kibbutz Kinneret on the Sea of Galilee. Her family had come from Vilna, Lithuania, which was a center of Talmudic learning and known as the Jerusalem of the North. Shemer found it difficult to compose a song for Jerusalem. Songs had been written about the holy city ever since the time of David and the Psalms—but during the past nineteen years while the city was divided and the Old City was in Jordanian hands, nothing had been written. Shemer says, "We are experts at sweeping things under the carpet. It was a kind of taboo."

One night Shemer's song was born out of a Talmudic legend she knew from childhood: Rabbi Akiba and his wife Rachel were very poor and lived in a barn. Once he was brushing the straw out of her hair and promised Rachel that someday he would buy her a "Jerusalem of gold"—a piece of jewelry in a shape symbolizing the city. Shemer called her song "Jerusalem of Gold."

To sing it at the festival, Shemer chose an unknown girl soldier, Shuli Nathan. The slim nineteen-year-old girl stood alone on the stage in a white dress and played her guitar and sang. The effect was electric. Everyone joined the last refrain. "Jerusalem of Gold" swept across Israel and became the folk song of this moment of crisis and of the city.

Three days later, on Thursday, May 18, Nasser formally requested U Thant, the Secretary General of the United Nations, to remove the 3,400-man United Nations Emergency Force (UNEF) that since 1956 had been posted on Egyptian territory, including Sharm el-Sheikh and the Gaza Strip. U Thant immediately complied.

In Amman, Jordanian Premier Saad Juma, supporting Egypt's request for the UNEF's withdrawal, announced that Jordan was "on the side of its sisterly Arab states against the common danger."[6]

On Friday at 4 P.M., two hundred UNEF soldiers in blue berets—men from Sweden, Canada and India—lowered the UN flag at their station in the Gaza Strip. A turbaned Indian band played bagpipes as the flag came down. The Palestine Liberation Organization took over Checkpoint King's Gate and the desolate border post. The Arab farmers working the nearby fields did not raise their heads to watch the fanfare.

Late that night, thousands of Israeli reservists at home on the Sabbath received mobilization messages. Both Egypt and Israel called up their reserves. Observing the activity across the Green Line in Israeli Jerusalem, Governor al-Khatib felt that battle was imminent.

Brig. Gen. Atta Ali Hazzáa, who commanded the Fourth or King Talal Infantry Brigade in Jordanian Jerusalem, says, "When Nasser pulled the UN troops from Sinai, the Middle East was charged with the expectation of war. War was on the horizon." Each of Brig. Gen. Hazzáa's three battalions was given a fourth infantry company of recruits; and antitank platoons, armed with 106-mm antitank guns, were strengthened by an extra squad.

On Monday, May 22, Jordan's chief of staff, Maj. Gen. Amer Khammash, flew to Cairo; he found the United Arab

15

Command totally impotent. That same day, while U Thant was hurrying to Cairo to try to hold the fragile peace, Nasser announced that he had closed to Israeli shipping the four-mile-wide Strait of Tiran linking the Gulf of Aqaba to the northern end of the Red Sea. Israel had won the right of passage there as a result of the 1956 Sinai campaign. Now Nasser's blockade would cut Israel's single lifeline to the east through its new port of Elat at the top of the Gulf of Aqaba.

The Cairo newspaper *Al Ahram* quoted Nasser: "The Israeli flag will not pass through the Gulf of Aqaba, and our sovereignty over the gulf entrance is not negotiable. If Israel wants to threaten us with war, they are welcome,"[7] The UN's F. T. Liu felt, "The point of no return had been reached."

Israeli Prime Minister Eshkol called the blockade an act of war. He told journalist Michael Elkins: "We are going to war." But, he said, he could not fight a war with a divided Cabinet and an uncertain country. The National Religious Party, the left-wing Mapam Party and powerful members of the Labor Party opposed any military reaction. Israel needed time to mobilize and prepare.

War was exactly two weeks away.

"The crucial point came when Nasser declared he had closed the Strait of Tiran," says Governor al-Khatib. "When this occurred, I became sure that war was inevitable. The Israelis would not allow the straits to be closed like this. As a matter of fact, they were not closed; it was a bluff. In Jerusalem, there was tension. I invited the nine Arab consuls in Jerusalem to my office and told them that war is coming very soon."

But the government in Amman was not planning to go to war. Jordan expelled the Syrian ambassador, severed diplomatic relations and ordered the Syrian embassy in Amman and the consulate in the Old City of Jerusalem closed.

Certainly, the sixty-five thousand people of Jordanian Jerusalem were not prepared for war. Governor al-Khatib, who was responsible for the whole Jerusalem area including Bethlehem and Jericho, began to organize food and water supplies and convert some basements into makeshift shelters.

In the imposing square-towered Augusta Victoria Hospital atop the long ridge east of the Old City, Dr. George Farah, the hospital's medical director, prepared for the possibility of war. With officials of the United Nations Relief and Works Administration (UNRWA), it was decided that the Austrian Hospice near the Fourth Station of the Cross in the Old City would be the collecting point for casualties inside the walls and Augusta Victoria, outside.

German Kaiser Wilhelm II had come to Jerusalem in 1898 and built the Augusta Victoria for German Protestant pilgrims and the Abbey of the Dormition on Mount Zion for German Catholics. After World War I, Augusta Victoria became the British headquarters from 1920 to 1927; and it was here in 1921 that the British colonial secretary, Winston Churchill, met with Abdallah, Hussein's grandfather, and created the Arab State of Transjordan, east of the Jordan River.[8]

Augusta Victoria was first used as a hospital by the British when they were fighting at El Alamein in World War II. After the war, Count Folke Bernadotte turned it into an International Red Cross hospital for Palestinian Arab refugees. When UNRWA was born, the Lutheran World Federation ran the hospital and UNRWA supported it. Members of King Hussein's family came there for treatment. After 1948, the hospital was no more than a hundred yards from the Israelis' isolated enclave on Mount Scopus.

Dr. Farah, the medical director, was a sixty-one-year-old Greek Orthodox, born in the Old City. His ancestors had lived in Jerusalem for at least 950 years. He was a member of the city government of Jordanian Jerusalem and had been the director of the 135-bed Augusta Victoria for twelve years.

Among the ordinary citizens of Jordanian Jerusalem, tension grew. Propaganda sought to convince them that Israel was weak and vulnerable and at the same time bellicose and menacing, but the Arabs in Jerusalem knew they were living on an exposed and vulnerable border. Many resented Jordan's prohibition against bearing arms and felt naked to the Israeli danger. The threat of war loomed over their lives, their families and their businesses. They watched the buildup of warlike forces totally beyond their control.

Speaking to the Knesset, the Israeli parliament, Prime Minister Eshkol called on the world powers to maintain the right of free passage to Elat. The United States tried to work out a

17

political settlement, and President Lyndon Johnson declared the Arab blockade of Israel to be "illegal and potentially disastrous to the cause of peace."[9] The British government said it would join an international attempt to keep the Gulf of Aqaba open to all ships. Portugal and the Netherlands supported the pathetic effort. During the next two weeks, the Egyptians built up their army in the Sinai and the Israelis sharpened their reserve units.

The tension also increased among the Israelis in Jerusalem. They feared that every day their enemies grew stronger and their chances for survival more precarious.

"For two weeks before the war," says Colonel Eliezar Amitai, the forty-two-year-old, Polish-born professional soldier commanding the Sixteenth Infantry Brigade defending the Israeli sector of the city, "we were mobilized. Our political leadership was undecided. We had the feeling that we were encircled by people who wanted to kill us—again. Hell, we thought, why don't we do something about it?"

Under the Armistice Agreement, the Israeli military was not to keep in Jerusalem any weapons heavier than 3-inch mortars; but Colonel Amitai's command was armed with English 25-pounders, 155-mm guns and 24 120-mm mortars. Its infantrymen carried stubby, gray-metal, Israeli-made 9-mm Uzi submachine guns and Belgian FN automatic rifles, which fired standard NATO 7.62 cartridges.

Colonel Amitai's Sixteenth Infantry Brigade, the overstrength territorial reserve unit, included the "Jerusalem Brigade." Unlike most Israeli army units, his Jerusalem Brigade was designed to fight in a particular area: Jerusalem. It had four first-line battalions and four second-line battalions of older and less physically able men. The second-line units were supposed to guard the border and the first-line units to attack the enemy.

Of the first-line battalions, the 163rd commanded by Lt. Col. Michael Peikas and the Sixty-eighth commanded by Lt. Col. Zvika Opher guarded the Corridor that approached Jerusalem from the population centers to the west. In the city itself, the other two battalions—the 161st commanded by Lt. Col. Asher Driezin and the Sixty-second commanded by Lt. Col. Gidon Rothschild—held the Green Line, ready to attack across it.

The 161st guarded the border from Mount Zion south to Kibbutz Ramat Rachel. Lt. Col. Driezin's greatest worry was the ridgetop leading past the United Nations' headquarters at Government House south of the city, because the road there offered access for Jordanian armor into Israeli Jerusalem. He wanted to place troops in no-man's-land to plug this hole; but General Uzi Narkiss, commander of the Israeli Central Command, denied his request. Driezin kept his battalion headquarters in a school west of the ridge.

In Israeli Jerusalem, the Arab harangues and preparations for war aroused fear. A people who had long lived with danger in Europe, in the Arab countries and in Israel itself—a collection of survivors—felt threatened again with destruction. They were once more at risk. They waited for the blow to fall and for the anguish of the mourning ahead. In Jerusalem, the rabbis sanctified parks to be cemeteries.

Civilians were instructed how best to prepare for war. They were told to keep essentials near them when they went to sleep. And to store first-aid supplies, mattresses, jerry cans of water and enough nonperishable food for about seven days. Bathtubs were to be filled with water, candles placed in every room and all windows taped and covered with blackout curtains. Air raid shelters were to be stocked with cans of water, candles, matches, first-aid kits and benches. People were asked not to smoke in the shelters and not to leave the shelters until permitted by the person in charge.

The care of casualties was a particular concern. This was the immediate responsibility of a bulky, slouching forty-year-old army captain named Uri Khassis, who had graduated in the Hebrew University's first medical class and also had a degree in hospital administration from Columbia University. Haifa-born Dr. Khassis was now the medical officer in charge of the population in Jerusalem and as far to the west as Latrun and Beit Shemesh. Under his command were one thousand people from doctors to ambulance drivers. He worked with the Jerusalem Brigade, with the police and border police, civil defense personnel and the Red Cross-like Magen David Adom. At central points in the city he set up operating theaters under surgeons from Hadassah Hospital. Countless volunteers came in and hundreds of the most able were added to his gathering force. They had to improvise.

Recognizing that the tension of this so-called Period of Waiting would grow even more severe in case of war, Dr. Khassis organized "a psychological counterattack." He gathered a team in his home, and using a psychological warfare manual from the Korean War, they created a program they called Psychological First Aid. They established a headquarters that anxious civilians could call and assigned psychologically trained people to the field hospitals and the public shelters. They tried to spread a sense of calmness over the radio. And they organized a system for visiting the homes of the killed and wounded.

The mobilization and the tension radically changed life in the city. People began stocking supplies and preparing their basement shelters. Buses stopped running as their drivers were called up. Youngsters helped to deliver milk and newspapers and sort the mail in Israeli Jerusalem's Central Post Office. On May 23, the United States and British embassies advised their nationals to leave Israel. Airline offices were jammed with people trying to get out; and incoming planes were almost empty, bringing only returning Israelis and journalists and broadcasters. Hotels were soon less than half full. By the end of the week, eleven thousand visitors had left Israel by air.

Intelligence reports tightened the tension in the Israeli establishment. Yehuda Avner, who had joined the Haganah, the pre-1948 Jewish defense force in Palestine, after seeing children survivors of the Holocaust in a camp near his home in Manchester, England, and who had fought in Jerusalem in 1948, now at thirty-eight years of age was working for the Foreign Office, primarily writing speeches and letters in English for Prime Minister Eshkol. He remembers: "Yaacov Herzog [the director of Eshkol's office] put on the prime minister's table an intelligence report indicating that the Egyptians had introduced gas units into Sinai. Prime Minister Eshkol asked me to get hold of [Foreign Minister Abba] Eban quickly, and he said to him in Yiddish, 'Tell the President of the United States we are dealing with animals. Gas!'"

This news was based on "soft" intelligence information, according to General Aharon Yariv, Director of Military Intelligence; and, in fact, the Egyptians never used poison gas in the coming war. But the report aroused gut-tearing fears among the Israeli leadership. Twenty thousand gas masks were bought from West Germany and distributed to the frontline troops who would face the Egyptians.

Dr. Uri Khassis was given the job of meeting the threat of poison gas in Jerusalem. That very day in a ceremony at the King David Hotel, the vice-president of the Democratic Republic of Madagascar honored him for establishing medical facilities and training medical personnel there. Suddenly, Dr. Khassis switched from memories of that constructive medical work to plans to prevent mass destruction. He directed chemists at the Hebrew University to start making antidotes, and he had simplistic gas masks devised for civilians. These preparations were kept secret to avoid panic.

"There was an immediate shock from this piece of information," says Yehuda Avner. "I remember seeing documents of the estimates of the casualties that there were going to be. And I remember keeping this all to myself, not a word at home." Avner had a special reason for not alarming his wife, Mimi. She was the younger sister of Esther Cailingold, who had been Avner's friend in the Haganah. Esther had come from London to teach at the English-speaking Evelina de Rothschild Girls High School in Jerusalem. She was killed defending the Jewish Quarter of the Old City in 1948. The twenty-two-year-old was buried on Mount Herzl.

"The Period of Waiting was a period of agony," says Avner of 1967. "These were the days of massing forces; these were the days of retaliations; these were the days of air clashes, knocking down Syrian planes; these were the days of the attempt to divert the headwaters of the Jordan; these were the days of summit conferences. These were the days of Nasser."

The tension wound tight by the threat of war erupted in divisions among Israel's political leaders. Levi Eshkol, now seventy-two, had replaced David Ben-Gurion as prime minister in June 1963 and adopted a policy of strengthening relations with the United States and the Soviet Union. To some, this looked like weakness. Many Israelis did not believe they could depend on the non-Jewish world. They would have to save themselves.

Eshkol was a powerful, patient man who had come to Palestine from the Ukraine in 1914 at the age of nineteen and had devotedly worked the land. In time, he became Ben-Gurion's right-hand man and as both minister of agriculture and minister of finance developed settlements and the nation's water system.

The aging Ben-Gurion—short, stocky, still imposing with his large leonine head and his wild mane of white hair recognized around the world—was unable to sit quietly in retirement at Kibbutz Sde Boker in the Negev desert. By 1965, his adherents, led by Shimon Peres and Moshe Dayan, resigned from the government and formed the dissident Rafi Party. In May 1967, Rafi's leaders aroused public opinion against what they saw as the government's indecisiveness in the crisis. Rafi wanted to bring back Ben-Gurion, now in his eighty-first year, as prime minister and make Dayan minister of defense.

Ben-Gurion himself became one of Eshkol's severest critics. He feared that Eshkol was vacillating and did not know how to handle politics and war; he did not respect Eshkol's desire for conciliation. And he misjudged Eshkol's fiber that gave the Israel Defense Forces time to prepare and led to the bold and dangerous preemptive strike that would start the war. Ben-Gurion helped create public panic about Eshkol. Many people felt that Ben-Gurion's instincts were right; they had followed the Old Man so often in the past.

Late one night in the Dan Hotel in Tel Aviv, Eshkol sat with his feet up and his shoes off and said to a journalist: "I never thought to be prime minister. I never wanted to be prime minister. But I sit in the chair and I am the prime minister and he [Ben-Gurion] talks of me as a *schmuck.*"

The infighting grew so ugly that on May 29 the *Jerusalem Post* was inspired to publish a front-page editorial titled simply "Leadership." It said: "This is not the time for coalition negotiations. The specter of political bargaining, often dismaying in normal times, is an affront to a nation under arms. . . . Such a nation, which had put aside its own inner divisions, ought not to be made to witness the sight of discord among its political leadership." The editorial urged the national government to follow the example of Jerusalem's municipal leaders who the day before had formed an emergency administration.

The political factionalism paralyzed the government. When Nasser closed the Strait of Tiran, the Cabinet was split down the middle on whether to go to war. The National Religious Party on the right and the Mapam Party on the left and Labor Party leaders like Abba Eban and Pinhas Saphir opposed military action. General Yariv, who thought Israel should have fought then, says, "If the government had said, yes, we understand that we have to go to war, but we need time for making preparations, that would have been something else. But the decision was not to go to war. I thought that time is against us, that the more time passes the better prepared Nasser would be and the more Arab forces would come into play. I thought we should go as early as possible. I don't blame Eshkol personally. He himself was strong. He did not lose his nerve."

Behind the political machinations was a deeply ingrained anxiety that the politicians both shared and exploited. Erwin Frenkel, who was to become the coeditor of the *Jerusalem Post*, later explained the trauma of those fearsome days:

"The Jew's image of the Arab was that he was bloodthirsty, and maybe the Arabs saw the Jews in the same way. We felt we were being choked and being left hanging until we just fell. The UN had pulled out. We had been given international assurances about freedom of navigation. And [President] Johnson [who met with Foreign Minister Abba Eban on May 26] did try to whip together some kind of international blockade, but nobody was buying it. He couldn't do it unilaterally. It confirmed for the Jews that when the Jews had to fight, in the end they had to rely on themselves. That was part of the anti-Eshkol syndrome: 'If he thinks we can rely on the *goyim* to do something, he's crazy.'

"I remember thinking the night after the 1967 war started how important it was that Ben-Gurion had been the prime minister and had been concerned with building a goddamn army. Now in Jerusalem we needed an army. When you think they are going to attack, you are thankful for the tough hardliner who had been there. B-G in his last years was very abrasive. He was wrong about Eshkol and the war. But he was a very careful man; he feared war."

One man who suffered especially from the tension and the political haggling was Yitzhak Rabin, the Israeli Chief of Staff. The responsibility for the nation's safety was his. He was a career soldier who had commanded the Harel Brigade of the Palmach, the Haganah's strike force, in the 1948 War of Independence and who, as his responsibilities as an army officer increased, gained a reputation for management and precision.

23

How well the Israel Defense Forces would perform in this war had to be credited to his years of thorough and intelligent preparation.

Rabin's parents had come to Palestine separately from Russia. His father had spent twelve years in Chicago as a tailor before joining the Jewish Legion in World War I. Yitzhak had been born in Jerusalem's Sha'are Zedek Hospital.

In the summer of 1966, Rabin had to deal with a political crisis. Tall, lean Ezer Weizman, with a flashy reputation as an air force officer, pressed Prime Minister Eshkol to make him Chief of Operations to General Rabin, forcing the head of Rabin's staff, Haim Barlev, into exile. Barlev was sent to Paris to study political science.

Rabin says of the incident: "Barlev was my number two for my first year as chief of staff. Then Eshkol decided, against my will, that he would like Weizman in that position. I said I am against it but you are the prime minister and the minister of defense. You have the right. I called Barlev and Weizman and said that this was the decision. I told them that I opposed it. I told Weizman I opposed it."

As the war with Egypt neared, Rabin came under strong personal attacks from Ben-Gurion, who harbored a long-standing hostility toward former Palmach officers, and from Interior Minister Moshe Chaim Shapiro, the leader of the National Religious Party.

On the night of May 23, after Egypt announced the Strait of Tiran closed to Israeli shipping, Rabin collapsed. He felt depressed and guilty that somehow he had failed his nation—put it in danger. He suffered from the heat of the blunt assaults on the government and on his civilian superior, Levi Eshkol.

Feeling under extreme pressure, Rabin telephoned Weizman and asked him to come over to his house. He shared his deepest doubts with Weizman and asked him if he should resign as chief of staff. Weizman encouraged him not to resign. But Weizman quickly notified Eshkol of Rabin's condition and summoned and ran a meeting of the General Staff without Rabin's knowledge. Rabin's doctor gave him a sedative so that he slept until noon the next day. He returned to work on the twenty-fifth.

Rabin is candid about what happened to him on May 23: "I felt tired and bitter. As a military man you need clear-cut instructions of what to do. It was not Eshkol. People really undermined his position and talked about mistakes that he had made, which was total nonsense. Ben-Gurion attacked him. Abba Eban was the man who undermined Eshkol. I am not a great admirer of Eban except for his English. When it comes to any way of thinking, he didn't and doesn't understand.

"I felt that I had much weight of responsibility, and I realized that we were put in a position that was worse from Israel's point of view. There was tiredness, frustration. For twenty-four hours I stayed at home and then I was fine.

"I made a mistake that I talked to my number two, Weizman. Weizman has never had the patience to be number two more than six months.

"When the tension started [on May 15], Barlev sent me a letter saying that he felt that Paris was not the place to be. And if I had no command post for him, he is a good tank crewman. I wrote him that if we face war I will call him. On the twenty-third I sent a cable to him to come: I don't know what you'll do but come. He came that evening."

Rabin's aide-de-camp met Barlev at the airport at 11 P.M. and told him that Rabin was not well; the story was given out that he was suffering from nicotine poisoning. Barlev went immediately to General Headquarters of the Israel Defense Forces in the Kiryah of Tel Aviv, and Weizman welcomed him wholeheartedly. Barlev says, "After all, he's an airman and he was relieved by the fact that I was there." Barlev would worry about the ground forces and Weizman, the Air Force.

Barlev spent the twenty-fourth with the divisional commanders on the southern front and late that afternoon visited Rabin at his home. The chief of staff was in his pajamas. "He was sitting on his bed but very fragile. He was very uncertain, unconfident. I tried to paint an objective picture that was encouraging. I had seen the units and the plans." Rabin came back to his post, but much of the burden of command fell on Barlev. On the thirtieth, the forty-two-year-old Viennese-born Barlev was appointed Deputy Chief of Staff. Weizman, furious, threatened to leave—on the brink of war. Barlev says, "But he calmed down."

Barlev concentrated on developing final plans, but his main role was to take charge. He says, "My contribution, I believe, was that in the lack of a chief of staff and due to the fact that the minister of defense [Dayan] was new and was out of the army business quite a few years—I believe ten years—my contribution was in the war itself. I think I contributed to the morale of the forces who felt that in the headquarters Ezer Weizman is not in the business [of ground warfare] and Rabin is neutralized, so they found someone who knew the ropes and was not neutralized."

On May 26, Nasser made his goal vividly clear: ". . . our basic objective will be to destroy Israel."[10]

The next day, King Hussein, more than half of whose subjects were Palestinians, visited the Old City of Jerusalem. He and Sherif Nasser Ben Jamil, Deputy Commander in Chief of the Army, held an hour-long meeting with Governor al-Khatib.

That night, the Israeli Cabinet debated what action it should take against Egypt. Its members knew that France's President Charles de Gaulle had warned Israel against firing the first shot and President Johnson had asked for time to organize an international patrol to break the blockade of the Strait of Tiran. The Israeli Cabinet was virtually evenly divided between taking immediate action and waiting a bit longer. Eban recommended a forty-eight-hour delay before taking a deciding vote. The Cabinet decided to give the United States and others a chance to put the international naval plan into effect. Eshkol finally recessed the meeting until the next afternoon, Sunday, May 28.

At eight-thirty Sunday evening, after a five-hour Cabinet meeting, Eshkol, exhausted and stumbling, made a radio speech that much of the tension-stretched public, listening intensely throughout Israel, found lacking in self-confidence. He urged continuing diplomatic action by the Great Powers. The people's worry increased. The political attacks on Eshkol gained credence. The nation seemed imperiled. All the people could do was to go about their daily lives, prepare their shelters and listen to the radio news from morning till night. They felt that war was now inevitable and that every day they waited would make it more hazardous and cost more lives. They exchanged bitter jokes; the most famous was that at Lod Airport a sign read: "Will the last one to leave please turn off the lights."

After Eshkol spoke and following the news, another voice came over Kol Yisrael. This was retired Maj. Gen. Chaim (Vivian) Herzog, former Director of Military Intelligence and

Commander of the Jerusalem District. The director of the Israel Broadcasting Service asked him to serve as a military commentator and explain to the public what was happening. The Irish-born, articulate Herzog had long interpreted military events; he had visited Vietnam in 1962, reported on the German army and seen the war in Nigeria.

"The government had lost contact with the public," Herzog says. His job was to provide the people with information within the bounds of security and to reassure them. In that first broadcast, he referred to the Arab broadcasts dominating the airwaves and urged everyone to "take a cool look behind the bombastic and scurrilous barrage of hate, threat and vilification which fills the ether today."[11]

In the next few days, his quiet explanations reached the nation apprehensive of annihilation. "I turned an entire nation on," says Herzog. "I never understood that." And after the war was over, General Rabin said, "For eleven days, hundreds of thousands in Israel waited impatiently to hear his voice and absorbed his every word."

Actually, the broadcasts were a sideline for Herzog. In the military reserves he was in charge of military government in the Central Command, but no one took it very seriously. Herzog says, "Right up until the war we had no vehicles, no typewriters, no right to requisition vehicles. We had literally nothing. Not a table. So much for Israeli aggression."

King Hussein, in the first interview he had given since the crisis began, told United Press International bluntly, "If Israel attacks any Arab state, we will fight."

On Tuesday, May 30, Hussein flew to Cairo and signed a military pact with Nasser under which Egypt's chief of staff would command both Jordanian and Egyptian forces in case of war. This was a shocking switch. Nasser had wanted to dethrone Hussein in the name of Arab pan-nationalism. Nasser's radio had been calling Hussein insulting names—"the little king," "imperialist hireling"—and Hussein's propaganda had been hitting back at Nasser for hiding behind UN troops and after the UNEF was removed asked, "Where are you, great hero?" But in the end, Hussein could not stand up to Nasser's strident call for Arab unity; the king had not joined the Arab cause during the 1956 Sinai campaign. When it became clear that the United States was not going to stop Nasser, he buckled.

Before Hussein flew back from Cairo to Amman, Nasser embraced and kissed him at the airport. Hussein took home with him, at Nasser's insistence, Ahmed Shukairy, the Jerusalem lawyer who was the first leader of the Cairo-based Palestine Liberation Organization.[12] Born in Acre, Shukairy had represented Saudi Arabia and Syria at the United Nations, served as assistant secretary general of the Arab League and in Jerusalem in 1964 was chosen to head the new PLO.[13] He called for "driving the Jews into the sea."[14] The story was told that when a journalist asked Shukairy what he would do about the Jewish problem if war came, he replied, "There's not going to be a Jewish problem." The Jews feared another Holocaust. They felt their backs were to the sea.

Of Hussein's "dramatic flight to Cairo," the *Jerusalem Post* editorialized: "Hussein changed sides in a dramatic reversal of roles which in any other part of the world would have seemed well-nigh impossible. Only a week ago Hussein had been called 'traitor,' 'prostitute,' and many worse epithets by the person he now called his brother. And only a week ago Shukairy, who would have toppled his throne and killed the young king—the same Shukairy is now an invited guest in the king's throne room."

That evening in Amman, cheering crowds met the king who had just reversed his allegiance and pledged his people's lives to the service of Nasser. Chaim Herzog told Israel on the radio: "This agreement is not innocuous, and we dare not treat it lightly. Within our capital city there is now an army linked by treaty with Nasser."[15]

The next day, Iraq, to support Hussein, moved troops into Jordan. In Amman, Shukairy, stirring up his Palestine Liberation Army which Hussein had banned from Jordan six months earlier, said grandiloquently that it was "most likely" that his men would fire the first shot.

To demonstrate the Jordanian army's virility to foreign reporters—many of whom had the idea that it was pretty hapless since it had gotten rid of its British leaders in 1956—a unit, wearing camouflage uniforms and carrying United States M-1 rifles, was sent to demonstrate its skill with U.S.-made 3-inch mortars in a grove five hundred yards from the Inter-Continental Hotel on the Mount of Olives.

In Jordanian Jerusalem, the army set up gun emplacements. Car headlights were painted blue to offer less distinctive targets at night. And the Arabic newspapers started calling for a *Jihad*, a holy war, against Israel.

The Nasser-Hussein pact and their kiss at Cairo's airport signaled the Israelis that there would be no turning back. They felt surrounded and endangered. Intelligence Chief Aharon Yariv says, "We saw it as Nasser's intention to use Jordan for strategic reasons against Israel. This was another sign of offensive intentions. Nasser embraced a man with whom he was on very bad terms. The important point was that Hussein agreed to establish in Amman an advanced command post of the United Arab Command for strategic coordination. That was why it was very dangerous. They were inside Jerusalem and on our borders. Jordanian troops were five hundred yards from the Knesset.

"Hussein had been against Nasser and his pan-Arabism. Now, we were sure there was going to be trouble with the Jordanians—with that kiss. Hussein was under strong pressure, not so much from the Palestinians as from the army. There were demonstrations. Everyone was saying that Israel was very weak and we would be annihilated."

It was Yariv's job to know Israel's enemies, their strength and weaknesses, their politics and their intentions. He had been Director of Military Intelligence since the beginning of 1964. Born in Moscow, he had come to Palestine in 1935 when he was fourteen and served in the Jerusalem Brigade of the British army through most of World War II. He was demobilized as a captain and joined the Haganah in 1947.

If Jordan was now a danger, the General Staff would have to find enough units to fight a two-front war. Narkiss' Central Command updated its contingency plans to seize the West Bank but did not have the forces in hand to carry them out. The military equation seemed clear to Deputy Chief of Staff Barlev: "We did not plan to attack the eastern front. We had basically only forces necessary to defend this front. We wanted to commit to the eastern front the minimum military force. Uzi Narkiss was very cooperative and calm. He understood the needs of other places. Had he panicked, we would have given in and sent another brigade to Jerusalem. If you had put Arik Sharon there, I am 100 percent sure he would have said without one more brigade it is impossible to secure the city."

That same Tuesday, Shimon Peres, the vigorous secretary general of the breakaway Rafi Party, announced that it was prepared to rejoin the government if an agreement could be worked out. This Rafi decision was made against the stubborn Ben-Gurion's advice.[16] Moshe Dayan, now fifty-two and the Rafi's Knesset faction whip, became its prime candidate for a position of power in the Cabinet. The National Religious Party also wanted the government enlarged to include the Rafi and the right-wing Gahal political groups.

The next forty-eight hours of intense political maneuvering and bargaining left Dayan "pessimistic and depressed."[17] He refused Eshkol's offer of the deputy prime ministership, which would have given the Ministry of Defense to Labor Minister Yigal Allon, who as a young Sabra was the commander of the Palmach and the leading hero of the 1948 war. Dayan, Allon's longtime rival and Ben-Gurion's protégé, announced, with a show of great self-confidence, that he would only join the nation's leadership if he were made defense minister or given command of the Southern Front. The army's leaders objected earnestly to taking Dayan from the reserves and putting him in control of the battle against the Egyptians; it would suggest that the government mistrusted the army.

On May 31, the Wednesday before the war, Yehuda Avner put into action a personal plan that he and his brother-in-law had agreed on. He took his wife, Mimi, and their young son and three daughters to Haifa so the two families would be together in the crisis. He says: "I came back from Haifa to Jerusalem in a taxi. The roads were chockablock full with army convoys. The taxi went via Lod Airport. I was the only Israeli in the taxi; the four or five others were tourists getting out of here. Sitting there, I felt nothing means anything if all this around us, as we drove through the coastal plain, is destroyed; and there is nothing too precious to protect this little bit of something that we have done here. I felt happy. I had made peace with the reality of the threat.

"I went straight to Mount Herzl. Esther had been killed at the end of May, and every single year her father had visited her grave at that time. But this year he was sick and I was the single representative of the family at Esther's graveside. I recited a prayer in my heart.

"I went from Mount Herzl to my office. The deputy director general in charge of administration and personnel said there was a request that I leave for New York as soon as possible to beef up the consulate. The debates were beginning in the United Nations. He said let your family go ahead and you pack up the house and then go. I must leave in forty-eight hours. I was the man who had been driving from Haifa to Jerusalem with those thoughts and convictions. Suddenly, I am told I am not going to be part of it.

"My wife and children, the oldest was thirteen, went off to London; and I began to pack up the house to leave on Sunday. On Saturday I worked through the night. I told the administration people I couldn't leave Sunday; I would have to leave Monday. Sunday night I was given the job of writing up an analysis of events that had taken place from Independence Day up to that Sunday night. Later, I realized it was the rationale for what was going to happen the next morning. I went home at four o'clock Monday morning."

On Thursday, June 1, the Israeli political infighting came to a head. The pressure on Eshkol to turn over the Defense portfolio to Yigal Allon had shifted. Now, the drive was to create a unity government including the Rafi Party and the two branches of the right wing, expansionist Gahal Party. And Dayan, as a popular leader of the Rafi, became the foremost candidate for minister of defense. Public demonstrations demanded his appointment. The stress on Eshkol became intense.

Yigael Yadin, the lean, mustached professor of archaeology at the Hebrew University who had been Israel's Chief of Operations in the War of Independence and Chief of Staff from 1949 through 1952, tells the story: "I went to Mr. Eshkol's office and like others there tried to persuade him to appoint Mr. Dayan minister of defense. He was very, very reluctant. He didn't want to do that for two reasons: First, he thought he could handle the situation rather well; secondly, he didn't trust Dayan. They were from two completely different factions within the party and were also different mentalities. But I pressed him very hard and explained, 'I think the morale of the people demands that, and I think Dayan—not that he is the best, there are others—is very capable to do this job.' He suggested to me that I should take the Ministry of Defense, and I said to him that this is not the problem.

"While we were there, Allon came in and he thought he should be the candidate for the minister of defense. I said to him quite frankly, 'Look, there are three here, and I think each of us could do it; we've each had the experience.' I explained to him I had recommended to Eshkol that Dayan should take it because of his reputation in the '56 war and so on. That was what was needed. The army had actually planned the whole operation. Anyway, I said no.

"That night, Eshkol agreed to accept Dayan. But he said to me that he had a condition: that I should be his military advisor. Until now the prime minister was always the minister of defense. Now we were going to have a new situation with a prime minister, a minister of defense and a chief of staff. He said, 'I would like you to be my military advisor with the main job of coordinating to see that everything works all right.' Of course, after having met with Rabin, I agreed."

After the war was finished, Dayan gave his version of this political struggle: "Eshkol did not want me. The people wanted me. Eshkol was forced to accept me. When the crisis came, he offered me a post as vice premier and military advisor. I replied that I was not interested in the titles. If it was to be a Cabinet post, I wanted Defense. If not, mobilize me and give me forces in the Negev fighting the Egyptians. I told him I knew the Egyptians and how to fight them.

"Eshkol did not want me in his Cabinet. He wanted Yigal Allon as his defense minister, but when he proposed Allon as his defense minister to his party Secretariat, they told him 'The hell with it—we want Dayan.'"

It became apparent that the world powers were not going to intervene. Nobody stopped U Thant from withdrawing the United Nations forces; no international armada challenged Nasser at the Strait of Tiran. Watching the scene from his catbird seat in New York, Israeli Consul General Michael Arnon said, "There were twenty-six things that could have been done and weren't. There was a great deal of talk, a very honest groping for doing something. But nobody was able to come up with anything real. Days were going by and nothing was happening. It became evident that this was not going to be resolved by international diplomatic action of any kind, and therefore we had to act."

Thursday night, a unity Cabinet was quickly formed. The Rafi's Dayan, the charismatic darling of the people, was finally given the post of Minister of Defense. And the leaders of the two elements of the right-wing Gahal Party, Yosef Saphir, sixty-two, and Menachem Begin, fifty-four, came in as Ministers without Portfolio. Begin, who ruled the Herut wing of Gahal, had been the leader of the Irgun Zvai Leumi underground before Israel was formed. Saphir, a longtime mayor of Petah Tikva, led the General Zionists or Liberals who had joined with Herut to form the Gahal coalition. They brought into the government parties that held substantial strength in the Knesset.

It was a patchwork solution. The outsiders joined the government only for the war and did not negotiate positions on the government's program. Their goals were to close ranks, broaden the government's base and tear away from Eshkol control of both the prime ministership and the Ministry of Defense.

Clearly, in the light of the events on the horizon, the appointment of Dayan was the most significant of these moves. A loner with a brilliant military record, he drew little support among Israel's political leaders and he haggled with Eshkol over his new prerogatives. But, as Yadin says, "Dayan was at the height of his popularity and he was brought in, so to say, by a *vox populi*." He attracted vast popular support with his intelligence, magnetism, trim, bald, soldierlike appearance, and his eye-patch trademark.

Dayan had great personal courage, although his military peers found him hesitant when it came to final, irreversible strategic decisions. He had played a key role in the War for Independence and been the hawkish leader in the Sinai campaign of 1956. But lately he had been more politician and dilettante archaeologist than soldier, and he had no influential role in the military preparations for the 1967 war. The credit for them goes to Yitzhak Rabin. But Dayan was a symbol of toughness to a nervous and frightened people.

The next day, three men lunched together in a Tel Aviv hotel: Dayan, Yadin and Zvi Zur, who had preceded Rabin as

Chief of Staff. Dayan had immediately fired Eshkol's man as Deputy Minister of Defense and named Zur his special assistant. Yadin remembers: "We had lunch and it was then decided that the war would have to start. We would have to take the initiative either Sunday or Monday because we were afraid that any day the Egyptians would launch their attack. Of course, this had to be approved by the government; but that this action should be taken was a decision of ours."

Friday night, Eshkol called a meeting at his home in Jerusalem. Some of the more dovish leaders still hoped that war could be avoided. Dr. Yosef Burg, the Minister of Social Welfare and member of the National Religious Party, says, "I thought perhaps there could still be a resolution; nothing is eaten as hot as it is cooked."

Long after midnight, they agreed that Israel must attack. At the meeting, the possibility of a battle in Jerusalem was not seriously considered. Yadin says, "I don't think Jerusalem was even in the mind of anyone there."

As was his responsibility, Chief of Staff Rabin was alert to the danger from the east. He says, "The Jordanian army was the best disciplined threat in all the Middle East even though they were not in possession of good equipment. Their tanks were inferior to our best. After Hussein went to Cairo and signed the defense pact, [the Egyptian] General [Abdel Moneim] Riad became the commander of the eastern front. He was very good, one of the best the Egyptians had.

"We did not believe then that it would be possible for Israel to combat two major offensives on two fronts. Only Egypt carried out an act of war before the war started—the expulsion of the UN and the blockade of the Strait of Tiran. Therefore, the policy was to limit the war to the Egyptian sector. When the war started, we were allowed [by the government] to start only against Egypt. We had to wait to see whether Syria, Jordan and Iraq would decide to go to war. In the beginning the strategy was to win over Egypt. Everything else was of secondary importance."

The policy of the Israeli government was to defeat the danger from Egypt, which had massed men and armor in the Sinai and cut off the lifeline from Elat. The government's aim was to keep Jordan and the other neighboring Arab nations out of this fight and to concentrate its strength against Nasser. Israelis in power did not seek to reunite Jerusalem or conquer the West Bank; they were willing to live with the divided city half in Jordanian hands. Their goal was not conquest by survival; all their energies were focused on the perceived threat that Egypt would accomplish what it proclaimed—to bomb and shell Israeli centers of population and destroy the Jewish nation.

Dayan demobilized a good part of the army, both to relax the nation and to deceive the Egyptians. The fear of war seemed to ordinary Israelis to subside for the moment. Pictures were published of soldiers and their families spending the Sabbath on the beaches. Men removed the covers from their cars. But Dayan's cleverness would make for casualties and confusion when war did come to Jerusalem.

Dayan held a brilliant news conference on Saturday afternoon. He said he thought diplomatic action was not enough. Israel could not accept the closing of the Strait of Tiran. But he warned that war would be "costly." The whole nation listened on the radio. This was Dayan's forte. He gave the people heart.

The dice were quickly cast. In a nation fearing for its survival, the final Cabinet decision was made Sunday night, June 4, in Jerusalem:

The Israeli Air Force would strike first, destroy the Egyptians' aircraft and airfields in a surprise attack, and the Israeli ground forces would plunge across the Sinai desert. H-hour would be 0745 on Monday, June 5.

In the south Sunday evening, troops and tanks were in place. And songwriter Naomi Shemer was flown from Beersheva by Chief of Operations General Ezer Weizman, piloting his small plane, to sing to Brig. Gen. Ariel "Arik" Sharon's armored troops on the border waiting for the word to go.

Most of the people of Jerusalem went to their beds that Sunday evening unaware of the events stamped for the coming morning. Teddy Kollek, the mayor of Israeli Jerusalem, and Mrs. Ruth Cheshin, his young director of tourism for the city, drove to the King David Hotel to visit a foreign guest. In normal times, the grand, high-ceilinged lobby of the King David was a kind of indoor Roman Forum, where all of Jewish Jerusalem and visitors from abroad came and went and mulled about and met and talked endlessly over coffee.

Tonight was different. The weeks of tension, the threat of war, had virtually emptied the old hotel. Ruth Cheshin, a seventh-generation Jerusalemite, remembers: "The city was very sad. I went with Teddy to visit at the King David, and the hotel was dead—no one in the lobby and very little light. It felt as if you were entering a deserted home. A miserable atmosphere. The King David was always so full of people—now suddenly this emptiness."

Then they drove to visit the old, sick owner of the Holy Land Hotel. Mrs. Cheshin says, "The city was dark. He was seriously ill and Teddy wanted to comfort him. There was nobody at the hotel; the same emptiness, quietness. We felt as though the whole world had deserted us and we were a lonely island in the middle of a stormy sea. The feeling was loneliness. You had no one to turn to. You are alone and you have to fight for your life."

Prime Minister Eshkol and his wife Miriam drove down to Tel Aviv. Miriam Eshkol had lived in the Eshkol household like a stepdaughter and worked in the Knesset as a research librarian. After Eshkol's first wife died, Miriam and Levi were married. She recalls: "I was a daughter in their house. His late wife was a kind of mother to me. God, if anyone had told me that after so many years I would be Eshkol's wife, I would have sent him to an asylum. That's life.

"He was thirty-four years older than me, but he was a hundred years younger. All of a sudden at home that Sunday evening, he started walking up and down and saying, 'You know, tomorrow there will be widows and orphans, and it's my responsibility.' Then he said, 'We'll have to take it back.' I said, 'What do you have to take back?' He said, 'We have to take back Jerusalem.'"

— Chapter 3 —

MONDAY MORNING—
ISRAELI JERUSALEM

At eight o'clock on Monday morning, Jerusalem was already hot and bright when the sirens feebly wailed an alert. At that moment, Mrs. Yael Uzay, the Secretary of the Israeli Cabinet, received an urgent telephone call in Jerusalem from Aviad "Adi" Yaffe, Prime Minister Eshkol's secretary. Yaffe was with the prime minister in his office in Sharona, a onetime German suburb of Tel Aviv. They were waiting in extreme tension for news from the Air Force's preemptive strike against the Egyptian Air Force—until they knew that 188 of Israel's 200 planes commanded by General Mordechai Hod had caught the Egyptians on the ground and destroyed nearly 250 Soviet-built MIG fighters and Ilyushin 14 transports—the entire Egyptian Air Force, all its runways and key radar positions. When the first of three air strikes had been launched against eighteen Egyptian air bases, Yaffe told Mrs. Uzay, "Please inform all the Cabinet members that the skies of Israel are clean."

This was the first word Jerusalem received that the Israelis' surprise attack had been sprung against the Egyptian Air Force. And it was Top Secret. Mrs. Uzay was instructed to tell each minister to keep the news secret and to convene the Knesset at seven o'clock that evening. Then, the prime minister would report to the parliament. In the meanwhile, the Cabinet members should ignore the news coming over the Arab and other foreign broadcasts.

With all the ministers, except Eshkol and Dayan, still in Jerusalem, Mrs. Uzay and her staff started telephoning. She

37

did not expect war in Jerusalem this morning: "Nobody thought Hussein would be so foolish."

When Dr. Yosef Burg, the Minister of Social Welfare and an ordained rabbi whose mother had died in a Nazi concentration camp, heard the news, he drove from his home in the affluent Rehavia section to his office in King David Street, almost opposite the King David Hotel. He says, "All these years in this office, I was not allowed to sit in certain rooms because there were snipers on the other side."

The ministry's security officer herded the bureaucrats into the basement shelter. Burg remembers: "The civil servants immediately divided into two groups: one that said prayers and one that listened to the transistor news. There was cultural interchange between them.

"Mobilization came over the radio. If it played 'The Blue Danube,' you knew you had to go to your unit; but if it played 'La Vie En Rose,' then I knew I had to go." The man who had been his driver for twenty-two years came to him and said they had played his song. Before he left he painted the headlights of Dr. Burg's car blue.

When Ya'acov Shimshon Shapira, the sixty-five-year-old Minister of Justice, received word that war had begun, he walked across Jaffa Road from his office to pay his respects in this moment of crisis to the members of the Supreme Court sitting in the Russian Compound. Soon, the justices called a recess and they all went down into the shelter.

Another Israeli official in Jerusalem, Yehuda Arbell, had started the hour-long drive to Tel Aviv when he heard the news on his car radio. He turned around and went back to his office. Arbell says, "It was a relief. The waiting period was wearing down the nerves of everyone. People were much more worried before the fighting started than after. When it starts, you have the feeling that it will be over."

The man specifically charged with the defense of Jerusalem, General Uzi Narkiss, commander of the Israeli army's Central Command, was not in Jerusalem at all, but in Ramla down on the coastal plain. At 6:30 A.M., when he had left his home in Zahala, the suburb of Tel Aviv favored by certain generals and politicians, he knew the Israeli air strike was coming. But he

38

told his wife only to be careful, something might happen today. It was a hot, sunny Middle East day. As he and his driver reached Ramla, Israeli jets were already screaming overhead on their way to bomb the Egyptian air bases.

Narkiss' headquarters was in an old building roofed with red tiles and built by the Germans for the Turks before World War I. As soon as he walked into his office at 8:15, General Barlev, the Deputy Chief of Staff, called from the underground bunker of the Operational General Headquarters of the Israel Defense Forces. He said, "Uzi, it's started. The war is on." Narkiss ordered the alarm sounded; and thrilled with the news, he telephoned Colonel Amitai, commander of the brigade in Jerusalem, and proposed a toast of champagne because the tension was broken and the fighting had begun.

The Central Command's orders were strictly defensive. Narkiss commanded only reserve units and had been instructed that if trouble erupted on his eastern front to try to calm it down. He told Amitai to come to a full alert and wait. Israel's leaders remembered that in the 1956 Sinai campaign the border with Jordan had remained quiet. They hoped it would again. They wanted to defeat Egypt and keep Jordan out of the fighting if possible.

Narkiss' most worrisome military problem was to protect Mount Scopus, the vulnerable Israeli enclave beyond the Green Line in Jordanian territory. Mount Scopus was a peak of the ridgeline that overlooked and dominated Jerusalem from the east. On it, Titus' Roman army had camped before he conquered the city in A.D. 70. Mount Scopus was the site of the now-deserted Hebrew University and Hadassah Hospital. Since the end of the fighting in 1948, the Israelis clung to that isolated knob, even though the Jordanians held the rest of the ridge: French Hill to the north, and Augusta Victoria and the Mount of Olives to the south, as well as the Kidron Valley to the west of the Old City. For nineteen years the Israelis had kept on Mount Scopus a small garrison under the command of the Jerusalem Brigade, changing the men every second Wednesday with armored convoys under UN supervision. If King Hussein decided to fulfill his pact with Nasser, it was unimaginable that the Jordanians would not strike Mount Scopus.

Narkiss says, "I was worried for Mount Scopus because it

was famous all over the Christian world and the Arab world. Secondly, it was easy to capture. We didn't have there more than 120 people—100 soldiers and 20 civilians.

"If Mount Scopus were captured, it would have been a terrible blow to the morale of Israel and Jews all over the world. Nothing in the Sinai Peninsula could compensate for the loss of Mount Scopus. I knew that if Mount Scopus were taken from us, they would ask after the war who was responsible; and I would be the scapegoat."

He feared that King Hussein might seize Mount Scopus and then declare peace and the Israeli government might accede: "This is a political thought, but a general in Israel has to think politically."

The men of the small Israeli force on top of Mount Scopus were not thinking politically. They were well aware that they were exposed and that they were the trigger point. If war came to Jerusalem, they felt, they would be the first hit.

They were commanded by Major Menachem Sharfman, a tough, voluble, stocky, pistol-packing forty-one-year-old professional soldier with a mustache and an intensity that he communicated to his men. He had been in charge of the Israeli defense of Mount Scopus for two and a half years; his men called him the King of Mount Scopus.

Although the agreements between Israel and Jordan and with the United Nations severely limited Israeli access to Mount Scopus and prohibited its use as a military base, the Israelis had, in fact, over the years built up a defensible position there. Its 120 men, mostly young, able-bodied soldiers, had smuggled up four recoilless rifles, three Jeeps with recoilless rifles and machine guns, eighteen .30 caliber machine guns, ten .50 caliber machine guns and four 20-mm cannons. The men were armed with Uzis and FN rifles and well supplied with mines, both antitank and antipersonnel. They also had six mortars, including four 81-mm. All these were illegal. Legally, the men were supposed to be policemen armed with old British Enfield rifles. But the Israelis meant to hold this hilltop.

Major Sharfman was in direct radio contact with Colonel Amitai of the Jerusalem Brigade (also illegal and secret), and Sharfman's artillery officer was in communication with all the brigades in the Central Command and with the Air Force. He could direct fire from the ground and air.

The "King" of this small, tight fort was a Sabra born in Yavniel, an old *moshav,* or farming community, in the Galilee, the home of a number of Israel's best known warriors. The people of Yavniel were land-rooted farmers who spoke fluent Arabic. Sharfman himself came from Russian parents and had fought in the War of Independence.

During his months as commander of Mount Scopus he had alternated with Captain Yosef Shaki every two or three weeks, traveling to the hilltop in buttoned-up trucks under UN guard. If he had to make a special trip, he was blindfolded and transported in a UN car. He had come up most recently on May 23 and on arriving learned that Nasser had closed the Strait of Tiran. Three days later, he received orders to lay mines in the area. Although he had experienced very little fire on Mount Scopus, he expected that he would be attacked as soon as war came.

He figured that because the Jordanians did not know of the Israeli strength on Mount Scopus, they would assume it to be an easy mark. All his arms were out of sight and only twenty picked men within his force knew all the secrets. UN visitors were escorted into a special guest room and never inspected the rest of his area, which covered 1.2 kilometers by 2.5 kilometers, with Hadassah Hospital at the north end and the Hebrew University at the south. Sharfman himself slept in the university's mathematics building, where he had his communications equipment. Captain Shaki stayed in the university's Magnes Building, the tower of which was the highest point on the hill and served as the unit's observation post. The command center was in the house of the director of the Hadassah Hospital who had been killed in the ambush of the Jewish medical convoy on its way to the hospital nineteen years before. Although Sharfman was totally surrounded, he felt confident that his position was strong enough to survive.

This Monday, Sharfman was up at 6 A.M. and, after a breakfast of salad and yogurt, climbed to the top of the Magnes tower. By eight o'clock he saw that Jordanian soldiers were in all their positions around Mount Scopus. They had not been before. He alerted his men, who slept near their weapons, and radioed Jerusalem Brigade headquarters at Camp Schneller in the city. From the tower Sharfman had a 360-degree view and for days he had watched Jordanian convoys bringing up troops, tanks and supplies to the West Bank and Jerusalem.

At 8:15 he heard on the Air Force radio net of the Israeli air victories against Egypt. As soon as Sharfman realized Israel was at war, he ordered the UN flags above the Magnes Building and the Hadassah Hospital lowered and Israeli flags raised. The pretense of neutrality was finished.

Suddenly in midmorning his communications with the Jerusalem Brigade went dead. Colonel Amitai was moving his headquarters and it was more than an hour before Sharfman could communicate with anyone. Then he heard from the Central Command that he had been switched from the command of Amitai to Colonel Mordechai Gur's paratroop brigade.

The UN had one last connection with Mount Scopus. At 8:30, Walter Klement, a square-faced, forty-year-old soldier in the Austrian army stationed at Government House, the headquarters of the United Nations Truce Supervision Organization and in Mandate days the residence of the British High Commissioner, south of the city, drove alone with a large tanker truck carrying five thousand liters of water through the Mandelbaum Gate and up to Mount Scopus. The Israeli garrison received its water from the UN each day; and because the UN did not work on Sunday, the Israelis received two truckloads on Monday. Klement, dressed in his summer blues, brought the first load from Government House and then refilled his truck near the Mandelbaum Gate. When he drove up the second time, he noticed the presence of Jordanian soldiers and that the shops were closed. He says, "I had a funny feeling but knew the UN would notify me if there was any danger. They didn't."

The loudspeakers on the minarets of the mosques in Jerusalem were quiet. For two days, the wind from the west had carried to Mount Scopus the agitating cries from the loudspeakers: "Slaughter the Jews! Don't leave even one!" The Arabic word for slaughter sounded on the wind like "Et-bakoo." Now they were silent.

The Mount Scopus garrison began taking incoming artillery and machine-gun fire. Sharfman could see that it came from Anata to the east and Tel el-Ful in the north and from near the monastery at Mar Elias to the south. The Jordanians were targeted on Mount Scopus.

When the shooting started, Walter Klement called Government House from the radio in his truck. He was told war had started between Egypt and Israel and he should stay on Mount Scopus. Klement hid under his tanker truck. He called Government House repeatedly until its radio was silenced. For the first few hours, he hugged the ground under his truck; and then Sharfman came out and brought him into an underground kitchen.

The Mount Scopus garrison joined the battle. At first, Sharfman had held his fire. He walked the area, carrying his Uzi and wearing his helmet, to see that everything was ready to meet an attack. Each building had been reinforced with thick walls of earth and stone. Toward 10:30 the unit on Mount Scopus began to answer the Jordanian fire and called for supporting fire from outside on the Jordanian positions. By noon, Israeli fire, spotted from Mount Scopus, silenced momentarily the Jordanian artillery fire aimed at Mount Scopus. But the machine-gun and rifle fire continued. Mount Scopus was holding out.

In addition to his worry over Mount Scopus, General Narkiss was obsessed by a private emotional commitment to capture the Jordanian section of Jerusalem, and especially the Old City. His eagerness was rooted in a personal memory. On the night of May 18, 1948, the Israelis had assaulted the Arab-held Old City in an effort to save the Jews besieged in the Jewish Quarter. Narkiss had led the Fourth Battalion of the Palmach's Harel Brigade, the brigade then commanded by Yitzhak Rabin. Narkiss' force was assigned to take Mount Zion—sacred to the Jews for the Tomb of David, to Christians for the site of the Last Supper and to Muslims for both places. This attack on Mount Zion was to be a diversion for the Haganah's main assault on the Jaffa Gate. Rabin vigorously opposed the plan of the Jerusalem commander; he called the idea "idiotic"[1] and proposed encircling the Old City from the north and east rather than attacking its strongest point. The desperate, ill-conceived main attack at Jaffa Gate failed, but Narkiss and his men seized Mount Zion.

Narkiss attacked again the next night. David "Dado" Elazar led the assault with twenty-two volunteers, smashed through the Zion Gate and brought ammunition and supplies and momentary hope to the Jewish Quarter's remaining defenders. Uri Ben-Ari commanded the men guarding Mount Zion during the attack. But the force inside the walls was too small to hold the Quarter; it withdrew. The Jewish Quarter surrendered to the Arab Legion ten days later. Rabin says, "I watched the surrender of the Old City from Mount Zion. Bear in mind that I was born here."

In 1967, the bitter memories of Rabin, Narkiss and Ben-Ari still clawed at them. They felt they shared the blame for the Jewish failure. These deep and personal feelings would play a role in the events unfolding now.

Narkiss says, "I was the commander who retreated from Mount Zion on May 19, 1948. Why? Because we were so few and so poor." When he ordered Colonel Mordechai Gur to take his paratroop brigade up to Jerusalem on June 5, 1967, he told Gur with great emotion: "I hope you will erase the shame of 1948."

By 9 A.M. Narkiss knew that Israeli armor was nearing El Arish, the Egyptian base nearest Israel on the Mediterranean coast of the Sinai. Destroyed Soviet-built tanks and trucks and dead Egyptian soldiers littered the desert sands. The Israeli armor had thrust far ahead of the General Staff's schedule. The battle reports made Narkiss euphoric; he felt certain that what the General Staff wished to avoid on the eastern front would happen. He started thinking not defense but offense.

Colonel Amitai, the commander of the Jerusalem Brigade, called to order an 8 A.M. meeting of his unit commanders at Camp Schneller, his headquarters in the northwest part of the Israeli sector of the city. Schneller had been a German orphanage that the British had made into an army headquarters during the Mandate. Major Yosef Langotsky, leader of the brigade's crack reconnaissance unit, came from a midnight exercise. Lt. Col. Asher Driezin had been at a late-night party celebrating the appointment of Moshe Dayan as Defense Minister. Amitai told them all that the war had started in the south and reviewed plans for the defense of the city—in case. The commanders raced off to alert their units.

During those first hours when Jerusalemites arrived at work and children at school, sporadic firing of rifles and machine guns crossed the Green Line inside the city. At first, Colonel Amitai was not particularly concerned; frequently during the past tense weeks shooting and occasionally fire fights had broken out across the border. But this morning, the small-arms fire seemed to spread along the entire city frontier. Then it escalated to shelling by recoilless weapons and artillery.

The Israelis and Jordanians could still communicate through one direct channel: the Mixed Armistice Commission, a UN organization under General Odd Bull's direction. It had its headquarters in no-man's-land inside Jerusalem, 150 yards north of the Mandelbaum Gate crossing between the two sections.

The MAC house had a western entrance through which the Israeli delegate to MAC would arrive and an eastern door through which the Jordanian delegate would enter. Similarly, a Jordanian handyman entered each morning through the east door and an Israeli cleaning woman through the west. The handyman was there this Monday morning and spent the battle with the MAC officers; the cleaning woman, who had lost many members of her family to the Nazis, did not arrive before the battle started. By the time she could come to the MAC house on Friday, it was a shambles with all its windows shot out.

In command of the commission was Lt. Col. Murray Stanaway, a six-foot New Zealander—cold, formal but extremely enterprising. He had been decorated for bravery in the Korean War. Stanaway had some forty officers under his command, including a nucleus at headquarters, officers out investigating claims and complaints and those stationed at four outstations. This morning in the MAC house were five UN officers in addition to Stanaway, who was known as the Chairman, plus eight of the headquarters staff.

Both Jordan and Israel had assigned liaison teams to work with the MAC over the years. Heading the Israeli team as its senior delegate was Lt. Col. Shmuel Gat. The Israeli junior delegate was Major Shimon Levinson, a thoughtful, quiet thirty-four-year-old Jerusalemite. His family had lived in the city for six generations, ever since his mother's ancestor, a rabbi in Suwalki, Russia, had come to Jerusalem. Levinson had served with the MAC from 1951 to 1962 and had been recalled to his post in April of this year.

Over seventeen years, Levinson had become a close friend

of the senior Jordanian delegate, Colonel Mohammad Daoud, who had served in his liaison job for more than a decade. In the years before the war, relations between the liaison teams had deteriorated; and the first thing Levinson did was to restore the direct telephone line between Daoud's office in the Jordanian sector, on a side street two blocks from the Rockefeller Museum, and his own office across Wallach Street from the Israel Foreign Ministry.

Levinson and Daoud trusted each other. Daoud was able and intelligent and an ascetic. He also was a Jerusalemite from an old family. He was a proud nationalist Palestinian but totally loyal to Jordan, in which many Palestinians held high positions of responsibility. He had served as a noncommissioned officer in the British Mandatory Police and risen in Jordanian service. As a teenager he had been required by Muslim tradition to marry his brother's widow, a woman fifteen years his senior.

On May 31, Lt. Col. Stanaway had called a meeting of the MAC; and both sides signed an agreement that whatever happened there would be no firing in Jerusalem. In the days just before the war, the agreement was violated several times. On June 1, the Jordanians fired on Israelis near the MAC building; and on Sunday, June 4, they fired on an Israeli plane that violated Jordanian airspace over the northern part of the city.

On Monday morning at about 8:45, Major Levinson received instructions from General Headquarters to meet Colonel Daoud. Levinson was to tell him that the Egyptian Air Force had been knocked out; but that Israel had no warlike intentions against Jordan; and if Jordan remained quiet, nothing would happen on their front.

Levinson called Daoud on the direct telephone and also notified Stanaway in the MAC building basement. Levinson and Daoud met at the MAC house at 9:15. Levinson delivered the message. He says, "If it had been in his hands, I am confident he would have said we won't interfere." Daoud could only assure him he would send the message to Amman.

When Levinson left the MAC house at ten o'clock, there was still no shooting. He drove his military Jeep to Jerusalem Brigade headquarters at Camp Schneller. Colonel Amitai complained to him that his hands were tied; he could do nothing, not even put soldiers into the Israeli experimental farm just west of Government House.

Prime Minister Eshkol was trying to convince King Hussein to stay out of the war. He instructed Yosef Tekoah, a deputy director general of the Ministry of Foreign Affairs who was with him in Tel Aviv, to telephone Jerusalem. He was to tell the veteran Deputy Director General Arthur Lourie to pass a message to the king through UN General Odd Bull, promising that if the Jordanians remained neutral, Israel would not attack them. But if Jordan attacked, Israel would hit back hard.

As soon as the UN political advisor, F. T. Liu, reached his office in Government House at 8:15, he received Lourie's call. Liu told him that General Bull and he would be over at noon, as was their custom in such cases. Lourie insisted that the matter was urgent, and Bull, Liu and Liu's deputy, Hubert Noel, a large, enthusiastic Frenchman, drove to the Foreign Ministry immediately. There, according to Liu, Lourie told them that the Egyptians had attacked Israel and the Israelis had reacted. Bull asked if that meant there was fighting on Israeli soil, and Lourie said, no, they had quickly pushed the Egyptians back.

General Bull was given the message for King Hussein. It read: "We are engaged in defensive fighting on the Egyptian sector, and we shall not engage ourselves in any action against Jordan unless Jordan attacks us. Should Jordan attack Israel, we shall go against her with all our might."[2]

The UN officials returned to Government House. In the car, Bull commented that this was the first time he had ever heard of an attacker fighting on his own soil. To avoid delay, Liu and Lt. Col. Floyd M. Johnson, Jr., went directly to see Colonel Daoud. Hussein received the message before 11 A.M. Amman time (10 A.M. in Jerusalem).[3]

"It didn't help," says Yosef Tekoah. General Aharon Yariv, the Israeli director of military intelligence, also felt the appeals to Hussein were useless: The king would not believe the report of the elimination of the Egyptian Air Force and he was determined to share in the victory that Nasser was broadcasting. Yariv says, "We had no interest in opening a front unless he attacked."

By the time Eshkol's messages reached King Hussein, events had moved forward. At Nasser's urging and loyal to his pact, Hussein made his decision to fight. His Hawker Hunters attacked Netanya on the Mediterranean. He replied to General

Bull: "They started the battle. Well, they are receiving our reply by air."[4]

An astute Israeli official in Jerusalem, Yehuda Arbell, was shocked when the Jordanians started shelling Israeli Jerusalem. "I didn't believe the Jordanians would interfere. I think most people—including the army evaluations—agreed with that. Hussein made his biggest mistake by interfering. Had he kept quiet, he could have been one of the most powerful rulers right after the war. Jerusalem would not have been united."

General Narkiss telephoned Mayor Teddy Kollek in the City Hall on the very frontier of Israeli Jerusalem—within yards of the Green Line near the northwest corner of the Old City wall. When Kollek had taken office on December 1, 1965, he had scrapped his predecessor's plan to move the City Hall to a safer location. It was his gesture signifying that he did not accept the division of the city as permanent. He had faith that Jerusalem would some day be reunited, but he had no expectation that it would come so quickly and by an act of war.

"Teddy," Narkiss said, "the war has started. Everything in the south is okay. You might become the mayor of a united Jerusalem."

Heavy-set, vitally energetic, Kollek sat behind his big desk in his top-floor office for a few moments, thinking. A charismatic man, he had come as a youth from Vienna to Kibbutz Ein Gev on the Sea of Galilee. With great courage during the Nazi years, he had rescued Jews from Europe and in 1939 had a face-to-face meeting with Adolf Eichmann that saved many young Jewish lives. After World War II, Kollek had run the Haganah's gun-smuggling mission in New York and later served as director of Prime Minister Ben-Gurion's office.

On this Monday morning in Jerusalem, Kollek was in no mood for the routine work of managing the city. For weeks he had supervised preparations in case the crisis did bring war. Encouraged by the older City Council members who remembered the horrors of the siege in 1948, he pushed the city's people to dig trenches and build shelters and planned to evacuate those who lived on the border. He brought in food supplies and organized the able-bodied volunteers who had not been mobilized. Many of his aides had gone into uniform. Even his driver had been called up, and he was now being driven by an elderly man with an ulcer. They had been out early that morning, before Narkiss' call, checking on safety and defense work.

Ronnie Feinstein dropped his six-year-old-son, Ofer, at his kindergarten and drove to the City Hall and his job as the mayor's public spokesman. Feinstein was in uniform and driving a military Jeep because he was a major in charge of personnel at the Jerusalem Brigade's headquarters. His father had been killed in World War II and his mother's second husband had been killed in the 1948 war. All her family had died in Nazi concentration camps.

When the shelling began, Feinstein picked up his son from the kindergarten and took the boy with him to Schneller. There they got in a Jeep with a driver and a sergeant and started to take Ofer home. A shell landed five yards from the Jeep; it was thrown against a wall but no one was hurt. An armored bus, normally used for the convoy run up Mount Scopus, came by and took Feinstein and Ofer home, where the boy was placed with his mother in the shelter. Feinstein went to his army job.

Mishael and Ruth Cheshin left their home in Balfour Street together to go to work. Misha was a deputy attorney general in the Ministry of Justice and Ruthie worked in the City Hall nearby. She was eight-months pregnant with their second child. They dropped off their five-year-old daughter, Efrat, at her kindergarten; and as they drove on, they heard over the radio that the war had started in the south. Mrs. Cheshin worried whether they had done the right thing leaving Efrat at the school but decided that life had to go on as usual.

Mrs. Cheshin went out from the City Hall with Mayor Kollek to visit the people living in the border area of Mamillah just to the south. They stopped at the last Israeli guard post on the frontier. She says: "We were really two steps from the Jordanian soldiers. You could see them sitting on top of the Old City wall. They were so close. I was afraid; but, of course, I pretended that I wasn't."

Back again in the City Hall, Mayor Kollek closed his door and caught a catnap. He was able to work incredible hours by sleeping briefly between appointments. Mrs. Cheshin recalls: "Then, all of a sudden, the whole thing started. We didn't know where the shooting was coming from. It brought me back twenty years. I had been in Jerusalem during the whole War of Independence. I was a child then, but I remembered the noise a bullet makes when it goes past your ear and hits a wall.

"The first thing I thought of was my daughter in the kindergarten. What had happened to her? I took my car, but Efrat wasn't at the kindergarten. I went home and found her there; one of the mothers had brought her home. I rushed her to my mother-in-law's. They had a shelter there. Then, I left the car and walked back to work. The streets were empty. In the garden in front of the City Hall, bullets were flying. But I reached the office."

Half a mile west of Kollek's office, at eight o'clock the American Consul General Evan M. Wilson climbed to his office above his residence in the old Arab-built consulate building on Agron Street and promptly learned that the war had started against Egypt. Wilson had been involved in the Middle East since 1938, when he had been posted in Cairo as a young Foreign Service officer. He had been an American secretary to the Anglo-American Committee of Inquiry in Palestine in 1945 and '46. The consulate, which had been established in 1857, had been the first, and for long the only, American representation in the area. Now, when the Jordanians began shelling the Jewish sector of the city, the consulate's six-man Marine Security Guard commanded by Gunnery Sergeant Samuel Cuevas started piling a barricade of furniture on the inside of the building facing east.

Erwin Frenkel, the young news editor of the *Jerusalem Post*, Israel's only English-language newspaper, sensed from the eight o'clock radio news that the war had started, even though no word of the Israelis' air strike was broadcast. "Suddenly, I was elated and confident, and at the same time there was this Holocaust trauma in me. I had grown up on stories of the Holocaust. The Jordanians were right there," says Frenkel, an American who had studied for the rabbinate, given it up and in 1960 had moved to Israel.

With many of the *Post*'s staff mobilized, he felt a special urgency to get to the newspaper office off Zion Square in the heart of Israeli Jerusalem. He told his wife to pack food and extra clothes for their three young children and to go into the shelter of their apartment house. The eight families who lived in the small building had already taped their windows and prepared storage space in the basement. One of his neighbors said this was his fourth war: World War II in Poland, Israel's War of Independence, the 1956 Sinai campaign and now war once more.

At the *Post*, the remaining staff, mostly older men and women and a few foreigners—like Pennsylvania-born night editor Charles Weiss, Englishman David Landau and American Malka Rabinowitz—gathered to start putting out the paper. The military correspondent telephoned and let Frenkel know the war against Egypt was going extremely well.

When the Jordanians began shelling the city, the pounding drove some people at the *Post* down into the building's shelter. After an hour or so, they began feeling sheepish and drifted back upstairs. Reporters started coming in with reports of civilians wounded, either by direct hits on their homes or because they had been concerned about their children in school and had ventured into the streets. The home of Ted Lurie, the *Post*'s American-born editor, was hit. Staff members worried increasingly about the fate of their families. News was thin; the Israeli authorities were unwilling to tell the world how well the war was going.

Charles Weiss, who had come to Palestine as a very young crewman on an illegal immigration ship in 1947, had three young children in school; and his wife Varda telephoned him at the *Post* to say she could not locate their eight-year-old daughter Noa. Since the No. 5 bus had stopped running, Weiss walked across town from the *Post* to Rehavia. He found Noa in the shelter of a friend's home and walked her home. They passed a brand-new house with a shell hole in the ground-floor apartment. Weiss counted more than twenty mortar shells that had landed within a hundred yards of his house. He ate lunch quickly and walked back to the *Post*.

Mrs. Yochevet Tubiana had just left her first-floor apartment at 13 Yefe Nof Street near the Beit Ha-Kerem section when the sirens sounded. A neat, little, brown-eyed lady who had spent three years in a British prison for her activities in the anti-British Irgun, she thought the sirens were just a test. Her

51

husband, whom she had met in the Irgun, was on duty as a bomb disposal expert in the civil defense; and their four children were in school.

The night before, Mrs. Tubiana wanted to bring her mother to the safety of her home; her Persian-born father would not leave his pupils in the religious school where he taught. Mrs. Tubiana's sister talked her out of moving their mother and thus saved her life.

Monday morning, despite the alarm, Mrs. Tubiana walked the three-quarters of an hour to her job as a medical secretary in a mental hospital in Talbiya on the southern side of the city. When the shelling started, she helped move the patients to the ground floor.

At about 9:30, a dust-covered Israeli military officer, up from the Sinai desert to report to the Cabinet, stopped at the home of journalist Michael Elkins in Bene Berit Street to clean up before meeting his superiors. Elkins heard him singing in the shower and his curiosity was aroused. When his friend came out, Elkins pressed him for news. He was told nothing; but because of the man's particular job and his joyous singing, Elkins realized the Israelis must have scored some really enormous air victory.

Elkins, who had been born on Hester Street on New York City's Lower East Side, had come to fight in the 1948 war and had stayed. Now a stringer for the BBC and a correspondent for CBS and *Newsweek*, he tried to figure out the news before the Israeli authorities would release it. An hour later, he was at the Knesset. He says, "Everyone was gathered in the basement. I eavesdropped and heard enough bits and pieces to put it together. Then I went to Ben-Gurion in the basement of the Knesset and told him what I had. He said, yes, it was accurate. I asked him if he would record a message to the Jewish people because Eshkol was busy and wouldn't see me. The only thing he would say was, 'Tell the Jewish people not to worry.'

"About three hours after the war started, I broadcast that the war was won. I knew of the air strike on the Egyptian airfields and planes. It was obvious that by fighting in the Sinai desert without air cover the Egyptians couldn't win. It was equally obvious that with the Egyptians quickly defeated, the Syrians couldn't stand. Jordan hadn't started.

"I took this story to the censor who said, you must be out of your mind. I said, no, it's true; and he began crying. There was great fear here, real fear. The censor said I couldn't send it. I said there are millions of Jews who are weeping now out of fear. The Arabs are broadcasting that they bombed Tel Aviv and so on. He said, well, find a way to do it.

"I found a way. I simply said that I could not report precisely what happened, but it was fair to say the Egyptian Air Force no longer existed, and Israel had discovered the nearest thing to a formula for instant victory ever found. They let that through.

"Nobody believed it. I had worked for CBS for eleven years. They held up the broadcast, and then they used it and sent me a telex: 'Your instant victory broadcast widely used radio television coast to coast creating nationwide sensation. There is no support from any other source. You'd better be right.' I thought, the bastards!

"I was brand-new for BBC, and people in London said that's what you get for having a Jew report from Israel. They did not carry me in voice for the first hour or two because they felt that—as they put later in a report—I had spoken with the tongue of the prophets and the exhilaration showed. It probably did. Part of it may have been compounded from just having this beat. But part of it was my own feeling. The BBC's military advisor was a guy I knew in Yugoslavia; they asked him if it was feasible, and he asked who said it. When he heard I said it, he said it must be true. That was nice of him. Nobody else had the story until that evening; *Ma'ariv* [the Israeli daily] put out a special edition saying the Egyptian Air Force had been nearly destroyed, and the *Jerusalem Post* had it. They were the first after me."

At 10 A.M., Raphael Levi, the District Officer of Jerusalem who represented the Foreign Ministry in dealing with the Jordanians and who was in charge at Mandelbaum Gate, began his usual Monday morning meeting with his Jordanian counterpart. Their task was to make arrangements for Muslim and Christian families who had members on both sides of the border. The families would wait in the open area on each side of the Green Line while the officials discussed their fate in the UN's MAC house.

By 10:10 A.M. they decided to disperse; and Levi, who came

from a family that had roots for three hundred years in Hebron south of Jerusalem, hurried back to his office in the Generali Building in downtown Israeli Jerusalem.

While Chaim Herzog drove from his home in Zahala to his office in Tel Aviv's Shalom Tower, he heard that the war had begun. He rushed over to the journalists' house, Beit Sokolov, and at 10 A.M. he was on the air. "A new chapter in the wars of Israel has been opened," he began. "If I refrain for the moment from reporting the conduct of the war, the reason is self-evident. The fog of war hinders the enemy, and so let us leave him with it rather than dispel it." And he closed his broadcast saying, "Deep in the heart of each and every one of us at this moment when we think of those engaged in the struggle, there is, irrespective of whether we normally pray or not, a prayer that the 'Guardian of Israel shall neither slumber nor sleep.'"[5]

Shortly after 10 A.M., Carmella Yadin, the wife of Yigael Yadin, in their home at Ramban 47 in the Rehavia section, received a telephone call from her husband. He was at General Headquarters in Tel Aviv, sitting just behind General Morde-chai Hod, the commander of the Israeli Air Force; and he knew precisely the enormous success of the Air Force. He told his wife, "I think Israel was reborn just now."

He returned to the immediate questions at hand: "There was a big debate then whether or not we should announce immediately what had happened to the Egyptians to deter Hussein. It was clear that the war was won as far as the Egyptians were concerned. At the end, Dayan's decision was not to announce anything. I don't think Dayan's purpose was to lure Hussein, but he thought the whole idea to announce was premature. If we should announce after a few hours of war what we had destroyed, it would be boasting. By then it was quite clear that even if Hussein will join the war, our Air Force would be free to deal with him. Everyone felt he was given fair warning and we really shouldn't try anything else. Mr. Eshkol had person-ally, through the UN and other means which we had, appealed to King Hussein not to interfere, but, of course, to no avail, and immediately shelling was started on Jerusalem." At that moment, it was still the policy of the government of Israel to maintain the status quo with Jordan, the West Bank and the divided city of Jerusalem. Events were about to change policy.

— Chapter 4 —

"THUS, YEHUDA,
THE WAR BEGINS"

WHEN THE JORDANIANS' MORTAR AND ARTILLERY FIRE started to strike Jewish Jerusalem, the sirens roared their warning—a rising and falling wail lasting three ear-pounding minutes. This time—unlike the weak, uncertain alarm at 8 A.M.—the signal was loud and clear.

"The alarm went off at 11:15," remembers Shaul Rosolio, the forty-three-year-old Sabra who was Israeli Jerusalem's chief of police. "Mothers went into the streets and collected children—no matter whose children—into shelters and homes, until somebody came and took them. Everybody knew everybody else would be taking in children and they would be fed and taken care of—without any kind of organization.

"A funny side of this country is that when everything is all right, all the red tape is impossible. But once things are really tough, it's beautiful. No problem. Everything is efficient. Everything. The people do wonders."

At the Foreign Ministry, Yehuda Avner, who had worked until 4 A.M. and been awakened by the sirens four hours later, was reviewing with another official the analysis he had prepared of the events leading up to the war. They began to hear the firing of machine guns and artillery in the distance. "My dear colleague stood up and, always correct, said, 'Thus, Yehuda, the war begins.'

"Now I couldn't leave for New York. I was so happy. When the sirens sounded again, people started going into the trenches we had dug on the grounds. As I made my way out, another colleague of mine said, 'We have shot down over two hundred Egyptian planes.' It was beyond belief."

The Jordanian shelling struck not only Jerusalem but also the suburbs of Tel Aviv and Netanya on the Mediterranean coast, and Jordanian planes got in one effective strike near Tel Aviv.

The shelling brought up sharp the decision makers in Israel's military headquarters. It took them time to realize the shells were from Jordan. First they thought that it was an aerial attack and then that the shelling came from the sea. In an hour, the Israeli commanders eliminated those possibilities and recognized that Jordan was in the war with both feet. Haim Barlev says that with the shelling of Tel Aviv by American-made 155-mm guns, "It became clear it was a major decision." The Israeli General Staff had to turn its attention to the eastern front and Jerusalem.

To make the decision to fight in Jerusalem was not simple. An hour after the Jordanians began firing, the Israeli Cabinet met and unanimously decided to ask Hussein once again to stop through the UN and the United States embassy. The Israeli government still wanted to confine the war to the Egyptian front. But when Jordan, Syria and Iraq made their first air strikes, the Israeli Air Force, already refueled and rearmed and ready, counterattacked.

"When Jordan opened fire it was an opportunity for us to change our plan and to improve our position in Jerusalem," says heavy-set, ruddy-faced Colonel Israel Le'or, Prime Minister Eshkol's military secretary.

"We had military plans and had war games about every eventuality," says General Rabin. Regarding Jerusalem, he adds, "After the war started with Jordan, I knew we would take it. A day more, a day less. No one would allow the situation to remain this way. Instead of arguing, we had to change the military realities to create enough incentive in the political leaders to do it."

Three Israeli brigades—two that had been earmarked as reserve units for the Egyptian front (including Colonel Gur's paratroop Fifty-fifth Brigade) and one brigade from the northern front holding against Syria—were shifted to strengthen the central front against Jordan. The northern brigade was aimed at the West Bank, freeing Colonel Uri Ben-Ari's Harel Mechanized Brigade to support the Jerusalem Brigade. Barlev says, "When it became clear that Jordan had joined the war, what we had at hand along the front was not enough." He decided to send Gur and Ben-Ari to Jerusalem.

General Narkiss' mind was always on Mount Scopus, isolated and vulnerable. He figured the best way to send a relief force there was by pushing armor through Jordanian territory north of Jerusalem to Tel el-Ful on the Jerusalem-Ramallah road east of the Israel-Jordan border. A few days before, Narkiss had gone to the hill called the Castel with Moshe Dayan—he was not yet the defense minister—and surveyed the area. They saw that the problem was to get Israeli tanks up the rugged hills and cut the Jerusalem-Ramallah road before Jordan's superior Patton tanks could reach Tel el-Ful and command the northern access to Jerusalem. Narkiss now called Colonel Ben-Ari and told him to get his tanks to Tel el-Ful by 5 A.M. Tuesday.

By late Monday morning, small-arms and machine-gun fire was heavy in the city. The Israeli artillery did not retaliate to the Jordanians' fire at first, hoping that King Hussein would demonstrate his symbolic solidarity with the Egyptians and let it go at that.

Each side knew in detail the other's positions, built up over nineteen years; but the Jordanian gunners seemed to be shooting into the Jewish sector at random. The firing picked up momentum, especially from the south and from the Old City walls. Yehuda Arbell says, "It was exactly as it was in '48. They were shooting at random into the middle of the city—anywhere."

Because Camp Schneller not far from the border was being subjected to intense fire, about noon Colonel Amitai moved the headquarters of the Jerusalem Brigade farther south to the prepared basement of the Evelina de Rothschild Girls School in Rehavia. The school had once been the mansion of a Swiss banker who had built houses in the religious neighborhood of Me'a She'arim and in the process had gone bankrupt.

The Jerusalem Brigade reservists, who were charged with defending the city and holding the Green Line, were firing back. There were machine-gun duels and crackling battles between Jordanian snipers on the Old City walls and Israelis behind sandbags in buildings and on roofs along the border. Israeli artillerymen began groping for the Jordanian guns farther beyond the line.

While the Israeli radio remained stubbornly silent, the Egyptians trumpeted about victories against their Jewish enemy, claiming to have attacked Tel Aviv and the oil refineries in Haifa. Listening in their shelters, the Israeli civilians feared the worst.

At the MAC house, Lt. Col. Stanaway was desperately trying to arrange a cease-fire. He sent two UN observers in a vehicle with a radio to Major Levinson's office to maintain radio contact in case the telephones failed. At 11:22, the first mortar round hit near the MAC house. At 11:25, Stanaway notified Levinson he would ask Daoud for a cease-fire and fifteen minutes later called back to say Daoud agreed to a cease-fire at noon. Five minutes later, Levinson informed Stanaway that General Headquarters agreed to the cease-fire. An Australian major who was with Stanaway in the MAC house says, "I felt that in the early hours both sides were keen to effect a cease-fire. I think there was genuine desire on both sides not to have a war."

Noon came and passed and the Jordanian shellfire continued. The Israelis were now returning the fire with all the resources they had.

At 12:20, Major Roger C. Hagerty, a United States Marine who was the operations officer at Government House, called and told Levinson that Stanaway was having trouble reaching him by telephone and wanted a cease-fire for 12:30. But at 12:30 Israeli orders were given to silence the Jordanian batteries with the until-then secret, short-range Lascoff rockets. At 1:32, Hagerty called again and passed the message that Stanaway asked for a cease-fire at 1:30. Levinson replied, "How can we agree to a cease-fire for 1:30 when it is now 1:32?"

At 2:45, Stanaway proposed a cease-fire at 3:00 and again the Israelis agreed to a halt in the firing. The Israeli government still wanted to keep this a one-front war; but General Narkiss says, "At that time I felt that this was the moment we might conquer Jerusalem."

By now time was running out. Although Stanaway doggedly

kept trying for twenty-four hours, the battle for Jerusalem could no longer be stopped.

The Jordanians were heartened by the Egyptian broadcasts. Not only did Jordan shell Israeli Jerusalem, but at about noon its aircraft attacked the Sirkin air base near Petah Tikva, Lod Airport and the Ekron air base. The planes did little damage but destroyed a transport plane on the ground at Ekron.

Jordan had only twenty-four fighter aircraft; and once they attacked the Israeli bases, Israeli aircraft, on their way to smash an Egyptian base, were diverted to attack the Jordanian Air Force at Amman and Al Mafraq, the site of an air base northeast of Amman. Israeli Mirages, Mystères and Super-Mystères flew nineteen sorties against Amman and twenty-seven at Al Mafraq and put out of action a radar installation at Ajlun, northwest of Amman. The battle was one-sided. Jordan lost 21 of her 24 fighter aircraft as well as 6 transports and 2 helicopters. In all, the Israeli Air Force would destroy 170 Jordanian tanks, 550 trucks and 80 armored vehicles. Israeli air losses against Jordan were 6 aircraft, 3 destroyed on the ground and 3 from ground-air attacks; 3 Israeli pilots were killed and 2 wounded.

The Israeli jets strafed the airport outside Amman for twenty minutes, machine-gunning and rocketing installations at low levels and flying between the seven hills on which Amman is built. Just before dusk, the Israeli fighter-bombers bombed Amman again for about an hour and knocked out its radio transmitter. The Jordanians had to switch radio operations to their station at Ramallah. King Hussein later protested that the Israeli planes tried to hit his palace in Amman. But the Israeli Air Force insisted that its pilots had no orders to attack the palace or any other civilian installations. The king's palace was not hit.

The Israelis also attacked three air bases in Syria with 67 sorties and a base known as H-3 in Iraq with 19 sorties. The Syrians lost 61 aircraft and the Iraqis lost 43.

After Dr. Uri Khassis visited the clinics he had set up in various parts of the city, he drove through the poor, shabby Musrara quarter along the Green Line northwest of the Old City. He heard shooting and hurried to his command post in the basement of the Generali Building in Jaffa Road near the post office. He immediately ordered ambulances spread throughout the city. When the Jordanians on the heights of Nebi Samuel fired at Israeli army units on Mount Herzl, he radioed ambulances to go there; they arrived in minutes. The small military hospital at Camp Schneller, the headquarters of the Jerusalem Brigade, was hit and moved to the Magen David Adom station in the Romema quarter farther west.

With the five regular male drivers mobilized in the army, only one ambulance was driven by a professional: Siema Hazan, a dark, trim, third-generation Jerusalemite. Throughout Monday she gathered wounded civilians and brought them to the hospitals. She even carried wounded neighbors from Shemu'el Hanavi Street on the border where she lived with her parents. She left the ambulance near the King David Hotel and walked down into the Yemin Moshe section, despite the shelling, to help a frightened woman, who refused to leave her shelter, give birth. The woman produced her first son after four girls, and Siema convinced her to go with her baby to the hospital.

The French Hospital, right on the border and across the street from the New Gate at the northwest corner of the Old City, had been evacuated during the preceding days of tension. This morning it contained only one last patient, an elderly blind man; and Dr. Israel Lichtenstein wanted to take him to an old people's home on the southern side of the city. The French Hospital, which had been built by the French order of St. Joseph of the Assumption to care for the residents of the Christian Quarter inside the New Gate, was a dangerous place. It had long been a target for sniper fire from the Old City wall. Dr. Lichtenstein said, "They shot people—doctors or not—in this Christian house of charity. It's like they have cholera in India. Here they have shooting. It's a kind of endemic disease in this country."

Dr. Lichtenstein, a short, vibrant, athletic man, walked with crutches. Although he had been a doctor in Paris, his birthplace, and was now thirty-four years old, he had volunteered for the paratroopers. He made his seventh training jump the previous December at night in a storm; of the fifty-five paratroopers in his plane, eight had been injured. Dr. Lichtenstein broke his left hip and spent months in the hospital. As soon as he could, he went to work on crutches.

Although he could not walk, he could drive his beige Peugeot; and he set out with his blind patient. He started on the most direct way past the King David Hotel, but the Jordanians shot at him from the Old City wall so he detoured through Rehavia. Shells started falling; he drove in a wide circle to the west and then to the old people's home in the Ge'ulim section. Dr. Lichtenstein dropped off the old man and went to his own home nearby in Bethlehem Street. ("I lived in Bethlehem Street and I had never been in Bethlehem," he says wryly.)

He and his wife, Hannah, who had been born in Morocco and whom he had met in Paris, took the car to get their two sons, ages four and five, who were in kindergarten fifty yards from the border. They were fired on from the Mar Elias Monastery; there the Jordanians had an artillery position near the road to Bethlehem and Hebron south of the Green Line which swung back to the west. Under fire, Dr. Lichtenstein says, "I thought: My parents died in Auschwitz. I can die here in the Holy Land."

In his wallet, Dr. Lichtenstein carried a picture of himself as a ten-year-old boy wearing a dark jacket with a yellow Star of David. When his parents were taken to Auschwitz (his mother actually survived but died soon afterwards), he had been placed in a Jewish orphanage in France and had escaped and hid in a small village. He had worn the yellow star in occupied France. He says, "It is a reason to be here. It is a reason to go to the army. It is a reason to do crazy things. It can explain Israel."

The medical units around the city came under increasing pressure. A military truck loaded with ammunition was hit near Mount Herzl and blocked the road to Hadassah Hospital. Dr. Khassis moved medical personnel to the Biqqur Holim Hospital off Jaffa Road nearer the city center. When the Jerusalem Brigade counterattacked Government House in the south, radio instructions shifted ambulances there to care for the wounded and to evacuate a home for physically handicapped children in Talpiot, which came under fire. When the Harel Brigade came up toward the northern end of the city, he sent it medical supplies. Dr. Khassis adds, "When the paratroopers attacked that night, our people were right behind them."

At 3 A.M. on Tuesday, he was in the Generali Building basement, answering telephone calls, moving ambulances and allocating beds. He says, "I had a driver named Aram and he asked me if there was anything he could do. Foolishly, I said I'd like something to drink. Twenty minutes later he came back with a cold drink. He had gone through the shelling to his sister's home to get me a drink."

Civilians in Israeli Jerusalem were hit and moved smoothly from first-aid stations to the hospitals. They and the wounded soldiers began to fill the hospitals as the battle gained momentum.

Monday morning, the wounded began arriving at the great Hadassah Medical Center in Ein Karem, west of the city. The hospital was ready. At about 9 A.M., Dr. Jack Karpis, the fifty-nine-year-old South African pediatrician who was the hospital's associate director, had received telephoned orders from the army to enter Stage Three: Get ready to receive emergency cases and move as many of the six hundred civilian patients as possible to the underground shelters. "Each patient had to be seen by a doctor and instructions written out for treatment," says Dr. Karpis. "By that time the battle was on."

During the war in Jerusalem, Hadassah Hospital's skeleton staff, depleted of its younger doctors, would receive more than a thousand wounded soldiers, both Israelis and Jordanians, and perform 350 operations. "The next day and a half were an absolute nightmare of confusion," Dr. Karpis says. "Operating teams in nine operating rooms worked for fifty-four hours solid. They were twelve hours on and twelve hours off, but there wasn't much chance of being off. In fact, two doctors, older people, had coronaries in the operating rooms.

"By mere accident, we had put in charge of seeing patients when they first arrived our best surgeon, the chief of surgery. This saved the situation. Here was a man with judgment who was able to say on the spot this man needs an immediate operation, this man needs a blood transfusion and so on." The chief of surgery, Dr. Nathan Saltz, fifty-four years old and born in New York, had served as a medical captain in the U.S. Army in North Africa and Italy in World War II and received the Bronze Star. His hearing was damaged in the Salerno landing and he wore a hearing aid. He and his wife, Armen, an anesthetist, came to Israel in 1952.

Actually, Dr. Saltz, a large, square-faced, bespectacled surgeon, a commanding figure, had stationed himself at the entrance of the large hall, which had been designed for the possibility of becoming a clearing space for casualties, "because I realized it was important to put the most experienced persons in the receiving area, where the casualties first come, to direct the flow of traffic and see that the casualties that needed the first therapy got it immediately and were operated on in time. The problem is called triage, choosing what has to be done first, and this takes experience."

Several times, Dr. Saltz left the controlled confusion of the receiving area to help surgeons operating on difficult cases with inexperienced support. He says, "We worked steadily through those three days. I didn't believe that it could be done. People caught catnaps between the waves of casualties that came in. Fortunately, it did not last longer."

Most of the wounds they had to deal with were the ripping, multiple type torn by shells, mines and high explosives. But, fortunately, the casualties in this battle could be brought directly from the battlefield to a major, fully equipped hospital that never ran out of blood or supplies. "This made a big difference," says Dr. Saltz. And Dr. Karpis credits the take-charge surgeon for what Hadassah was able to achieve. "The experience he had in World War II was brought into play. I am sure he was responsible for saving many, many lives. Of the more than a thousand patients brought to us, only five died."

Volunteers poured into the hospital. Retired nurses and visitors from abroad showed up to do what they could. The staff made use of the most helpful. One white-haired professor from California vigorously helped carry stretchers. A volunteer who impressed everyone was a tall, strong, silent man who moved beds and heavy equipment about single-handedly. He came from the Baptist village near Herzliya, but he never told anyone his name and after the crisis he disappeared as quietly as he had come.

Because many of the hospital workers had no one to leave their children with, the hospital was swamped with children. A day care center was suddenly created in an underground room of the dental school, and volunteers were assigned to take care of them and feed them.

Soon wounded soldiers, just minutes from the battlefield, were overflowing into the corridors; and mothers who had just given birth were lying on mattresses because their beds were occupied by soldiers. Staff members searched the newly arrived faces anxiously, looking for sons and brothers, and then turned back to their work.

As the activity heightened, up drove Mrs. Nily Gur, eight months pregnant, for her checkup appointment. She says, "When I came to Hadassah, I felt terrible. I think I was the only one who dared to come for a regular checkup. They looked at me like I had committed a crime. Everyone was preparing beds for the war. They saw I was quite worried so they did the checkup.

"Then I drove myself home. The motor made such a noise I did not hear the siren warning of the shelling. I was stopped by the civil defense and when I opened the window I heard the alarm. I left the car in the street and went into a public shelter. I was worried about my six-year-old daughter, Nivi, who was in school; I knew they were prepared; but if they sent her home, she would find no one there. My husband, Shlomo, was a lieutenant in the Jerusalem Brigade. They didn't let anyone out of the shelter; but after an hour and a half, I couldn't stand it anymore and just left.

"I drove to the school near the wall of the Old City. While I was on my way the bombing started up again. When I got to the school, it had no shelter, only some foxholes outside. I drove behind the school, left the car and ran down into the valley toward the school. Everyone was gone, just a few workers were there digging trenches. They were frightened because they were in an open area and there was shelling. I couldn't leave because of the shelling and shooting from the Old City wall and had to stay about an hour. Then I got in the car and drove out of there in reverse. When I reached home in Keren Hayesod Street next door to the American Cultural Center, Nivi was in the shelter with the neighbors. My husband had come three times looking for me and he finally came again for two minutes just before his unit moved out."

About 11:30, the Hadassah Hospital began to be hit by Jordanian artillery shells. One penetrated the outpatient department, and two other shells struck the premature care unit. Shells exploding in the parking lot tore holes in four of the twelve world-famous 11-by-8-foot stained glass windows by Marc Chagall in the hospital's synagogue. Miraculously, no patients were hit.

As Jordanian wounded arrived, they were treated along with

the Israelis according to the seriousness of their wounds; but Dr. Karpis received orders from the army to put them in a separate ward. He says, "There was no antagonism on the part of our staff. There was not a single murmur against treating the Jordanian soldiers. Blood was given freely. They were treated exactly like ours. A wounded person is a wounded person. He's a human life that has to be saved."

At 3 P.M., orders arrived to evacuate the civilian patients. Buses were standing by and the patients organized in groups according to where they lived. In half an hour they were on their way home.

Late that afternoon, Dr. Karpis looked out of his office window to the distant northern height of Nebi Samuel and saw an Israeli armored column approaching the ridge. He did not know until later that commanding one of the half-tracks he could see was Sergeant Charles Karpis, his son.

At 6 P.M., it was still light when Dr. Karpis was relieved for the night and drove home to the Talbiya sector. He was shocked to pass in the Valley of the Cross an Israeli artillery battery firing steadily into Jordan. He spent the night in the shelter of his apartment house with twenty-one others. The water tanks on top of the building were hit, and he climbed up and shut off the water. At 6 A.M. Tuesday, he went back to the hospital for an even busier day of struggling to keep the wounded alive.

One of the first Jordanian shells Monday morning hit a technical school for electronics on the hill of Abu Tor near the Green Line just south of the Hinnom Valley from the Old City. Avi Ella was playing basketball with other students in the school yard. He was sixteen and had been born in Jerusalem just after his parents arrived from Iraq. When the shell struck, everyone fell to the ground and no one was hurt. The principal called the army and was told to take everyone to the center of the Israeli part of the city. Led by three soldiers, a line of 250 teachers and students snaked its way on a long, roundabout hike through the Katamon section of the vicinity of Sha'are Zedek Hospital. Since he lived nearby, Ella ran home to 72 Jaffa Road. It was about 1 P.M. He found the residents of the building, including his parents and younger brother, in the shelter.

After about three hours, Ella says, "I couldn't stay there anymore. I went up to the roof to see what was going on. I didn't tell anybody because if my mother knew I was going up she would have been angry. But I couldn't sit there. None of us knew what was going on. From our roof you can see the Old City and the new city. I saw that our guns were firing from the Valley of the Cross and no guns were firing from the east. I stayed about an hour; and when I came down, I told the people that they could be calm because the shells they heard were ours. We felt better."

But the Jordanian shelling damaged hundreds of houses. When the alarm sounded, Mrs. Eve Zarhaya had just finished ironing in her ground-floor apartment at 5 Rehov Ha-Qeshet. She went down into the shelter and soon she felt the building shake. After noon she climbed upstairs and found the building a shambles, with a gaping hole letting in the daylight and most of her furniture destroyed, except for her ironing board and television set. She went back down to the shelter badly upset. Nearby, 10 Rehov Chopin, across an empty lot from where the President's official residence was to be built, was hit four times; the red tile roof was wrecked and three apartments struck. A car in the street outside was completely crushed.

Shattered branches lay across the half-circle entrance to the King David Hotel and several employees were slightly injured. Three buildings in Magnes Square and a new tall building in Ben Maimon Street took direct hits. Shelling was heavy in the Musrara section near the border.[1]

Fortunately, most of Jerusalem is built of stone. Police Chief Rosolio says, "You had a city being shelled and bombarded at pointblank range. Because it is built of stone, it doesn't burn, it doesn't crumble. Houses had holes through both sides but didn't collapse. Had this happened in Tel Aviv, it would be a different story."

The Sha'are Zedek Hospital in Jaffa Road had gaping holes torn in its stone facade. One shell landed in a storage space overlooking the corridor of the maternity ward where there were twelve mothers and their babies. The shell neither rolled forward nor exploded. Engineers later defused it.

Mayor Kollek, who visited the hospital, recalls: "It was a direct hit on the hospital. This was in the first hour of the war, and it was obviously aimed at the hospital to demoralize people.

We didn't think the shelling was so random—the hospital—the museum—the district where the prime minister lived. On the whole, it was very well pinpointed. They had good British army training.

"By the time we arrived at the hospital, they had already received a few civilian wounded. In the war, we had about fifteen or twenty civilians killed and maybe a hundred wounded in Jerusalem, some in the streets but mainly in their apartments where they felt safe. Some people wouldn't go to the shelters and their apartments were hit."

Mayor Kollek told his remaining staff to start calling schools to send their children home whenever they could. He dragooned Daniel "Danny" Bloch, a twenty-five-year-old Jerusalemite and local reporter for *Davar*, the Mapai Party newspaper. Bloch's army information unit had not been called up, and Kollek asked him to help with the inpouring foreign journalists. Bloch had worked against Kollek, the Rafi Party candidate, in the 1965 municipal election; but now he pitched in to assist the energetic mayor.

When Kollek toured the city in his green Dodge Dart and checked the shelters, Bloch went with him and from time to time other journalists joined them. Bloch says of Mayor Kollek: "He had the instinct to do the right thing. The first thing he did was to order his driver to put the mayor's flag on his car. Until then he had never flown it. His idea was to boost morale. Women and children alone in the shelters in the border quarters like Katamon would see the mayor is there. Mainly we drove along the Green Line."

When the sirens sounded, the eight hundred children and forty teachers of the Ge'ulim School at the southern end of Jerusalem were in their classrooms. For days before, they had filled sandbags and stacked them around the building's glass doors; and they had covered the doors and windows with curtain material stuck on with glue made of flour. Now they moved well drilled to the basement.

The school had been started in 1948 by Polish-born Shlomo Doron, who had fought in the Jewish Brigade of the British army in World War II and been severely wounded in the Israeli War of Independence. He was now fifty-five and still the principal. He had named the school Ge'ulim, which means Redeemed, in honor of one group of children in the school he had run in 1945 in a British camp near Lecce on the heel of Italy's boot. The children in that school were all survivors of the Holocaust, collected from concentration camps and monasteries and private homes throughout Europe. They were eventually brought to Palestine, most of them illegally. Doron says, "I loved the Ge'ulim group more than any other in the school because they were unlucky. We made a lottery and those who were lucky left the camp and went to Palestine. The Ge'ulim group never won the lottery. One night, these children, eight to eleven years old, packed all their belongings and took the train to the port of Bari and boarded a British ship. They were sure they were going to Palestine. Of course, the English sent them back the same day."

So when Doron was asked to establish a school in the empty Arab neighborhood of Bak'a west of Government House, he asked that the school be named Ge'ulim. In time the whole neighborhood, right on the border with Jordan, acquired that name. It was an area of new immigrants from Yugoslavia, Bulgaria and the Arab countries. Poor and eager to adapt to their new life, they made the school the core of the neighborhood. It grew rapidly and the school became one of the largest in Jerusalem.

This Monday morning, five minutes after everyone was in the school's basement, Jordanian shells destroyed two classrooms on the third floor. Other shells landed outside. Residents of the neighborhood who did not have shelters at home began piling into the basement. Shlomo Doron could not turn them away. He says, "It was very crowded in the shelter, but we managed. If people love, even if it is crowded, you can always manage. If there is no love, even if it is comfortable, it always seems crowded.

"You cannot imagine what happened to those people in a few hours. Everybody changed his character. Everybody was ready to do whatever he could for his friend and for a stranger. There were no buses, but whoever had a car used it as a bus. Some people opened their shops and gave everything without money. I have never seen such an understanding that everybody showed to his neighbor."

Mayor Kollek soon appeared at the school. He came down to the shelter to reassure everyone. He said, "Don't worry.

Everything will be all right. The school will be repaired. We are going to win the war." Then he drove to some of the children's homes to tell their parents that they were safe.

Whenever the bombardment eased, teachers led groups of children to their homes. Sometimes they took hours to make their way between volleys. Many children, including those from the border kibbutz of Ramat Rachel, could not get home until late on Tuesday. None of the schoolchildren here was hurt during the battle.

The shelling of the school and neighborhood came from the Jordanian artillery position to the south near the Green Line at the ancient Greek Orthodox monastery of Mar Elias, named for the prophet Elijah. Tuesday morning about noon, an Israeli Fouga Magister jet trainer bombed and knocked out the artillery position. No one in the monastery was hurt. Jordanian anti-aircraft fire killed the plane's pilot, Lieutenant Dan Givon; and the plane crashed into the hillside across the road and broke into hundreds of pieces. Givon was a twenty-one-year-old kibbutznik from Sha'ar Ha'amakin east of Haifa; and after the war, the Ge'ulim School adopted with reverence the memory of the young blond flier.

Another early Jordanian artillery shell struck the Israel Museum, the handsome complex that Teddy Kollek had pushed to completion two years earlier. The museum sits on the hilltop above the Valley of the Cross where many Christians believe was cut the wood for the Cross used in the Crucifixion of Jesus. Among the trees in the valley, near the Greek Orthodox theological seminary in the Monastery of the Cross, the Israelis had now set up a major mortar position.

The Jordanians could have been aiming at the mortar battery or at the Knesset atop the very next hill. No one knew. Shells broke several of the museum's windows and caved in the roof of the archaeological pavilion. One hit an empty spot in the outdoor Billy Rose Art Garden but did no damage to the sculptures there. The museum's most valuable art objects had been rushed down to the basements as soon as the war started and were not harmed.

Under the direction of Mrs. Elisheva Cohen, the museum's chief curator, and Yohanan Beham, the acting director, every object had been tagged with one of three colors according to its importance—red marking the most valuable. A crew of young people and volunteers had worked swiftly to bring the pieces to safety. In addition to moving the permanent collection, they had to carry down a large collection of African art on loan from the Paul Tishman family in New York. By 10:30, before the shelling started, the job had been done.

Among the young people who worked demonically to protect the art was twenty-seven-year-old Martin Weyl. When the museum was built in 1965, Weyl was a student at the Hebrew University and as a construction worker helped put together the eighteenth-century Italian synagogue which was rebuilt inside the museum. Born in Holland, young Weyl was a survivor of German concentration camps; he and his parents were liberated from Theresienstadt when the Soviet army overran Czechoslovakia. After the war, he graduated from high school in Holland. Although he experienced no anti-Semitism in Holland, he came to Israel in 1959—against his family's wishes. He says, "I felt it was not good not to be able to defend oneself and to be taken away just like that, especially since I came from a very assimilated family that was sure nothing would happen to them and didn't believe in being Jewish at all. In Holland I was allowed to be the child Jesus Christ in the school Christmas play because I was Jewish. I was something special because I was Jewish and this always bothered me."

Monday morning he left his eight-month-old son, Ory, with neighbors, because his Sabra wife, Tamar, was visiting her sister in a Negev settlement town. Tamar that morning was frantically trying to hitchhike back to Jerusalem against the flow of military traffic. She caught a ride on a truck full of oranges and ammunition. As they drove past hordes of vehicles filled with soldiers heading south, she threw oranges to them. She finally reached Jerusalem that night.

Another young worker at the museum this morning was a guide named Meira Perry, a twenty-two-year-old Sabra who was also a student at the university. When she arrived at the museum, she learned the war had started. Martin Weyl calmly explained to her some of the paintings as they carried them to safety.

When they thought everything essential had been put away except for the unmovable sculptures of the Billy Rose Art Garden, everyone gathered in the museum's two basement shelters. Among the group was the pregnant French wife of the Norwegian craftsman who was casting and erecting in the Billy Rose Garden a twenty-foot-high concrete Picasso sculpture, the gift of donors in Antwerp.

Weyl says, "Someone suddenly shouted: 'The Dead Sea Scrolls!' and several of us ran outside. The bombing had already started, and we ran through it and took the scrolls under our arms and put them in the cellar of the main building." The huge Isaiah Scroll on a drum in the center of the Shrine of the Book building was supposed to be handcranked into a cavity in the ground and sealed, but they had trouble lowering it to safety.

At the end of the morning, Meira Perry—whose husband was in the Jerusalem Brigade and later fought at Abu Tor— left the museum shelter and went to help her aunt tape her apartment windows. When Meira reached King George Street, the shooting grew heavier and she spent the next hours in the shelter of a store. She finally reached her aunt's home and stayed there until Wednesday. By that time, Weyl had volunteered to drive a garbage truck and bring milk and food to the people in the Musrara section on the border.

Meanwhile, in the museum shelter, which had first-aid supplies and water but no food, people were starting to get hungry. About four o'clock, when the firing seemed to decrease, Yohanan Beham drove off to search for food. All the shops were closed, but he saw a bread truck, stood in line and bought ten loaves. In the Mahane Yehuda Market, he found a felafel stand still open and bought all the felafel that was ready. Back in the museum shelter, everyone's mood picked up. Beham says, "The felafel was a bonus."

After dark he went home, stopping at the apartment of Mrs. Willem Sandberg, the elderly wife of the museum's artistic advisor who was abroad. Beham found her sitting in complete darkness because she didn't know how to lower the shutters. He completed her blackout and turned on the lights; but she had no food, so he returned to the museum and brought her half a loaf of bread.

In Beham's ground-floor apartment in Shalom Aleichem Street, his wife, Bea, and daughter, Sash, had taken the glass from the windows and put it under the beds. They were terrified because strange men were wandering through their garden.

They didn't know whether they were Israelis or Jordanians. They turned out to be members of an Israeli defense unit that was forming in the street.

Along the Green Line in the city, the Jerusalem Brigade's second-line units of older men sat in trenches to defend the Israeli sector from attack. About a hundred soldiers in the Third Company were positioned north of the Old City and across no-man's-land from Nablus Road. When the first man was wounded on Monday, the corpsman who rolled up his sleeve found his arm tattooed with a number from Auschwitz. They were of that generation.

The company was commanded by an unlikely soldier named Chaim Guri. A Sabra who had been in the first class of Israeli parachutists trained in Czechoslovakia, he was now forty-three years old and a poet and essayist known throughout the country. Before the war, intellectuals, writers and academics, who had not been mobilized because of poor health or foreign citizenship, gravitated to him, asking to be taken into his company. At first, Captain Guri refused to accept them; it was against regulations and he felt he could not be responsible for them. But as it happened, his battalion commander was a student of some of the professors who wanted to join; and they told Guri that if the battalion commander didn't accept them, he would not pass his exams. This mild bit of blackmail seemed to work. The battalion commander finally told Guri to accept anyone who had papers from earlier army service; he would take care of the formalities later. The Third Company, although it still consisted in the main of ordinary workingmen, came to be known as "The Professors Company."

One man who showed up just before the war without papers of any sort was a professor of economics, Robert Shershevsky. He was thirty years old; two years in a bunker in the Warsaw Ghetto had damaged his lungs, disqualifying him for Israeli military service. When Guri turned him down, Shershevsky said he would stay anyhow; and Guri assigned a veteran to show him how to use the Israeli weapons. On the evening before the war, Guri and the young professor sat and talked about what would happen. Shershevsky, who was a pacifist, said he believed the war that was coming was inevitable and just. On Monday afternoon when the battle in Jerusalem was under way; the economics professor lifted his head above the trench and was shot between the eyes. The poet-commander wondered about a survivor of the Warsaw Ghetto who came to Jerusalem and was killed. Why was this his fate?

The place where Guri's company held the line was destined to be one of the Israeli army's breakthrough points before dawn on Tuesday. In front of the men stretched the mined and barbwire tangle of no-man's-land, beyond which the Jordanians were dug in, waiting. Next to the company's trenches stood a house where five women and a few children still lived; their men had gone to war. Years before, these families had come from Persia to Palestine illegally and the barbwire of the Green Line stretched right in front of their home. They lived always on the very edge of danger.

Early Monday, Guri and the other company commanders had been summoned to brigade headquarters and warned that the Jordanians might use poison gas. Guri thought it was a macabre joke: the gas was supposed to be Russian and the gas masks were German. Since women and children constantly visited the men in his company and people from the neighborhood brought them coffee and sandwiches, Guri feared that word of the gas threat would spread panic through the city. He did not tell his men of the possibility. It depressed him deeply.

Shells hit near Mayor Kollek's apartment in the Rehavia section, possibly aimed at the home of Prime Minister Eshkol in Ben Maimon Street nearby. Kollek drove home to see if the occupants were safe. He found his wife, Tamar, and their seven-year-old daughter, Osnat, in the basement shelter. Their nineteen-year-old son, Amos, was with his army unit. Osnat had walked to school as usual that morning; and when the shelling began, the grandmother of a girl across the street had brought her home.

In the shelter were a number of children: grandchildren of neighbors, the daughter of a woman who worked for Sabena airlines and could not get home. Kollek brought to the shelter the young daughter of the widowed maid who worked for them.

"People didn't think the Jordanians would attack," says Tamar Kollek. "We listened to the news as much as possible. The children slept. Teddy came around and told us what was going on. More than frightening, it was a kind of relief that the fighting had finally started. Chaim Herzog came on the radio; he was wonderful, very reassuring."

Mrs. Kollek knew how a Jerusalem shelter compared with being under attack in the frontier kibbutz of Ein Gev on the Sea of Galilee, where they had lived years before: "Even though Jerusalem was on the border, you did not feel the isolation you did in Ein Gev. It was very different in an outlying settlement on the Syrian border. I remember in 1938 and '39 Ein Gev was attacked when it was still stockade-and-watchtower and you could hear the bullets hitting the wall."

Because the Israeli army had ordered radio silence to prevent the enemy from gaining information, Egyptians' exaggerated reports of victories dominated the airwaves and frightened many Jerusalemites. Mayor Kollek went from shelter to shelter, telling the occupants that the Egyptians were lying and the Israeli cause was progressing well. He saw that the apartment houses along the Green Line, occupied mainly by Jewish immigrants from Arab countries, were being hard hit.

Not everyone could seek safety in the shelters. In the government offices, employees were instructed to go to the basement; but Mrs. Uzay, the Cabinet Secretary, and her secretary, had to stay at their posts relaying telephone messages from Eshkol and his staff in Tel Aviv to the ministers in Jerusalem. She says, "It was a big shock when the Jordanians started firing. I didn't believe my ears because I knew they had been warned."

A young neighbor in the German Colony telephoned Yehuda Arbell and asked if he would take her to the kindergarten to pick up her daughter. He said the child was safer in the school's shelter, but she insisted. "The feeling of people was that they wanted to be together," he says. He picked her up in his Peugeot and drove toward the kindergarten. A shell landed twenty yards in front of the car. They ran into a shop, waited a couple of minutes and then drove on.

The school was engulfed by shells and smoke. While he turned the car around, she dashed into the building and came running back with the child in her arms. Then he drove her home. "On the way, I told her this was completely crazy, because it was an unnecessary risk for her and her child."

Before Arbell returned to his office, he stopped at his home and saw that his wife and their two daughters were safe. They had cleared a basement room.. His daughters were running around outside picking up pieces of shrapnel. He was confident that his wife could manage; she had been born in Warsaw and had escaped at the last minute before the Germans came.

At the new Hebrew University campus in Givat Ram, west of the city center, was set up an emergency civil defense center directed by Shemaryahu Talmon, a Polish-born associate professor of Bible. A shell struck the parking lot nearby and shattered the windows of every car there.

One member of this civil defense unit was Dr. G. Douglas Young, an American clergyman of the Evangelical Free Church of America. He had founded the Institute of Holy Land Studies on abandoned property of the Church of England to enable young clergymen and other students to come and study the Holy Land and Biblical history. Dr. Young says, "As a Christian, I wanted our clergymen to be familiar with the silence of the Christian church in the Holocaust."[2]

Monday morning, the gray-haired, quiet-speaking Dr. Young drove the institute car out to the edge of Jerusalem to bring back members of the civil defense unit; no buses were running. On the way back, they came under Jordanian fire from Nebi Samuel and passed a large truck that had taken a direct hit and was blazing.

Later in the day, Jordanian prisoners of war started arriving at the university and were concentrated on the tennis courts. One Jordanian told Dr. Young that he was getting tired of being a prisoner of the Jews; this was the third time he had been captured. According to Dr. Young, the prisoners were well treated. One soldier who had lost a buddy in the fighting kicked a POW and was immediately arrested and locked up.

Monday afternoon, a recent immigrant from England came to fetch his wife, a doctor at the mental hospital in Talbiya; and Mrs. Yochevet Tubiana, the medical secretary who had walked so far to work, hitched a ride with them. In the shelling, the couple picked up their daughter from a kindergarten and then drove themselves home. From there, Mrs. Tubiana still had a long walk to her own home.

As she neared her house she saw a crowd. She wondered why they were not in the shelter. She saw her husband and their children carrying things out of the building. A shell had come through the wall of the Tubianas' bedroom, crossed the apartment and buried itself in the kitchen wall. Mrs. Tubiana could only think, "If I had brought my mother here, she would have been in the room that was bombed. I thanked God nobody was hurt.

"We went up to the third floor to my neighbor. Behind the trees is the military cemetery on Mount Herzl. In the background we heard the song, 'Jerusalem of Gold.' We saw the military cars carrying the victims of the war, and we knew the price we had given for the right to live here. In this cemetery you see that everyone in this land was a soldier and took part in this great thing. All the history of the Jews is a continuation. You can't say we start something and we finish it. From your birth until death, which I hope will never be, it's one story."

Just north of the university, the large building of the Hebrew University Secondary School was hit by four or five shells shortly after the alarm sounded; more than a thousand students and teachers filed into the basement shelters. All the shells but one struck in a few minutes of each other; the final one hit hours later. They smashed the assembly hall, a downstairs corridor and the glass-fronted entrance hall. Windows were splintered, but the fabric that everyone had pasted on the glass held the fragments. No one was injured.

Dr. Meir Shapira, the school's long-time director, lay on the floor in the main hall outside his office when the shells hit. A deadly piece of shrapnel landed a few feet from him. He was glad he had drilled the school for emergencies and equipped the shelters with first-aid supplies, water, biscuits and candy. He judged that the shelling came from the heights of Nebi Samuel north of the city and must have been aimed at a military installation in the valley beyond the school but fell short.

A thoughtful, precise man, a mathematician and physicist by training, Dr. Shapira was responsible for this special academic-oriented high school, most of whose graduates went on to the university. He had been with the school since 1944 and its director since 1953. In this morning of crisis, he was surprised that he felt very calm: "There was not even fear. It reminded me of when I was a boy studying in Vilna; when I prepared for an examination, I was tense; but when I entered the hall to start the examination, I was absolutely quiet. Before the war, we were in tension; but when the war broke out, everyone in this building from the oldest to the youngest sat and sang. Unbelievable! Not only calm but cheerful."

During the afternoon, parents arrived to pick up their children and volunteered to take other youngsters home. Since the students came from all over the city, it took until seven o'clock to empty the building. The graying director was the last to leave. Civil defense people painted over his headlights, and he drove home to Bet Ha'Karen.

The calm in the high school was not typical of what was happening in the shelters of Israeli Jerusalem that morning. Mayor Kollek says, "The men were all in the army; there were only women and children, mainly immigrants from Iraq and Morocco. They heard the Egyptian radio's reports of one tremendous victory after another. Tel Aviv had been shelled and Haifa had been burned. There was no Israeli radio news. The people got extremely nervous.

"In some cases their children were in school and in separate shelters. The parents heard the shelling and worried whether anything had happened to the children. Couldn't they get the children? Of course, the most dangerous thing was to move people from one shelter to another. This was the one thing we didn't want to do. In some cases, it was sixty or seventy hours before children and parents were united again."

With his usual candor, Kollek later said, "In the rush and excitement of those first hours of war, it never occurred to me how absurd it might later sound that the mayor of a city under attack was dashing around carrying messages between parents and their children because the phones were out. But the truth of the matter is that I really had nothing better to do, and it still seems to me that personally helping to promote calm in the city was far more constructive work than sitting in the mayor's chair pretending to do something important."[3]

He adds, "There was always something to do—shelters, sandbags, traveling around at night and seeing that people kept the blackout—satisfying lots of needs and worries. There was no time for long, historical thoughts."

Just before noon, Kollek went home and changed his white shirt for a dark one so he would not be a conspicuous target. Near the Knesset, he stopped at the municipal kitchens that prepared meals for the schools and grabbed a bite. Then Kollek visited Narkiss' Central Command headquarters, which was now in a bunker deep beneath Jerusalem's Convention Hall.

The tension, the fear, the sense of isolation wore on people's nerves. Into one shelter in a building on Chell Street above the Monastery of the Cross, Mrs. Esther Bachrach, a tall, blond interior decorator and wife of microbiologist Uriel Bachrach, who was on reserve duty at Amitai's headquarters, brought their two children, Zelila, eleven, and Gilad, four and a half. They spent three days and nights in the crowded basement. People dashed out at times to bring food and lemonade to the mortarmen in the valley. Once, Esther took Zelila with her; they were caught in a renewal of the gun duel, dropped their offerings and ran back to the shelter. The shelling shook the house. Esther says, "It was like a concert—a terrible concert."

People in this shelter grew increasingly frightened. One woman who had gone through the Holocaust was particularly afraid. They listened to the Arab broadcasts announcing attacks on Tel Aviv, Netanya and Haifa. Little Gilad was terrified; he asked, "Mommy, how do you think they are going to kill us, with knives or with guns?"

Her husband, who had fought as a demolition expert in Jerusalem in 1948, was now deputy commander of civil defense in the northern part of the city from Jaffa Road to the Pagi border section. He sent milk and food to the shelters in the border communities, crowded with poor immigrants who ran out of supplies. The shelling resulted in desperate calls to help the wounded all along the border. The civil defense lost contact with its posts in Pagi, and Lieutenant Bachrach went out to investigate. The firing had cut the telephone line. He told the people in the shelters of Pagi that the Egyptian Air Force had been destroyed, and their spirits rose.

— Chapter 5 —

MONDAY—JORDANIAN JERUSALEM

AT EIGHT O'CLOCK ON MONDAY MORNING, AS WAS HIS DAILY custom, Brig. Gen. Atta Ali Hazzáa visited the governor of Jordanian Jerusalem, Anwar al-Khatib, in his office. "Around nine o'clock I heard of the attack on Egypt," says Brig. Gen. Hazzáa. "At the same time, the West Bank commander, Maj. Gen. Mohammad Ahmad Salim, informed me that the battle had started, that our artillery was engaging targets inside Israel and to be prepared to execute our defensive plan." King Hussein had already moved two armored brigades with Patton tanks across the Jordan River into the West Bank.

Hazzáa, a dark, short, animated and forceful soldier of forty-five, was responsible for the defense of Jordanian Jerusalem. He was proud of his men and called the Fourth or King Talal Infantry Brigade, which he had commanded for two years, "one of the best trained infantry brigades in the Jordanian armed forces."

He was an experienced soldier. Born near Al Mafraq in the north of Jordan, he had joined the army in 1938 as an illiterate Bedouin private and in World War II served in the Arab Legion in Palestine and Iraq; he rose with loyalty and dash to sergeant major and lieutenant. In the 1948 war with Israel, he commanded the company that seized the Mandelbaum Gate and was decorated for gallantry.

Now he commanded fifteen hundred men in three battalions of infantry, with the Ninth Field Artillery Regiment in support. His infantry were armed with American M-1 rifles, 3-inch mortars and 106-mm antitank guns.

80

The Fourth Infantry Battalion held the northern end of his sector—from Shu'afat on the road to Ramallah south to a point just north of Mount Scopus. In the center, the Second Infantry Battalion was positioned from near Mount Scopus south through the Sheikh Jarrah and Wadi el Joz quarters to the Damascus Gate of the Old City. The Eighth Infantry Battalion held the Old City and the southern side of Jerusalem to Abu Tor.

Strangely, the brigade's headquarters was at Ar-ram, north of the city and east of Qalandiya Airport. Brig. Gen. Hazzáa was unhappy with its location and kept an operational headquarters at Al-Azariyah (Bethany), east of the Mount of Olives toward Jericho, and a forward command post in the Wadi el Joz quarter inside the city.

Another Jordanian organizational arrangement was also disadvantageous to Hazzáa. He had no control over forces either north or south of the city. The troops south of Jerusalem received their orders from the Hebron commander and the troops on the north, from the Ramallah commander. The strategic height of Nebi Samuel should have been commanded by Hazzáa's headquarters in Jerusalem but was subordinate to the command in Ramallah. Says Governor al-Khatib candidly, "In my opinion this was not correct."

Even earlier, at 7 A.M., Lt. Col. Floyd M. Johnson, Jr., of the United States Marine Corps, left his third-floor apartment in the Kaloti building half a block east of the Anglican St. George's Cathedral and two blocks off Nablus Road in Jordanian Jerusalem. Dressed in khakis and his blue United Nations beret, he drove his white UN car, license plate number 4, to Government House in the neutral zone south of the city. "Mick" Johnson, a six-foot-six native of Fort Worth, Texas, had been serving for a year as the deputy to the Norwegian Air Force General Odd Bull, the Chief of Staff of the United Nations Truce Supervision Organization based in Government House.

The United States Marine, now forty-five, had been a naval attaché in Baghdad through the bloody revolution of 1958. Graduated from Rice Institute, he had seen three years of combat as a Marine in World War II—starting as a member of the 4th Marine Raider Battalion under Major James Roosevelt, the

President's son. He received the Legion of Merit commanding a battalion of the First Marine Division in the Korean War.

During the winter of 1966–67, Johnson had been in charge of Government House after Odd Bull had flown home with hepatitis. Bull only returned to Jerusalem in April when tension between Syria and Israel began to heat up.

Lt. Col. Johnson was often frustrated with General Bull. He felt that the gentlemanly, honest Bull was too cautious and too dependent on instructions from the ponderous UN bureaucracy at headquarters in New York. Johnson said of his chief, "He doesn't react to things forcefully." Although Bull, a tall muscular man, was not especially dynamic and was reluctant to step into the unpredictable maze of UN politics, he had a long and respected military record. He had been one of the few fliers who survived when the Nazis overran Norway and he rose to head the postwar Norwegian Air Force. He was a leader of the United Nations Observer Group in Lebanon when the U.S. Marines landed there in the summer of 1958.

About 8:30, Lt. Col. Johnson's wife Alice drove their private off-white Chevrolet through the Mandelbaum Gate to her weekly appointment at the hairdresser on the Israeli side of the city. Alice, who came from Corpus Christi, Texas, was of the King Ranch family on her mother's side. She had been a reporter on the *Wall Street Journal*, using the byline A. K. Estill, before she and Mick had been married in 1949. For the past three days, they both had been organizing the evacuation of some 350 UN wives and children by convoy to Beirut and by plane to Cyprus. The UN had been reluctant to order the families to leave and thus increase the tension; Johnson says, "I wasn't; their lives were at stake." The battle-smart Marine felt that Israel might preempt the situation.

In the Israeli sector this morning, Alice Johnson found people busily taping their windows. Her hairdresser had been called to his reserve unit. The streets were empty of taxis, buses, cars. While she was there, the shelling started. She drove south to Government House and through the compound's west gate to consult with Mick. She thought of remaining in Government House, but they decided she should go back and stay at the apartment. Mick figured the UN people were experienced "line-crossers," and he would be able to get word to her—which was not to be the case. Alice drove swiftly out of Government House's east gate.

As the sound of machine-gun and later mortar fire echoed up to the hill atop which Government House stood, the local staff of a hundred or so Palestinian Arabs grew increasingly worried about their families in the city. They asked permission to go home.

General Bull conferred with Dennis Holland, his chief administrative officer, and decided to let them go. "We knew things were close," says Holland, a large, affable and incisive Englishman who was responsible for the UNTSO staff. London-born and now forty-six, Holland had served in the Royal Signals during World War II and at Cambridge University rowed for Queens College (from which Anwar Nuseibeh had graduated earlier). He joined the United Nations and in 1962 took charge of the United Nations Relief and Works Administration (UNRWA) field operations in Amman. His district had a second office in the former Police Training School on the Green Line in Jordanian Jerusalem. After a tour in New York, he came back, rather reluctantly, to Jerusalem as UNTSO's chief administrative officer. By this Monday morning, his wife "Sanie" and their three children had already been evacuated to Beirut.

Holland saw most of the Jordanian staff off in their cars and the staff bus. Later in the morning under fire, the staff driver managed to bring the bus back to Government House, where it was subsequently destroyed.

As the battle built up in Jerusalem, the UN foreign staff and the families that had come to Government House—some ninety people in all, including a few remaining women and children—sought shelter in the main corridor on the first floor. It seemed safest there protected by the building's heavy stone walls.

In Jerusalem, when news of the attack on Egypt reached Governor al-Khatib, he summoned Hassam al-Khalidi to his office. Al-Khalidi was the director of tourism for Jerusalem and the West Bank, but his importance was much greater than his title suggested. His family had been Jerusalemites since A.D. 537. He had studied at Heidelberg University until forced out by Hitler's anti-Semitism and served as an officer in the

British army from 1940 to 1946. He became the first commandant of Syria's military academy and in 1948 commanded the Second Syrian Brigade against the Israelis. He was in charge of the United Nations Relief and Works Administration in the Damascus area and then spent several years as an official of the Royal Dutch Shell Group. This spring he had been in Germany as Jordanian Jerusalem's director of tourism and arrived home at 11 P.M. the night before the war started.

The governor told al-Khalidi that he feared the Israelis might invade the West Bank and asked him to stay with him during the crisis. The governor told him that at lunch the previous day the Jordanian Chief of Staff had told him five brigades were in Jerusalem. Al-Khalidi felt confident such a force could hold Jerusalem for a month.

They heard rifle and machine-gun fire. All the civil servants in the governor's office departed, without orders. The only person left was the governor's civilian law clerk.

At 10:15, the governor, at Brig. Gen. Hazzáa's request, moved to the army's forward command post in the concrete room in the basement of the police headquarters behind the Rockefeller Museum and near the Ritz Hotel. Al-Khalidi borrowed the governor's driver and sent him for his shaving kit and additional underclothes. He expected they would be busy for some time. His wife thoughtfully sent along three bottles of cognac.

The command post had two telephones and a World War II radio, which was in contact with police headquarters in Amman. Over it came a string of belated instructions about civil defense measures. At 10:40, King Hussein called the governor to inquire about Ahmed Shukairy, the PLO leader, and Maj. Gen. Wajih al-Medany, a Palestinian who was the PLO's military commander and a veteran of the Kuwaiti army. Al-Khatib told the king that the two PLO leaders had just left the Ambassador Hotel and were headed for Jericho. That upset the king. Then, he asked about conditions in the city, and the governor assured him that morale was high and "they would fight the Jews with their nails if need be."

A few minutes later, Brig. Gen. Hazzáa received orders to distribute arms to Jerusalemites who would resist the Israelis. Some six hundred Canadian rifles were stored in the Old City, but it would take hours to remove the heavy grease in which they were packed.

The governor and al-Khalidi soon realized that the city did not have five brigades. When the governor asked the general directly, he said they would have five brigades by evening. Al-Khalidi feared for the city in the meanwhile.

The general ordered that Israeli Jerusalem be shelled. The artillery fired mostly at random, and al-Khalidi felt it was wasteful and useless against Jerusalem's stone buildings. At first, the Israeli guns did not reply.

Before noon came an order from Amman to capture the hill on which Government House stood. Al-Khalidi was worried. The attack was ordered for one o'clock; but when Brig. Gen. Hazzáa asked him, al-Khalidi recommended that it be postponed until the end of the day. By then their reinforcements should arrive, and the Jordanian troops could seize the hill and lay antitank mines under the cover of darkness and before the Israelis could counterattack. But the general said orders were orders.

The Jordanian brigade had only five 106-mm antitank bazookas; and because Brig. Gen. Hazzáa could not locate his engineer officer, no antitank mines were prepared.

Shortly before noon, the king telephoned Governor al-Khatib again. This time he sounded alarmed; he declared that the defenders of Jordanian Jerusalem should be bold and courageous and fight to the end.

Town Clerk Salah Jarallah, who had served as a municipal civil servant in Jerusalem under both the British and the Jordanians, had walked early this morning from his home two hundred yards inside the Lions Gate through the Old City's narrow alleys, which his family had known for eight hundred years, to his office just inside the Jaffa Gate. His wife, Amineh, was a head teacher at the UNRWA school for refugees in the Jewish Quarter. It still seemed a normal working morning. The forty-seven-year-old town clerk sat at his desk, routinely listening to taxpayers argue about what they had to pay.

Jarallah thought of himself as a Palestinian and resented Jordan's treatment of Jerusalem and its people. He was not alone in this feeling. As early as 1951, Anwar Nuseibeh, then the member of the Jordanian parliament for the Jerusalem region, had written the prime minister, protesting Amman's discrimination against Jerusalem.[1]

Jarallah says, "All through the nineteen years of the regime, they did not treat the inhabitants as Arabs. The people were all the time in revolt against them. Jerusalemites never carried any arms because the Jordanians did not allow even guns for hunting. They levied severe punishment against those they found with a bullet. They might hang them.

"The Jordanians did not care for Jerusalem as they should have. Jerusalemites who wanted to build a project or a factory were asked to go to Amman. East Jerusalem was not helped under any circumstances. Taxes were negligible and services were very poor. Water supply was very difficult. Road construction was only a bit of maintenance. The Old City was still using the very old Turkish sewers."

Of the situation in the spring of 1967, Jarallah says, "In Arab Jerusalem, the tension was not felt by the ordinary people, only by the government officials. Any precautions that should have been made were made by the military. No sandbags were made by the civilians. We never had any shelters; we counted on the basements of buildings. There were no public shelters at all in East Jerusalem. All through the nineteen years, the Jordan regime built a shelter only in two government buildings.

"Immediately after the war started, the army forced civilians to help carry sandbags and ammunition. At about eleven o'clock we began to hear bombs and gunfire all around the city."

The Christian community in Jerusalem was deeply affected by the morning's events. At about 10 A.M., the Greek Orthodox Metropolitan of Caesarea Vassilios, Greek-born and forty-four years old, drove up to the Mount of Olives to fetch His Beatitude Benedictos, the seventy-five-year-old Bishop of Jerusalem and Patriarch of Palestine, from his home and bring him to the Patriarchate near the Church of the Holy Sepulcher in the Old City. Vassilios told the Patriarch, who led the oldest church in Jerusalem, that he had heard on the radio that the war had started. They hurried to see Governor al-Khatib, who tried to reassure them. They went on to the Patriarchate and collected the sixty-odd brothers in the basement of the stone building. That evening, Vassilios was praying in his room. "The planes were flying low and screaming, and I was so afraid

I left my room and left praying and went down again to the basement. I was alarmed."

When Dr. George Farah, the medical director of the Augusta Victoria Hospital, heard of the war on the radio at about 10 A.M., he thought his hospital was both safe and sacred. It was flying the UN flag and the Cross of the Lutheran World Federation.

"When we heard the news about the war, we were happy," says Dr. Amin S. Majaj, the hospital's forty-six-year-old chief of pediatrics. An Anglican Arab, Dr. Majaj had, like Dr. Farah, studied medicine at the American University in Beirut. Dr. Majaj was a political activist and had been shot in the right leg by French Marines during a demonstration in Beirut. He says, "I believe very much in Arab unity and Arab nationalism." But he was not anti-Jewish and as a boy he had a Jewish violin teacher in Jerusalem who became his closest friend. Dr. Majaj had been a deputy mayor in East Jerusalem, a member of the Jordanian parliament and minister of health. He became a distinguished researcher in the anemia of refugees, supported by the U.S. National Institutes of Health and later by King Hussein. This was a bright, practical man who could look at the evidence objectively, despite the strength of his feeling for the Arab cause. He did not think Jordan was strong enough to win a war against Israel.

Dr. Majaj had flown home, cutting short a vacation in Vienna, when the war seemed imminent; and this morning at 9 A.M., when he drove to work from his home near the post office in Salah ed Din Street, he had sensed confusion in the Jordanian section of the city and saw that people were listening intently to their radios.

Dr. Farah had been sending patients home for several days so that now only thirty-six remained. They were moved to the grand festival hall on the main floor. The hospital was undefended except for fourteen policemen paid by UNRWA and barracked across the road and an eight-man Jordanian army unit with mortars and two heavy machine guns entrenched just north of the hospital.

When the firing began from the area of the Mount of Olives, the Augusta Victoria doctors went out on a balcony where they

87

could see what was happening in the city. Their own ordeal had not yet begun.

In Brig. Gen. Hazzáa's command post, Governor al-Khatib heard the firing and ordered the streets evacuated. He sent out loudspeakers telling everyone to go home and dispatched messages to the schools instructing the principals to send their children home. He says, "Some people misunderstood my instructions and said the governor had declared a curfew. That was not true. There was a great difference between asking the people to go home and a curfew. It made some panic.

"Before the war started, the foreign consuls instructed their people to leave; and this also created a sort of panic. Odd Bull had come to my office and said, I want to protect my men and their families in the Government House and I hope that both sides will respect the neutrality of this zone. I assured him on behalf of my government that we would respect the zone. He said he would remove his families in the night so that people would not see that they were evacuating. I thanked General Bull very much for this and assured him that the Jordanian government would respect the United Nations flag.

"I gave him my word because it never occurred to me that that part of Jerusalem would be attacked by anybody. But unfortunately and for the sake of history the Jordanian army started attacking that point.

"Later when I went to Amman, I was told that this order was given by General Riad, an Egyptian officer; and the Jordanian government did not interfere. They gave him freedom to attack any position. He was a very capable officer but why he attacked there is a mystery to me. The first target was to be Mount Scopus because it was a thorn in our back. Everyone agreed. But to my personal horror they started attacking Government House, the place I had given my word of honor should be respected. I tried my best to convince the commanding officer to stop attacking Government House. He said, these are my orders from Amman and I can't do anything. I tried to contact the king; I wanted the king to stop the attack on Government House. I could not get the king on the phone.

"There is a second point that is very important. At about two in the afternoon I received a call from Colonel Mohammad Daoud, who was the Jordanian liaison with the Mixed Armistice

Commission. He said there is an effort to declare a truce in Jerusalem—what is your reaction? I said I accept immediately but the final word is not with me. The final word is with the authorities in Amman. Whether the Israelis were serious in offering this truce, I did not know, but now I believe they were not serious. They wanted Jerusalem by force. It was their dream."

The Jordanians had long developed a plan to defend the West Bank in case of war with Israel. One of their first objectives in the Jerusalem area was to seize Jabal Mukaber, the dominating hill south of the city and the site of the United Nations' Government House. Just before the war, the Ussamah Bin Zeid Infantry Battalion of the Imam Ali Brigade, which was in reserve between Jerusalem and Hebron, was attached to Hazzáa's brigade and brought up to Abu Dis, east of Jabal Mukaber. It would take the hill if war started.

On June 3, Brig. Gen. Hazzáa and Major Badi Awad, the commander of the newly attached battalion, reconnoitered the area. Major Awad, who was now thirty-eight, had fought as an officer cadet in the Old City of Jerusalem in 1948. He had been wounded twice in the head and once in the leg and thigh. Hazzáa explained the plan to him: "As there was nobody but the UN on the hill, they could take the hill easily. I instructed him to place his antitank guns facing the approaches of enemy armor.

"Forty-eight hours before the war, His Majesty King Hussein visited my operational headquarters. He discussed the situation and I explained to His Majesty that, because of my experience in Jerusalem in 1948, I knew the enemy well and needed more troops to support me. So the rest of the Imam Ali Brigade was placed in support of my brigade. It was located on the road from Jericho."

On Friday, June 2, Anwar Nuseibeh, the Cambridge-educated lawyer who had retired earlier that spring as Jordan's ambassador to the Court of St. James's, was in Kuwait on business. He received a telephone call from his wife in Jerusalem, urging him to come home immediately. She was fearful; everyone was talking about war. He did not think there would be a war, but he flew to Amman and drove home to Jerusalem.

The Jordanian countryside was bright with poppies and green from the spring rains.

Nuseibeh says, "On the morning of the fifth we really had no idea there would be a war. I was planning to drive my car to Amman where I had some work to do. I happened to turn on the radio and heard the news about the attack against Egypt. So I decided against going to Amman."

He returned to his home at 49 Nablus Road, a hundred yards south of the American Colony Hotel. He had lived there many years; his father lived next door and his sister, across the road. They were a distinguished and respected Jerusalem family, and Anwar Nuseibeh had read law in the office of a prominent Jewish lawyer who had sat on the city council with Anwar's father. In 1948, when Anwar Nuseibeh, a civilian, was secretary of the National Committee in Jerusalem, he lost his left leg in the fighting near his home.

The Green Line ran through the garden behind his house. The garden contained a bunker from which Jordanian soldiers watched over no-man's-land and in times of tension fired machine guns into Israeli Jerusalem. They had been billeted in the house next door since 1949.

Back home on Monday morning, the first thing Nuseibeh did was to telephone Ahmed Shukairy, the PLO leader. Shukairy had come to Jerusalem the Friday before the war to pray at the al-Aksa Mosque on the Temple Mount, and the crowd had carried him away on their shoulders. Shukairy was a spellbinding orator who appealed to Arab crowds—although he only raised most Westerners' hackles. At least one ardent Arab Palestinian nationalist felt he did the cause more harm than good. Nuseibeh called Shukairy at the Ambassador Hotel to see what he could do to help. "He wasn't there. That convinced me that Jordan at least was in no mood to go to war. He had already left. Later, I heard that he had gone to Amman and Damascus. So I telephoned Governor al-Khatib and asked him if there is anything one can do. He said we are meeting at police headquarters and trying to organize something.

"I went there, and they were still talking about organizing groups of resistance, issuing rifles, things like that. The day the war was on! Well, there wasn't much that one could do in that kind of situation. I told them that I am at home; you can telephone me. And I came back home.

"In the afternoon, the soldiers next door came and insisted that I leave. It was extremely good advice because we would have had no hope of surviving if we had stayed." He and his wife and Saqr, the youngest of their four children, went to a relative's house across the road. With them went their house-guests, the Egyptian consul general and his wife. Before the fighting was over, Nuseibeh's house was riddled with gunfire, doors broken, rooms shot up. His father's house burned to the ground.

That morning, the fifty-four-year-old lawyer and diplomat was still convinced that King Hussein did not want war. "There was some shooting, mainly mortars aimed at the Hadassah compound [on Mount Scopus]. One had the thought it would be occupied by the Arab Legion to protect the northern flank of Arab Jerusalem. The Jordanians were in no position to cross over and attack. I don't think they intended to.

"In fact, the whole thing as far as the Jordanians were concerned seemed to me to be a demonstration of solidarity. I don't think the king had many illusions about the situation. I think he knew that he couldn't carry out a successful war. He said the Arab armies were not ready for a war against Israel at that time. He was taking a tremendous risk, but I think he had very little choice. Once the situation on the southern front became known, the king would be in real trouble. There would be public resentment, public outcry, demonstrations, very, very serious trouble that I don't think the king would have been able to contain. And I think the Israelis would have taken that as an excuse to occupy the West Bank on the pretext that they could not allow unrest so close to their demarcation line.

"The November before, they had attacked the Arab village of Samua near Hebron on the pretext that there was unrest and *fellahin* [Arab farmers] were coming in from that area and bothering the Israeli settlements. They attacked Samua with army and air force and killed a lot of villagers and destroyed a lot of houses. So perhaps the king felt the Israelis would come over—either way. 'Let me do at least the right thing from a national point of view, because the result would be the same either way.'

"And I don't think President Nasser was prepared for war. I think he was trapped into a position where he couldn't save face and avoid a confrontation. What he did, was, again, a

91

demonstrative act and not an act of war. He put two old Turkish guns [at the Strait of Tiran] that would not stop anyone, and the Israelis knew it. The Israelis knew his troop movements were not intended for attack. They were gestures. There were some among them who knew very well that Abdel Nasser did not want war.

"Of course, while Abdel Nasser did not want war, it was a fact that the propaganda and speeches were so tense that it created an atmosphere of war. I think President Nasser would have liked to keep it as political warfare. He was very, very good at that. He didn't want the United Nations to pull out completely; he wanted a limited pullout. However, the United Nations decided to pull out. He couldn't tell them, 'For God's sake, don't pull out.' How could he? He knew the risks. He was not very happy with the prospects. In fact, I remember I was in Kuwait listening to him on television when he said if this means war, I welcome war. He did not sound very convincing. One felt that he didn't really want war and at the same time he was too proud to give in.

"It was my feeling that no Arab leader wanted war, but I did not at that time know what the Israeli feeling was. The Israelis themselves have admitted that their own internal situation was extremely difficult, that they had to explode somehow. And this atmosphere of tense political warfare gave them, I think, a very useful pretext for exploding. Of course, afterwards they said they did it in self-defense, but in their heart of hearts I believe they know very well that it wasn't a case of self-defense, that they could have defended themselves very, very well without going to war. If they had been willing to pursue the diplomatic initiative, possibly war could have been averted. But knowing the Israeli background, I don't think they were very intent on avoiding war. War to them was a convenience."

In Amman at 8:50, King Hussein, waiting for breakfast with his wife, received a telephone call from his chief aide-de-camp informing him that the Israelis were attacking Egypt's airfields. Without breakfast he jumped into his personal car and drove himself to General Headquarters of the Jordanian armed forces, where he switched to a Jeep with a two-way radio. In the neon-lit concrete basement operations room, he met with General

Abdel Moneim Riad, the professional Egyptian soldier who now commanded the joint Egyptian-Jordanian military command in Amman. Riad was not well known to Israeli Intelligence but was reputedly a competent officer. He received orders in code from Marshal Abdel Hakim Amer, commander of the Egyptian armed forces in Cairo, to open a second front from Jordan. General Riad told the king that he had ordered the Jordanian artillery to "occupy the front lines"[2] and an infantry battalion of the Imam Ali Brigade to seize Jabal Mukaber, the site of the headquarters of the UN Truce Supervision Organization.

"We knew that Jerusalem was the most vital spot for both sides," says Colonel Yousef A. Kawash of General Riad's planning and operations staff and senior member of the United Planning Board. The Israeli and Jordanian military strategies toward Jerusalem were similar: attack the city from its flanks.

Colonel Kawash was a Palestinian born in 1923 near Safad in the Galilee; and his Palestinian family history went back five hundred years. He had graduated from the U.S. Army school at Fort Leavenworth, Kansas, in 1959; and since the United Arab Command had been set up in Cairo in 1964, he had been a colonel in its operations branch for the eastern front. On June 2, he had flown to Amman. By 8:30 on June 5, the officers of the combined command in Amman learned of the attack on the Egyptian airfields. Colonel Kawash says, "After war broke out, maybe after ten o'clock, His Majesty appointed General Riad to command the Jordanian armed forces. We sat together with the Jordanian command and started to work together."

At about 11 A.M., Jordan officially started military action against Israel. Jordanian artillery began bombarding Israel. At 11:20 the bombardment opened along the eight-mile-long border inside the city of Jerusalem. The small Royal Jordanian Air Force attacked previously selected targets and was quickly eliminated by the Israeli Air Force. Colonel Kawash says, "After we committed our Air Force we were at war."

Governor al-Khatib says, "Eshkol at that time sent a wire to King Hussein telling him that if you don't start attacking, we will not do anything to your Western Bank. The king admitted receiving this cable from Eshkol but he said it was too late.

"He had no other alternative. Two-thirds of his subjects

were Palestinians and it was the battle for Palestine. How could you expect the king to remain indifferent? Many people blame King Hussein because he took part; but if he didn't take part, all the people would blame him that because he didn't take an active part, they lost the war. He couldn't behave otherwise. He couldn't. So the refusal of accepting the truce, so the attack on Government House. It never occurred to me that everything would be over in a few hours."

Brig. Gen. Hazzáa remembers: "At around 11:15 the Israelis started firing on our infantry positions. I informed Maj. Gen. Salim, and he said I should return the compliment. At the same time, the Ussamah Bin Zeid Battalion should occupy its target—Government House—at once. I passed the code word to the battalion commander: 'The Omen of Good Luck.'"

Sammy S. Mustaklem, the chief officer of the Fire Brigade in Jordanian Jerusalem, was up north of Jerusalem inspecting the electrical power station in Shu'afat when he heard of the fighting between Egypt and Israel. At first, he didn't believe it. There were no signs of war; everything was quiet. The radio confirmed the rumor.

He drove to his office in the fire station down the steep hill that drops abruptly eastward from the Rockefeller Museum and the northeast corner of the Old City wall. At the fire station the road bends sharply right around the sheds of the city wholesale produce market and climbs straight toward the Augusta Victoria Hospital atop the ridge to the east. This fire station was responsible for all of Jordanian Jerusalem including the Old City. Mustaklem even responded to alarms from Ramallah and other towns in the West Bank. He had charge of three engines and eleven men. There was no fire alarm system; calls for help were telephoned to the fire department.

Mustaklem was a professional. His training included four months in London and Manchester in 1959 and another four months on Welfare Island in New York City in 1964. His family had been Jerusalemites for more than four centuries and belonged to the Greek Orthodox Church.

About ten o'clock, Mustaklem heard distant rifle and machine-gun fire. He telephoned all his firemen at their homes; and, since he was also chief of the municipal inspectors, he

94

called the inspectors on his force. Twenty-eight men gathered at the firehouse across from the market.

In midafternoon a 2-inch Israeli shell slammed into the firehouse, sped through two walls and burned up a fireman's bed and clothing. No one was hurt. Mustaklem led his men into the storeroom in the basement.

A Jordanian army Land Rover came barreling down the hill and was hit right in front of the firehouse. The driver managed to put the Rover next to the firehouse before he died. A second soldier in the vehicle was wounded. Mustaklem shouted to him to come into the firehouse, but the man ran around the corner of the building and disappeared. Later, they found him lying in the garden.

Around 2 P.M., Mustaklem received a call from the suburb of Al-Azariyah that a shell had made a direct hit on a car and it was burning. He sent a fire truck which put out the flames and made the four-mile trip without incident.

About 6 P.M., Mustaklem received a call from the Old City reporting a fire near the Lions Gate. He sent an engine with three men. As they climbed the hill toward the Old City, they were shelled and shot at. The fire truck was damaged, but the men escaped and ran into the Old City. From there they telephoned Mustaklem and reported that the fire had been small and had been extinguished before they arrived. They said their fire truck could still run and they would return to the firehouse. But he ordered them to take the engine and set up a fire station in the Old City near the Lions Gate.

The men in the firehouse were isolated without water, food or a radio, as the battle around them grew in intensity. One of the men, a chief clerk from the health department, suffered a heart attack. He begged for water. After dark, Mustaklem stole outside to a water tap. It was dry; the water tanks on top of the building had been split open. Mustaklem could see another tap across the road by the market, but a body was draped over it. He was afraid if he ventured that far he would be shot.

Sometime later, Mustaklem heard a voice speaking Hebrew, which he could not understand. Shortly afterward, a neighbor knocked on the firehouse door and said, "The Israelis are here. They went through my house and ordered me out. So I came here." With Israelis in the area, Mustaklem feared that any noise would expose his men to danger. Mayor Rouhi al-Khatib, the mayor of Jordanian Jerusalem since 1957, had been telephoning from time to time to inquire about the situation. Mustaklem worried that the ringing telephone would attract the enemy. So he telephoned the mayor and said, "We are surrounded by Israeli soldiers and I don't know what fate we are facing. I am going to close down the telephone bell so nobody hears it." The mayor said, "God be with you. That's all I can say."

Priscilla Hall, the wife of the consul in charge of the American Consulate in Jordanian Jerusalem, Deputy Consul General McGinnis Hall, remembers that the firing started at 11:22 A.M.

There was an American Consulate on each side of Jerusalem, both of them in charge of Consul General Evan M. Wilson, who had his headquarters on the Israeli side. Because the United States still recognized Jerusalem as a *corpus separatum*, Wilson reported not to the embassies in Tel Aviv or Amman but directly to Washington.

The East Jerusalem building under Hall's care was a solidly built, old Turkish structure surrounded by a garden and a three-foot-high wall topped with iron grillwork. The consulate stood near the Mandelbaum Gate at the intersection of Nablus Road and Shemu'el Hanavi Street. It was due to see its share of this war.

The Halls learned of the war in the Sinai from the BBC during breakfast, and "Mac" Hall dashed over to the consulate on the Israeli side to confer with Wilson. His official blue-gray station wagon would not start; so he drove over alone through the Mandelbaum Gate in his personal blue Ford Mustang. Because his wife wanted to use the Mustang, after meeting with Wilson, Hall hurried back through the gate. If he had tarried, he would have been caught on the Israeli side when the Jordanians began shelling the city. He just made it back before the shelling started.

"Mac" Hall was a forty-nine-year-old Kansan and a descendant of the first rector of Yale University, from which Mac had graduated in 1940. In World War II, he had served as a lieutenant commander of the old battleship *Nevada*, a resurrected survivor of the attack on Pearl Harbor; at Okinawa, his ship was badly damaged by Japanese land batteries and a kamikaze.

When the shooting began in Jerusalem, fifteen people were in the Nablus Road consulate: the Halls; Mrs. Hall's father and stepmother, Mr. and Mrs. Amasa Maynard Holcombe; three vice consuls—David M. Morrison, Denis R. Regan and Chester M. Polley; the USIA Cultural Affairs Officer Richard F. Ross, who was there from the Israeli side; five Arab employees, and two American tourists who were caught in the building.

Mrs. Hall's elderly parents had been on a Mediterranean cruise and had insisted on coming to Jerusalem despite the prewar tension. When the war began, the Halls were concerned about their safety. But her father, a Washington lawyer and brother of Arthur Holcombe, the former chairman of Harvard's government department, had reassured them. "Mac," he said, "it's the most exciting time of my life."

The second floor of the consulate was the Halls' residence; the offices were downstairs. Everyone stayed away from the windows. They closed the steel shutters, but the steel proved useless against machine-gun bullets.

The group in the building collected on the first floor; there was no basement. At least the ground floor was partially shielded by the compound wall against the intermittent small-arms fire. At noon they heard over the radio connection with the consulate on the Israeli side that the United Nations was trying to arrange a cease-fire, but the shooting continued. The cook laid out a cold lunch. The Holcombes managed to nap in the downstairs apartment used by Consul General and Mrs. Wilson when they had to stay in Jordanian Jerusalem after the Mandelbaum Gate closed at 8 P.M. They played bridge to pass the time until the tension drove them from the table.

In the afternoon, two Jordanian soldiers came to the back door to tell the gardener that his house had been struck by a shell. He went with them to help care for his family, and the two trapped American tourists took the opportunity to leave with them. Then there were twelve.

When Alice Johnson, the wife of General Bull's U.S. Marine deputy, returned to their apartment that looked over to Augusta Victoria, she searched for a spot that would put as many masonry walls as possible between herself and the danger outside. She decided on a little hallway next to the kitchen. She collected a folding garden chair that opened into a lounge, blankets, a bucket of water, toilet paper, a radio, a can opener and some cans of soup; she made herself a snug base camp that would be her home for the next three days. She was glad their son was at Deerfield Academy in Massachusetts and away from the gathering war.

The apartment building was six stories high and used as an observation post by the Jordanian army. An Israeli bazooka shell plowed into the building and finally stopped against the wall of the Johnson's apartment. It was a dud. The two men who lived in the next apartment, where the shell had landed, came over and invited Alice to see it. She took one horrified look and ducked back in her hideaway.

Meanwhile, Lt. Col. Johnson was sitting on the roof of Government House with a panoramic view of the entire city. He says, "I thought I could see our building being destroyed. It was hit but not destroyed. The Jordanians had machine guns mounted up there. When the Israelis came into the area on Tuesday, two men were still on the roof and tried to come down the stairs. They came to the third floor; and the Israelis killed them with hand grenades, right outside our apartment."

After the Israeli army swept over the area where the Johnsons lived, two soldiers tried to commandeer their Chevrolet. Alice yelled at them from the balcony; but they broke a window, climbed inside and tried to start the car by crossing wires. They couldn't get it started. Alice was furious.

During this time, for two days, Mick Johnson didn't know whether Alice was alive or not.

The Jordanian artillery that pounded Israeli Jerusalem on Monday morning were mostly the 25-pound guns of the Ninth Field Artillery Regiment commanded by Major Mohammad Saleh Salah. Three months before the war started, the regiment had been supplied with American 155-mm howitzers. But, fortunately for the Israelis, the artillerymen lacked sufficient ammunition for the new guns; and when they moved over to the West Bank in mid-May, they left the howitzers behind. They brought forward only their older, lighter British 25-pounders, which had a range of thirteen thousand yards but were not effective against buildings, tanks and armored vehicles.

The regiment's three batteries were positioned east of Jerusalem to support the three infantry battalions of Brig. Gen. Hazzáa's brigade. The First Battery, commanded by Captain Mohammad Fayyadh, an especially experienced officer, was the southernmost. Stationed at the village of Anata, it supported the Eighth Infantry Battalion and faced Government House. The Second Battery, commanded by twenty-nine-year-old Captain Shawkat Jawdat, a native of Nablus, was positioned at Hizma to support Major Mansaur Kreishan's Second Infantry Battalion, the Hussein Battalion, in the center. Farthest north, Captain Khalid Hafez's Third Battery and Major Salah's regimental headquarters were protecting the Fourth Infantry Battalion and the historically vulnerable northern reaches of the city.

When the war broke out, Major Salah conferred with his battery commanders. They decided that if they were attacked by Israeli aircraft, they would keep the guns silent and the men in their trenches. They stood by on alert and set up forward observation posts.

Lieutenant Mohammad Ali Khreisat, a twenty-three-year-old native of Taflah, and his observation team for the First Battery took a position in a public school a hundred yards from the Benedictine Monastery on a strategic height south of the city and east of the village of Silwan. His job was to stay with the infantry and call in fire to support the Eighth Infantry Battalion. Lieutenant Kaman Jaradat and his observation team of the Second Battery were stationed near the border in the Sheikh Jarrah section north of the Old City. And Captain Abdel Wahab Mahadin was the forward observer for the Third Battery at Shu'afat north of Jerusalem. The three observers communicated over the battalion radio net.

Captain Jawdat remembers: "The observers could see no live military targets. The Israelis had kept very silent in the last few days. So we were forced to choose known military targets."

The men were expecting action. "We were eager to start it, in fact," says Lieutenant Khreisat. "Everything was prepared for war." When the regiment's batteries were ordered to engage their targets, they knew where the Israeli troops and guns were concentrated; and the punishing shelling of Israeli Jerusalem began.

By noon, Israeli artillery and aircraft attacked the batteries to try to stop the shelling. In the north, Captain Hafez's Third Battery was particularly hard hit; trying to change its position, it came under Israeli counterbombardment and took severe losses.

At noon, Ted Yates was standing with a group of newsmen inside the lobby of the Inter-Continental Hotel atop the Mount of Olives. An award-winning television producer-director for the National Broadcasting Company, Yates, now thirty-six, had been a U.S. Marine Corps combat correspondent in the Korean War and headed a five-man NBC crew covering the Middle East crisis. Suddenly, machine-gun fire sprayed the hotel. The attack was a total surprise. While the others dived for cover, Yates remained standing to see what was going on and was struck in the head by a machine-gun bullet. He died the next day in the hospital of the Austrian Hospice in the Old City.

At about the same time, Private Samara Muniezel of the Jordanian army had just fired his two-inch mortar into Israeli Jerusalem from his position next to the Mandelbaum Gate when an Israeli bullet struck him in the head. His platoon commander, Lieutenant Ghazi Rababa, who had just arrived on the scene, ordered him put in an ambulance; but in five minutes Private Muniezel died. "His mistake," says Lieutenant Rababa, "was he did not change his position after firing."

Rababa, who was twenty-three years old and had been in the army four years, had been caught away from his platoon the morning the war started because he was in a month-long officers' infantry course. In his absence, his platoon was in charge of Officer Cadet Hamed Melkawi. Early Monday, courses were canceled and Rababa was ordered to report to his unit. He was driven to the headquarters of the Second Battalion, the Hussein Battalion, of the King Talal Brigade, in the Rockefeller Museum, just outside the northeast corner of the wall of the Old City. The battalion commander, Major Kreishan, ordered him to go quickly and take command of his platoon of the Third Company at the Mandelbaum Gate.

The Mandelbaum Gate in the center of the city was not really a gate at all but the site of the home of a merchant named Mandelbaum at the junction of Shemu'el Hanavi and St. George streets on the border between Israel and Jordan. For the past nineteen years, this so-called gate had been the only legal crossing point for diplomats, United Nations officials, pilgrims, journalists and convoys going to Mount Scopus. It had none of the grandeur or history of the gates of the Old City; it had become an ugly symbol of the permanence of the division of Jerusalem. At the Mandelbaum house on May 19, 1948, the Jews had stopped the Arab Legion's armored attack on the city from the north.[3] In 1967, each side had a checkpoint and a small unit here. Because the position was under fire, Rababa had difficulty reaching his command post, the "red building" one hundred yards from the gate and near the UN's MAC house north of the gate.

As soon as he had seen the mortally wounded Private Muniezel into the ambulance, Rababa entered the red building, which was already partly destroyed. The more powerful Israeli communications was overpowering his radio, so he talked by telephone with Cadet Melkawi, who was in a building by the gate itself. Melkawi told him that there had been heavy firing between his men and the Israelis in a building twenty yards away. Four of his soldiers had been killed and several wounded, and he had sent them out by ambulance. Rababa had fifty men left under his command, including twenty-five reservists led by 1st Lt. Haikel al-Zaban. Jordanian platoons were usually undermanned; the army was short of manpower.

The exchange of fire, the Jordanians charged, had begun at 10 A.M. with an Israeli machine-gun burst at the Jerusalem district office of the United Nations Relief and Works Administration (UNRWA). This office was housed at the former Police Training School of the days of the British Mandate, nearly a mile due north of the Mandelbaum Gate.

The firing caused no Arab casualties; but after half an hour, Major Kreishan gave his company commanders permission to return fire, aiming only at Israeli uniforms. "Minutes after that, hell broke loose," says Maj. Gen. Ma'an Abu Nuwar, the head of police and civil defense for Amman and all the West Bank including Jerusalem. "Enemy soldiers were seen evacuating forward trenches and observation posts."

At the Mandelbaum Gate, Rababa told his men to be careful. They stayed in their trenches and the Israeli fire went over their heads. They could not see the Israelis, but Rababa ordered his men to fire anyway to keep up their morale. They fired a bazooka at the Israeli position several times and thought they had silenced a machine gun. Rababa says, "The Israelis had good fire control. They would fire a volley and then keep silent." The dueling went on until sunset.

As Monday wore on, tension grew among the civilians on both sides of the Green Line in the city. At his office inside the Jaffa Gate, Town Clerk Salah Jarallah was trying to make do. "We organized ourselves for first aid and rescue, even though we didn't have any equipment. We were asked to stay in our offices and sleep there. We spent Monday night in our offices, listening to the explosions. We saw airplanes overhead. Some said they were Iraqi; others, that they were Jordanian. We were confused. We had only rumors. The radios of the Arab countries were misleading us. When we listened to the Israeli radio, we did not know what to believe. Is this true, or is that true?

"By Tuesday morning, the Old City walls were closed up entirely, and the employees who lived outside did not come to work. The Old City was disconnected from the area outside the walls. Things became worse, and employees, one by one, started leaving the office. There were explosions and airplanes in the sky, and you could hear the machine guns. Mayor Rouhi al-Khatib went to a safe place in the Latin Convent. I walked home through the Old City. I was expecting to get a bomb on my head." At their home near the Lions Gate, Jarallah's wife and three young sons were waiting for him, desperately afraid.

For the ordinary citizens of Arab Jerusalem, war had come into their homes, threatening, brutal. Their relations with Jews before the State of Israel had always been a mixture of friendships and antagonisms. Since 1948, Israel had been the armed enemy a rifle shot away. And still it was not simple. Palestinian Arabs in Jerusalem like Salah Jarallah were ruled by the Bedouin kingdom based in Amman; with some exceptions, the Arab army defending their city was made up of Bedouins from across the Jordan River—outsiders. Jerusalem's Arabs might share the stirred-up hatred of Israel, but they had little control over the deadly battle they now had to endure.

Chapter 6

TEN RUBLES IN HIS POCKET

WHILE OPPOSING ARMIES SWUNG INTO BATTLE IN THE MIDDLE East, in New York at the United Nations the world powers were starting to bring their pressures and self-interests to bear on the combatants.

At 7:45 A.M. precisely, Yosef Tekoah in Tel Aviv placed a telephone call to New York, where the city slept ignorant of the violence that had erupted in the Middle East. Tekoah, the Foreign Office's deputy director general in charge of international affairs and Israel's former ambassador to the Soviet Union, was now, at forty-two, responsible for Israel's relations with the United Nations. He was calling New York on instructions from Foreign Minister Abba Eban.

In the darkened apartment 17D in the twin-towered building at 300 Central Park West in New York, it was 1:45 A.M. when the telephone rang next to the bed of sleeping Gideon Rafael, the fifty-three-year-old Berlin-born Israeli ambassador to the United Nations. Tekoah, calling from the headquarters of Prime Minister Eshkol and the General Staff, told Ambassador Rafael the war had started and asked him to find a pencil and write down his instructions and the announcements that Tekoah had drafted. Rafael's wife, now fully awake, asked her husband what was happening. He said simply, "The war has broken out."

Tekoah told the ambassador to ask for a meeting of the UN's Security Council. So his immediate job was to notify the president of the Security Council, who for that month was the Danish representative, Hans Tabor. Tabor was not at his official residence in suburban Pelham, New York, and Rafael finally located him in the city. Tabor agreed to convene the Security Council.

Rafael telephoned his driver. "Shmuel, saddle the horses," he said. "The war is on." At the office at 11 East 70th Street, where he had been assigned barely a month, Rafael received cabled and coded orders to stall for time and, he said later, "strict instructions not to reveal any military information and not deny any Arab boasting." He also received word that the Egyptian Air Force had been destroyed. He started preparing a statement he would read to the Security Council at nine o'clock.

Meanwhile, Michael Arnon, the Israeli Consul General in New York, was also awakened by the news. He dressed hurriedly and in the dark drove his car, which was parked outside his apartment building three-quarters of a mile south of Rafael's home on Central Park West, to the consulate adjoining Rafael's UN Mission in East 70th Street. By 6 A.M. he was watching the incoming cable traffic and had checked with the Israeli Defense Mission in New York and the embassy in Washington. The bulky, bespectacled Arnon, a former journalist and an experienced diplomat with a Viennese sense of humor and a keen ability to analyze complex political situations, spent the day besieged by the press, officials from Jewish organizations and anxious Israelis.

In Ambassador Rafael's office the telephone rang incessantly. One of the most troubled callers was Arthur Goldberg, the United States ambassador to the UN. When Goldberg's secretary Maureen Corr put him on the line, Rafael says, "He was frightfully worried about Israel and the military equation. Our friends in the Western world were concerned for Israel's survival. Arthur Goldberg did not call only because of his Jewish emotions but because of United States concern."

Rafael was asked by his government to try to delay a vote in the Security Council for a half day, and he exuberantly replied, "I promise you at least two days before a cease-fire." When a Security Council vote on a cease-fire could no longer be avoided, he was to try to prevent a cease-fire that demanded a withdrawal to the original lines before combat started. "Everything else the good Lord and the army of Israel will take care of."

When he went to the Security Council chamber, Rafael was fortified by two things. First, he did not share the anxiety in Israel over a United Nations proclamation. He says, "Our people thought this is like a court and they can't oppose a judgment." Secondly, his goal to delay a cease-fire matched that of the Arab representatives, who heard from the bombastic radio in Cairo, Damascus and Amman that the Egyptian forces were approaching Tel Aviv, that Haifa was burning and that Jordan had invaded and taken over Jerusalem. Believing their own propaganda, the Arab ambassadors wanted to delay a cease-fire as much as did Rafael.

It was 3 P.M. in Jerusalem and 9 A.M. in New York when the Security Council sat down to business; a lot had already happened in the Middle East. But the diplomats in Manhattan had very ragged and conflicting information about the course of the war. India and the Soviet Union wanted both sides to return to their positions before the fighting began and the UN to condemn the Israeli air attacks and the death of three Indian members of the deactivated UN Emergency Force in the Gaza Strip area. The United States, Canada, Denmark and Brazil were among those that wanted a resolution simply calling for a cease-fire—without insisting on a return to the original lines and a condemnation of Israel. Secretary General U Thant told the council that Jordanian troops had captured the Government House compound.[1]

Israeli Consul General Arnon says, "The Arabs and Russians were misinformed and thought they had all the time in the world. By the time they caught themselves, it was a long way down the pike."

Rafael remembers: "Later, the Dane Hans Tabor, a great friend of Israel who felt sincere anxiety about what was going to happen to the Jewish people, came over to me and said the only riddle in this situation is: Why were you so composed while Israel was burning? You didn't show a trace of anxiety.

"I said: Look, I'll tell you a Jewish story. On the eve of Yom Kippur, a stranger, a Jew, comes into a little town and goes to the head of the Jewish community and says, 'I'm a stranger in town and don't know where to go to pray. I have no place to stay, no money.' He was invited in; and shortly before they went to the service, the stranger says, 'Let me have ten rubles.' The leader says, 'Why do you need ten rubles? You won't eat; you'll sleep here. You're my guest. There is no opportunity to spend ten rubles.' The stranger was insistent. So he gave him the ten rubles and he pocketed them. The next night, he took out the ten rubles and gave them back. The leader asked him, 'Why did you insist on having these ten rubles?' He said, 'My dear man, with ten rubles in my pocket I pray so much better.'

"I told Ambassador Tabor that before I came to the Security Council I had an 'eyes only' telegram that we had shot down 250 Egyptian airplanes. I was sworn not to reveal this, but I knew that if there were no limits in the sky, there were no obstacles on the ground. Therefore, I could feel rather quiet. I was sitting with my ten rubles in my pocket.

"Since I knew in which direction the momentum of the war was advancing, I had to provide Israel with the political and diplomatic time. Space was the army's problem; my problem was time. We had enormous support from the United States. We had enormous support from our direct enemies, who were completely confused. They became the victims of their own lies. They were feeling very cocky. They really believed they were advancing and they were also playing for time. I had a more reliable source of information.

"Arthur Goldberg asked me in the middle of the day, 'Gideon, what do you want me to do?' I said, 'I want time, nothing else.' He understood that and it apparently fitted American objectives. President Johnson was a very realistic man. So we got our time.

"The Egyptians did not understand the immensity of their disaster. The Russians also made a fatal mistake. For the whole day of the fifth of June, the Russian representative, Nikolai Federenko, with whom I had some unfriendly exchanges, was unavailable. He also did not know in which direction the war was moving. If the Egyptians were approaching the gates of Tel Aviv, there was no hurry to stop them. Certainly not to adopt a resolution of withdrawal to the original lines.

"By five o'clock in the evening, Federenko popped up as though he were stung by a hornet and looked for Arthur Goldberg. I told Arthur Goldberg, 'You are not so available for the next few hours.' By that time, the Soviets had become aware of the realities on the ground. They implored the Egyptian representative, a man by the name of Mohammad al-Kony, to make a statement that they had agreed to a cease-fire. He was brought with two Soviet representatives on his arm, like a Soviet defector being put on an Aeroflot plane, put in his seat and with tears in his eyes announced the end of the glorious Nasser venture.

"The United States said they would veto a resolution that included withdrawal. They said the main thing is to bring the fighting to an end. Anything that would delay it could be discussed at a later stage." Tabor, Federenko and Goldberg met privately through most of Tuesday before the Soviet Union agreed to a simple cease-fire resolution.

Although the political leaders in Israel were concerned about the fate of Jerusalem once King Hussein moved against Israel, Jerusalem was not on Rafael's mind during his diplomatic maneuverings. He says, "Jerusalem surprised all of us completely. This foolhardy king attacked us, and we had no strategy at that time. As a matter of fact, even after the shooting had started, we were pleading with him to keep out." Rafael was not trying to win time so the Old City could be conquered. He says, "I can't carry out the tactics of a nonexistent strategy."

— Chapter 7 —

"THE OMEN OF GOOD LUCK"

BY MONDAY MIDDAY, THE JORDANIAN ARMY WAS ADVANCING toward the Israeli sector of Jerusalem. The first men to try to stop it were not Israelis but a young Burmese named U Than Aye, whom everyone called "Charlie" and who was a distant cousin of the UN's secretary general; the United States Marine Lieutenant Colonel "Mick" Johnson; the Chinese F. T. Liu; the Englishman Dennis Holland, and the Norwegian General Odd Bull.

This strange opening scene occurred because the Jordanians did not first attack Mount Scopus, as the Israelis expected, but instead assaulted an undefended hill south of the Old City. The Israeli government, fully occupied with the war against Egypt, was hoping for quiet on the Jordanian front. When the Jordanian army advanced and the artillery and mortar duel of the morning became a battle on the ground, that hope was smashed.

The attack came against a long windswept ridge where the Israelis had prepared no defense. The ridge ran through no-man's-land and on its crest a road led directly into the southern reaches of Israeli Jerusalem.

On top of the eastern end of this ridge, in no-man's-land, stood the lands and buildings of the United Nations Truce Supervision Organization. The UNTSO had seven hundred fenced-in acres at the heart of which—like an English manor house on a large estate—stood Government House, the grand residence built of solid yellow Jerusalem stone for the British High Commissioner of Palestine in Mandate days and that was now UN headquarters.

To command the ridge and the road, the Jordanians had to pass through this neutral compound of the UN. Because the ridge was the best level route into southern Israeli Jerusalem, because it was undefended and because it was the highest ridge on that side of the city, it became the first battleground for Jerusalem in this war.

The ridge had a long history. It was known as Jabal Mukaber, the Hill of Evil Counsel. Jews hostile to the British and later to the UN thought the name appropriate. A much older account says that on this hill Judas betrayed Jesus for the pieces of silver. Another story says that here grew the hackberry tree on which Judas hung himself.[1] And a tradition has it that here, in his summer house on the hill, the High Priest Caiaphas gave counsel which led to the Crucifixion of Jesus.[2]

North from this strategic hilltop sweeps a magnificent, sun-washed, unimpeded panorama of the Old City. Government House stands with its various outbuildings, mechanics shops, parking lots atop the eastern tip of the ridge which drops directly downward in three directions. Below it to the northeast the Arab village of Silwan clings to the steep slope above the Kidron Valley. On the south stretches a long, deep valley beyond which sits the hilltop Arab village of Sur Bahir. To the west, the ridge sticks straight as a spear into modern Israeli Jerusalem.

The Jordanians wanted to seize the high ground of Jabal Mukaber in order to possess the only level route over which they could send armor into the southern side of Israeli Jerusalem. It was an easy target, undefended and neutral ground. The Israelis had no force nearby.

The nearest Israelis to Government House were the five men of a squad of the 161st Battalion of the Jerusalem Brigade. The squad, wearing the uniforms of border police, was stationed in a two-story stone house, nicknamed the Lonely House and tucked down the hill in a grove of pines thirty yards west of the UN compound.

Six hundred yards southwest of this outpost was Kibbutz Ramat Rachel—right on the Green Line at the southern end of the armed border dividing Jerusalem. The kibbutz, founded in 1926 on then empty land, had been the target of repeated Arab attacks in 1929 and the 1930s and had changed hands half a dozen times during the 1948 war. The site had already been inhabited in 1000 B.C. and a millennium later by the Tenth Roman Legion. In the fifth century A.D., a church had been built there because, Christians believe, Mary rested here on her journey to Bethlehem, where her son Jesus would be born.[3] Now, a four-man border patrol unit—a corporal and three privates—was posted on the kibbutz. When the Jordanian artillery started firing, they took shelter in a 1948 trench.

West of the Government House compound, on the main road between Jerusalem and Bethlehem, stood the Allenby Barracks. It had been a British army and then an Arab Legion camp and was now a reserve unit depot. Here, a second-line battalion of the Jerusalem Brigade was mobilizing. The men, whom Dayan had sent home a few days earlier, were being hastily reformed under shellfire. Lt. Col. Bill Aaronson, the battalion commander who had served in the British army in India, refused to take shelter. Shrapnel ripped his abdomen and he was carried away bleeding profusely. One of his company commanders, a thirty-seven-year-old geophysicist named Captain Uri Amitai, was approaching the camp on foot when a shell exploded in a tree overhead and a steel fragment drove into his skull. Still conscious, he was bundled into an army vehicle and rushed to Hadassah Hospital and operated on immediately. He was one of the first military wounded treated there. In the 1948 war, Amitai had been wounded six times while protecting the convoys coming up to Jerusalem. The men at Allenby were ordered out of the zeroed-in camp into stone buildings across the road.

At 10:30, Radio Cairo and Radio Amman announced that the Jordanians had captured Jabal Mukaber. Israeli officers watching the area reported seeing no action; but up the chain of command and in the General Headquarters bunker, officers recognized the import of the radio news. What had been announced as already accomplished would soon be attempted.

When a Jordanian shell hit near the square concrete guard house at the far eastern or Jordanian entrance to the UN compound, U Than Aye, the UN guard on duty there, threw his overweight body under a table and was deluged by dirt, splinters of wood and glass from shattered windows. Other shells hit deeper into the compound.

North across the valley near the Benedictine Monastery,

Lieutenant Khreisat, the observer of the First Battery of the Jordanian Ninth Field Artillery, was registering his targets. The 25-pounders had no trouble reaching Jabal Mukaber and even Sur Bahir farther south. Although Khreisat wanted to miss Government House itself, some of his gunners were coming very close.

General Bull already had assurances from the Israelis that they would not attack Government House. This morning he had Lt. Col. Johnson call Colonel Mohammad Daoud, the Jordanian liaison officer to MAC. Johnson says, "Daoud gave me an absolute assurance that morning that the Jordanian military would not attack Government House; the area would be regarded as inviolate." But Daoud's word was not upheld in Amman.

Jordanian shells struck the UN compound, smashed into the gardens, outbuildings, garage, mechanics shops and storehouses. Lt. Col. Johnson telephoned the battered guard house and was surprised to find U Than Aye still alive. Johnson asked him if he had seen any troop movements. He had not.

Jordanian Major Badi Awad and the 650 men of his Ussamah Bin Zeid Infantry Battalion received their orders to move out and occupy Jabal Mukaber. The code signal for the operation was "Sabeel Al-Saad"—"Omen of Good Luck."

At 1 P.M., it was a pleasant seventy-five degrees when Major Awad and his men reached their formation area on the slope of the steep, bare, dun hill, three hundred yards southeast of the UN compound. With Major Awad came Captain Mohammad Fayyadh, commander of the First Battery, and a forward observer.

Major Awad's mission was to seize Jabal Mukaber. He had to pass through the vast Government House compound to achieve his objective. His zero hour was 1:30. Then, the major said later, "I started my battle."

Now, U Than Aye saw marching up the road 150 armed Arabs, followed by teenagers lugging boxes of ammunition. He alerted the UN duty room and walked to the red and white pole across the dirt road at the eastern entrance to the compound. He told the leading Jordanian officer that he had reached UN territory. But the Jordanians moved around the barrier and

111

entered the compound. General Bull called it "one of the biggest surprises of my life."[4]

The Jordanians spread out north of the road and simply took command of the undefended hill. They had Jeep-mounted 106-mm recoilless antitank guns and 3.5-inch rocket launchers, American made, plus the support of the Ninth Field Artillery. In the woods north and east of the compound, they dug in.

Inside Government House, Dennis Holland, the chief administrative officer, stopped by the third-floor office of Hubert Noel, the deputy political advisor, and said in his best British style, "Noel, we have visitors in the garden." Then Holland disappeared. Noel went to the window and saw Jordanian soldiers digging trenches in the UN garden.

From the top of David's Tower at Jaffa Gate on the western side of the Old City wall and the highest point in the Old City, Brig. Gen. Hazzáa and Major Mohammad Saleh Salah, his artillery commander, watched the action.

In his guard house, U Than Aye picked up the telephone, a Jordanian soldier grabbed him and another pointed a rifle at him. Four Jordanian border policemen, manning the permanent checkpoint near the UN guard house, intervened.

General Bull, F. T. Liu, Dennis Holland and an Arabic-speaking field service officer carrying a white flag rushed into the yard between Government House and the east gate. Shells were raining into the compound. They met Major Badi Awad and told him he was violating the agreements between the UN and Jordan. Awad said he was following his orders and had instructions to protect the UN personnel. Bull told the major to take his men out of the compound.

The major and his radio man accompanied Bull to the garage area where there was a telephone. Bull wanted to relay an emphatic protest to Colonel Daoud. While Bull was trying to call Daoud through MAC, Major Awad received a radio order to occupy Government House itself.[5]

In the main UN building were many civilians including women and children. Seven or eight UN families had chosen to seek refuge in Government House rather than escape to Lebanon and Europe. They were now getting ready for lunch in the dining room. Major Awad suggested that they be evacuated to the Jordanian sector of Jerusalem. Bull refused.

Major Awad and two soldiers came into the building. One

soldier walked into the code room just as the operator was informing New York: "Jordanian soldiers entering Government House . . ." Then the line went dead; that was the last word the United Nations received from Government House.

General Bull took the major to his third-floor office over Government House's main entrance and again called MAC. Angrily, he said that if the Jordanian troops were not withdrawn immediately he would call King Hussein himself.

The major and the two soldiers with him left the building. Three soldiers carried a machine gun up to the third floor, intending to set it up on the roof outside. They were met by unarmed UN officers led by Lt. Col. Johnson, Dennis Holland and Hubert Noel—all big men. Johnson says, "We were having at it hammer and claw. This was UN property. Get the hell off!"

One UN man at each elbow manhandled the three Jordanians with their machine gun down the stairs. "We gave them the bum's rush," says Holland. Noel comments, "This was very important because if we had not opposed the posting of a machine gun on the roof, Government House with the people inside would have been destroyed."

Downstairs, the Jordanians refused to leave the building. A UN field staff man, thinking quickly, dashed outside and came right back in and told the soldiers their commander wanted them outside. They obediently went out. UN personnel slammed and locked the large bright-green main door and barricaded it with furniture.

From the UN compound, the Jordanians opened fire on targets in Israeli territory. The Israelis now could have no doubts about Jordan's intentions. Hopes that King Hussein might limit his participation were wiped out. Yehuda Arbell says, "Nobody had believed that the Jordanians would use this weak spot, because it was extraterritorial and protected by the UN. They didn't give a damn about it. This was the most critical hour in Jerusalem."

The Israeli squad in the Lonely House just west of Government House first heard that the war had begun from the Arabs' loudspeakers on the Temple Mount. An Israeli private who spoke Arabic told the others what the Arabs were saying:

113

"This is your day. This is your chance to take back your country stolen by the Jews. Take up your weapons."[6]

The Israelis on the lower floor of the Lonely House could see only north to the Old City and west to Israeli Jerusalem. On the upper floor one window gave them a view eastward to the UN compound. Corporal Zvi Paz, the squad leader, climbed upstairs and from the window saw a Jordanian setting up a machine gun. He called down to his men to telephone Jerusalem Brigade headquarters and to hand up his Uzi. He wanted to get the machine gunner. Then Paz saw more Jordanian soldiers moving toward the experimental farm in the Israeli side of the demilitarized zone. The private who was manning the telephone reported to headquarters that an entire Arab company was moving toward Israeli Jerusalem and asked permission to pull back. Colonel Eliezar Amitai, the brigade commander, came to the phone and said that if a company was coming, they could go.

Corporal Paz started for the door and spotted a half dozen Jordanians advancing toward the house. He ran across the room to the window and jumped ten feet to the ground. He stopped to help one of his men caught in the barbed wire. The Jordanians opened fire. The five Israelis crawled through the scrub under fire and after forty minutes reached Israeli Jerusalem unharmed.

Jordanian soldiers moved across the fields toward the experimental farm at Hawwat haLimmud southwest of the UN compound. Colonel Amitai and Lt. Col. Driezin had wanted to place troops at the farm but could never obtain permission because it was in no-man's-land. So, as it happened, the first Israelis who actually fired weapons to stop the Jordanian infantry were a small, stocky woman named Rachel Kaufmann and an old auxiliary policeman, whose army days were long over. From the farm, they fired two Czech Spandau light machine guns at the Jordanians near the farm's mink sheds. The machine-gun fire halted the Jordanians and at a line of trees they started to dig in.

Normally, there were at the farm—which tested products like flowers, medical herbs and mink for hill farming—about twenty young workers and thirty students from the Hebrew University; but they had all been mobilized. This Monday morning, only five old laborers; the auxiliary policeman; a civil defense worker, and Mrs. Kaufmann, the wife of the farm director, were there. Mrs. Kaufmann's husband, Shalom, was

114

driving back to Jerusalem with Rachel Yanait Ben-Zvi, who had founded the farm as an agricultural training school for girls and whose husband had been Israel's second president. Mrs. Ben-Zvi, now eighty years old, had insisted on coming to the farm this morning; and while Shalom was taking her back, the Jordanians attacked.

At the farm under fire, Mrs. Kaufmann took charge. She had survived three years in Nazi concentration camps and fought in the 1948 war. She broke out a few old rifles and ammunition. Her husband had emplaced their two machine guns at the corners of the house to protect it against the Jordanian soldiers who were permanently posted in no-man's-land.

Mrs. Kaufmann did not know that the Lonely House had been abandoned and that she was in the forefront of the entire Israeli defense of Jerusalem. For more than an hour she tried to telephone the army's emergency number and got only a frustrating busy signal. She called the police; before anyone could reply, an explosion shook the building and the telephone went dead.

The old workers had never fired a weapon; they were terribly frightened and she hurried them into the basement. As the Jordanian soldiers approached from Government House, she and the auxiliary policeman manned the two machine guns and opened fire.

Suddenly, five Israeli reservists of B Company of the 161st Infantry Battalion of the Jerusalem Brigade burst through the farm building's rear door. One soldier (a father of four) had been hit on the way to the farm. The soldiers stripped off their packs and set up a machine gun. They were followed by young soldiers from H Company, an ROTC-like Academic Reserve unit of officer cadets at the Hebrew University. A shell exploded, killing one man and wounding two. Mrs. Kaufmann had them carried to the basement. Then, the Israeli army took over Mrs. Kaufmann's war.

Government House started to receive artillery fire from the direction of the Israeli kibbutz at Ramat Rachel. In his guard house, U Than Aye crawled back under his table. Several buildings and many vehicles in the UN compound were hit by more than twenty mortar shells. Part of General Bull's living quarters on the top floor of the main building was burning.

Anticipating an Israeli counterattack, General Bull at 2 P.M. telephoned the Israeli Foreign Ministry and asked that Israeli soldiers be kept away from Government House while he tried to persuade the Jordanians to leave the UN compound. The Israelis said simply that they would take care of it. Then the telephone went dead. The Jordanians had cut the wires.

At 2:45, the UN informed both sides that at 3 P.M. General Bull would be leaving the compound in a Jeep with a white flag to drive out and communicate with Amman and the king.

Colonel Amitai had already received orders from General Narkiss to counterattack. At 3:05, the Jerusalem Brigade reported to Central Command that it was attacking Government House. Almost immediately, in an attempt to respond to General Bull's request, General Headquarters ordered the attack called off. Jerusalem Brigade headquarters said the troops had already left.

The war in Jerusalem might still have been stopped, despite the Jordanian invasion of the UN compound. But the battle built up, propelled by the continuing Jordanian fire and by the eagerness of the Israeli commanders on the scene to get into action. They saw here both an opportunity and a threat. If the Jordanians moved west from Government House, the heart of Israeli Jerusalem lay open to them; if they brought up armor, the Israelis had nothing to halt them.

On Abu Tor—the only hill between Jabal Mukaber and Jerusalem—Lt. Col. Asher Driezin, the stocky, bantam-sized, thirty-four-year-old career officer who commanded the Jerusalem Brigade's 161st Infantry Battalion, was directing fire from bazookas and a bulky rocket launcher against Jordanian fortifications only yards away. Mortar fire destroyed Driezin's Jeep and radio, so when he decided his mortar platoon at Allenby Barracks should fire on Jordanian positions, he had to go on foot to give the order. Arriving there, Driezin assumed command.

Looking east from Allenby, across the top of Jabal Mukaber, Driezin could not see the UN compound. He ordered mortar fire to clear the road along the hill's crest; he was well aware that this was the prime entry point for Jordanian armor. As Driezin put it, "They could come into the belly of Jerusalem."

Over the radio came urgent word that the Jordanians were

approaching the experimental farm. Driezin sent B and H companies forward. B Company's commander placed Lieutenant Israel Stern and his men in front of the farm buildings with two machine guns.

Colonel Amitai had already alerted his reconnaissance unit and his tank company and now telephoned Driezin at Allenby Barracks, who reported that he had sent two infantry companies to the farm.

Driezin knew the contingency plan in case of an Arab attack on Government House—to react with tanks and half-tracks if the attack came in daylight. The vital positions to be seized were Antenna Hill, the ridge's highest point where the United Nations had erected its radio antennae, and beyond it to the east the junction of the road running east-west past Government House and a secondary north-south road between Jerusalem and Bethlehem. North of and below the ridge, the Jordanians had a small position at Salim-a-Ras; and in no-man's-land south of the ridge, a major complex of trenches and bunkers that the Israelis called "The Sausage." The Sausage was a difficult fortified position at least eight hundred yards long and might hold as much as a battalion of Jordanian troops.

Then, Driezin, his runner Gidon Halvatz and Sergeant Ruven Robert Haddad, who could spot the mortar fire, ran to the farm to direct the mortars more accurately. The machine-gun and mortar fire pushed back the Jordanian spearhead south of Government House and then aimed at the UN compound, where Jordanians could be seen digging in at the edge of the woods.

Driezin reviewed the plan with his officers. When tanks and half-tracks came, they would attack Government House and then Antenna Hill and the road junction. H Company would advance on foot into the woods just north of the Government House compound and take Salim-a-Ras. Then, whoever was ready would tackle The Sausage. But they could do nothing until the Israeli armor arrived.

Without waiting for orders from Central Command, Amitai immediately sent Driezin his recon unit. Reconnaissance Unit 90, a 125-man, all-volunteer team, the Jerusalem Brigade's elite strike force, was under the command of Major Yosef "Yossi" Langotsky, a strongly built, daring officer. Langotsky had been born in Jerusalem and knew the city intimately. Now thirty-three, he was a geologist and the deputy head of the Geological Survey of Israel.

Langotsky had commanded Reconnaissance Unit 90 since 1961 and whipped it into a superb fighting force. All its members were carefully selected and highly motivated; if they showed any inadequacies, they were sent back to other units in the brigade. His deputy, Captain Yoram Solomon, was a Ph.D. in biochemistry. Among the privates was the geologist who had been Langotsky's superior in the Geological Survey. Says Langotsky, "There was a joke in Jerusalem: You had to be at least a Ph.D. to join the reconnaissance unit." Langotsky, who had turned down the command of one of the brigade's battalions to stay with his unit, knew that if Jerusalem was attacked, the recon unit would be the first called.

The recon unit, as the motorized element of the infantry brigade, now had seven half-tracks, nine Jeeps with machine guns and four with recoilless guns. It was an exceptionally heavily armed assault force, with four recoilless guns, eighteen machine guns, eleven light machine guns, four mortars, four bazookas, fifty-one Uzi submachine guns and seventy-four rifles. Each man officially carried one grenade, but in fact everyone had at least three. While many of the brigade's weapons and much of its ammunition had been stripped for use on the Egyptian front, Major Langotsky had seen to it that his men were well armed.

They trained intensively to attack as a unit and with tanks. They familiarized themselves in the greatest detail with the whole length of the fortified border through the center of Jerusalem. They knew every house and alley along the frontier and gave each place a nickname to make it instantly recognizable. In the south, they covered Kibbutz Ramat Rachel but not Government House, which was in no-man's-land. Government House and the strategic Hill of Evil Counsel were the responsibility of Lt. Col. Driezin's 161st Infantry Battalion, and therefore Langotsky did not know them as well as he did the strongpoints along the Green Line itself.

Over the years, Langotsky had built a special four-man team around himself. This team was the most selected of the select. Corporal Zerach Epstein, thirty-three years old, a hearty, shrewd wheeler-dealer type, was independent and resourceful, and at six feet an inch taller than his commander and equally strongly built. A member of an old Hebron family, his grandfather had been a rabbi who escaped the massacre of the Jews there in 1929 and settled in the Old City. Zerach had been a demolition frogman in the Israeli navy in his regular service and was now Langotsky's driver. Also a member of the team was Sergeant Doron Bar-Adon, a twenty-seven-year-old sculptor whose mother had immigrated from Philadelphia in 1936. The sergeant possessed great powers of observation on which Langotsky depended. Bar-Adon was in charge of the command half-track and sat next to Epstein with a .30 caliber machine gun. The fourth man was the radio operator Avner Malkov, a curly-haired, gentle architect. The four had worked together for six years and trusted each other with their lives.

On Sunday, the recon unit spent the entire day exercising on the Castel, a strategic height north of Jerusalem, and at midnight hiked all the way back to its base at Tsuba, on a mountaintop west of Ein Karem, west of Jerusalem. After 3 A.M. the men completed cleaning their weapons and equipment and got to sleep.

Langotsky had three hours' sleep when Epstein woke him and drove him to an 8 A.M. meeting of commanders at Camp Schneller, the Jerusalem Brigade headquarters. Colonel Amitai announced to the officers that the war had begun. Langotsky, anticipating a long detailed planning session, sneaked out of the room and telephoned Captain Solomon to prepare to move out of the camp within an hour.

By 9:30, Langotsky and Epstein were back at the unit with instructions to move into Jerusalem. The men were ready to go. They sped to their deployment position in a Hadassah social workers' school near the Russian Compound in the heart of the Israeli sector and not more than five hundred yards from the Green Line. Along the way, people threw flowers and candy to the soldiers who represented a visible symbol of support and reassurance. At the school, Langotsky called the men together and said, "This is the beginning of the smoke and fog of battle. Nobody knows what is going to happen. Be patient."

The unit was well concealed and protected, but civilian casualties started coming in and had to be transported to hospitals. Next door, the wife of Dr. Young, the head of the Institute for Holy Land Studies, had organized a dormitory for the people of the neighborhood. The soldiers brought bread, milk and eggs to the shelter. And the neighbors brought the soldiers coffee and cake. One of the men later would marry a woman he met that morning.

Langotsky received an assignment from brigade headquarters to blow up bridges that night on the highway to Jericho to prevent the Jordanians from reinforcing their units in Jerusalem. Langotsky put together a force of twenty men, and to command the night mission into enemy territory chose Lieutenant Danny Bachrach, a happy-go-lucky, blond architectural student, whom he considered his best combat leader.

Plans made, Langotsky lay down to take a nap. He was exhausted and he wanted to demonstrate to his men that their commander was calm about the battle that was building up. He slept until he was awakened to receive a message.

The message was laconic: "The High Commissioner's Palace [the Israeli term for Government House] was captured by the Jordanians. They are now trying to attack the agricultural school at Hawwat haLimmud. Go to Allenby directly to attack the High Commissioner's Palace."

Langotsky was angry. He says, "This was not the only time that day that orders were so vague to be almost a disaster. It was a big mistake to give orders that can be explained four ways. What does it mean to go to Allenby? Where in Allenby? Allenby is a big barracks. Who are we going to meet there? What is the plan? Are we going to continue directly? Are we going to stop there? It was very unpleasant."

The men swiftly mounted their vehicles and, to protect their vulnerable half-tracks and Jeeps from the Jordanian snipers on the Old City wall, rushed to Allenby Barracks through the back streets. Langotsky saw children of friends and even some relatives. They shouted: "Where are you going, Yossi?" Langotsky felt strange driving to war through his own hometown— "It was crazy fighting in your home."

D Company was the lone tank company near Jerusalem. Its fourteen World War II-era, American-made, Super-Shermans with 75-mm cannon were commanded by Major Aaron Kamara, in civilian life the owner of the Jerusalem Arrow Driving School. Kamara, a stocky boxer-like man of Iraqi descent, had been born in Jerusalem in 1929. When he was sixteen, he had joined Lehi, the Stern Gang, the most extreme Jewish terrorist group fighting the British. They captured him and imprisoned him for a year at Latrun. In 1948 he was wounded while serving with small South African "tanks" in the Palmach, the Jewish striking force, and in the 1956 Sinai campaign had fought as a paratrooper captain.

Under the 1949 Armistice Agreement, his Shermans, which he had commanded since 1958, were kept just west of the city near Beit Zayit in the same area as Langotsky's recon unit. Just before the war began, he was reinforced with another seven tanks. All Kamara's men had to live in Jerusalem; they were on two hours' call. They were always alerted in moments of danger to Jerusalem.

After attending the 8 A.M. meeting at Camp Schneller, Kamara returned to his camp and met Langotsky, who knew no more about the situation than he did. When the shelling of western Jerusalem began, Kamara tried to telephone Colonel Amitai, could not get through and decided to move into Jerusalem without orders.

He brought eleven of his tanks into the city and left the remaining ten under his deputy, Captain Raphael "Rafi" Yeshaya, to defend the corridor connecting Jerusalem with the rest of Israel. Husky, thoughtful and bespectacled, thirty-three-year-old Yeshaya had been a tanker for fifteen years. In civilian life, he had been a lawyer in Ashdod since that port was new. His family went back seven or eight generations in Hebron; but he had been born and now lived in Jerusalem.

Kamara, riding in his Jeep through the Jordanian bombardment, led his eleven tanks to the Russian Compound, near the border. The Russian Compound was a large piece of land that had been purchased by the Grand Duke Constantine of Russia when he visited the Holy Land in 1859. On the site outside the Old City had been built a vast Russian complex: the green multi-roofed Cathedral of the Holy Trinity, a hospital, a hostel for pilgrims, a residence for the Russian consul and a monastery with a chapel.[7]

At the Russian Compound, Kamara was told a cease-fire was in force. He figured he would be court-martialed for bringing his tanks into the city. He drove to brigade headquarters; Amitai was delighted to see him. Kamara thought if he came any closer the colonel would kiss him. Amitai told Kamara the Jordanians had taken Government House and were moving on

Talpiot in the southern part of Israeli Jerusalem. Kamara's tanks were needed urgently. He ordered the major to move his tanks to Allenby. Kamara told his men, "We are going to the last war. We are making history."

Kamara led ten of his tanks south down King David Street, the most direct route, even though they would be exposed to fire from the Old City. The civilians they passed saw the tanks with astonishment and joy. Near the King David Hotel, he halted and ordered his tanks' guns turned to the left to answer any enemy fire. But the Arab guns were silent. The sight of the armor on the road seemed to extinguish the firing from the Old City walls.

At Allenby, Kamara found a scene of noisy chaos. No one knew what to do. The Jordanians were shelling the camp, and Lt. Col. Aaronson's second-line infantry battalion was being badly hit. "It was terrible to see," Kamara said. He met Corporal Paz from the Lonely House. They were old friends. Paz and his men told Kamara of their narrow escape. "Don't worry," said the battle veteran Kamara with a bit of reassuring bravado, "I'm here."[8]

A man on crutches pulled himself out of his car at Allenby Barracks and started caring for the wounded lying among the trees. Shells were still coming in. Dr. Lichtenstein had left his wife with their two young sons and driven over to see what he could do. He knew Allenby was an army post and thought they might need a doctor. They did. When he drove up, soldiers dashed over and asked if he could help the wounded. He said, "I can help but bring the patients to me because I cannot walk."

A soldier with a shrapnel wound was brought to him, and he treated the wound. A friend of his, Yehuda Arbell, drove up in his Peugeot. Says Arbell, "I told him, 'You are crazy. What are you doing fighting on crutches?' Then I went on my way and he went on driving around looking for wounded people."

Langotsky and Kamara found each other at Allenby and looked futilely for Colonel Amitai. Neither major knew who was in charge or whether they should attack the UN compound. Says Langotsky, "It was funny-tragic that Kamara and I came to that place and asked each other what was going on. Who is in command? Who is to do what? It was absolutely crazy. We didn't know if the agricultural school was captured by the

Arabs. We looked at each other and we didn't know what to do. Thank God, Kamara and I were good friends and respected each other."

They tried to communicate with headquarters and could not get through. It was nearly a half hour before they received vague radio instructions to move up the road to the experimental farm. There, someone would meet them and tell them what to do next.

— Chapter 8 —

COUNTERATTACK AT GOVERNMENT HOUSE

To ATTACK THE JORDANIANS ON THE HILL OF EVIL COUNSEL, Langotsky and Kamara had to cross open ground on the ridge crest exposed to Jordanian fire. Kamara's tanks moved on the road; and the recon unit's vehicles advanced on their right through the fields and orchards, partially shielded by the tanks. On the high ground, they took fire from Abu Tor, the hill to their left nearer the city, and from the Jordanian Ninth Field Artillery. Tanks were hit but not damaged by the light 25-pounders, even though Lieutenant Khreisat ordered eight hundred shells fired.

Waving his arms in the middle of the road at the entrance to the farm, Lt. Col. Driezin flagged down the advancing column. At Kamara's lead tank, he picked up the telephone by which a man outside could talk with the tank commander. Driezin took command of the operation. Kamara wanted to plunge straight ahead into the UN compound, but Driezin gave him more conservative instructions. Five tanks would go into the orchard of the experimental farm and three would attack the compound and sweep the area between the gate and the tall radio antenna south of the road on the peak of the hill. Another force would move ahead to hold the road junction east of the compound.

Then Driezin hurried over and met Langotsky, who was just arriving, a hundred yards from the gate of the farm. Langotsky wanted to review the attack and make a battle sketch so that the Israelis would not be shooting at each other in the very confined target area. He warned, "We're going to kill each other."

They were under Jordanian fire, and Driezin was afraid the vehicles would be hit and the attack stopped. Angrily, he pointed his Uzi at Langotsky and said, "If you are not going to go immediately, I'm going to shoot you."

Driezin says, "I wasn't joking. I was in a hurry."

Zerach Epstein stood up, looking very large and aggressive, and said to the colonel, "Take it easy. If not, I'm going to cut your throat."

Langotsky was furious; he remembers: "I said, 'Asher, you are in a panic.' I felt I must speak as slowly as possible to relax him. I said, 'Take it easy. You don't know what you are saying. Better to do it in another three minutes and save lives.' Zerach was standing there. I told Driezin, 'In an hour or a day you'll come and say I'm sorry.' It happened in an hour; he came and apologized. I said, 'Shit!'"

Driezin finally drew a sketch in the sand. He wanted to attack Government House through the main gate. Langotsky says, "I think it was very stupid. The Jordanians were waiting on the other side with their recoilless guns, and it was a miracle that they were not quick enough to finish the first tank and stop everything.

"Asher Driezin gave me very mixed orders. I had a problem to give orders to my unit, and it was a very big mishmash. We didn't have any maps; we didn't have any air photos. We had an excellent collection back at headquarters."

The basic idea was for a platoon of Kamara's tanks to break through the compound's main western gate followed by Langotsky's half-tracks. Each unit of half-tracks would attack a different section inside the compound and the tanks would stand and give covering fire. Langotsky's Jeeps would wait at the experimental farm under Captain Solomon until Langotsky called them up. One element of half-tracks would assault Government House itself, while another took the antenna area and prepared to attack The Sausage, the Jordanian trenches running down the south side of the hill. About sixty soldiers of the Academic Reserve H Company would clear the pine woods north of Government House.

The Jordanians in the compound were shooting at the Israelis. Langotsky, his vision blocked by the trees, could not tell if the fire was coming from the roofs or windows. He did not know whether Jordanians were inside Government House itself.

As Driezin started to put his plan into effect, brigade headquarters ordered him to hold his positions. Someone higher up was having second thoughts about an all-out battle on the Jordanian front. With his force under fire, Driezin feared a halftrack would be hit before they started—"It could mean we would not have the guts to continue." He spread out his units on the grounds of the experimental farm.

Kamara moved his tanks off the exposed road into a narrow path leading into the farm's orchard. "It was a mistake," he said later. The tanks were caught in the mud under Jordanian fire and could not turn around. He ordered them to shell Government House and Silwan and Abu Tor in the direction of Jerusalem.

Inside his Government House office, Lt. Col. Johnson tried to act as normally as possible; he sat between two windows that faced south and dictated to his secretary sitting across the desk. Suddenly, a burst of Israeli machine-gun fire sprayed the building. Bullets entered both of Johnson's windows and buried themselves in the plaster wall above the secretary's head. They both dashed for the door and the greater safety of the narrow center hallway.

Downstairs, where General Bull had placed Dennis Holland in charge, the building's civilian occupants crowded into the main corridor that stretched the length of the first floor. The building had no basement. Hubert Noel brought an armchair from the dining room so the aged and ill political advisor Henri Vigier could sit comfortably, if a bit dangerously, in the corridor.

An Israeli shell smashed through the front door and exploded against the wall of the corridor like a violet sunburst. People dropped to the floor; a second round put most of the rest on the floor. Holland says, "How everyone was not killed in that corridor, I still do not understand. It was like a wind blowing the wheat down."

He herded a good number of the people to the west end of the building and the rest to the former ballroom, with its arched high walls and parquet floor, at the east end. Artillery and mortar shells continued to hit the building, shattering windows and glass doors.

After nearly an hour, Driezin received a renewed order from brigade to attack. Kamara climbed out of his tank and into his command half-track immediately behind. Driezin joined him. The half-track plowed through the trees and regained the road. The branches of one falling tree struck Kamara. Three soldiers had to lift the tree off the major.

Kamara ordered the last three tanks, which had not entered the muddy path, to break into the UN compound. Under Jordanian fire, the lead tank, its main gun firing once, smashed through the closed steel western gate.

The Academic Reserve H Company tried to cut through the fence surrounding the compound to get at the Jordanians in the pine woods, which were now burning. The Israelis' pliers would not cut the heavy fence and they had no bangalores. So the company entered the gate and went into the woods that way. The delay gave the Jordanians time to recover and open fire; they killed Lieutenant Israel Stern, commanding the lead platoon, and wounded several soldiers. The company had trouble advancing.

On the crest road, Driezin looked northward at the city of Jerusalem below him; from one point he thought he could see the Western Wall.

Major Badi Awad had placed his battalion facing north toward Jerusalem. Although he had Jeeps with recoilless rifles that could destroy the Israeli tanks, he did not send them to cover the road leading west; they were not even positioned to protect the main western gate. And they seemed totally unprepared to do what the Israelis feared most: attack westward into Israeli Jerusalem.

As the Israeli armor attacked his left flank he called in artillery fire, which hit both sides indiscriminately. Under Israeli pressure, Awad asked permission to withdraw; and the Jordanians fell back to their formation area east of the Government House compound to regroup. Awad had five men killed and twenty-five wounded. Long-range fire killed another ten Jordanian soldiers near the monastery. Lieutenant Khreisat and his assistant were wounded by shrapnel from an Israeli tank shell.

At that moment, the Israelis controlled Jabal Mukaber. Major Awad radioed the commander of the Ninth Field Artillery to blanket the Hill of Evil Counsel, including Government House. Lieutenant Khreisat believed he saw six half-tracks destroyed. He directed the Ninth Field Artillery to fire across the entire front to the north, including Mount Zion and the King David Hotel. But the 25-pounders did little damage. With his remaining men, Awad courageously mounted a counterattack, advancing again the few hundred yards into the eastern end of the UN compound.

Passing burning vehicles and dead Jordanian soldiers, the Israelis approached the UN compound. Driezin, in Kamara's half-track, spotted three deserted Jordanian Jeeps, one of which was armed with an antitank recoilless rifle. Several Jordanians daringly raced to these Jeeps to turn the gun on the advancing tanks. Driezin grabbed one of the half-track's two heavy machine guns and with a long burst set the three Jeeps on fire and killed the Jordanians. A shell struck a tree near the half-track, and shrapnel severed an artery in Driezin's right forearm and lodged in his elbow. He pressed his upper arm to stop the squirting blood and had a corpsman apply a tourniquet. For the next ten hours Driezin fought with his wounded arm strapped across his chest.

The tanks destroyed eleven Jeeps in all. Two tanks rolled out the compound's east gate to the intersection with the secondary north-south Bethlehem-Jerusalem road. Kamara wanted to head directly for the Old City. He had pierced the border and he knew that there were no Jordanian positions between his tanks and the Old City. But Driezin ordered him to stay and clear the UN compound first.

From the height Kamara looked at the panorama laid out before him: "Until this day, we had never seen this view—the Old City from behind. And the desert. And the sun. We were so surprised. I am not an emotional man, but I said to my driver: 'Look at the view. How nice.' He looked at me, and said, 'Are you crazy?' But it was beautiful."

Three tanks assembled near the antenna facing east. Twenty yards downhill began the trenches of The Sausage; fire was laid on them to suppress any Jordanian resistance. Driezin leapt from Kamara's half-track and ran to the antenna, eager to attack

The Sausage and expecting to find men of the recon unit. None was there.

Langotsky's half-tracks were supposed to advance up the short, circular driveway of the main building; instead, they swept on toward the far end of the compound. Distances were so short inside the compound that the drivers did not realize they had passed their objective.

One platoon commanded by tall, twenty-five-year-old Lieutenant Menashe "Muni" Altman dug in at the woods northeast of Government House. To Altman, in his first battle, the June afternoon seemed dark and gray. Everything stood out in vivid relief. When Altman, who had been born in Hadassah Hospital on Mount Scopus and was a former paratrooper, had passed Government House in his half-track, he stopped momentarily and fired on the building with particular zeal. He hated the UN presence; in his mind, the UN personnel were strangers who had no business being here. The Arabs, he felt, at least were the Israelis' neighbors and cared about the city. But he had a special score to settle with them also; in 1956, the Jordanians had killed his uncle at Ramat Rachel. He eagerly wanted to pay them back.

From his position near the far end of the compound, Altman went to find someone who would give him orders. And he met Lt. Col. Driezin for the first time. Driezin, standing in the road near the antenna, shouting orders and waving his good arm, told Altman to go back to Government House and find Langotsky and determine what was happening there. Altman decided to leave his men where they were dug in and went alone.

Leading his unit in his command half-track, Langotsky stopped directly in front of Government House. Sergeant Bar-Adon, sitting next to Zerach Epstein, the driver, sprayed the windows in the front of Government House with bullets from his Browning light machine gun. Langotsky watched in amazement as the rest of the convoy passed him. "I was here alone. I didn't believe my eyes." He decided to attack the building itself. "There were hundreds of soldiers, Israelis and Jordanians, in a very concentrated area, shooting. I tried to be as calm as possible. I took Avner Malkov's microphone and said, 'We are going to attack the main building of the Government House in sixty seconds. I am asking all units to keep firing at the first floor for sixty seconds and then raise your fire to the second level and then the third level and stop firing on the House in five minutes.'"

He halted a half-track that had fallen behind. Under fire from the left, it had gone off the road and down a cliff and had been delayed reaching the road through the mines. Its commander was Platoon Sergeant Gershon Cohen, a strong, athletic, twenty-seven-year-old former paratrooper from Kibbutz Cabri in the Galilee, who had been working as a physical education instructor in Jerusalem.

Ordering Zerach Epstein and another soldier to cover them with his half-track's machine gun, Langotsky ran up the driveway with Sergeant Cohen, followed by ten soldiers. They advanced through the bushes and flowers of the small garden on either side of the main entrance. Jordanians and Israelis fired on each other. Langotsky saw several Jordanians shoot at them and start to run for a shelter in the garden. He hurled a grenade and killed them.

Israeli fire sprayed through the windows and French doors of the ground floor of Government House. Inside, the virtually unarmed UN personnel suddenly found themselves in the middle of a battle between armies. Lt. Col. Johnson says, "The Israelis attacked the building as though it were occupied. I would too. We were all just lucky as hell we weren't blown to bits."

The bright green wooden door of Government House was locked. Langotsky ordered it blown open. It was now 3:52. His demolition man put against the door an explosive "cross" consisting of two pieces of wood with explosive material at each end connected with wires. The Israelis crouched behind nearby rocks and blew a hole through the heavy door. They climbed over the furniture that had been piled against it and was starting to burn. The main corridor was empty. Opposite the entrance was the large, arched dining room with a sculpted stone fireplace. Expecting that the Jordanians were in the building, the Israelis swarmed over it, inside and out. They worked their way toward both ends of the main corridor. The rooms were locked. They hurled a grenade through the glass door of each room; and, after it exploded, they kicked in the door and fired their Uzis inside. Dennis Holland says, "They were very trigger-happy." The building started to fill with smoke. It was difficult to breathe.

There was one moment of levity. A Japanese security officer was sitting on a first-floor toilet when a machine-gun burst stitched the bathroom. With his trousers at half-mast, he ran out into the ballroom. Everyone shrieked with laughter.

In front of Sergeant Cohen, a door at the east end of the corridor opened and F. T. Liu shouted in English: "Don't shoot! We are UN." The Israelis held their fire. In the ballroom were about thirty people. A grenade flew in through a window; it bounced harmlessly under a bench—a dud. Kazuo Ohta, the Japanese World War II veteran in charge of the UN motor workshop, remembers that the Israelis ordered them to raise their hands and that some of the women secretaries and children were crying. The Israelis ordered everyone down on the floor.

Cohen called for Langotsky, who had started to climb the stairs to the second floor. He rushed down and was shocked by the sight of the civilians huddled in the ballroom and the kitchen in the midst of the battle. He said, "Don't worry. Stay in your room. I'm sorry but *à la guerre comme à la guerre*. Stay on the floor. Don't try to be wise. Don't interfere. We will try to do our best."

Dennis Holland objected to the Israelis firing on the UN building; Langotsky explained they presumed it was occupied by the enemy. He questioned the UN people in English about the presence of Jordanians in the building. An Indian UN field service secretary told him that several Jordanian soldiers had gone up to the third floor, but they had been quickly ushered out.

Distrusting these assurances, Langotsky climbed cautiously to the third floor. Two Israelis had already found General Bull and his senior staff sitting on the floor in Bull's office directly above the main entrance. One soldier went to the window and the other signaled the UN people to lie flat on the floor. General Bull greeted Langotsky politely and expressed concern for the UN's Arab employees. Langotsky gave his word that they would not be harmed. He was impressed with Bull's professional demeanor. Langotsky said later, "The one who really upset me was the Marine colonel. He spoke to me as the Brits used to speak to the natives. He was very unpleasant. He gave me orders instead of understanding that I was not there as a

Boy Scout, that I had soldiers and a mission, and first of all, I have to kill my enemy or he will kill my boys."

Johnson confirms the confrontation. He says General Bull was agreeable to evacuating the building under Israeli pressure, but "I was disagreeable as hell."

Good fortune had prevented extensive casualties among the UN personnel; the only one wounded was an Australian colonel who was nicked in the leg by a shell fragment.

The Israelis found no Jordanian soldiers in the building. They did no shooting above the first floor; but looking out an upstairs window, Langotsky saw many Jordanian soldiers moving through the woods. He could see none of his own men. He told Zerach Epstein to go to a balcony, wait until he saw the Academic Reserve H Company, assigned to clear the woods, and warn the men that the building was already in Israeli hands. "If you can show them where the Jordanians are, do it." Langotsky was worried that the Israelis would kill each other; "I wasn't afraid of the Arabs; I was afraid of the Jews."

He ordered Gershon Cohen to get a machine gun from a half-track and place it as quickly as possible in an upper-story window to support the approaching Academic Reserve company.

Cohen had trouble getting out through the burning furniture in the main doorway; and when he returned with the gun, he found the entrance blocked by flames. Despite a right wrist weakened from an old break received when he was a paratrooper, he grabbed the bars of a first floor window and with Sergeant Bar-Adon's help handed up the gun, still hot from the earlier firing, to soldiers on the second floor.

Then, Cohen climbed a rain pipe to the roof and leapt from roof to roof until he was on top of the three-story building. Arab guns from all over the area fired at him. He lowered the UN flag. Shots hit the water tanks and flooded the roof. He fell flat and impulsively called for an Israeli flag. None could be found so Major Kamara had his tank's signal flag with horizontal white and blue stripes passed up to Cohen. Lying prone under fire, Cohen tore holes in it with his teeth and raised it on the pole atop the building.

Inside on the first floor, the Israeli soldiers, obeying their orders strictly, would not let the UN people move about. In the dining room, some of the Israeli soldiers were helping themselves to lunch and beer. Langotsky told Holland, the ranking UN officer downstairs, to have the flames in the doorway extinguished with water carried in pots from the kitchen. Israeli soldiers helped carry the water. The UN's fire extinguishers were not working.

Langotsky radioed Colonel Amitai: "It's a crazy situation. I am here with fifteen of my soldiers. All the others are split up, on the hill and in the rear. Send someone to take charge of these diplomats." Shortly, the chief of logistics for the brigade arrived. But he spoke only Rumanian and Hebrew, and Langotsky had to continue with his diplomatic duties.

He was awed by the luxuriousness of Government House: "In one room I saw a very big collection of medals. Odd Bull's. I told one of my soldiers not to leave the entrance of that room until you are relieved. There is a fortune here. Nobody should dare to touch it."

Jay Bushinsky, a young American reporter for the *Chicago Daily News*, with Israeli press photographer Emanuel Pratt, had raced after the Israelis and taken two bullets through his car's roof. Bushinsky wrote: "Inside, the palatial headquarters building was in a shambles. The huge wooden door was burnt out and lay across the threshold. Carpets, drapes and woodwork were blackened by fire. The elaborate communications center had been blown up."

Langotsky remained in Government House less than fifteen minutes. Then, under Colonel Amitai's order, Langotsky informed General Bull that his people had fifteen minutes to evacuate the building. Bull declared that he wanted to go to the Jordanian sector of Jerusalem. Amitai refused his request.

The UN officials worried about what would happen when the Israelis discovered that the kitchen staff were Jordanians. Holland says, "So the best thing was to have them handed over officially." Langotsky collected the Jordanians' identity cards and reassured Bull that the Arabs would be taken care of. Bull shook hands with each of them as a gesture of loyalty and support.

Since General Bull's car had been one of the many UN vehicles destroyed, Langotsky ordered Sergeant Bar-Adon to drive the general to Jerusalem in a Jeep. Bull simply ignored the sergeant and told Langotsky he would be the last to leave.

Under Jordanian artillery fire, the UN people were herded into whichever of their vehicles would still run.

Langotsky then ordered Bar-Adon to see to the safety of the UN's Jordanian cooks and helpers. They started to walk west in front of Bar-Adon's Jeep. As they emerged from the compound, Jordanian troops fired on them. The Jordanian civilians fell to the ground and were not hurt. At the experimental farm, Bar-Adon turned them over to other Israeli soldiers. The Jordanians were jailed for about a week and then released.

A number of Americans were among the UN staff, including, in addition to Lt. Col. Johnson, Marine Major Roger C. Hagerty, the operations officer and the elder son of James C. Hagerty, who had been President Dwight Eisenhower's press secretary; several Army noncommissioned officers, and a U.S. Navy chief petty officer who served as corpsman. The others included Englishmen, Australians, Frenchmen, Danes, Austrians, Japanese and, of course, the Norwegian, General Bull.

The enforced departure from Government House angered several of the UN officials who did not believe the United Nations should leave its headquarters just because the Israelis told them to. They hastily collected some of their most secret code books and confidential files that had not been sent ahead to Beirut, and the finance officer brought out $100,000. Personnel whose cars were damaged tried desperately to change tires and get motors running. Holland says, "It was like a Mack Sennett comedy. No one wanted to leave his car there. All that were left were thoroughly looted."

Before 5 P.M., the UN people headed out in two convoys to the Israeli sector of Jerusalem. Most of them, including the women and children, drove out of danger to the western suburb of Ein Karem. Dennis Holland tried to go back into Government House and bring out more code books, but he was stopped in the corridor by an armed Israeli who hurried him outside. He found his official car was undamaged and followed the convoy to Ein Karem.

They headed for Ein Karem because Hubert Noel had a house there. Ein Karem was the traditional birthplace of St. John the Baptist.[1] Noel offered to take one family to his house and was surprised to find more than a dozen Jeeps following him. Most of the people were housed in the Catholic Convent of Notre Dame de Sion, although the Sisters were afraid their presence might compromise the convent.

A second and much smaller party, led by General Bull, Vigier, Liu and Johnson, drove directly to the Israeli Foreign Ministry to present a formal claim to repossess Government House. Arthur Lourie gave them sandwiches and a drink and put at their disposal rooms in the President Hotel. Once settled into the hotel, this group walked over to the U.S. Consulate in Agron Street and asked Consul General Wilson if they could hold a staff meeting there. "They didn't want to do it in the Israeli hotel for fear of surveillance," explains Wilson. "They had their meeting in my bedroom because we had thirty-five of our staff and dependents and had turned the living room into a dormitory. They asked me if I could send to Washington their report to the Secretary General and to Ralph Bunche of their eviction from Government House, and I did so. They joined us for a quick meal."

At the consulate, Johnson and another UN officer whose wives were in the Jordanian sector were the subject of much sympathy. Everyone thought that most of the Arab side had been destroyed and Johnson did not know whether Alice was alive until Mac Hall dared go out in the streets and check on her. Johnson says gratefully, "Hall is a gutsy little man."

They returned to the President Hotel. Holland and his chief security officer showed up from Ein Karem and they accounted for all the UN personnel except for U Than Aye. No one knew what had become of him. On a telex machine General Bull asked Ralph Bunche to start action to recover Government House from the Israelis. Bull and Holland went back to the Foreign Ministry, where Holland got into an angry row with an Israeli official because Israeli aircraft were strafing the Augusta Victoria Hospital, which had been one of his responsibilities when he was the UNRWA director in Jordan.

General Bull soon set up his UNTSO headquarters in the YMCA facing the King David Hotel, parking his vehicles and equipment on the YMCA soccer field.

Meanwhile, when Langotsky was busy sending off the UN personnel, the battle around Government House raced on to a swift climax. Zerach Epstein fought in the middle of it. He was an awesome figure. Brawny and powerful, he wore a

Browning pistol in a hip holster; carried two grenades, and had on crepe-soled shoes so he could move quietly in battle.

As Langotsky had ordered him, Epstein found the commander of the Academic Reserve H Company; a dozen of the men were exchanging fire with the Jordanians in the woods. Epstein joined the attack, shooting from cover. Two students followed him. He told them to fire their automatic weapons toward a shallow pit from which they were being shot at. Epstein swung wide and flung a grenade into the pit. He killed five Jordanians.

He was fired on by Jordanians both up the hill and lower down. He dove on top of the bodies and called to the two students, but they had disappeared. He was alone, surrounded by most of a Jordanian company in the woods. He climbed out of the pit and plunged straight at three Arabs shooting at him from forty yards. Epstein stopped, fired a rifle and killed the three soldiers with three shots.

His vision was blurred by enemy smoke shells; but he moved forward, firing into holes and flinging in grenades he took from dead Jordanians. A large Jordanian rose in front of him and lifted a wounded buddy on his shoulders and walked slowly away. Epstein let him go.

Near the edge of the road, a man charged him. Only when he was a few yards away was Epstein certain that he was a Jordanian. Epstein fired first. He returned to Government House, leaving at least nine dead Arabs on the hill.

Lieutenant Altman's men found a box of Jordanian grenades. They were British types and they had not been armed and were not ready for instantaneous use. "When I saw this box," Altman said later, "I realized that the Jordanians didn't understand the war. I passed out the grenades to my soldiers, and in the fighting later that day we gave them their grenades back."

The action at Government House was over. One Israeli was dead and several wounded. Kamara assembled his tanks at the antenna and waited for the infantry. His men found the Burmese guard, whom the Jordanians had left tied up in the east gate guard house. Kamara sent him in his half-track to the main building. U Than Aye was the last of the UN personnel on the Hill of Evil Counsel.

* * *

Once the Israelis seized Government House, Brig. Gen. Hazzáa left David's Tower and—with his intelligence officer, Governor Anwar al-Khatib, the director of police and Major Salah—returned to his tactical headquarters in the underground shelter in Wadi el Joz. All along the Green Line of the city, sporadic firing crossed no-man's-land, and the artillery of both armies continued to fire.

At 4 P.M., Brig. Gen. Hazzáa received a telephone call from Brig. Gen. Ahmed Shihadeh, commander of the Imam Ali Brigade, who said he had instructions from Maj. Gen. Salim, commanding the West Bank, to enter Jerusalem under Hazzáa's command and to support his brigade. Hazzáa told Shihadeh that, if he could advance despite the artillery fire and air attacks, he should bring his two remaining battalions north to Tel el-Ful and replace Hazzáa's Fourth Infantry Battalion, which he wanted to move to support his Second and Eighth battalions in the city. He estimated that Shihadeh could reach Tel el-Ful by about 8 P.M. But he never made it through the Israeli bombardment. Early the next morning, a few of his exhausted soldiers reached Tel el-Ful.

Long before that, Brig. Gen. Hazzáa ordered Major Badi Awad, the commander who had attacked the Hill of Evil Counsel, to return to his starting point at the suburb of Abu Dis on the road to Jericho. Awad kept one company on the road for a few hours to block any Israeli advance to the east. At Abu Dis, he lost radio contact with Hazzáa and by midnight reassembled his men at Et Tur at the southern tip of the Mount of Olives. No Israelis were near there. Out of communication with his brigade and the sole target in the area, Awad returned to Abu Dis.

At 1 A.M. he found the First Tank Company commanded by Captain Mamud Salim Abu Wandi waiting for him at Abu Dis. Eventually, they led the remaining nine tanks back across the Jordan River. "I was fighting a lonely battle," Major Awad says. He and his men retreated on foot, leading the tanks through rough country. Awad's battalion had suffered fifteen men killed and sixty-five wounded—25 percent of his men and 30 percent of his vehicles. The battalion was finished.

The operation with that ironic name—"Omen of Good Luck"—proved to be the trigger for the Israeli conquest of the

Jordanian sector of Jerusalem. Starting with this signal, the Jordanians initiated the battle on the ground for Jerusalem and enabled the Israelis to reunite the divided city under their flag.

The Israelis had to have justification—conviction that in their own eyes and the eyes of the world they had the right, by provocation and attack, to take Jordanian Jerusalem by force. They did not require much provocation, but they did require justification. Jerusalem had to be taken justly. If King Hussein had not ordered the attack on Jabal Mukaber, he would not have lost East Jerusalem and the Old City (or the West Bank). U.S. Consul General Wilson says: "The most foolish thing that the Jordanians did was when they decided to try to take Government House."

Why did the Jordanians do it? Because King Hussein felt he had to make a gesture of support to President Nasser? Because the Jordanians really expected the Israelis to make war on Jordan? To prevent the Israelis from taking the high ground south of Jerusalem and flanking the city? Because Jabal Mukaber was not defended and the UN personnel were unarmed? Because it was there?

Yitzhak Rabin has his view: "King Hussein was misled by Nasser. Nasser told him he was winning the war. Hussein knew Mount Scopus was a fortified position that could call for real fighting. Here, he took something that did not belong to Israel. Therefore, he didn't exactly challenge Israel and did not call for direct confrontation with the armed forces of Israel. And he could say he achieved a lot."

— Chapter 9 —

ADVANCE INTO JORDAN

HAVING FORCED MAJOR BADI AWAD TO WITHDRAW FROM THE Hill of Evil Counsel, the Israeli half-tracks advanced east beyond the UN compound to the road junction. The men stared at a breathtaking view of the bare, sand-colored hills stretching ahead into Jordan and to the Dead Sea in the distance. Below them to the north, golden in the sun, lay Jerusalem.

They waited at the crossroads for twenty minutes, met no enemy and turned back to the antenna. There, Lt. Col. Driezin was collecting soldiers to attack The Sausage, the intricate, twisting maze of trenches and bunkers extending south of the compound. He ordered them to set up a defensive line near the antenna. Jordanians approached and opened fire. A mortar shell decapitated one Jordanian and the rest retreated.

The recon platoon that Driezin had told to stay back at the farm under command of Captain Solomon, Langotsky's deputy, now advanced. These men had been under constant bombardment during the fight at Government House. Solomon tried to reach Langotsky or Driezin by radio without success. Finally, he took his men and a number of student-soldiers from Lieutenant Stern's former platoon and moved toward the battle on his own.

The Israelis prepared to attack The Sausage. Waiting for them in the trenches and bunkers and protected by a heavily mined wadi was part of a Jordanian brigade based at Hebron. The Sausage had been built to guard the border against an attack from Kibbutz Ramat Rachel to the west. But the Israelis were approaching The Sausage from its most vulnerable northern end.

The tanks assembled near the antenna to support the infantry attack. An artillery shell struck near Kamara's half-track, singed his face and eyebrows and threw him out of the vehicle and to the ground.

Driezin ordered Solomon to form three teams to attack The Sausage's three main trench lines. A total of twenty-four Israelis prepared to assault the long fortifications. One group led by Lieutenant Danny Bachrach cut through the fence surrounding the compound, entered The Sausage under cover of the tanks' fire and raced into an open trench.

Another squad came through the wire uphill. Shouting against the strong ridgetop wind, Bachrach pointed out to them the other two parallel trenches winding down the hill with spurs leading to bunkers. They all rushed into The Sausage and attacked it systematically as they had been trained. In each trench, two men led the way. The first fired his Uzi around the bend in the trench. When his magazine was empty, he pressed himself against the trench wall to reload while the second man took the lead. Bachrach followed the two lead "trackers" and sent the next men into the spurs to clear the bunkers.

A recon squad leader, Lieutenant Zvi "Zvika" Ginossar, went up one spur and then dashed back, yelling, "Grenade!" After it exploded, Bachrach saw a Jordanian rushing to them out of the spur. He did not have time to raise his rifle. He called "Zvika!" and Ginossar stepped forward and blasted the Arab with his Uzi.

Driezin was sending men from B Company into the trenches as fast as he could gather them. One platoon swept clear a secondary trench. A few more soldiers entered the main trench and mopped up bunkers that Bachrach and his men had bypassed. One Israeli came upon a Jordanian who had just pulled the pin of his grenade, grabbed the grenade from the man's hand and handed it to one of his own soldiers.

In one spur, three Israelis came up behind two Jordanians staring across toward Israeli Jerusalem. The Israelis killed them with grenades and then found five more Jordanians in identical positions. The Israelis flung in grenades and killed all five.

They had cleared only a quarter of The Sausage when they started to run out of ammunition. The road leading back to Allenby Barracks was cut by heavy Jordanian fire, making it impossible to send forward any "soft" vehicles. They took weapons and grenades from the dead Jordanians and continued the attack.

The Jordanians defending The Sausage seemed to be unled. Only one wounded officer was found; the rest had apparently fled. Lieutenant Avram Bernstein had wounded the remaining officer, a major, with a grenade and left him for dead. (Hours later he was heard groaning in the dark and discovered to be alive.) By 4:30 P.M., The Sausage was taken. In the trenches and bunkers lay thirty dead Jordanians—in addition to the forty in the UN compound. In The Sausage, the Israelis had only one man wounded and no one killed.

Then, Driezin received a radio message from brigade head-quarters asking if he was ready to attack The Bell position at Sur Bahir. This was a fortified Arab village atop the next rocky hill a mile south of Government House and on the border directly facing Ramat Rachel. In 1948, the villagers from Sur Bahir had repeatedly sacked the kibbutz. Driezin replied that he was ready but he was out of ammunition. He was told he would be sent more.

Colonel Amitai felt that if The Bell—which was named after the shape of its main bunker—was taken, any idea of the invincibility of the Jordanian army would be smashed forever. He radioed Driezin at Government House to attack Sur Bahir and The Bell and cut the main Bethlehem-Jerusalem road.

Driezin and his officers held a hasty briefing. They had only a small-scale map of the whole area; it did not show in detail the targets they would face. And not all the commanders could even see the map; some strained to read it over the heads of the men in front. All the detailed maps and aerial photographs had been left behind.

Driezin rounded up Langotsky's and Kamara's men for the attack. He would leave most of his force at Government House and The Sausage because he expected the Jordanians to coun-terattack. He wanted to arrive at the rear of Sur Bahir with tanks and half-tracks. Kamara insisted his tanks had to stick to the secondary Bethlehem road east of the UN compound. He would not take them into the deep valley and up the hill to Sur Bahir. "If you want to go down the valley," he said, "you go without me."

Driezin, Langotsky and Kamara planned their attack while sitting beneath a tree near the antenna under Jordanian shellfire. Although Langotsky's men had stolen ammunition from the depots before the war and had four times as much ammunition as they were supposed to, they still had only enough for four or five hours of fighting. As they waited and the men loaded into their vehicles, an armored bus usually used for the Mount Scopus convoys ran through Arab fire on the crest road with a new supply of ammunition. They could fight on.

It was still light at 6:30 when Driezin's jerry-built force moved out. Three tanks took the lead and two brought up the rear. In between were the recon unit's half-tracks. Several tanks remained behind to block any counterattack from Bethlehem and Hebron. Driezin left one tank and a half-track to guard the road junction.

The column passed around The Sausage, which had been so fearsome and which Israeli soldiers now held. Some of the tankers, thinking the soldiers in the trenches were Arabs, fired on them by mistake. But no one was hit. At the crossroad, Kamara reluctantly wheeled right, away from the target in his heart—the Old City—and toward Sur Bahir.

At the first turn, two Arab civilian cars blocked the winding, narrow road. Their frightened occupants were huddled in a nearby cave, and the Israelis let them be. Kamara sent his lead tank crashing over the cars. But the second tank swung left around the roadblock. From his half-track Kamara shouted to stop it but he was too late. The tank commanded by Sergeant Arik Kantor tumbled down the sheer drop and rolled over nearly a hundred feet into the deep wadi. All four of its crew were injured; the loader was crushed mortally. If the column was to attack The Bell before dark, it could not stop to help them.

Badly hurt, Kantor found an Uzi and he tried to radio the column. But since he was deep in the wadi, no one could hear his signal. With the Uzi, a flashlight and a flare gun, he started painfully crawling up the steep hill to the road. A head wound smeared his face with blood. At the top, he tried unsuccessfully to start one of the abandoned Arab cars to go back to Government House for help. He hobbled back toward the spot where his tank had gone over. In the dark, one of his men, fearing an Arab attack, fired on Kantor. A spray of bullets hit his leg, groin and stomach. He screamed to the soldier to stop firing, and the man dashed up to help Kantor. The soldier left Kantor lying by the side of the road and went down the hill again to hide himself. Kantor was alone for hours. If Arabs came, he was prepared to shoot himself rather than be captured alive.

The small Israeli column moved fast between Sur Bahir's barley fields and climbed into the confined winding village street, past windows that threatened to harbor a resistant enemy. But the Arabs had closed up their houses and did not try to halt the Israelis. Although no one was in sight, they fired hundreds of rounds into the windows to reduce the risk.

Sur Bahir's six extensive trenches and thirty-five bunkers—fortifications large enough to hold a company—were all on the far western side of the village facing the fields of Ramat Rachel on the same high, windy ridgetop. The men could see all the way north to Jerusalem and south across the desert to the ruins of Herodion, the mountain fortress and palace-tomb of Herod the Great overlooking Bethlehem.

It was almost dark. In the village a half-track broke down and blocked the rear of the column. Unaware, the two lead tanks followed by three half-tracks plowed ahead through the village to a low stone wall on the left of the road and opened fire on The Bell. The road ended in a small house; the first tank simply crushed it.

Langotsky was eager to strike before darkness closed in. His men were expert at trench fighting in daylight; but in the dark, it would be hell. "Where is everybody?" Langotsky wondered.

The attack was supported by powerful fire from four recoilless guns and ten Jeeps with machine guns at The Sausage and more distant covering fire from some of Kamara's tanks and from Driezin's men. But troops directly across the Green Line at Ramat Rachel, thinking Driezen's column were Jordanian reinforcements, fired on the Israelis.

Entering the battle, the force consisted of Driezin's small headquarters group, Langotsky and a few men and Altman's twenty soldiers. They faced sixty Jordanians in the position; fortunately, only some thirty stayed to fight.

Driezin and Langotsky knew that The Bell was entirely surrounded by mines and barbed wire. There was only one entrance at the rear. Langotsky jumped from the lead half-track and raced to the nearest trench, which ran parallel along the right side of the road. He called to the others to follow. Epstein and Bar-Adon were with him. Langotsky found the entrance and entered the trench. The walls were higher than a man and were carved out of natural caves reinforced by steel beams and concrete. Langotsky came upon a young Bedouin soldier facing toward Ramat Rachel. The Jordanians did not expect an attack from the rear. "I put my Uzi in his back and said in Arabic: 'Hands up!' He almost fainted. I took his carbine. I was alone. Zerach came up and I told him to give me his word that no one would touch the youth. I didn't come to collect prisoners. I came to fight. He was the only prisoner taken at that strongpoint." Epstein led the prisoner to the rear.

Driezin feared for Langotsky's small party trying to clear the Jordanian trench. Driezin ordered a tank to smash through a house and join Langotsky. The colonel thought soldiers were hanging back, afraid to follow Langotsky. He did not know that a major part of his force was immobilized behind the damaged half-track back in the village. Going on foot to the two half-tracks that had come forward with Langotsky, he angrily ordered the two drivers and two guards to go with him and clear the next parallel trench to the south.

When Epstein brought the prisoner back to the half-tracks, he found them deserted. He hiked through the Arab village to the rear element, left the prisoner and ran alone to rejoin Langotsky.

Always in front, the major raced along the trench and shot and killed two more Jordanians. Bar-Adon with his Uzi was right behind him. They cleared bunkers with grenades. A tank shell hit the main concrete bunker of The Bell. Langotsky and Epstein dashed up and dropped grenades into the bunker's firing holes.

It was now getting dark. Driezin sent out three groups to clear three more trenches. Langotsky was followed only by a dozen men from his half-track and Lieutenant Altman's. He sent Altman and his men to a bunker and trench on the right side. Altman calmly hurled a grenade and went in. Two scouts moved ahead to clear the position. Altman's section of the L-shaped bunker was empty. He fired his Uzi into the other part and killed a Jordanian; the barrel of the man's rifle was still hot.

From below them, a Jordanian called, "Who's there?" Sergeant Gershon Cohen was now in front of Altman, and the unexpected shout stopped him. Altman urged Cohen to move on, but Cohen's rifle was not operating. For a vital instant, the little group was halted. Altman hesitated a fraction of a second and then pushed past Cohen, ran into the bunker and with his Uzi wiped out its defenders and their light machine gun.

The Israelis advanced through the trench. Two scouts led the way; they and Altman would fire into a bunker and dash past it. A following fire team went in and mopped up the bypassed bunker. At one bunker just beyond The Bell, the recon unit suffered its first fatality, communications Sergeant Yehoshua Weltzer. Known as a quiet man, Sergeant Weltzer had been hidden with his brother and sister in a windowless basement in Belgium for two years during World War II by a Christian family. He was shot in the head only ten yards from where Langotsky fought. Near him at the bunker's entrance lay a dead Jordanian.

On the left, Lt. Col. Driezin spotted three Jordanians approaching through one of the trenches. With his wounded right arm still in a sling, Driezin fired the half-track's machine gun with his left hand. Then he sent four men into the trench and raced along the top himself. A grenade ripped his remaining good hand. His men killed the three Jordanians.

Zerach Epstein and another Israeli soldier entered the trench on the far left and worked their way back from The Bell. Epstein drew his pistol and killed two Jordanians who were shooting through a firing slit. He threw his last grenade into the next bunker and killed three more. He took grenades from the dead Jordanians, but at the third bunker he met two Jordanians coming out. Epstein's companion fired at them. They ducked back into the bunker, and Epstein hurled a grenade after them. He cleaned out another bunker at the end of the trench, while his partner wiped out one that Epstein had missed. They had cleared the farthest trench. His rifle clip now empty, Epstein killed two sergeants with his pistol. They were the twelfth and thirteenth Jordanians he killed in the trench. Before the fighting was done for the day, he would kill a total of twenty-seven Jordanians, a third of all those killed.

Now it was dark. Driezin heard firing but could not tell where his men were and where the Jordanians were. He concentrated all his soldiers and three tanks and two half-tracks near the now-silent Bell. There were still trenches and caves they had not cleared.

Brigade ordered an infantry company of the Sixty-second Battalion to open a path through the minefield from Ramat Rachel, two hundred yards away, to relieve the men at The Bell. By radio, the force at Ramat Rachel asked the men at The Bell to indicate their position with a light. Driezin ordered his men to cease firing and sent forward a man with a flashlight. Immediately shots rang out.

At first, the men thought they were being fired on by the soldiers coming from Ramat Rachel. Driezin and Kamara yelled at them to stop shooting. Then they made out five soldiers wearing Jordanian British-type helmets. And they heard shouts in Arabic. Intense firing broke out. The Jordanians killed two recon men: Sergeant Daniel Ashuri and First Sergeant Menachem Schraga. They had just volunteered to carry Sergeant Weltzer's body away from the battle site.

The five Jordanians attacked the small group of Israelis standing on the rise just to the right of The Bell. Driezin tried to release his Uzi's safety switch with his wounded left hand. His runner, Private Gidon Halvatz, a lean, long-faced electrical engineer, was shot through the head. Sergeant Ruven Robert Haddad, the Morocco-born forward fire controller who had originally joined Driezin to spot mortar fire, was also killed. Lieutenant Yaacov Barnes, a tank platoon commander, was shot in the eye. Langotsky was sprayed with shrapnel.

Epstein was the first to react. Lying prone directly in front of The Bell, he emptied a fresh rifle clip at the Jordanian muzzle flashes below them. Langotsky's and Kamara's Uzis joined the firing. Driezin ordered grenades dropped on the Jordanians and they killed all five. Grenade fragments ripped Driezin's left hand and arm—his third wound. He says, "We owed our lives to Epstein. If he had not shot immediately, nothing would have stopped them. We didn't know who was who."

The fight was now over. They found the bodies of seventeen Jordanians. With the help of the more distant covering fire, The Bell had been taken with five Israelis killed and eight wounded.

The handful of still battle-able Israeli soldiers were virtually out of ammunition. Langotsky shouted, "Anyone seen shooting will be the enemy." In the dark the men collected. Everyone had less than a magazine left. They conserved their fire. The two tanks were brought up behind The Bell, and the men on the windswept ridge formed a tight circle around them, with the wounded in the center. They rearmed with ammunition and grenades from the tanks and the dead Jordanians.

Epstein ran back through the village and brought up the men from the rear of the column. Thirty Israelis were now huddled there in the dark waiting for the company from Ramat Rachel, struggling through the minefield. They had to wait more than three hours.

Near to midnight, they finally started back toward Government House. The night was cold. The Israeli bodies lay on the floor of a half-track. A tank towed the broken-down half-track.

At Government House, Langotsky was horrified by what had happened to the luxurious building since the afternoon. The building had been looted and General Bull's medals had disappeared.

Later, after an investigation, the medals were located and returned to Bull. But over the next days, the Israelis destroyed and removed much of the United Nations communications system and looted UN personal belongings. Of the looting, Major Levinson, the MAC liaison officer, said, "This didn't help Israel." Israelis also made off with UN stores of food and liquor and removed or copied the UN files. Lt. Col. Johnson says, "I don't know what the hell they were looking for." From New York, Secretary General U Thant protested. Eventually, the UN recovered 179 of its 700 acres and Government House itself.

That night, Driezin assured Kamara he had picked up the men from Kantor's tank; but Kamara could locate only three of the tank's crew. Furious, he took three tanks back to Kantor's tank and found the fourth man, now dead. He was trapped under the tank's gun and a surgeon had to remove his arm to bring out his body.

The troops rode back to the Hebrew Gymnasium next to the Evelina de Rothschild Girls School in Rehavia. One half-track took the dead and wounded to Sha'are Zedek Hospital.

Very upset, Langotsky reported to Colonel Amitai and said loudly, "Who are those idiots sending us to fight without enough grenades and ammunition? Why was there so much hesitation—wait here and wait there? We waited hours to get permission to keep fighting." Langotsky did not notice that General Narkiss was in the room during his outburst. He was embarrassed when the general greeted him warmly and ignored his remarks. But the major was convinced that if they had moved more rapidly the Israelis could have finished the battle in daylight with fewer casualties. He was told there were political reasons for the delays.

Later he said: "We were lucky not to fight against a real good Arab unit. In The Sausage and The Bell they fought stupidly. The Jordanian firing positions were badly planned. They expected us only from one direction. Therefore, we were always fighting one against one. We came down The Sausage and attacked The Bell from the rear, and they were not smart enough to reorganize themselves to stop us. In other places, the Jordanians fought very bravely—like lions."

Driezin says, "We started to free Jerusalem with less than one battalion." He deployed his command and at 1 A.M. was taken to Hadassah Hospital to repair the artery that had been severed ten hours earlier. He was carried there in the same vehicle with the wounded Jordanian major who had been captured in The Sausage. Later, the two commanders talked about the battle. The Jordanian said he had stayed in The Sausage expecting his men to counterattack.

Colonel Amitai stationed first-line battalion soldiers at Government House, Sur Bahir and Ramat Rachel. He expected a Jordanian counterattack at dawn. He would be ready. The half-tracks and their drivers were sent to join the paratroopers' brigade.

In his evening broadcast to the Israeli people, Chaim Herzog said, "The first day of fighting is over and a new page in the history of Israel's wars has been opened. . . . King Hussein today made the mistake of his life because he believed Nasser's false estimate in regard to Israel's weakness and inability to stand up to all the Arab forces at once. . . . I would say that tonight Nasser is a very different person from what he was when he started work this morning."[1]

— Chapter 10 —

"DO WE DARE DO IT?"

THE FIRST WORD OF THE JORDANIAN ARMY'S ATTACK TO REACH Operational General Headquarters in Tel Aviv was garbled. Defense Minister Dayan, Chief of Staff Rabin and Yigael Yadin in the headquarters bunker heard from Jerusalem that the Jordanians had occupied the Hebrew University campus on Mount Scopus. Yadin says, "That was the first news we got. Later, it was corrected that they had attacked Government House. But that first news immediately triggered an alarm in the mind of each of us that the actual objective of the Jordanian army would be to occupy Mount Scopus. If the Jordanian army really wanted to attack in Jerusalem, it would have to attack there. From a strategic point of view, as long as we controlled the campus of the Hebrew University, we controlled the approaches to Jerusalem. It is the most commanding position. That was our main worry; if they captured it, we would have been in trouble in Jerusalem."

Although the Israeli government had not acted, the military leaders had to make immediate decisions. Yadin continues, "By then it was clear that Hussein was already in the war; his troops and armor were moving. Obviously, the troops we had allotted for the West Bank and Jerusalem were not sufficient. The decision was taken then by Dayan and Rabin—I was there— to bring in more forces. There were two available units. First of all, it was decided to move a reserve paratrooper unit commanded by 'Motta' Gur to Jerusalem as quickly as possible. Then there was another brigade, also reserve, commanded by Ben-Ari. These two brigades were ordered to Jerusalem. Ben-Ari was to occupy the ridges and to come to Jerusalem from the north, while 'Motta' Gur's brigade was actually to push

149

into Jerusalem to be a reserve for whatever happened, particularly for Mount Scopus."

When the Jordanians attacked Government House, Mayor Kollek wanted to see the battle for himself. He sat with his driver in the front seat of his car; in the back were Arthur Veysey of the *Chicago Tribune*, an Israeli newspaperwoman and an Australian journalist. Kollek told the driver to go from the King David Hotel straight along the exposed roads toward Abu Tor. Danny Bloch overruled him. "The city doesn't need a dead mayor," he said. They took a safer route. On a hill near the experimental farm, three machine-gun bullets pierced the rear of the car; one came within inches of Veysey. That was enough frontline curiosity.

At 4 P.M., Kollek held a press conference in his office for the flood of journalists who had rushed to Jerusalem. Bloch remembers, "For the first quarter of an hour of the press conference, there was no shooting at all. Then, suddenly, the Jordanians started to shoot. The foreign journalists could see with their own eyes that the Jordanians were shooting from the Mount of Olives. Teddy joked about having it staged. He and some of the journalists went up on the roof to see what was going on."

Kollek received a telephone call from Ruth Dayan, Moshe Dayan's wife, whose car had broken down at the gas station next to the King David Hotel. She asked if he would drive her to the Knesset for her husband's swearing in as Minister of Defense. She waited for the mayor in La Regence restaurant in the hotel's basement. It was the safest spot in the huge old building, even though it was in the very corner where British staff headquarters had been blown up by Menachem Begin's Irgun on July 22, 1946, killing ninety British, Arabs and Jews.

Kollek and Mrs. Dayan reached the Knesset about five o'clock and found the place teeming with politicians and journalists. They were milling around waiting for the Knesset to meet. They talked of the war and whether Israel should attack the Arab sector of Jerusalem.

As Shimon Peres said later in another context: "Every battle is a kind of test, in which the unpredictable must be expected."[1]

The idea was taking shape that the Jordanian entry into the war created a possibility to seize all of Jerusalem. Most of the politicians expressed enthusiasm for the idea, although they feared arousing world public opinion against Jewish control of the Christian and Muslim Holy Places. They remembered that after the Sinai campaign of 1956 the United States and the Soviet Union had forced Israel to surrender what it had conquered.

This Monday evening in the Knesset building, most important among the more cautious leaders was Interior Minister Moshe Chaim Shapiro, a Cabinet veteran and the leader of the National Religious Party with a reputation for honesty and prudence. He questioned, "Should we do it? Do we dare do it? What are the risks?"

Shapiro's colleague in the National Religious Party, Dr. Yosef Burg, says of Shapiro's view: "He was for all those years a dove. He was always for caution: We should not take too big risks. We should avoid having fallen soldiers. That was his line, but not the party line."

Kollek says, "People were worried about whether we would have a great fight with the world. Mr. Begin loves to tell the story that he had the decisive vote on this. He may have been for it, but he was a very junior partner at the time. There was general agreement that you had no choice and you had to do it. And maybe it was also a great historical opportunity. Although he was fully aware of the complications, Ben-Gurion was outspokenly for it. Everybody felt at the time that whatever we took we were ready to give back. But Jerusalem you just couldn't give back." So far it was still all political talk; there was no decision.

At seven o'clock, Antonique "Tony" Bakerjian drove his United Nations Relief and Works Administration car up to the Dung Gate on the southern side of the Old City. Bakerjian was responsible for a hundred thousand Arab refugees in the Jerusalem area and had had a harrowing day. From his office in Ramallah, he had distributed gasoline and drugs to the refugee camps. He advised the refugees to remain in the camps and sent home the students, some of whom came from all over the West Bank and Gaza, at the various vocational and teachers' schools in his charge. He could hear the firing of guns in the direction of Jerusalem.

About 5:30 he drove to his home in the Old City, stopping

at camps and schools on the way. He found the Dung Gate locked and banged on it until the gate was opened. At his home near the Zion Gate, his wife and fifteen-year-old son and mother were in an underground room with neighbors. They were very frightened.

Bakerjian lived on the edge of the Armenian Quarter across the street from the Jewish Quarter, which these days was occupied by hundreds of Arab refugee families for whose welfare he was responsible. Bakerjian, now forty-five, remembered the days before 1948 when he had Jewish friends across the street and his mother had breast-fed Jewish infants. "Our personal relationships with the Jews were far more intimate than people think they were," he says. In fact, he had an uncle who never married because he loved a Jewish woman who later married a man of her own faith. Just before the uncle died in 1959 he had asked his nephew to tell her someday that he had always been faithful to her. Bakerjian was able to give her his uncle's message after the Six Day War.

Although of Armenian heritage, Bakerjian was an Arabic-speaking Christian who was born and grew up in the Old City, identified as an Arab and as a Palestinian. He felt that anyone of any ethnic origin who lived in Palestine was a Palestinian. The British had promised the Jews a national home in Palestine in the Balfour Declaration of 1917 but had used the Arabs to help oust the Ottoman Empire from the area in World War I. In 1921, Winston Churchill had tried to settle Britain's debt to the Arabs by creating Transjordan east of the Jordan River.[2]

Bakerjian understood the Palestinian Arabs who felt the Jordanians failed to promote Jerusalem's economic development and should permit Palestinian Arabs to bear arms and defend their homes, especially after the Israeli army attacked the village of Samua in November 1966. Now on this Monday evening, all this unhappy history had brought Tony Bakerjian and his family to the basement of their house in the Old City while the Jordanians and Israeli artillery dueled over their heads.

Prime Minister Eshkol sent word that he could not arrive in Jerusalem before nine o'clock and asked that the Cabinet meet in the Knesset building at 6 P.M. without him. As the Cabinet ministers arrived, they were herded into the safety of the basement. Mrs. Yael Uzay bustled around and found a small, airless room where they could meet, sitting on small, uncomfortable chairs.

Here, in this informal basement meeting, the Cabinet for the first time discussed what action should be taken in Jerusalem. The Jerusalem Brigade had already recaptured Government House from the Jordanians, and the Harel Brigade and the paratroopers were on their way to the city. The army proposed to surround the Old City from both flanks but, to avoid damaging the Holy Places, would not attack the Old City itself. Dayan said, "Let them lift white flags and then we'll enter."

The Cabinet members discussed the delicacy of endangering the Old City. How could they take the Old City without damaging the Holy Places? The old Turkish city walls, built to keep out Bedouin marauders, were solid obstacles to modern warfare. Interior Minister Shapiro urged them to be careful.

Of the basement meeting, Minister of Justice Ya'acov Shimshon Shapira says, "There wasn't anyone there who didn't want Jerusalem united. It was a question of whether it could be done—what would be the outcome. Begin was very much for it and so was I. Dayan, I believe, was doubtful—not that he was against the conquest of Jerusalem but on military grounds he probably did not want to take the initiative." At least three members voiced doubts about whether they could take the city and then keep it.

The Cabinet members felt under tremendous pressure. They were intensely aware that they had only hours, maybe a day, to take their objectives before the outside world might interfere, perhaps with a United Nations cease-fire.

Justice Minister Shapira says, "It was decided we had to expedite the capture of the Old City. If it had to be done, it had to be done now. Jerusalem is so deeply rooted in every one of us that it is beyond discussion."

The Cabinet approved the army's plan to have the paratroopers attack across the Green Line. In the members' view, the political situation did not allow delaying the attack until the artillery and Air Force could prepare the way. "There was the feeling you have when you decide to undergo a very serious operation or when you join a war as a soldier," adds Justice Minister Shapira. "You feel that you are doing your duty—to

153

your nation, to the history of the Jews. You have to thank God that it is your lot to be among those who decided that.

"In such moments, people have a feeling of humility: 'Why should I be one of those who decided to take Jerusalem? There have been so many great Jews since the destruction of the Second Temple. Do I dare to compare with them? Of course, I don't.'

"I don't like great moments in the life of a people. We have had too many great moments. Of course, they are tragic. There is tragedy even in success. If it is not a tragedy for us, it is a tragedy for others. It is a tragedy for certain Christians—not for all of them."

For Israel, this basement meeting was historic. No minutes were kept, but great decisions were quickly taken. They felt that if they took the Old City they could never give it back. Justice Minister Shapira says, "There is no point in taking the Old City and giving it up in a few days. I think we would rather give up Tel Aviv than Jerusalem."

After the Cabinet meeting, the waiting seemed endless before Eshkol would arrive. Finally, Dayan, impatient and restless as ever, left. He told Mrs. Uzay, with a touch of exaggeration: "Please apologize to the President, apologize to Eshkol, but I have a war to run."

Shortly after 8 P.M. a shell exploded near the Knesset building and the concussion blew out the windows of the cafeteria. Everyone was escorted into the basement where, as the *Jerusalem Post* reported the next morning, "eminent personalities such as Mr. Kadish Luz [the seventy-two-year-old Speaker of the Knesset], Mr. Ben-Gurion and Mrs. Golda Meir sat with senior officials, with clerks, cleaning workers and a British TV technician clutching his tapes—all in high spirits and good humor."

Darkness closed in on the blacked-out city of Jerusalem, and those in the Knesset watched the explosions and tracer bullets of the continuing battle. "It was quite a beautiful sight," Kollek remembers. Suddenly, a huge spotlight that illuminated the monastery in the Valley of the Cross came on. No one knew why this single great light switched on, but it made the Knesset a brilliant target for the Jordanian artillery. Someone ordered the light shot out.

The army feared for Eshkol's safety. He was not permitted to take the direct road up to Jerusalem and was delayed by the roundabout route over secondary roads. When the three black cars of his entourage, accompanied by only a police escort, finally arrived in the city, he could hear the artillery firing.

The Israeli sector was still being heavily shelled. The dark streets were deserted except for tanks and military equipment; shops were locked tight. Some streets were flooded by broken water pipes. Tree limbs lay in the gutters. Along the border sat shrapnel-riddled cars. Says Colonel Le'or, "The feeling was we were waiting for something extraordinary. Everything was full of tension."

Eshkol's party drove directly to the Knesset, arriving at nine. Miriam Eshkol raced home to take a shower and pick up some clothes. Her telephone rang. A woman friend seeing a light in the Eshkols' home called and told Mrs. Eshkol that the Jordanians had tried to shell the Eshkols' house and had destroyed her balcony instead. Mrs. Eshkol, who was scurrying around with a small lamp because the house had no blackout curtains, said, "Let them bomb. Nobody is home." She took her shower and hurried back to the Knesset.

The prime minister met briefly with his Cabinet in the basement room. Colonel Le'or says, "The opinion of all the ministers was now that we had to take Jerusalem." Dr. Burg remembers, "There was no formal voting on this. It was, so to say, an atmosphere of consensus." The record of those basement Cabinet meeting says: "Fifth of June 1967. Eshkol said that the Cabinet wants Old Jerusalem. We have to see to it tomorrow. . . . Dayan describes the situation on the West Bank and proposes to take the Old City and maybe the whole [West] Bank."

The Knesset members did not want to meet in the basement, so they went up and crowded into the main hall. The windows were blacked out and the lights were dim. Eshkol spoke immediately: "I am happy to report to the Knesset that the sky of Israel remains the sky of Israel." The effect of his talk was electric. When he finished, all the members of the Knesset stood up and, on an impulse, sang the national anthem, "Hatikvah."

Then, Begin and Yosef Saphir were sworn in as Ministers

155

without Portfolio. Dayan was not officially sworn in as Minister of Defense for another ten days when the war was over.

President Zalman Shazar invited all the Cabinet members to his house for a reception after the Knesset meeting. He had the table laid and a speech carefully prepared for the occasion. None of the ministers wanted to go. When Eshkol was told of the reception, he said, "Leave me alone. I'm going back to Tel Aviv. I'm tired. I had a terrible day." At eleven o'clock, Eshkol and his aides set out for Tel Aviv.

Mrs. Uzay told the two new members, Begin and Saphir, they had to go to the president's house. She drove with Saphir through the blackout. Begin went in his own car with his driver and his wife, Aliza, and they got lost in the darkness. When only Saphir and Mrs. Uzay showed up, Shazar was deeply disappointed. Begin arrived half an hour later, and they all had a drink to celebrate the day's military achievements. It was nearly midnight when they left.

While Saphir and Begin returned to Tel Aviv, Mrs. Uzay went home to her apartment on the second story of a house above the Valley of the Cross, where the Israeli artillery was still pounding away. Her husband had prepared a place for them in the basement shelter. But Mrs. Uzay told him, "I am so tired, I don't care if I am killed. I am going to sleep in my own bed." And they did.

Late that evening, Fink's restaurant, the venerable bar that specializes in goulash soup and steaks just off King George Avenue and which the proprietor, David Rothschild, had long made a meeting place of significance, was deserted except for Rothschild and his wife, Tonka, and a couple of patrons who could not get home across the city. Israeli Jerusalem was buttoned up for the night. Mayor Kollek continued to tour the city until midnight.

At about 11 P.M., the Augusta Victoria Hospital on the Mount of Olives began to receive a severe shelling and bombing. Dr. George Farah, the medical director, had left the lights on and the windows open to identify the hospital; but the Israeli Air Force, believing a Jordanian artillery battery was emplaced next to the hospital, attacked the massive structure with bombs and napalm.

156

The three-story hospital was constructed with a tile roof supported by huge wooden beams. Between roof and beams was an insulation of straw. The bombs smashed the tiles and the napalm ignited the straw. Three quarters of the building's third floor was destroyed, including Dr. Amin Majaj's laboratory. The raging fire could be seen for miles. The flames melted the iron beds in the doctors' rooms above the children's ward. The fire was still burning at daylight. Dr. Farah says bitterly, "They knew we were a hospital."

Fortunately, the huge hospital was built of stone, and the fire did not spread below the roof and third floor. The thirty-six patients, including twelve children, and a hundred staff members were safe deep in the big, solid, arched basement. No one was hurt by the bombing, even though five of the very ill patients died during the battle. Dr. Farah heard on the BBC that the hospital had been destroyed and ten doctors killed—a false report. Smoke filled the cavernous basement, and Dr. Farah had its windows cleared of debris. "Everyone was afraid of being suffocated," says Dr. Majaj. "It was mad. It was really mad."

While everyone was in the basement, an Arab civilian with his bowels ripped open was brought in. But his companions could find no one to help and the man died.

Two Arab soldiers from the tiny unit outside came to the hospital and said the battle was hopeless and they were leaving. Finally, the last two soldiers asked for sanctuary in the hospital and were turned away. They returned to their trenches.

According to Dr. Majaj, the Israelis bombed the hospital for four hours in order to destroy that single squad outside. But the trenches and bunkers near the hospital suggested the presence of more Jordanian troops.

By now the hospital's telephones had been knocked out, and Dr. Farah walked down to his home in Bethany to try to get help. He managed to telephone Anwar al-Khatib, who told him no ambulances were available to evacuate his people.

It was daylight by the time Dr. Farah climbed back to the hospital. He and his patients and staff had to survive on tea, bread and potatoes. There was no electricity and the well water was foul.

Nobody slept much that night. The shelling continued. After

midnight, Danny Bloch walked home through the blacked-out, shell-torn city. His landlady and her husband were waiting up for him with a bowl of hot soup.

At the *Jerusalem Post*, the staff finally got out the paper. It carried a page one proclamation from Mayor Kollek:

> Citizens of Jerusalem! You, the inhabitants of our Holy City, were called up to suffer the vicious onslaught of the enemy, while our determined airmen and soldiers were battling with him in the air and in the South. Your homes also became a battlefield.... Nobody flinched. Nobody failed. You remained cool, calm and confident, while the enemy launched his assault upon you.
>
> You have proved worthy inhabitants of the city of David. You have proved worthy of the words of the Psalmist: "If I forget thee, O Jerusalem, may my right hand forget its cunning." You will be remembered for your stand in the hour of dangers.
>
> Citizens have died in our city and many have been wounded. We mourn our dead and will care for their families. We will tend our wounded...

And reporter Abraham Rabinovich described Jerusalem that night:

> Jerusalem was never more a city of peace than for a few minutes at dusk last night. In the Musrara section, the firing had dwindled and died, but the streets remained deserted. There were no street lights. There were no moving cars. There was no noise at all except a loud humming on one street where a transformer had gone berserk. It was only the fading light in the west and the silhouettes of tapering cypresses with stars emerging from a darkening sky. And silence. Across the valley a fire was burning in Jordan on the approaches to Mount Scopus.

About 2 A.M., Erwin Frenkel drove home, feeling his way in the total darkness of the virtually moonless night. He found everyone huddled in the shelter. People had come in from neighboring buildings that had no shelters. Many children were there, sleeping. He remembers that everyone was in good spirits. "In the back of some minds was the possibility that things would not go right. But in general there was tremendous confidence. There was fear and confidence—it was a paradox."

The Israelis in the shelters did not yet know the historic decision had been made: the Israel Defense Forces would conquer Jordanian Jerusalem. Jerusalem would once again be united. It would cost lives—Israeli and Arab alike—and Jerusalem would become again a focus of the world's attention and tensions.

Part II

THE
CONQUEST

— Chapter 11 —

CONTINGENCIES

DECIDING TO MAKE WAR IN JERUSALEM WAS FOR ISRAEL'S GOVernment a prolonged and painful process. Until *after* the Israeli air victory over the Egyptians early Monday morning, Jerusalem had been an issue to avoid. By midmorning it became central. King Hussein already held the jewel in the crown: the Old City and its Holy Places. Israel's government sought actively to prevent a two-front war; it wanted to erase the danger from Nasser, not to take East Jerusalem from Hussein. But event led to event, action sparked reaction—until the decision was made to conquer all Jerusalem.

Ironically, Israel's religious-political leaders, who might be expected to dream the strongest dreams for possession of the Western Wall and the Temple Mount, were, on the whole, the most reluctant to take the aggressive step. The generals, mostly secular and pragmatic, moved more rapidly to a decision to attack Jordanian Jerusalem. The political leaders, fearing outside hostility toward Jewish sovereignty over the Christian and Muslim Holy Places, had the greater doubts. They knew that if Israel took the Old City its surrender would be demanded; and they knew as well, Israel could never give it up. In the end, they needed to be provoked into action; and King Hussein, amazingly, provided the provocation and the justification.

Deciding is one thing, doing is another. In war, the latter is young men's work. As is the dying. Even before the Israeli government made its basement decision, the military leaders started to move the pieces on the board of battle. Repeatedly, they would act in haste and, as in every war, wasteful of young lives.

Israel's military leaders had started creating contingency

plans for the conquest of Jerusalem in the days after the 1948 war. Their basic strategy was to double envelop the Old City to avoid destroying the Holy Places inside the walls.

Yitzhak Rabin had pushed this concept during the 1948 war—to encircle the Old City rather than to storm it—but had been overruled. The attack on the Jaffa Gate was a disaster; Jordan occupied the Old City for the next nineteen years.

Throughout those years, Israel's main contingency plan remained to surround the Jordanian sector of the city in a pincers from the north and the south. The prime thrust would strike Jerusalem's northern side and capture the high ground east of the city. There, a steep, towering ridge of hills—Mivtar Hill, French Hill, Mount Scopus, Augusta Victoria and the Mount of Olives—forms a banana-shaped barrier embracing and looming above the city itself. Command of these guardian heights would prevent any Jordanian attack coming up from Jericho and the Jordan River Valley. Geography ruled all planning.

Armor—Jordanian or Israeli—could attack Jerusalem most easily from the north, where a plateau opens up on the city and allows room to deploy and maneuver. Long ago, Jeremiah the Prophet warned Jerusalem: "Evil appeareth out of the north, and great destruction."[1] It was still true. On all its other sides, the Old City was protected by deep, narrow valleys—the Kidron on the east and the Hinnom on the west and south. They were almost like moats.

As the Israeli envelopment plan developed on Monday, June 5, 1967, the Tenth Brigade, the Harel Mechanized Brigade, would assault the Jordanian-held ridges just north of the city and seize control of Tel el-Ful, the highest strategic point in the north. The Sixteenth Brigade, the Jerusalem Brigade, would advance around the Old City on the south. The Air Force would both fly close support and interdict Jordanian armor that might threaten to interfere. Chief of Staff Rabin says, "By no means was I allowed to attack the Old City."

The logic of these long-standing, carefully thought-out plans was distorted by the isolated enclave of Mount Scopus. To some of Israel's military leaders, Mount Scopus symbolized in miniature what West Berlin, deep in Communist East Germany, represented to the NATO commanders in Europe. It was essential to the top Israeli officers—especially those who had

164

fought in the War of Independence nineteen years before; in fact, it was a principle of emotional intensity—that Mount Scopus should not fall to the Jordanians. If war came to Jerusalem, the Mount Scopus garrison would have to be relieved as quickly as possible. The shortest route crossed the heavily defended Green Line inside the city and penetrated the Jordanian urban neighborhoods just hundreds of yards north of the Old City.

The topography of this small area centered on the narrow valley of Wadi el Joz that led to the base of Mount Scopus. Just south of the valley was the slightly higher section called the American Colony. Along the north side of the valley rose the steeper Sheikh Jarrah neighborhood and behind that the dominating rise called Ammunition Hill. Any direct attempt to relieve Mount Scopus by this route would require the conquest of Wadi el Joz and its protective ridges. Brig. Gen. Hazzáa's Second Battalion was dug in to prevent this.

But such an attack became possible when the Israeli Fifty-fifth Brigade, a unit of paratroop reservists which had been scheduled to support the battle in the Sinai desert, turned out to be superfluous in the south and was freed to be sent to Jerusalem instead. Under the pressure of battle, the Israelis' prewar plans were altered and the obsession with Mount Scopus was gratified.

This is how three reserve brigades of Israelis would conquer all Jerusalem and change the map and the history of the Middle East.

Chapter 12

THE TANKS—THE CRUCIAL
BATTLE

COLONEL URI BEN-ARI HAD THE REPUTATION OF BEING ONE OF Israel's best combat leaders. He was a Berliner by birth—tall, straight, lean, tough and a veteran. His family name had been Banner; they had been assimilated Jewish Germans. His father, a lieutenant in World War I, had won the Iron Cross; but he died in Dachau. Ninety-four members of Ben-Ari's family were killed in the Holocaust.

Early in 1939 when he was fourteen, Ben-Ari had been brought out of Germany and sent to Kibbutz Ein Gev on the shore of the Sea of Galilee. That was also Teddy Kollek's kibbutz; and, with the older Kollek, teenaged Ben-Ari helped guard the fields on horseback.

In 1946, he joined the Palmach, the Jewish military strike force, and was in Jerusalem on May 15, 1948, when the six Arab nations attacked the new-born State of Israel. He commanded A Company, Fourth Battalion of the Palmach Harel Brigade. By then, the battalion had been reduced to this one company.

On May 18, Ben-Ari commanded the defense of Mount Zion against the Arab Legion, while twenty Palmachniks of A Company stormed through Zion Gate into the Old City and brought food and ammunition to the surviving defenders of the Jewish Quarter inside the walls. Ben-Ari says, "The main aim that night was that the Jerusalem Brigade should break in through Jaffa Gate. That failed. Ours was only a diversion. We succeeded in breaking in, but we couldn't keep the Old City of

Jerusalem. We didn't have enough people left. We had to come out."

The Palmach Harel Brigade in 1948 was commanded by Yitzhak Rabin, the Israeli chief of staff in 1967. Ben-Ari says, "This was *the* brigade of the Israeli army which was fighting in Jerusalem—besides the Jerusalem Brigade. My company fought in all the places on the road up to Jerusalem. We took Mount Zion and went into the Old City. But we did not finish the job." Of the two hundred men Ben-Ari originally led up to Jerusalem, fifteen survived.

He studied German Panzer tactics and, despite Dayan's attempt to break up the tank battalions, became the Israelis' preeminent tank commander. In the 1956 Sinai campaign, Ben-Ari commanded Israel's only regular armored brigade and was the first to reach the Suez Canal. But shortly afterwards, while commanding the Armored Corps, he was accused of having covered up the stealing of some sugar years earlier. Prime Minister Ben-Gurion made an example of him. Ben-Ari resigned from the army and went into the publishing and printing business. Many Israeli officers are still certain that this able, skilled leader would have become Israel's chief of staff.

On June 2, 1967, just days before the war, Ben-Ari, now forty-two and beginning to gray, came back from civilian life to command the Harel Mechanized Brigade—the Tenth Brigade. Except for one battalion, the 106th, which was camped near Kibbutz Hulda, the brigade was assembled in the Ben Shemen forest north of Ramla on the coastal plain in the vicinity of Lod Airport. Ben-Ari took charge immediately. "I had to shake up the brigade because it was not in good shape," he says. "In 1956, it had not done well and its name wasn't the best in the army. I had four days to bring it into shape. I devoted twenty-four hours a day to it. I drove them crazy." He ran repeated drills timing how fast the tanks, half-tracks and men could get ready to move.

A reserve brigade, the Tenth consisted of one battalion of tanks and two of infantry motorized in half-tracks. The infantrymen carried Uzis and Belgian FN rifles, and the half-tracks were armed with machine guns and occasionally 20-mm cannon. Altogether, the brigade had five companies of sixty Sherman tanks and one company of twelve new British Centurions. Most of the Shermans were World War II-type American-made;

the Israelis had intensively rebuilt them with larger 75-mm French guns, longer turrets, diesel engines and new communications and optical systems. The guns were not the Israelis' most powerful; their best had been sent to the Sinai.

Ben-Ari's deputy commander was a regular tank officer: Lt. Col. Eldad Avidar, an excellent staff officer who had been wounded in the 1948 war and again while fighting the Palestinian Arabs of Yasir Arafat.

The brigade's 1967 mission if Jordan should attack was to defend the plain northeast of Jerusalem from Netanya through Jerusalem south to Lakhish, halfway between Tel Aviv and Beersheva. As the only mechanized brigade in the Central Command, it had to protect the main population centers and Israel's narrow waist where the Jordanian border came within a dozen miles of the Mediterranean.

In the weeks before the war, morale in the brigade had been low. The officers knew that Israel would not attack on its eastern front, and they feared that if Jordan took the initiative they would have to fight in the suburbs and streets of Tel Aviv. Lt. Col. Yigal Ben-David, the small, forty-two-year-old commander of the 104th Armored Battalion, says, "It was a very bad feeling until Uri [Ben-Ari] came." The new brigade commander told his officers that if the Jordanians attacked, some units of the brigade would bypass them and slash into Jordan itself; by counterattacking, they would force the Jordanians to pull back. This may have been wishful thinking, but it gave the men new purpose and hope.

One of Ben-Ari's tank companies had special self-confidence. P Company of the Ninety-fifth Tank Battalion had just finished its annual training in southern Israel. Major Uri Berez, a tall, hawk-nosed, thirty-two-year-old native of Hadera and now the manager of a truck company in Ashkelon, was the commander of the tank company's one hundred men and fourteen tanks. By the time they reached the brigade's base near Ramla, he felt, "The company was as ready as it could be."

Ben-Ari says, "Then the war started. I was called to Central Command headquarters at Ramla at nine o'clock on Monday morning; and at about ten, Uzi Narkiss told me Jordan had started to shell Jerusalem."

The Israeli High Command worried about the two Jordanian

armored brigades already on the West Bank, and by 10:30 decided to give Ben-Ari a new mission. He would move up into the Judean hills, cross into Jordan and seize Tel el-Ful—the highest hill overlooking the road between Jerusalem and Ramallah. Ben-Ari would thus attack north of Jerusalem, cut off the city from the northern reaches of the West Bank and close to Jordanian tanks the roads from Jericho up to Jerusalem. Says Barlev of Ben-Ari's mission, "His task was basically to isolate Jerusalem."

To perform this task, Ben-Ari would have to move his entire brigade swiftly eastward up from the coastal plain into the Judean hills. Because the Arab-populated West Bank was possessed by Jordan, Jerusalem stood at the end of a narrow "corridor," sometimes less than eight miles wide, that had been won at heavy cost in 1948. On both sides of the corridor Jordanian forces stood ready to squeeze off this thin neck and crush the Israeli half of the city at its head. Ben-Ari would have to move nearly a thousand vehicles eastward and upward in the corridor. Then, short of Jerusalem he would turn abruptly left or north and cross the Green Line into Jordan-defended hills to reach the ridgetop road that would take him to Tel el-Ful.

The Israeli armor would break through the Jordanian lines near Kibbutz Maale Hahamisha, climb the hills to the ridgetop, cut the Jerusalem-Ramallah road, take Tel el-Ful and then turn south and clear the heavily defended Mivtar Hill and French Hill overlooking the city.

The plan was strikingly similar to Operation Jebussi of 1948, which sought to capture the height of Nebi Samuel, attack through Jerusalem's Sheikh Jarrah quarter to Mount Scopus, conquer the Mount of Olives ridgeline to the east, and drive around the southern side of the city, encircling it. In 1948, the plan had failed.[1]

General Narkiss impatiently pressed the General Staff for permission to attack; but until after noon on Monday, Chief of Staff Rabin refused. Then came word of the Jordanian assault at Government House. That unleashed the Harel Brigade.

The most dangerous of Jordan's two armored brigades west of the Jordan River was near Jericho. Other elements were north near Ramallah and south between Hebron and Jerusalem. About 2 P.M., the Israeli Air Force sent small Fouga Magister training aircraft with rockets against the Jordanian American-made A-48 Patton tanks.

An Iraqi armored brigade was spotted east of the Jordan River, heading toward the bridges. The Israeli Air Force hurled Fouga Magisters, Mystères and even Mirages at the Iraqi tanks and prevented them from crossing the river. The Air Force, with the resources it had, was making an all-out effort to protect Jerusalem.

And the Harel Brigade was sent up into the Judean hills. The two armored forces—Jordanian and Israeli—would race to reach the Jerusalem-Ramallah road at Tel el-Ful and control the vulnerable northern entrance to Jerusalem. The Israelis could not allow the Jordanians' superior Pattons, which outgunned the Israeli Shermans, to get there first. "If the Jordanians' Sixtieth Armored Brigade was to reach Tel el-Ful before Ben-Ari's brigade, then the whole story would be entirely different," says Rabin. "I realized then that this would become the crucial issue to the whole sector of Jerusalem—that our brigade reach the crest before the Sixtieth.

"We decided to use the Air Force with the help of flares to disrupt all the movement of the Sixtieth—to delay it, to destroy as many tanks as possible, to destroy supplies, to make real havoc. I don't believe they expected it. The success of the Air Force that night was tremendous. It was a magnificent job, after they had to fight the Egyptians and the Syrians and the Jordanians and attacked the closest air base in Iraq. That night was crucial."

"We had to be at this place at sunrise—five o'clock Tuesday morning," says Ben-Ari. "This place controls the approach to Jerusalem from all the northern part of the West Bank and there is a road coming up from Jericho. It was to be a contest between the two brigades. Whoever is there first would govern Jeru-salem. It doesn't matter what happens *in* Jerusalem. This is where one breaks into Jerusalem and whoever holds this place governs Jerusalem. So that was the idea."

Early Monday afternoon, Narkiss telephoned Ben-Ari to start moving up toward Jerusalem and to be at Tel el-Ful before dawn. Narkiss figured the Jordanian armor would wait for daylight to attack.

Dayan wanted Ben-Ari's brigade to bull straight to Mount

Scopus through the wadi inside Jerusalem just north of Ammunition Hill.[2] But Narkiss knew that the mine-filled wadi was dominated on both sides by the Jordanians dug in on Mivtar Hill and Ammunition Hill. Running such a gauntlet would cost many Israeli lives. Instead, Narkiss had the brigade cross the border where it was thinly defended and strike down on the Jordanians from the rear. It would be faster and cheaper.

Narkiss ordered Ben-Ari to advance up both the main road and a secondary road to the hills in the narrow corridor northwest of Jerusalem. Once he crossed into Jordan, he would have to fight through a series of fortified positions to reach his mark—Tel el-Ful.

Ben-Ari's advance would follow an ancient, historic route among the Judean hills. All sorts of people seeking the way to Jerusalem had followed it. It had been used in Biblical times by Hebrews coming to the Temple on the Jewish festivals, by the Pharaohs of Egypt, the centurions of Rome, the Crusaders and throughout the ages by devout Jewish, Christian and Muslim pilgrims to Jerusalem.

Ben-Ari broke radio silence to give the order to move out. Not wanting to name the destination of Jerusalem over the air, he told his units to move to the city that was the home of Israel's Nobel Prize-winning writer, S. Y. Agnon.

They would go through Lod, the Old Testament town where St. Paul cured the sick man Aeneas and where St. George, the patron saint of England, was born. In 1948, Moshe Dayan, in a surprise attack, had taken Lod in open Jeeps with machine guns spraying bullets left and right, cowboy-style.

As soon as the order arrived to head for Jerusalem, Ben-Ari sent his tough, brawny driver, Corporal Yuval Pasternak, who in civilian life worked in Tel Aviv's rugged central produce market, to round up his officers. When Lt. Col. Ben-David heard Pasternak's message, he remembers feeling "very worried because I thought Jerusalem was being attacked." It was his hometown.

Engines started roaring, and the Harel Brigade started moving south through Ramla and then east into the Judean hills. The tanks traveled on their treads. At Sha'ar Hagai, the 106th Armored Battalion from Kibbutz Hulda and the brigade's twelve 120-mm mortars, commanded by Major Benjamin Arad, followed the secondary road to the south, while the larger force advanced on the main road. Ben-Ari detoured to Narkiss' head-quarters for one final conference. He told the general, "Once I leave the road between Tel Aviv and Jerusalem and move into the mountains, I do not want to stop. I want to go and that's it." Narkiss agreed. Then Ben-Ari sped off to catch up with his column. Over the radio he gave each battalion commander his first target and urged them all forward at full speed. He would meet them on the road and explain their orders in detail. He had little time, little daylight.

Under his plan, the brigade would break off from the Tel Aviv–Jerusalem corridor at four points just short of the city. Here the armistice Green Line, which set the entire border between Jordan and Israel, ran east and west. The brigade would cross the border north into Jordan. "I wanted to break through in four places to make sure that I'll make it in one. These places had been fortified for nineteen years. We would have very hard fighting in each one."

The brigade had to advance twenty-eight miles and climb two thousand feet in less than four hours in order to launch its four-pronged attack by 5 P.M. Then each of the four elements would wheel left, cross the Jordanian border and climb into the hills up to a dirt road that ran east on the ridgetop through Biddu to Nebi Samuel, where it became asphalt, and then through Beit Hanina until it met the Jerusalem-Ramallah road, the main north-south road of the West Bank, at Tel Zahara, opposite Tel el-Ful.

The column churned up the old road past the cement factory at Ramla, which had been the Arab capital of the area from the eighth until the eleventh century, when the Crusaders destroyed it. From a tower here in 1799, it is said, Napoleon watched his soldiers attack Jaffa and decided not to assault Jerusalem but instead to head north for Acre.

At the gas station in Ramla at 2:30, Ben-Ari met Lt. Col Zvi "Zvika" Dahav, the handsome, thirty-four-year-old commander of the Ninety-fifth Tank Battalion, who had served under him in 1952 as a lieutenant. Dahav was now a Paz Oil Company executive in civilian life. Ben-Ari quickly gave Dahav his orders. He would cross the border farthest east, climb a boulder-strewn hill called Khirbet Talila and then follow a goat path only a mile west of the Jerusalem-Ramallah road. Months earlier, a patrol had scouted the path and reported optimistically that tanks could use it. Dahav took off in his Jeep to reconnoiter his impossible-sounding assignment.

On schedule at 5 P.M., the brigade was in its four positions ready to attack. Says Ben-Ari, "That was something wonderful."

Farthest west, the 104th Armored Battalion—commanded by Lt. Col. Ben-David, a mustached, rather dashing and experienced armored infantry leader—a farmer in civilian life—was a mixed unit of one company of tanks and two of half-tracks. It left the Tel Aviv road at Abu Ghosh, a village of Israeli Arabs and a place with a long history, ten miles from Jerusalem. Across the road is the site where the ancient Hebrews' Ark of the Covenant stayed for twenty years after it was recovered from the Philistines, until David brought it to Jerusalem.

From Abu Ghosh, the 104th Battalion would jump off through the border kibbutz of Maale Hahamisha, attack the Jordanians at the so-called "Radar" positions and climb to the Arab crossroad village of Biddu. Ben-David worked out the details while moving up in his half-track.

The 106th Armored Battalion, commanded by tall, heavy-set Lt. Col. Aaron Gal, a professional and skilled tanker, would attack from the Israeli settlement of Mevasseret Yerushalayim (Herald of Jerusalem), move on the Jordanian position of Sheikh Abdul Aziz eight hundred yards above the main road and meet up with the 104th at Biddu.

The Forty-first Reconnaissance Company, led by Major Amnon Eshkol, a young, dark, mustached kibbutznik, would fight through the Jordanians at the small village of Beit Iksa. The company's French armored AML cars with their 90-mm guns would dash for the ridgetop road east of Nebi Samuel.

Finally, on the right flank, the Ninety-fifth Battalion, under Lt. Col. Dahav, would maneuver up Khirbet Talila along the goat path. The Ninety-fifth gave one of its four tank companies of thirteen Shermans to each of the other two battalions and acquired in exchange two infantry companies in half-tracks, plus the hastily formed company of Centurion tanks commanded by Captain Aaron Shatz.

Ben-Ari commanded the attack from the Castel, the hill with the first Arab village that had been captured—by the original Harel Brigade—during the 1948 war. The round, high hilltop dominated the Tel Aviv road and the valley below and had been fortified even in the times of the Romans and of the Crusaders.

The Harel Brigade faced two enemies in its race against time to cut the Jerusalem-Ramallah road. One was the Jordanian defenders—each fortified position was held by at least one company. The other was the minefield that had been planted over the years on both sides of the border. No one any longer knew where all the mines were placed, but they blanketed the roads and deep stretches on both sides.

The brigade was handicapped for the coming battle. All its minesweeping equipment, most of its bangalore torpedoes for use against the mines, and the night-sighting equipment for its tanks' guns had been sent to the Sinai for the massive battle against the Egyptians.

Ben-Ari's attack started at 5 P.M.; it was still daylight. First, the tanks bombarded each and every Jordanian bunker at the four breakthrough points. The men could see the bunkers, and most of them had earlier been spotted and were marked on the brigade's maps. Jordanian fire from those bunkers was completely silenced before any forward movement started. At Kibbutz Maale Hahamisha, the first four tanks positioned themselves off the road near the cow shed and the chicken coops to get the best angles for pinpoint fire on the Jordanian fortifications.

Then, the infantry, and the engineers commanded by able Major Micha Ma'or, went into action. The infantry of each spearhead advanced on foot with Uzis and machine guns. At the beginning of their attack, they had five minutes of close support fire from the Israeli Air Force. Although many of the Jordanian officers fled, their soldiers stood without leadership or organization and fought bravely.

Simultaneously, the engineers tackled the minefield on both sides of the Green Line. They carried no equipment for locating and detonating the mines; they dug them out with bayonets, sticks, the cleaning rods of their Uzis and whatever tools they had.

The engineers continued their dangerous job in the almost moonless dark. Ben-Ari says, "It took hours, clearing another mine and another mine, antitank mines and antipersonnel mines.

Every half hour or so someone had a leg or both legs blown off. Somebody else took over until the whole thing was cleared." Only after ten o'clock could the tanks and half-tracks move forward and join the infantry which had taken the Jordanian positions.

In the attack farthest west, Lt. Col. Ben-David's 104th Battalion faced the formidable Jordanian positions called the Radar. There on three hills beyond the border, the British had constructed a radar station in World War II when German Field Marshal Erwin Rommel was charging toward the Suez Canal. Later, the British used it to spot ships bringing Jews into Palestine illegally. In 1948, Ben-Ari's Palmach company attacked the then Arab-held Radar five times: "Many of my friends died there."

A narrow dirt road led through steep hills from Kibbutz Maale Hahamisha two miles up to the Jordanian village of Biddu. The road was filled with mines, which could not be cleared because of the fire from the strongly fortified hills called Radar 1 and Radar 2 just behind the border. All their bunkers were underground.

Ben-David's four tanks pounded the bunkers with direct fire. The brigade's mortars on the Castel reached for them. One 120-mm round hit Radar 2, the main position, and it burst into flames. Two Israeli planes strafed it.

Ben-David ordered two infantry companies to take the Radar hills against heavy Jordanian machine-gun fire. The Israelis were led through the minefield by a tank that exploded antipersonnel mines harmlessly with its treads. The tank missed an antitank mine, which stopped the following half-track with Ben-David aboard.

From the beginning of the minefield to the base of the hills of Radar 1 and 2 was only two hundred yards, but it took three hours to clear them; three engineers lost their legs and many others suffered lesser wounds. Where the men could not follow the vehicles, they tried to jump from rock to rock to avoid the soil that might conceal a mine.

The infantrymen cut through the barbed wire and reached Radar 1 on the left side of the road. By now the position was deserted, the barrels of its machine guns still hot. Fire from Radar 2 wounded four Israelis at Radar 1.

As a second force approached Radar 2, its men discovered they had no wire cutters. A lieutenant chopped up the barbed wire with his Uzi. When the soldiers charged into Radar 2, it too was deserted. By 8 P.M., both positions were taken without an Israeli killed.

The conquest of these positions marked an historic moment. Here was the first War of Independence battlesite that had been lost in 1948 and was retaken nineteen years later. Ben-Ari felt a sense of continuity, the triumph of an earlier defeat wiped clean. When the capture of the two long-hated Radar positions—"this damn hill," Ben-Ari called it with passion—was reported over the army's radio net, men from the old Palmach Harel Brigade came on the air from the Sinai to the north and joyously congratulated the excited Ben-Ari. They had not forgotten.

As though to make their achievement permanent, Ben-Ari forced Ben-David and his 104th Battalion to stay and hold the Radar hills for two hours. Until 2 A.M., the engineers probed the ground in the darkness to uncover the Jordanian mines beyond the two Radar positions. Explosions mutilated unlucky soldiers and unnerved the engineers. They tried to use their few bangalore torpedoes, long pipes filled with explosives, to set off the mines. In all, fifteen men were wounded by mines at the Radar. For a time, it was impossible to move out the wounded.

Ben-David's force was joined by Lt. Col. Michael Peikas, who commanded the 163rd Battalion of the Jerusalem Brigade. His battalion was posted in the Jerusalem corridor to guard the approaches to the city; it had trained to take these very hills, and Peikas wanted to share in the action. He was a short, strong man with great energy and had taken charge of the 163rd Battalion as his wartime "emergency assignment," leaving his regular job as deputy commander of the officers training school of the Israel Defense Forces.

He marched his men to Maale Hahamisha; and with two radiomen, he climbed up the Radar road. An engineer stepped on a mine, and fragments cut Peikas above the eye. His face was covered with blood when he reached Lt. Col. Ben-David and asked to join the fight.

Peikas' battalion surgeon, First Lieutenant Uri Freund, a

thirty-two-year-old Sabra and a protégé of Dr. Nathan Saltz, chief of surgery at Hadassah Hospital, wrapped a bandage around Peikas' head. A lean, athletic tennis player, Freund was the son of a carpenter; and his parents' families, except for two of his aunts, had all been killed in the Holocaust. Uri Freund was a bright and determined young man who was to be one of the heroes for the battle of Jerusalem. He had served in the army as an infantryman and fought in retaliation raids in the 1950s. After the 1956 Sinai campaign he left Kibbutz Ga'aton in the Galilee to go to medical school at Hebrew University. He paid his way by driving a heavy tractor sixteen hours a day in the Negev desert through four summers. When this war began, he was doing his residency in surgery under Dr. Saltz.

Freund hurriedly set up a first-aid station in a field by the road near Kibbutz Maale Hahamisha to help Ben-Ari's men who were being injured by the mines. The Harel Brigade's doctors were already forward in their half-tracks. Freund treated more than twenty soldiers there in the field and rushed them to Hadassah Hospital in any vehicles he could find.

Ben-David radioed Ben-Ari, who agreed to let Peikas' men attack Radar 3, the Radar position deepest in Jordanian territory. Peikas chose for the attack his company commanded by Major Yacov Even, a thirty-year-old, experienced career officer whom he had brought with him from the officers training school staff. Even, who was the eighth generation of his family in Palestine, had been in the army since he was sixteen, fought in the Sinai campaign and been cited in Syria in 1962: "I had been under fire several times and was not at all a virgin."

Because Peikas had no command open for Even in the weeks before the war, Peikas had instructed him to form his own company. He had collected the battalion's recon platoon and several others from the Academic Reserve units at the Hebrew University, less than eighty men all told, and drilled them hard until he felt they could fight well as a unit.

When Peikas ordered Even to assault Radar 3, he led his men on a long detour around to the left. Radar 3 was lightly defended; only one of his men suffered a chest wound. They took the Jordanian trenches. Even was elated: "I was in the middle of my enemy's land with a license. Once I had spent thirty days in prison because some suspected that I had done something forbidden across the border. Here I was with a license, a company, mortars. I was really happy about it." The Jordanians above them at Biddu started to counterattack. Even's company held them off with long-range fire, and the Jordanians could not close on them.

Meanwhile, for hours in the darkness Ben-Ari's engineers cleared a path through the Jordanian minefield. Then they confronted an antitank ditch eight feet deep, backed by antitank barriers. Ben-David ordered the ditch filled and joined the men throwing in rocks. The job was done by 2 A.M. and the road was finally opened to Biddu.

At that Arab village, the Jordanian army stood and fought. It was their main fortified position on the ridge. The Israeli infantrymen had to dismount and attack a bunkered hill near the village. Captain Avi Keren, commander of C Company and a citrus farmer in Rehovot in civilian life, led the assault over terrain they did not know. They fought in the dark trenches, hand-to-hand. Twenty Jordanians and one Israeli were killed.

The commander in the lead tank scanned his searchlight in front of him and at the entrance to the village spotted a Jeep with a recoilless rifle waiting in ambush on the side of the road. Instantly, a shell from the tank destroyed the Jeep. The tank entered the village square; it was empty. The ridgetop crossroad at Biddu was in Israeli hands.

Five miles to the east, Lt. Col. Aaron Gal's 106th Armored Battalion, with its tanks out front, ran into a 300-yard-wide minefield and heavy mortar fire. A mine blew the tread off Gal's lead tank; he shifted to the tank behind. His infantry advanced on foot in the tanks' tracks. Fifteen men were killed and sixty wounded by the mines and enemy fire.

Lt. Col. Gal's second in command, coincidentally named Major Moshe Gal, a tall, long-faced, thirty-two-year-old bus driver born in Sofia, Bulgaria, kept moving back and forth through the minefield helping the wounded, carrying them out. Most men were relieved to traverse the minefield once; Moshe Gal did it repeatedly.

T Company was in the lead, commanded by Captain Assa Yaguri from Kibbutz Yagur near Haifa. His deputy commander, Lieutenant Adi Rosen, a young architect from Kibbutz Ein Gev, showed Moshe Gal where a Jordanian bullet had pierced his helmet without harming him. If this can happen, he told the major, nothing can hurt me.

Captain Yaguri saw the tanks getting stopped in the minefield. He told Lieutenant Ze'ev Merenstein, a German-born platoon leader, to have his men clear the way for the tanks. The soldiers walked cautiously on the rocks single file in front of the tanks, probing for mines with their Uzi cleaning rods. One man stepped out of line; Merenstein tried to shout at him to get back, but it was too late. He lost a leg.

Beyond the minefield, they rushed through a plum orchard and into Sheikh Abdul Aziz. Yaguri sent Merenstein's platoon to the right, another platoon straight forward and he led a third to the left. Merenstein found himself inside a trench higher than his head. Ahead in a bunker a Jordanian was talking on a radio. Merenstein killed him with a grenade. Inside the Jordanian position, Yaguri and his men moved carefully among some buildings. Suddenly, several Jordanians popped up and killed Yaguri and Sergeant Pinchas Goldberg. Lieutenant Rosen shouted to Merenstein, and he went after the Jordanians. Merenstein and his men trapped them in a T-shaped trench; they killed seven Jordanians with grenades and Uzi fire.

When it became dark, the Jordanians started shelling; an artillery observer was posted a hundred yards farther north on a higher fortified peak called Khirbet Lausa. An armored infantry company and three tanks finally went up and took the peak. The Jordanians had fled.

The 106th Battalion organized to defend Sheikh Abdul Aziz from a counterattack. It grew cold on the hill, and one soldier collected blankets the Jordanians had left. The Israelis rested there, trembling with cold; and toward dawn they started moving up to Biddu.

The 106th left seven of its eleven tanks disabled on the hill. Lt. Col. Gal led the remaining four through the hills for Biddu with a pistol in one hand and a flashlight in the other. The 106th Battalion entered Biddu shortly after the 104th. The forces reorganized; and the 106th, with the tanks in front followed by the half-tracks, headed east.

Despite its difficult route and massive antitank barriers, Amnon Eshkol's Recon Company moved swiftly and reached its objective, the village of Beit Iksa, without a fight.

"Infantry took the hills," says Ben-Ari. "They were fired

on coming through the minefields and barbed wire and into the trenches. They destroyed all the positions from which the Jordanians were firing. Not one was left. The Jordanian officers ran away but the soldiers remained and fought. We found sergeants but not one officer. The Jordanian army fought well. The best soldiers in the Arab world are the Jordanians. They are Bedouins, most of them. Even the lower-grade officers are very good. They ran away when they saw there was no chance whatsoever." The Israelis took no prisoners.

On Ben-Ari's eastern flank closest to the brigade's objective, Lt. Col. Dahav's Ninety-fifth Battalion—the tank battalion with two companies of Shermans, one of Centurions and two of mechanized infantry—quickly ran into trouble. The twelve Centurions had joined the brigade only two days before the war. They carried larger guns than the Shermans. Although the Centurions were an improvised unit and the Israelis were not used to these newer tanks, they led the battalion up the hill so they would be in position to meet the Jordanian Pattons first.

At 5:30 P.M., Dahav's tank spearhead began crossing the Green Line under long-range fire. There were no mines on Khirbet Talila. And no Jordanians. The steep, rocky hill was so treacherous that the Jordanians (and the Israelis) had been convinced that no attack could be mounted here.

The tanks could not spread out. The goat path proved no wider than a single tank tread. The inexperienced Centurion tank commanders and drivers could not master such rugged terrain. Although the Centurions had more ground clearance than the Shermans, every Centurion got caught on the boulders. Ben-Ari says, "After an hour, twelve Centurions were sitting on their bellies on the rocks, their treads turning in the air. They could not move forward or backwards. They were out of the war the minute they started. It was a shame."

Major Berez's P Company started climbing at six o'clock. With scouts out in front, Berez led the company from the lead tank. They moved up the hill in the darkness. They could see nothing until the Jordanians started shelling them with 25-pounders. Berez had fifteen years' experience in tanks, but on this steep, rock-strewn hill even his tank got caught on a boulder; and he shifted his command to the next Sherman for the final climb up Khirbet Talila.

Listening on the radio at the Castel, Ben-Ari feared that Dahav had taken the wrong approach. Ben-Ari and his brigade intelligence officer, Major Chagai Man, jumped into a Jeep and found the Ninety-fifth Battalion, viewed the Centurions' predicament and sent one company of Shermans to Aaron Gal's 106th Armored Battalion where the terrain was easier. Lt. Col. Dahav moved on with only his half-tracks and Berez's P Company of 14 Shermans.

Ben-Ari returned to the Castel and was trapped there until eight the next morning. The minefields bordering the road prevented him from passing the line of vehicles up ahead. Totally frustrated, he called for a helicopter; but until it came, he could only stay on the Castel in radio contact with his force moving forward to the decisive junction at Tel Zahara.

By 10 P.M., Captain Abdul Wahab Mahadin, the observer for the Jordanian Ninth Field Artillery Regiment at Shu'afat on the Ramallah road north of Jerusalem, reported to Captain Taysir Mohammad Ali, the twenty-eight-year-old regimental adjutant, a native of the West Bank, that he heard and saw a column of Israeli tanks moving up from the direction of Jerusalem toward the height of Nebi Samuel. The entire artillery regiment concentrated on the tank column for fifteen minutes. The Third Battery fired from a position near regimental headquarters at Neve Yaacov; the Second Battery from Hizma, and the First Battery from the crossroads near Anata (the birthplace of the prophet Jeremiah). The regiment had held these positions, all east of Jerusalem, since June 1 to protect Jordanian Jerusalem. Captain Mahadin thought he saw several Israeli tanks hit. Certainly, they were stopped. But the artillery fire could not halt the column.

Major Berez's tanks struggled to the ridgetop and frequently, when the slope became too sheer, had to back off and find other routes. They felt their way through the darkness, lit only by exploding shells and flares. Some of the Shermans were caught on rocks, others broke treads or burned out their motors. A few men climbed out and led their tanks. One soldier stuck a white undershirt in the back of his belt to guide his driver. It took them four hours to climb the last thousand yards. When Major Berez reached the top of the ridge at 2 A.M., six tanks joined him; the other seven could not make it. The seven on top assembled on the asphalt road leading east from Nebi Samuel. Muslim tradition says this village of a dozen houses and a mosque is the site of the tomb of the prophet Samuel; here the Crusader King Richard the Lion-Hearted wept at his first sight of Jerusalem. The lead elements of the Ninety-fifth Tank Battalion—seven tanks and six half-tracks—had needed eight hours to climb the mile and a half to the ridgetop road that led to Tel Zahara.

No one was close behind them, and Dahav ordered Berez to wait for more units to catch up. The soldiers went to sleep for an hour—in the middle of enemy territory. About 3 A.M., they were joined by a few more half-tracks with soldiers and by Major Eshkol's Recon Company. Then, Ben-Ari radioed Dahav to move on to the intersection with the Jerusalem-Ramallah road.

With the recon unit in the lead, the brigade's tiny spearhead set out for Tel Zahara. In Beit Hanina, a village of Christian Arabs, Berez's tank slipped into a ditch and again he transferred to another tank. Dahav and Berez rumbled forward with six tanks.

From the east, up out of the Jordan Valley, two companies of M-48 Pattons were moving toward the same junction with the Jerusalem-Ramallah road on orders of Major Khlaif Awad, commander of the Jordanian Fifth Tank Battalion of the Sixtieth Armored Brigade commanded by Colonel Zaid bin Shaker, one of Jordan's most distinguished armor leaders.

When the war had broken out, the Jordanian tanks had been on the West Bank between Jericho and Jerusalem, a few miles south of the traditional tomb of Moses near the Jordanian base at Baggá. Monday morning, Major Khlaif Awad went with Colonel bin Shakir on a reconnaissance to the south; they still expected to link up with Egyptian forces.

At 6 P.M. Monday, the three tank company commanders of the Fifth Tank Battalion met with their superiors and were given orders to support the infantry battalions of Brig. Gen. Hazzáa's King Talal Brigade defending the Jordanian sector of Jerusalem. The First Tank Company under twenty-eight-year-old Captain Mamud Salim Abu Wandi, a native of Maien-Madaba on the East Bank, was instructed to move to Abu Dis and support the battalion from the Imam Ali Brigade that had been attached to the King Talal Brigade south of the Old City. Wandi's mission was to attack the Israelis in Jerusalem.

Captain Dib Suliman, a twenty-eight-year-old native of Irbid near the Syrian border, was ordered to go with his Second Tank Company and an infantry battalion to support the Thirty-third Infantry Battalion at Anata, northeast of Jerusalem. Suliman had graduated from the U.S. Army's basic tank course at Fort Knox, Kentucky, and returned to Jordan only two weeks before the war started.

And thirty-year-old Captain Awad Saud Eid, the short, mustached son of a nomadic tribe on the border of Jordan and Saudi Arabia, was directed to take the fourteen Pattons of his Third Tank Company and move with an infantry battalion to the Tel el-Ful–Shu'afat area. Captain Eid had been astounded by the outbreak of war. His first inkling had been the sight of Israeli aircraft overflying his position near Baggá to strike Jordan's air bases. His men fired their .50 caliber machine guns at the planes futilely.

At 7 P.M., all three tank companies moved out. Israeli aircraft lit their way with flares and brought them under attack but at first caused no casualties. The road was littered with destroyed and burning military vehicles, which the tanks sometimes had to shove out of the way.

They refueled at the Abu George road junction, where the treads of one of Captain Eid's tanks broke. Aircraft continued to harry them on the road. At midnight, Major Khlaif Awad's tank battalion headquarters reached the infantry battalion he was to support in the Tel el-Ful area.

By 5 A.M. on Tuesday, Captain Eid reached Anata and while advancing up to the Jerusalem-Ramallah road was taken under artillery fire, which he thought came from the vicinity of Nebi Samuel and west of Sheikh Jarrah. Near Shu'afat, three of his tanks were destroyed by a napalm air attack. The Israeli Air Force was effective. He pushed his ten remaining tanks to within yards of the Jerusalem-Ramallah road. Captain Suliman brought up his Second Tank Company on Eid's left. There, Eid's company met the Israeli tanks.

Meanwhile, at first light, Lt. Col. Dahav's spearhead, led by the Recon Company, advanced through ancient olive groves on the hills and reached Tel Zahara on the west side of and overlooking the Jerusalem-Ramallah road. Now the Israeli army had a fragile handhold on the high ground north of Jerusalem. The hill of Tel Zahara was actually a stone quarry with dangerous holes thirty feet deep. Two of Berez's tanks got stuck, and in the end only four Shermans commanded the Jerusalem-Ramallah road. Lt. Col. Dahav felt alone and nervous. Ben-David was still at Biddu and Gal, at Nebi Samuel. Of the entire 2,500-man brigade, less than 70 men—short of fuel and ammunition—stood atop the hill at Tel Zahara.

Ben-Ari says, "We did it. But what was the brigade? Four Sherman tanks and some half-tracks and the vehicles of the recon unit. The reconnaissance unit was a very good one. It led the battalion to this hill. The objective of the brigade—to cut the road between Jerusalem and Ramallah by sunrise—was achieved by P Company of the Ninety-fifth Battalion."

With the greatest difficulty, Lt. Col. Dahav arranged his four tanks and his half-tracks in an arc slightly below the crest of Tel Zahara. All was silent. From their position four hundred yards west of the main north-south road, their fire could stop all traffic on that road.

Just before dawn, two troop-laden Jordanian trucks came down the road toward Jerusalem. Berez's tank shells set them on fire. This awoke the Jordanians of the Ninth Field Artillery near Neve Yaacov to the fact that the Israelis had penetrated the northern side of Jerusalem.

A unit of 106-mm recoilless guns moved south trying to reach Jerusalem, and Berez's tanks knocked them off one by one. Once the Israelis were on Tel Zahara, not a single Jordanian vehicle got by to reinforce Jerusalem. The road was closed.

Dahav could see across the road, looming over him on the much higher hill of Tel el-Ful, the unfinished summer palace that King Hussein was having built on the site of the ancient palace of Saul, the first King of Israel.

Lt. Col. Avidar says, "We came on Jerusalem from the high ground and surprised the enemy, who were prepared to fight our forces from Jerusalem, not from an Arab place. The way we came was not for tanks; it was for infantry. The Jordanians were shocked."

The Jordanians at Neve Yaacov, a pre-1948 Jewish agricultural settlement slightly more than a mile north of Tel el-Ful on the Jerusalem-Ramallah road, went into action. Berez's tanks came under the fire of Jordanian 25-pounders and machine guns until the Israelis suppressed much of it. Then the Ninth Field Artillery Regiment, which had been firing through the night, ordered its Third Battery commanded by Captain Khalid Hafez to move away from Tel el-Ful and Neve Yaacov.

Captain Taysir Mohammad Ali remembers that when they started moving, the regimental headquarters and the Third Battery were under heavy fire from mortars and artillery. "When we approached Anata, which was our way to the east, our convoy came under heavy air raids. The raids lasted about an hour and a half and destroyed the whole convoy on the road to Anata. Some of our chaps were killed.

"At that moment, I was told over the radio that the Israelis were occupying places in Arab Jerusalem. They had reached Herod's Gate, approached Abu Dis and crossed the Sheikh Jarrah area and Wadi el Joz to Mount Scopus and Hadassah.

"At about 1 P.M. we received orders to change the other gun positions—the First and Second batteries—and set up new positions at the Abu George road junction. We remained there until about 5:30 and then received orders to concentrate at Baggá toward the Dead Sea. So ended our battle for Jerusalem."

Of the artillery regiment's 550 men, eight had been killed—one officer and seven men—and seven wounded. The regiment had lost nine field guns and a large number of vehicles.

With Lt. Kaman Jaradat, the observer of the First Battery, dead and Captain Mahadin, observer of the Third Battery, captured, Lieutenant Khreisat, south of Jerusalem, was the Ninth Field Artillery's only observer still functioning. He now had to control the firing of the entire unit—what remained of it—often against targets he could not see. Sometimes support was urgently requested by the infantry units, and at other times brigade headquarters gave him targets.

Khreisat says, "I had now only five guns near Anata. We fired on the enemy and our troops also. The last target I fired on that morning was the Rockefeller Museum. After that, enemy planes, tanks and mortars fired on the guns, so about 10 A.M. they withdrew to the east and tried to establish another firing position. My battery commander was at Abu Dis with the infantry unit that had pulled back from the Government

House area. I stayed at the monastery because the enemy did not advance from Government House. My battery commander radioed me that Iraqi troops would come and to stay in my position. We hoped that Iraqi troops would arrive and we could start the battle again." Khreisat remained at his post until Wednesday; his only job was to spot targets for the infantry's 106-mm antitank guns. He had no artillery.

Ben-Ari says, "We had won the race with the Jordanian tank battalion that was in Jericho. We were in position. They had Pattons and we had Shermans; they had 90-mm guns and we had 75s and it was an old gun."

Waiting for the Jordanians was Ben-Ari's tiny spearhead of four tanks and half-tracks commanded by Lt. Col. Dahav. At 6 A.M. on the hill of Tel Zahara, Major Amnon Eshkol of the Recon Company, looking into the rising sun, called to Major Berez in his tank turret: "See there, three Pattons."[3]

The Shermans opened fire on the Jordanian Third Tank Company 1,100 yards to the east, coming up the road from Jericho. Lt. Col. Avidar says, "The situation was good for them. The sun was at their backs. And they were higher and their tanks were better."

The Israeli gunners were accurate, but the Shermans' shells bounced off the Pattons. The Israelis could see the shells hit and fall. Captain Eid's second in command, Lieutenant Hamza al-Azab, suffered a severe head wound. And one Jordanian tank commander was killed by machine-gun fire. At that range the Pattons' guns could penetrate the Shermans, and Dahav pulled his tanks back from the crest.

The Pattons started firing at the Israeli half-tracks and hit three. Then they opened on the Shermans. A shell struck the main gun of one Sherman and wounded its commander. A metal fragment killed Sergeant Yoram Portnov, one of the recon men—the spearhead's first fatality. The damaged tank withdrew and its crew got out. The pin of the gun of another Sherman broke. Berez stayed on the crest directing fire. The two remaining tanks fired and moved their positions and fired again. Their shells had no effect on the Pattons. When Jordanian shells landed near one of the Shermans, Berez ordered it to fall back behind the crest. There was not room for all the vehicles behind the hill. One abandoned half-track burned and three more half-tracks were hit. Twelve Israelis were wounded and several killed.

Captain Eid did not know how vulnerable a spearhead he faced nor how devastating his fire had been. He felt he could not fight his Pattons in this built-up area and close on the Shermans at Tel Zahara. He pulled back behind Tel el-Ful. When the firing stopped, the crew of the Sherman with the damaged gun climbed back into their tank. Now three Shermans stood between the Pattons and Jerusalem. They would turn the war around.

A few minutes later, six of Captain Eid's Pattons again appeared on top of Tel el-Ful. They swung left to join Captain Suliman's Second Tank Company. Shells from the Shermans ricocheted off their sides. But the turn revealed extra benzine fuel tanks attached to the Pattons' sides and rear. Sergeant Eitan, commanding the Israeli tank whose cannon did not work, opened on the Pattons with his turret's heavy machine gun. The bullets crept closer and closer to a Patton and finally struck its outside fuel tanks. The Patton burst into flames. The crew of a second Patton deserted its tank. Captain Eid's tank suffered a direct hit from Israeli aircraft and he was wounded in the back. Three Pattons were destroyed.

The Israelis jammed the Jordanians' radio net so the tanks could not communicate with each other. Captain Eid says, "This was one of the factors that won the war." Because of the jamming, only one other troop of three tanks followed him. The tank of Lieutenant Mohammad Abad, the troop commander, took a direct hit; his crew was killed but he was thrown clear from the turret and survived. Lieutenant Abad could see many Israeli tanks in line on the ridge west of the main road. Captain Eid now had six tanks left as they moved to join the Second Tank Company. They headed south to reach the high ground above the Israeli position. Israeli planes destroyed three more Pattons and the Shermans fired on the Jordanians in their flight. Israeli jets pursued the Pattons with rockets as they headed back down the road toward Jericho.

This was the crucial moment of the entire battle for Jerusalem. If the Pattons had broken through to Mount Scopus and the city, the outcome of the battle for Jerusalem would have been different. Avidar says, "At this moment, the question of Jerusalem was settled."

Yitzhak Rabin adds, "The Patton M48A1 could only move for five hours; but some people—I don't know whether they were from the Pentagon or the Jordanians themselves—attached fuel tanks to the tanks' decks. One Israeli used high explosive shells and aimed them at the barrels of gasoline. This is how we won that battle with fewer tanks, just by the mistake of putting on additional fuel."

By 8 A.M., Ben-Ari finally was able to fly to a spot near Nebi Samuel in a two-seater bubble helicopter that had been flown up from the Sinai in reply to his urgent demand for mobility. He and his intelligence officer conferred with his commanders under an olive tree. He sent Lt. Col. Avidar back to the Castel to command the rear element and collect the stranded and damaged tanks, half-tracks and artillery. And he ordered Lt. Col. Gal's units forward to Tel Zahara.

There, Ben-Ari met with Dahav and ordered Gal to advance immediately across the main north-south road to seize Tel el-Ful. Ben-Ari commanded the advance in Major Eshkol's half-track. The 106th Battalion crossed the road, climbed Tel el-Ful and from the hilltop fired on the rear guard of the retreating Pattons. Two Israeli armored cars were hit and several men killed. Two more Pattons were destroyed. In all, eight Pattons were knocked out. By nine o'clock the battle was over.

As the Israeli tanks crossed the road, Captain Eid found Captain Hamid Mohammad Flayeh, second in command of the Fifth Tank Battalion, and his adjutant. They joined Eid in his tank. They moved two miles east to the road leading to Abu George junction. One of the tanks got stuck on a huge boulder. Eid had no communications with regimental or brigade headquarters. With his last two tanks, he reached Anata junction about 11:30. His company of forty-eight men had five killed and eight wounded.

"They decided enough is enough," says Ben-Ari. "And we achieved our goal—not to have a Jordanian armored battalion at Tel el-Ful."

When T Company of the 106th Battalion reached Tel el-Ful, Lieutenant Adi Rosen, the young architect who had taken over the company after Captain Yaguri was killed and whose helmet had been pierced by a bullet without harming him, found the plans to King Hussein's unfinished palace and enthusiastically told his buddies he would come back after the war and see how he could finish the palace.

About 2:30 at Anata, Captain Eid was joined by Major Khlaif Awad, commander of the Sixtieth Armored Brigade's Fifth Tank Battalion, and by Captain Suliman, commander of the Second Tank Company. Suliman still had nine of his original fourteen tanks. They refueled and rearmed at a supply point north of Anata. Then, under Israeli air attacks and artillery fire, the whole group withdrew and by dusk reached its base at Baggá. Wednesday under air attack Suliman lost five more tanks. He says, "The fight was tank against aircraft. We had no antiaircraft."

One Patton with a broken tread had been left on the road. Colonel Zaid bin Shaker, the Sixtieth Armored Brigade commander, who was frequently up forward and whom his men admired for his courage, passed by and had the tank towed to safety. The Jordanian tank officers felt that despite the heavy odds and the absence of any antiaircraft weapons, they had fought well. Colonel Ben-Ari agreed.

On Tel el-Ful after winning his battle against the Jordanian tanks, Ben-Ari was ordered to move south into Jerusalem and take Shu'afat, Mivtar Hill and French Hill, because the paratroopers of the Fifty-fifth Brigade were in trouble on Ammunition Hill near the Green Line in the city. He was told not to cross the valley to Mount Scopus and the eastern ridge.

Ordering Dahav to stay at Tel el-Ful and block the road coming up from the Jordan Valley, Ben-Ari told Aaron Gal to move his 106th Battalion forward swiftly.

The wounded were carried back to Beit Hanina, and Avidar sent two helicopters there to lift them back to the Castel.

Ben-Ari gave Gal everything available from the Ninety-fifth Battalion at Tel Zahara and ordered three infantry companies and three tank companies south toward Jerusalem. They reorganized and before 10 A.M. some elements overran Shu'afat, the village just south of Tel el-Ful. Firing left and right through Shu'afat, Ben-Ari and Gal dashed ahead with four tanks and four half-tracks down the long main road toward Mivtar Hill and French Hill.

Charging into the deep cut that splits Mivtar Hill, Ben-Ari's spearhead, led by the tanks, came under intense fire. A Jeep was hit on the road and four Israelis were killed. Gal was restricted to using only his machine guns for fear his main guns would accidentally hit Mount Scopus.

He advanced fifty meters beyond the crest of heavily fortified and bunkered Mivtar Hill, from which the Jordanians were shooting down at the paratroopers on the smaller Ammunition Hill eight hundred yards away and one hundred yards lower down. The Jordanians on both sides of Mivtar Hill blasted him. He halted with two tanks in line on the road and two off the road to the left. He could see Jerusalem before him now with the Dome of the Rock shining golden in the morning light. Gal's battle was not finished.

Captain Raphael Yeshaya, Major Aaron Kamara's deputy, spent Monday morning waiting outside Jerusalem with the reserve element of the Jerusalem Brigade's tank company. The movement of the Harel Brigade toward Jerusalem had eliminated Yeshaya's mission to guard the corridor leading from Tel Aviv to Jerusalem.

About 3 P.M., after pressing brigade headquarters, Yeshaya was ordered to bring his tanks into the city. He was joined by the tank that Kamara had left at the Russian Compound. He now commanded eleven Shermans. Jerusalem Brigade headquarters told him to report to Colonel "Motta" Gur and support the paratroopers' Fifty-fifth Brigade.

Through the dark early hours of Tuesday, while Ben-Ari's tanks were fighting in the hills north of Jerusalem, Yeshaya's fought with the paratroopers in the city itself. And after the terrible battle on Ammunition Hill, two of his tanks that had fought there, commanded by Sergeant Ben Gidi, moved north toward where the Ramallah road enters Jerusalem. It was a tiny force against any Jordanian armored attack from the north. The two tanks shelled Mivtar Hill from which the Jordanians were still firing on the paratroopers on Ammunition Hill.

About 10 A.M. Tuesday, paratroopers on the roof of a hospital next to the road called to Sergeant Gidi that four tanks were coming from the north. Almost out of ammunition and fearing that the approaching tanks were Jordanian Pattons, the two sergeants commanding the tanks pulled into ambush po-

Mayor Teddy Kollek discusses medical preparations in Israeli Jerusalem before the battle. *(Israel Government Press Office)*

General Odd Bull (in beret, center) and members of his staff with soldiers of the Jerusalem Brigade, June 5 at Government House. *(Israel Government Press Office)*

Tanks and half-tracks of Ben-Ari's brigade approach commanding height of Tel el-Ful on the horizon. *(Israel Government Press Office)*

The trenches of Ammunition Hill after the battle. *(Dan Arazi)*

Wounded paratrooper being evacuated from Sheikh Jarrah.
(Yossi Shemi)

Jordanian prisoners of war. *(Dan Arazi)*

Israeli tank makes turn to head for Augusta Victoria. This is point where tanks missed turn on night of June 6 and ran into Jordanian ambush. *(Bahamane)*

Paratroopers climb the hill to Augusta Victoria, June 7. *(Yossi Shemi)*

Paratroop brigade command group on Mount of Olives giving orders to attack Old City. Seated bareheaded is Colonel "Motta" Gur and standing center is Major Stempel. Morning of June 7. *(Israel Government Press Office)*

Israeli paratroopers pour into the Lions Gate of the Old City, past burned out Jordanian bus. *(Yossi Shemi)*

General Narkiss, Defense Minister Dayan and Chief of Staff
Rabin, left to right, enter Old City through the Lions Gate.
Turning his head in center is "Gandhi" and bareheaded
between Dayan and Rabin is Moshe Pearlman. June 7.
(Israel Government Press Office)

Captain Yoram Zamush (right) hangs flag from Jewish Quarter in 1948 on fence above the Western Wall. *(Bahamane)*

Paratrooper brigade section in Mount Herzl Cemetery immediately after the war. Graves are still marked only with wooden signs. *(Yossi Shemi)*

sitions in a small street. When the four approaching tanks were three hundred yards away and started to turn toward Mount Scopus, Sergeant Gidi opened fire.

The tanks were Gal's. One was hit by Israeli tank fire from the front and by the Jordanians on Mivtar Hill. Four Israeli Mystère jets screamed overhead. Ground-air communication failed. Gal pulled his hatch partways closed. Shrapnel ricocheted off the inside of the hatch and ripped his back painfully.

The Jerusalem Brigade tank and the Jordanian fire knocked out the lead Harel Brigade tank, and one of the Mystères destroyed a second tank and two half-tracks. The one tank burst into flames in the road and the other on the east side of it. The men trying to climb out were killed.

Ben-Ari, in the half-track behind Gal, was hit in the elbow by a stone hurled up by the Israeli jet. Under the unexpected attack, he ordered the remaining two tanks and half-tracks to pull back to Shu'afat. The Air Force hit them again.

The Air Force said the Harel Brigade tanks were in a "dead zone" and were presumed to be Jordanian, but Ben-Ari was enraged: "They should have known better. They should have recognized Shermans, which the Jordanian army did not have. I had coordinated it twenty times before we crossed the cut. The Israelis were firing at us. The Jordanians were firing at us. Mainly, the Israeli Air Force was attacking us. We retreated into a built-up area where it was difficult for the Air Force to recognize where we were. Chagai Man was shouting into the radio, trying to reach the airplanes; but, of course, it didn't work. He called our rear headquarters on the Castel and told Avidar to reach the Air Force. Avidar had to radio Central Command. I was furious, but you have to understand that things like that happen in every war. Of course, you are mad."

Taking fifteen minutes to reorganize and assemble greater strength, Gal attacked Mivtar Hill again. This time, the tanks stayed on the crest and the infantry went down and seized the hill from the rear. It was heavily fortified to 360 degrees in the British style with bunkers and deep trenches. Aaron Gal sent Lieutenant Rosen and T Company to the right side of Mivtar Hill. Following Rosen, Lieutenant Merenstein saw a Jordanian with a heavy machine gun, killed him and took over the gun. He fired at the Jordanians who were in the trenches and running down the hill. Rosen's half-track was hit by a

Jordanian grenade; it killed the young architect who thought no harm could come to him after he had survived the bullet through his helmet. The half-track's driver rapidly drove back in search of medical help for his load of dead and wounded.

Merenstein was now T Company's third commander. For a moment there was quiet on Mivtar Hill as he and his men watched some forty Jordanians flee north toward Shu'afat, throwing away their weapons. In the bunkers on Mivtar Hill, the Israeli infantrymen found thirty-seven antitank guns, many of them mounted on Bren gun carriers.

Suddenly, twelve Jordanian soldiers appeared with their hands up. For the first time in the battle, the Harel Brigade collected prisoners. Merenstein turned them over as POWs and led his men back toward Shu'afat to find his battalion.

Gal sent out Merenstein and T Company and a tank toward French Hill. In three half-tracks, the men climbed among the hill's Arab villas. The tank came upon a huge hole in the ground; and in the tension of battle the men fired the tank's machine guns into the hole—wildly, madly. Merenstein shouted for them to stop; and once the firing halted, out of the hole climbed twelve children. None was hurt. The Israelis gave them water. Jordanian soldiers came in and gave themselves up. Soon a dozen prisoners were sitting there. There were no Jordanians left on French Hill. The Israelis did not know what to do with their prisoners, so finally around noon they showed them the direction to Jordan and they walked off through a wadi.

The brigade had a life-and-death problem with its wounded. It could not take them down into Arab Jerusalem and it could not carry them all the way back through Tel Zahara and over the rugged ridge to an Israeli hospital. Dr. Hanoch Bar-on took blood from the men of an armored infantry company for the wounded, who were eventually flown out by helicopter.

In its share of the battle for Jerusalem, the Harel Brigade had 169 casualties; of these, thirty-nine were killed (five officers and thirty-four enlisted men) and 130 were wounded (four officers and 126 enlisted men).

As the units of the brigade came forward, they rapidly refueled and rearmed. A half hour after taking Mivtar Hill, Ben-Ari received orders to turn north and capture Ramallah. He left behind Gal's 106th Battalion, which had fought five battles in less than twenty-four hours—at Sheikh Abdul Aziz, Khirbet Lausa, Nevi Samuel, Tel el-Ful and the Mivtar.

At midafternoon, Mayor Eytan Arieli, a kibbutznik and an expert tank company commander, was ordered to take ten of Gal's tanks, including those that had survived the Israeli Air Force's and Jerusalem Brigade's attack, over to the paratroopers' command post in the Rockefeller Museum at the corner of the Old City. At dusk they moved out. Six of the tanks lost their way through the dark, traffic-clogged city streets; and only the first four led by Major Arieli made it to the museum. They were assigned to fire on the Augusta Victoria Hospital atop the ridge east of the city on the assumption that the massive building was being used as a military position by the Jordanians. Arieli's tanks would play one more dramatic role in the conquest of Jerusalem.

Meanwhile, the Jordanian Fifth Tank Battalion's commander, Major Khlaif Awad, and his twenty-three-year-old intelligence officer, Lieutenant Tayseer Kilani, a native of El Karak, made their way to the Sheikh Jarrah sector of East Jerusalem and witnessed the Israeli paratroopers' attack on the Jordanian infantry there. About noon Tuesday, the two officers moved on to Anata; and Major Awad sent Lieutenant Kilani and the command tank back to join the Imam Ali Brigade east of Tel el-Ful. Arriving there at 2 P.M., they came under heavy air attack and lost contact with Major Awad and his command.

Ben-Ari rejoined Lt. Col. Dahav at Tel Zahara and organized a force of three tank companies, one mechanized infantry company and the reconnaissance company to attack Ramallah.

Ben-David's 104th Battalion was still at Biddu, protecting the brigade's rear and the western approaches to Jerusalem. As far as Ben-Ari knew at the time, Latrun was still in Jordanian hands and he was exposed from that side. In fact, the Israeli Fourth Infantry Brigade had already taken Latrun and was also advancing on Ramallah, which was crucially important from a military viewpoint. When matters were straightened out and Ben-Ari started for Ramallah, he was given command over both brigades. By three o'clock, he was on his way.

Ben-Ari's three tank companies entered Ramallah and systematically fired a shell into every building as they rumbled through the streets. There was no opposition.

Ben-Ari's Tenth Brigade, aided by the Israeli Air Force,

had prevented the Jordanians from bringing armor up from the Jordan River Valley. King Hussein had lost his battle for Jerusalem.

The romantic popular conception of the Israeli conquest of Jerusalem in the Six Day War is that the battle was won by the paratroopers. Certainly, their role was courageous and bloody. They plunged through the center of Jerusalem and dashed dramatically into the lightly defended Old City. They got the glory. But the public perception of a paratroop victory was essentially false. It is important to realize that the paratroopers' fight was improvised hurriedly and, in truth, a terrible mistake. This reality detracts nothing from the bravery with which they carried out their assignment. But the crucial and definitive fact is that the skillful joint effort of Ben-Ari's brigade and the Israeli Air Force prevented Jordanian reinforcements and armor from reaching the city and made the downfall of Jordanian Jerusalem inevitable.

The U.S. Embassy in Amman secretly cabled Secretary of State Dean Rusk that the "Jordanian Air Force [was] destroyed" and the Jordanian army "was losing tanks at rate of one every 10 minutes." The Embassy told Rusk that the Jordanians said their army casualties were "unbearably high."[4]

— Chapter 13 —

THE PARATROOPERS

SHORTLY AFTER NOON ON MONDAY, ISRAELI GENERAL HEAD-quarters called General Narkiss and asked him if he wanted a battalion from the Fifty-fifth Brigade of paratroopers commanded by Colonel Mordechai "Motta" Gur. This reserve brigade had been scheduled to jump into action in the Sinai desert behind the Egyptian lines near El Arish, but the Israeli forces' rapid advance had eliminated its mission. Although the Fifty-fifth Brigade was new and had finished its initial training only six months earlier, Narkiss immediately accepted its battalion. He was short of men in Jerusalem.

The offer of a battalion of paratroopers gave Narkiss a fresh and trained assault force. He was assigned the Sixty-sixth Battalion commanded by Major Yosef "Yossi" Yaffe. Yaffe was a legend in the army, powerful and thoughtful. He had absorbed six bullets on the major night retaliation raid against the Jordanian border town and police station of Kalkilia in October 1956, when twenty-seven Israelis and forty-eight Arabs had been killed; and he still walked with a limp in his left leg. One of his officers said, "Yossi had no time, and he had time for everybody. He was everywhere. He led by example."

Five minutes after the first call, Narkiss was informed he could have not one but two paratroop battalions and a few minutes later was given Colonel Gur's entire Fifty-fifth Brigade. He asked that Gur come to him at Ramla and was told he would be there in twenty minutes.

Since Gur's military car was not working, he and his operations and intelligence officers drove from their base near Lod Airport in a rented Oldsmobile. In his war room, General Narkiss gave them a brief military order to move up to Jerusalem and he defined their sector and their two prime objectives:

Mount Scopus and the Jordanian strongpoints north of the Old City.

The Fifty-fifth Brigade was one of the Israeli army's three paratroop brigades—the regular Thirty-fifth Brigade, now fighting in the Sinai, and two reserve units, the Fifty-fifth and the Eightieth. Their men were recognizable to all by their red jump boots.

The colonel being shifted to Jerusalem was a stocky, agile soldier with bright, smiling eyes that shielded a streak of exceptional stubbornness. Many of his paratroopers worshipped him, but others thought him impulsive and hasty in his judgments, and some saw in him an arrogance that covered up deep uncertainties.

"Motta" Gur was now only thirty-seven, young for a brigade commander, but a veteran of military service. He had been born in Jerusalem of Russian parents and grew up in Rehovot. When he graduated from high school in the spring of 1947, he had a scholarship to go to London and study to become a teacher. But he was given command of the Haganah youth organization in Rehovot. In the War of Independence he served in special recon units of the Palmach operating behind enemy lines. In 1954, after he spent three years in the university, terrorist infiltrations from Jordan and Egypt increased and retaliation operations built up. "I just couldn't stay anymore in the university," Gur says, "and as most of the activity was being done by the paratroopers, I volunteered to the paratroopers."

The men of the Fifty-fifth Brigade had assembled from all over the country. Men even took themselves out of hospitals. They felt a compulsion to join their unit; as paratroopers, they felt they were members of an elite.

The brigade was made up of three battalions: the Twenty-eighth led by Lt. Col. Yosef "Yossi" Fradkin, the Sixty-sixth commanded by Major Yaffe and the Seventy-first led by Major Uzi Eilam. Gur was greatly aided by his deputy, Major Moshe "Moishele" Stempel, a small, round man with a reputation as a great, cool fighter. Each battalion had four infantry companies plus one support company. Each infantry company numbered one hundred men, more or less—four infantry platoons and a fifth that included a bazooka squad, a 52-mm mortar squad and a command squad. But in a reserve brigade like Gur's, units were seldom fully manned. The basic infantry squad had six to eight men armed with Uzi submachine guns, Belgian FN automatic rifles and a light machine gun. Each platoon also had a bazooka team.

The brigade camped in a citrus grove of a kibbutz until dysentery swept through the troops and they moved five miles up into the foothills of the Judean hills near Beit Shemesh. The reservists ran exercises there and among the buildings of an old British army camp in the sand dunes on the Mediterranean. Major Uzi Eilam, commander of the Seventy-first Battalion, wrangled permission to use a school at Beit Shemesh for a day and put his companies through built-up-area training. "The most important thing," Eilam says, "was we had enough time to know each other." He replaced two company commanders.

Sunday night, June 4, the whole brigade moved down to Giv'at Brenner to be nearer the military airport close to Lod. Lieutenant Karni Kav, a woman soldier, says, "It was a very special evening. People were, on the one hand, very much afraid of the war and, on the other, were trying to settle themselves and make an impression on the others that they were not afraid. And, of course, thinking about their homes. They would start laughing suddenly with no logical reason; they told dirty stories—actions that were controlled by nothing but sentiment and fear."

Some paratroopers were sent to a musical show in Tel Aviv as a small part of Moshe Dayan's tactic to reassure the Israeli people and to give everyone the impression that war was not imminent. By the time Sergeant Amram Gabai, a member of the brigade's 100-man scout unit returned from the city at 1 A.M., he knew that something serious was afoot. There was no time for sleep.

Sergeant Gabai, a twenty-six-year-old native of Tangier, had come to Israel when he was nine. He was supposed to arrive with a planeload of Jewish Moroccan children; but just as he was prepared to leave home, his mother gave birth to her first daughter after six sons—and Gabai missed the flight. The plane exploded in the air and all the children aboard were killed. Gabai eventually reached Israel and settled with about twenty other children on Kibbutz Cabri in the Galilee. He had worked in the cotton fields, married and had a daughter, who was one year old on May 24, the day her father was mobilized in 1967.

Captain Nir Nitzan, who was deputy commander of the Sixty-sixth Battalion's B Company, was to play a special part in the battle for Jerusalem. The son of Russian-born parents, he remembers how he felt before the 1967 war began: "I was a father of three children, and as every father and as one who fought a little before, I wasn't eager to fight. All of us were eager for peace and quiet. When Mr. Begin told Mr. Ben-Gurion he would join a national unity government, we embraced each other. We started to feel we were united and stronger."

Nitzan had been a squad leader on retaliation raids and in 1955 was shot three times by a Syrian officer. He killed the Syrian and kept his 9-mm Browning pistol. He jumped as a paratrooper at the Mitla Pass in the Sinai desert in 1956 and afterwards became a civilian athletic instructor. Now, although already thirty-three, he was a physically powerful blond of medium height, square-jawed and with pale gray eyes. A strong youth, Nitzan had graduated from the Wingate Institute, a renowned school for physical culture. The institute was named for British General Orde Wingate who had been killed in Burma in World War II. In the 1930s, as a captain, Wingate organized picked squads of the Haganah, which fought Arab guerrillas and developed into the Palmach, the Haganah's elite striking arm.

Monday morning, the paratroop commanders were briefed at the airport for their Sinai combat jump and then went back to camp and waited. When the men were told they would go to Jerusalem, some were pleased. One sergeant said afterwards, "You don't feel good jumping from an airplane when you know it is a real battle. You are a good target. Nobody likes the idea." But others, keyed up to jump into the Sinai battle, were disappointed by the change of assignment. They knew from the pilots, who waggled their wings as they returned to the military airfield, that the war against Egypt was going well. But many paratroopers felt they were merely going to defend the Israeli sector of the city; they would miss the fighting. They were mistaken.

About 2 P.M., General Narkiss decided to go up to Jerusalem. "Why should I give someone else the honor, the pleasure, to command the capture of Jerusalem? So I went to Jerusalem." When his mobile command group of three cars and a half-track passed the Castel, they came under enemy fire. In Jerusalem, they set up Central Command headquarters in the Convention Hall near the entrance to the city and went to the observation post on top of the Histadrut Building in Nathan Strauss Street, the highest point in Israeli Jerusalem. Narkiss says, "Only the Jerusalem Brigade knew the front in Jerusalem. But when I decided to penetrate the urban line and go through Sheikh Jarrah, Ammunition Hill and the Police Training School, I did not think the Jerusalem Brigade was up to it. I was scared."

Under this decision, for which Narkiss claimed credit, he asked Colonel Amitai if his Jerusalem Brigade could attack the Police Training School, which was believed to be strongly fortified and manned. Amitai said it would be difficult. So Narkiss looked for another weapon; Gur's brigade was his solution.

The key question for the Israelis became whether Ben-Ari's brigade should plunge down on Mount Scopus and Jordanian Jerusalem from the north or whether Gur's paratroop brigade should slash through the heavily populated and heavily defended Arab quarters inside the city. In retrospect, the decision to send Gur against Sheikh Jarrah and Wadi el Joz was wrong— but it was comprehensible under the political pressures facing the commanders. Colonel Amitai says, "We had plans for everything, but this was not according to plan. This was a diversion of the plan."

Narkiss' mind was always on Mount Scopus; he wanted to attack on the most direct route to that exposed enclave. To charge through Sheikh Jarrah and Wadi el Joz was the shortest way on the map to Mount Scopus, but it threw the Israelis directly at the Jordanians' strength. It would cost lives.

Still, it did have a rationale. Yitzhak Rabin says, "I believe that the positions at the Police Training School and Ammunition Hill and the Rockefeller Museum had to be taken in the first stages to make it clear to the Jordanians that they had no hope."

Colonel Gur agreed with the decision. He says, "The General Staff decided to go [against the Jordanians' strength] because it wasn't just a military front. They were shooting at civilians—finish it fast, that's all. I believe that was one of their reasons for the decision to go straight ahead in Jerusalem. It started in Jerusalem because the Jordanians attacked Government House, and you had to counterattack. And they were shooting at population, and you had to stop it as fast as possible. I am not only talking about our front; we attacked all over and I think it was a good decision. There were at least six brigades that operated all along the line. Any fight in such a close area [as ours] is a tough fight. The decision to go in that area was decided by the General Staff and Territorial Command, which I accepted."

But once Ben-Ari turned back the Jordanian armor at Tel el-Ful and shoved the Jordanians off Mivtar Hill, eastern Jerusalem was indefensible. The Jordanians along the Green Line could have been taken from the rear. Even Ben-Ari, who believes that the paratrooper attack started out correctly, says it should have been stopped because he could have neutralized bloody Ammunition Hill very quickly. Although the Israeli attack succeeded, it would prove wasteful of lives.

Maj. Gen. Chaim Herzog, the former head of military intelligence and commander of the Jerusalem District, says, "Ben-Ari's concept was the right concept. Gur's attack cost a lot of good lives, wonderful people." He adds, "They had blinkers on because they were looking straight up at Mount Scopus."

Narkiss says, "Gur had to break through the urban line to get to Mount Scopus. Thinking politically, I told Motta, 'This is your main effort, but bear in mind that at any minute we might be called to penetrate into the Old City, so [also] turn to the right and occupy the Rockefeller Museum.'" The museum stood just outside the northeast corner of the walled Old City.

"In my opinion, Gur's was an impossible mission. They were not prepared. They came to Jerusalem directly from the airport. They were equipped to jump; they didn't have the material for ground fighting. They took a new mission from the Jerusalem Brigade. This is something that doesn't happen. There were so many paratroopers who had never been to Jerusalem; there were many, many commanders who had never visited the line. And everything happened so fast, the decisions were taken quickly by me and by Gur and by the others. They didn't have any time to plan it.

"And they made a few errors—Ammunition Hill and the division of forces. Two companies broke through in battle and came immediately to Sheikh Jarrah, while two others got stuck at Ammunition Hill. If we had had one more day, we should have planned to attack Ammunition Hill with the whole battalion." Or they could have bypassed it. "But we didn't have enough time. The hurry was also political. Everything that touches Jerusalem means that everybody, internationally speaking, is interested. Everything that is done here in wartime and in peacetime interests the whole world.

"In Jerusalem time runs against us. If you plan to do something today and you postpone it to tomorrow, maybe tomorrow never comes in Jerusalem. That was the reason to hurry. The whole time I was afraid of being obliged to stop either by my government or by other governments, by Russia, by America, by the UN. I thought to myself if we were stopped on Ammunition Hill or any other place, we would not be able to accomplish what we had started nineteen years ago. What would everybody say—and history? I would be the accused."

Israeli Intelligence had collected exact, detailed information about all the Jordanian defenses in and around Jerusalem—knew their positions and guns, had maps and aerial photographs. "Down to the last detail," says General Aharon Yariv, the Director of Military Intelligence, who masterminded the intelligence side of this war. "It was so close you had to be deaf, dumb and blind not to know. Here was the place where we had more information than anywhere else."

The information was efficiently filed in special folders in Central Command headquarters. But through human error, the kind of mistake that happens in war when units are shifted and attack suddenly, Yariv says, this information never reached the paratroopers. "It didn't get to Gur. Narkiss' intelligence officer had all the information—not for himself only but for the troops in case of war. If I had been Gur's intelligence officer I would have raised hell to get it. I would have told Gur, don't move before you have it. You are going to attack a fortified position and when you attack a fortified position you must show your

201

soldiers where the enemy is. A fortified position is a set-piece attack. They didn't take time to prepare a set-piece attack."

General Barlev agrees: "The paratroopers did not get all the updated information before they attacked." They had full information on the area around El Arish, but they were not briefed to fight against the well-prepared defenses in Jerusalem. Yariv says of this costly lapse, "They were switched at the last moment and this is where it all starts. Sometimes it is better to lose two hours. It loses less men."

Their main problem, Gur and his staff believed, would be the no-man's-land between the Israeli and Jordanian sections of Jerusalem..Ranging from about twenty to one hundred yards wide, it was a deadly maze of mines, barbed wire and deep bunkers. Major Arie "Arik" Achmon, the athletic, charismatic young kibbutznik who was the brigade's intelligence officer, says, "It was the most fortified line anywhere on the border of Israel."

This operation called for street fighting in a city unfamiliar to most of Gur's officers and without time to plan the attack skillfully and in detail. It would prove to be an exercise for which the paratroopers were unprepared. Their mistakes, as a result, were costly, despite their courage. Major Langotsky of the Jerusalem Brigade wondered why they did not use his street-wise recon unit. He says, "It was a very big mishmash."

"General Narkiss ordered us to make the breakthrough at midnight that same night," Major Achmon remembers. "Usually it took twenty-four hours for a brigade to prepare, but we had to do it in less than ten. So we had to get to Jerusalem with the battalion and company commanders before dark—to see the place. It was amazing. Our biggest problem was not to find our way in the Arabic side; most of us knew those streets better than our side.

"On the Saturday before the war started, Motta thought the war would begin with the change of units on Mount Scopus." Gur was wrong. He did not know that on this same day, June 3, the Israelis agreed to send only supplies to Mount Scopus next time because of the tension.

"We were sure that if something happened here, the army would pick us to fight in Jerusalem," Achmon continues. "So we went, Motta and me, and we sat with Colonel Amitai at

Shemu'el Hanavi Street and thought and thought what we would have to do if we have to rescue the unit from Mount Scopus.

"Opposite us was the Nablus Road. We saw the low wall on the near side of this main Arab road from Jerusalem to Ramallah and decided our place of crossing would be a big eucalyptus tree near the gas station. We knew from an aerial photograph that there was an opening in the wall there. And we decided, *if* we had to rescue the unit, we would break through from this place and go through the hole into the valley of Wadi el Joz, the shortest way to Mount Scopus. On our left was Ammunition Hill and the Police Training School, the highest place in all the area. We would have to capture them too.

"We didn't even dream that two days later we would come here to fight a war. We only made a plan to rescue the unit on Mount Scopus. How things go! This became our main plan after that. We were planning a rescue operation but the problem was the same—to get to Mount Scopus. In the car from Ramla to Jerusalem on Monday, we made our plan because we had seen the place with our eyes for another purpose."

While the troops waited for buses to carry them to Jerusalem, their commanders raced ahead to the city to organize their attack. On the road, they were shelled near the Castel and passed Ben-Ari's tanks already bombarding the Jordanian bunkers in the hills across the Green Line. They reached the city about two hours before dark, drove up Jaffa Road and met at the Schneller military barracks because everyone knew where it was. Schneller was under heavy shelling, and they had to run through the courtyard. Since the Jerusalem Brigade had already moved its headquarters to the Evelina de Rothschild School, they found only a few officers and soldiers at Schneller. They tried to get some maps. Gur arrived, and so did Captain Yeshaya, the Jerusalem Brigade tank officer who had been assigned to support the paratroopers.

Then, they moved through the back streets to the corner of Zefanya Street and Bar Ilan Street. There, Bar Ilan Street dropped down until it deadended in the Pagi section on the border. From the top of the street, they had a clear view of the Police Training School–Ammunition Hill area they were to attack.

Major Achmon says, "I remember I had a mental problem

not to go to Zefanya up a one-way street—Amos Street. In the middle of the war! None of us knew the way here.

"At the end of Zefanya we were under heavy fire. We could not cross Bar Ilan Street. On a staircase in a building on the corner, Motta gave his orders. It was about six o'clock.

"Then everybody went to Bar Ilan to stick his nose out and have a look. Each commander had about an hour to go and see his exact place for the breakthrough and make his plans. We put our headquarters in that building. I placed my intelligence unit in a small open lobby to the building where there was a civilian telephone. To get Motta in these hours you had a number of a civilian telephone here."

That vital telephone had been connected for only a few days in the home of the Elitzur family; and now when the paratroopers arrived, Rami Elitzur, a son who was an electrician, hooked it up downstairs. The corner house at 72 Zefanya Street, on the crest of the hill overlooking the Green Line, became brigade headquarters.

The Elitzurs were Persian Jews who owned a neighborhood grocery in the Bukharim section down the hill. Joseph and Sarah Elitzur had six children. When the shelling had started that morning, Sarah had been at the grocery. She brought home an Arab woman from Abu Ghosh who worked in the store and now stayed with them, badly frightened. Joseph had fetched their daughter, Dalia, from school and brought her home through the back alleys. Simon had been taking a math test in the Alliance School across Jaffa Road and the teacher had sent them all to the shelter. During the afternoon he and some other kids had broken a locked back door and run home. Tuesday was Simon's seventeenth birthday and he would always feel that the paratroopers freed Jerusalem sort of as a birthday present for him.

After a five-minute briefing, Colonel Gur took his battalion and company commanders and staff down from Zefanya Street to survey the scene of the breakthrough from a roof in the Pagi section on the border. Young Aryeh Elitzur went along in Gur's Jeep to show him the way. Later, Eli, another son, who had been released from the army as an airplane mechanic only three weeks earlier and had not been called back, showed Gur's driver how to reach the Mandelbaum Gate area by the back roads. The paratroopers were already in strange territory.

In Pagi, some of the officers were emotionally moved to meet the poor, stalwart immigrants who had for years faced the dangers of border life. Their gray concrete fortlike buildings had small windows with steel shutters that they could close in case of attack and their roofs had narrow firing slits. The inhabitants, after years of shooting and tension, were heartened by the appearance of the paratroopers and confident that now their lives would be saved.

On the roof, the officers could see the Jordanian guns firing from Wadi el Joz. They were told they would break through the Green Line at two points. Their missions were to sweep the valley of Wadi el Joz, which in years past had been famous for its walnut trees, and the American Colony sector and the Police Training School and to link up with the men on Mount Scopus. And they were to be ready to take the Old City if the order should come eventually.

Facing the hazardous no-man's-land and the Jordanian fortifications, some officers had the feeling that the entire Israeli army was in the Sinai and Jerusalem was going to be a disaster area.

The most crucial question the officers discussed in Pagi was the timing of the attack. This was highly controversial; it would decide the fate of many men. The main issue was that a daylight attack could be supported by aircraft and adequate artillery bombardment, while a night attack would have to be made by the soldiers alone. In daylight, aircraft would supply their cover—at night, the darkness. Gur believed that the Arabs fought less well at night and that his paratroopers had been specially trained for night fighting. And he feared that the Jordanians would strengthen their forces in the city if he delayed until dawn.

Barlev and Narkiss had discussed the options on the telephone, and Barlev finally said the commanders on the spot should decide. Later, Narkiss called Barlev back. Barlev was napping at the time, grabbing a few minutes to refresh himself. Narkiss told him they had decided not to wait for the Air Force. Barlev approved the decision. "I also thought it would be better to use the night," he says. "After all, it's a built-up area and you couldn't make good use of the Air Force and tanks and artillery without really destroying the Holy Places."

Also favoring a night attack were the political pressures. Colonel Le'or, Eshkol's military secretary, says, "Some people were critical. Maybe it would have been easier to attack after some shelling first. But every delay could affect the decision from a political point of view, and nobody wanted the responsibility for shelling the Holy Places.

"The main consideration was we knew we had only twelve hours or twenty-four, no more, because of the pressure from Russia, from the United States, from the other countries. Every hour was very important. This was not the usual war we study in history or in war schools." In the end, the fear of political pressure ruled; and Gur stormed East Jerusalem in the dark.

While their superiors were worrying about the worldwide implications and risks of delay, the paratroop officers in Pagi made their decision on a purely military basis. Says one who was present, "We hesitated whether to do it at night or to wait until morning. We preferred to do it ourselves—without a lot of cooperation and adjustments. We wanted to catch the Jordanians in their positions. We figured they would fight in their positions anyway, so even if we came with tanks, we would have to clear house after house, post after post. It was better to do it at night. Some officers argued for waiting for morning. The decision was finally made by Yossi Yaffe." General Yariv, the Director of Military Intelligence, says it was a mistake in judgment.

Major Eilam, commander of the Seventy-first Battalion, had a second decision to make. His job was to break through into the American Colony sector. He had two choices: He could attack through the Mandelbaum Gate or three hundred yards farther north. At the Mandelbaum Gate, he would need tanks to overcome the fortified Jordanian border posts; and Gur could let him have only three of Captain Yeshaya's. The rest had to go with the Sixty-sixth Battalion against the imposing Police Training School. So Eilam concentrated on his northern option.

The commander of A Company of his Seventy-first Battalion was a tall, lean Sabra named Yoram Zamush. His family had fled Berlin and Hitler in 1936 to the religious Kibbutz Yavne south of Rehovot. He grew up in that fervent tradition; and early in 1967, because his kibbutz did not feel he was pious enough to meet its standards, he had been sent to a yeshiva in Jerusalem. The twenty-five-year-old captain was the only religious commander in the paratroop brigade.

Now on the Pagi rooftop, he went over to Gur. Zamush was deeply touched by the prospect of sharing in the capture of the rest of Jerusalem and the Temple Mount. He felt that the other officers saw before them only a military problem. To him it was much more: "Our plan was to fight in Sinai. Then suddenly we were in Jerusalem. Once we had a chance to take the Temple Mount, it was no longer a coincidence. It was our destiny."

Zamush said to the brigade commander that if they entered the Old City, he wanted to take the Temple Mount and the Western Wall with his company. "Don't send any of the animals, the kibbutzniks who don't know anything about Jerusalem. I understand what it means. If we take it, I want it to be me." Gur promised him he could.

After the rooftop meeting, Major Eilam took his company commanders and went down into the Jerusalem Brigade trenches near the point where he planned to break through. It was just becoming dusk and in the last rays of sunlight they were able to spot most of the important installations in the Jordanian line opposite them.

Later that evening, Zamush and Major Eilam were sitting in a shade-drawn apartment in the Beit Ha-Kerem section near the new Hebrew University campus. A soldier told the apartment owners, a Mr. and Mrs. Cohen, that the next day they would be in the Old City. Mr. Cohen went in another room and came back with a flag, which had been made in the Jewish Quarter where his mother had been during the 1948 siege. He asked Zamush to hang the flag there again. Zamush took it and put it in his pack.

The commanders assembled at the Evelina de Rothschild School in Rehavia to propose their detailed plans and have them approved. At about ten o'clock, they met at the command post in Zefanya Street for a final briefing. General Narkiss showed up and they decided together to postpone the attack from midnight to two o'clock Tuesday morning. It was taking the brigade time to assemble and get into position to jump off.

At headquarters, Rabin recognized the danger of the delay.

It meant that the paratroopers might be fighting in the Jordanian border positions when daylight came. He asked Uzi Narkiss if he wanted to wait for the morning and close air support. "He said no. I left it to Narkiss after consultation with Gur. When they said they preferred the night, I said all right. I believe in such a case you have to rely on the commander who has the task. But at that time, I realized it was going to be late; and I was afraid that at least part of the fighting was going to be after dawn."

At 11 P.M., Colonel Amitai, Lt. Col. Fradkin and Major Achmon gathered on the top of the Histadrut Building with Maj. Gen. Rechavam Zeevy, Weizman's Assistant Chief of Operations in General Headquarters, who had come up to Jerusalem on his own initiative. The colorful Zeevy, a tall, lean hero from 1948 and graduate of the U.S. Army Command and General Staff College at Fort Leavenworth, Kansas, was known universally as "Gandhi" because as a young soldier in the Palmach he had cut his hair short, draped a white sheet over his skinny frame, put on glasses and led a goat—all as a joke—and the name had stuck.

Zeevy, now forty-one, was a fifth-generation Jerusalemite. When he heard that Government House had been attacked, he got into his military Plymouth and drove himself from Tel Aviv, skirting Ben Ari's tanks and half-tracks, to the city. He says, "In our army, the experience is to get the best information not only through the ordinary channels but to jump from one front to another to get first impressions on the battlefield itself." So he sent himself to Jerusalem. He felt it was important for him to be in the city; like Narkiss, he had grown up there. "For many officers in the Israeli army, the dream to complete the mission of '48 was in our heads. For us to take part in the day when Jerusalem can be liberated—not occupied but liberated, I emphasize—it was a big dream."

After visiting Narkiss at his Convention Hall headquarters and his mother in a shelter in the Romema section, Zeevy had gone to the Knesset, talked with Dayan and was asked to brief the Cabinet in the basement. Then he went to the observation post atop the Histadrut Building.

When, because of the delay in H-hour, the paratroopers had to reconsider their timing, Achmon remembers: "'Gandhi' asked us whether we still preferred to attack in the night with all the arrangements not finished or to postpone the attack until eight in the morning when we could have air support. We decided to attack at night because in this area with such close lines the effect of air support is very little and we needed the dark to cross the line. I believe we saved a lot of lives because we only had five persons killed in the breakthrough. Afterwards, there was a lot of argument about this decision."

The men of the brigade arrived in Jerusalem at about ten o'clock. They came up in civilian Egged buses, trucks and Jeeps; and, because the tanks and half-tracks of Ben-Ari's Harel Brigade filled the main road, they took secondary roads through Beit Shemesh and Kibbutz Zubah.

Most of the officers and noncoms had been in action before, but many of the less experienced men seemed unnerved. Their officers reassured them; and when everyone in the buses started singing the popular new song "Jerusalem of Gold," the crisis passed. Captain Nitzan says, "You can't imagine what that song meant to us."

After the long roundabout trip, the buses reached Jerusalem through Ein Karem to the west and drove up Herzl Boulevard to the Beit Ha-Kerem section near the Hebrew University. There the men waited, as soldiers always must. Some slept on the sidewalks. Some even telephoned their families. Sergeant Gabai of the scout unit called the secretary of Kibbutz Cabri and jokingly told him they were all the way down to the Dead Sea at Beit Ha'arava, which had been the first home of the kibbutz before the Jordanians seized it in 1948.

Sergeant Yuval Beham, a twenty-seven-year-old member of a special mortar unit attached to the brigade, was one of the few whose home was in Jerusalem. Before the war he worked for the civilian Security Service and knew the city intimately. From Beit Ha-Kerem he called his young wife, Miriam, "Mickey," to check on her and their year-old-son, Allon. And when he called his parents, his father, the acting director of the Israel Museum, immediately drove over; but by the time he reached the university the paratroopers had left. His son was gone.

As the units spread out into the small streets around the religious section of Me'a She'arim, the men sat and talked. One paratrooper remembers, "There was no food. We were

very hungry. Some of the people, when they saw the paratroopers, dared to open their windows and doors and brought
us food. They were poor people and had been under Jordanian
shelling and were quite fearful."

A few members of the brigade, including the handful of
women soldiers, came up to Jerusalem in private cars. When
the brigade was mobilized, it had more than thirty women
reservists. Lieutenant Karni Kav, in charge of the women soldiers, says, "When the brigade was training, the girls had
nothing to do, except for some girls in specific jobs like intelligence, mapping or secretaries to certain officers. All of the
rest of them were just walking around. It called for a lot of
trouble." So Lieutenant Kav convinced Gur to let most of them
go home. The girls were not parachute-qualified. When the
brigade's mission was changed to Jerusalem, the few women
still around had no orders. Lieutenant Kav made her own way
to Jerusalem in a light blue British Ford that belonged to Sergeant Major Jacob "Waxey" Barnea of Major Achmon's intelligence section. He had left his car with the women soldiers
when he expected to jump in the Sinai.

Barnea's Ford was driven to Jerusalem by an administrative
soldier, with Lieutenant Kav, two other women and two male
soldiers. Reaching Jerusalem exhausted, they parked, and Kav
changed seats with the driver to let him stretch out. She fell
asleep; her head hit the horn until a passerby shook her awake.
She had not even heard the noise. A dud shell fell within ten
yards of the car, and they scrambled into the basement shelter
of a nearby house. Kav says, "It was packed with people and
mattresses and babies and old people. It reminded me of the
stories of the Second World War in the British Underground.
There was a lot of noise and tension and fear."

On orders, the men climbed back into the buses. Those who
had come up to Jerusalem in Jeeps and cars left them and
crowded into the buses. It took another two hours to move
from Beit Ha-Kerem to their jump-off points. It was difficult
for the civilian bus drivers to maneuver through the narrow
streets. They did not know the way; a few buses had Jerusalem
Brigade officers aboard to guide them. Half of one battalion
got lost in the maze of city streets and arrived in place only at
the last minute. After a shell landed too near to one of the

Seventy-first Battalion's buses, its frightened driver turned around and headed away from the border. Unfortunately, this bus carried B Company, the battalion's assault company, and the bangalore torpedoes that were supposed to destroy the barbed wire in no-man's-land.

Major Eilam also lacked enough mortar ammunition. To strengthen his own mortars, he had been assigned the mortar platoon from the Twenty-eighth Battalion; but the mortar ammunition had been stowed on the aircraft for the Sinai drop. They had only two hundred rounds with them and that would not last long. Not until ten minutes before the bombardment was scheduled to start did Eilam learn that his men had found another thousand rounds in an armory. With them, his mortarmen knocked out the Jordanian mortar positions in Wadi el Joz.

Once the buses came close to the border, they received Jordanian sniper fire, and the men sought shelter.

At 72 Zefanya Street, the Elitzurs served the headquarters group tea and food. They had stocked their house with provisions and water because they remembered the siege of 1948. Colonel Gur caught a nap for half an hour. The Elitzurs gladly let the soldiers use the telephone to call home. For some it was the last time they talked to their wives and parents.

Later, the Elitzurs heard the rumble of tanks, and Sarah went outside and counted seven tanks followed by about a hundred soldiers in single file. The Jordanians across the Green Line also heard the tanks and started firing in their direction.

Captain Yeshaya tried to slide his tanks down the steep incline of Bar Ilan Street without using their engines, but they made so much noise anyway that Yeshaya ordered the motors turned on. As he says, "We moved to our positions and the war started."

The tanks stood in Pagi near the Green Line pumping shells for more than two hours into the Police Training School and other targets. The Jordanians fired back, mortally wounding one crewman. The battle was joined in the heart of Jerusalem.

After 1:30, Gur's command group decided to move from Zefanya Street, where they could see only one breakthrough point, to a location where they could watch both of the two spots they planned to attack. The headquarters—about fifty

211

men, mostly commanders and communications men—moved to the top of an apartment house in Yoel Street on the edge of the religious neighborhood Me'a She'arim. From there, they had a panoramic view of Ammunition Hill and the Police Training School and Mount Scopus and Wadi el Joz and to the right the Mandelbaum Gate.

While they stood on the roof, two shells hit the building wall and several people were wounded. Major Achmon says, "It was very quiet except for the shelling and the shooting. The people who lived there were all in the basement shelters; I don't believe anyone slept. The units of paratroopers were going through all the streets to their starting points.

"It was a night of darkness and confusion and not knowing exactly what we were supposed to do. We had this feeling *very* much because we fought not according to plans but after the enemy, after the fire. When we met fire, we fought there. It was confusion."

The firing grew so intense that Jordanian Brig. Gen. Hazzáa was convinced that the Israelis were making repeated attempts to break through the line at Shu'afat and in the American Colony sector around St. George's Cathedral and the nearby Tomb of the Kings. The tomb was supposed to be the burial ground of the kings of Judah but was actually the tomb of Queen Helena of Mesopotamia, who converted to Judaism in the first century. Hazzáa sincerely believed that the Israelis were coming and that his men repeatedly repulsed them. In fact, the paratroopers were not quite ready.

In the police headquarters above Brig. Gen. Hazzáa's command post, Governor al-Khatib tried to sleep in one of the beds used by on-duty policemen. But the bed was infested with lice so Hassam al-Khalidi took the governor to the Ritz Hotel and insisted he get some sleep. Al-Khalidi managed to sleep for a couple of hours; the governor could not.

Far to the east beyond the Mount of Olives could be seen the flares dropped by the Israeli Air Force, as its planes stopped the Jordanian tanks and men trying to come up from Jericho to relieve Jerusalem. Al-Khalidi urged Hazzáa to order the reinforcements to leave their vehicles on the bombed roads and make a forced march to the city. But by now, Hazzáa's radio could no longer reach his forward units or the West Bank

Command north of Ramallah and was only in intermittent touch with the police department in Amman.

As the Israeli paratroopers neared their zero hour, Yaffe's Sixty-sixth Battalion prepared to cross no-man's-land and attack the Police Training School and Ammunition Hill. Major Achmon says, "From a military point of view, Ammunition Hill was the strongest and dominating place of the area of the city line that we had to cross. If you hold that ground, you hold the whole area."

Farther south along the line, Eilam's Seventy-first Battalion would cross in the valley of the Bet Israel quarter near the American Colony, charge through Wadi el Joz and move directly to Mount Scopus by the shortest route—through the valley under Ammunition Hill. Fradkin's Twenty-eighth Battalion would follow the Seventy-first through the gap, turn right after the breakthrough and rush to secure the northern side of the Old City. Captain Yeshaya's tanks of the Jerusalem Brigade would support the paratroopers' attack.

— Chapter 14 —

THE BREAKTHROUGH

THE PARATROOPERS' ATTACK WAS NOT SUBTLE. THEY WENT strength against strength—out of plan and mistakes. It was gutsy; it was brave; it was overwhelming; it was successful. Was it necessary?

Why send infantry in haste and without air support against the strong center of the enemy's defenses? Why force a fight at the Jordanian stronghold of Ammunition Hill—like U.S. Marines assaulting Tarawa?

In the south, the Jerusalem Brigade had already thrown back the only Jordanian ground attack—against undefended Government House. In the north, the Harel Brigade's tanks were breaking through the Jordanian line above the city, preparing to pound down on Jerusalem. Was the costly assault through the center essential?

These, of course, are questions one asks after a battle—especially a battle pockmarked by errors. Decisions are made on the spot with little time for discussion and none for second-guessing. They are made by flesh-and-blood men moved by complex judgments and emotions—esprit, ambition, glory, guilt, fear, courage. To apply hindsight to their decisions is not the point. To tell their story is. This is what happened.

The paratroopers of the Seventy-first Battalion attacked the Green Line eight hundred yards south of where the Sixty-sixth Battalion assaulted no-man's land in front in the Police Training School. Major Uzi Eilam, commanding the Seventy-first, was a bright, thirty-three-year-old Technion-graduate engineer who the year before had returned from a Ford Foundation fellowship at Stanford University. Born of Russian-immigrant parents on Kibbutz Tel Yosef south of Nazareth, he had had a heart murmur and had to struggle to join the paratroopers. Since then he

214

had made 150 jumps and fought in the Sinai campaign. Now in civilian life he was the production manager of an appliance manufacturing company. A veteran combat officer who had been wounded in action, he had been given command of the battalion just six months before the war.

Eilam was the only one of Gur's commanders who knew Jerusalem well. He had lived there for two years while his wife, Naomi, studied medicine; and for two months in the winter of 1957 he had been a company commander along the Green Line in the city. As deputy commander of the paratrooper scouts he had studied the border. On an old archaeological map, he was shown an ancient water tunnel that ran from near the Histadrut Building in Israeli Jerusalem to the area of the Rockefeller Museum in Jordanian Jerusalem. He and two other officers, disguised as telephone workers, crawled through the tunnel and found that it was still passable.

Only he and his deputy battalion commander, Major Dan Ziv, were veterans. The rest of his 500-man battalion were young and new to war. But they were a select group; 80 percent of the battalion had had higher education.

Opposite the paratroopers, on the Jordanian side of the Green Line from Ammunition Hill south to the Old City, stood the Bedouin soldiers of the Second Infantry Battalion of the King Talal Brigade. Major Achmon says, "They were really good fighters. They fought like hell. They fought till they died."

Where the paratroopers of Major Eilam's Seventy-first Battalion attacked, the Jordanian main line was dug in along a low stone wall in front of Nablus Road which paralleled the border. The Jordanians had strongpoints hidden in buildings in front of the wall. No-man's-land between Shmu'el Hanavi Street and Nablus Road was planted with mines and obstacles. If the space had been empty, a man could have walked across it in a couple of minutes; but as a fortified border from Ammunition Hill on the left to the Mandelbaum Gate on the right, it made a fearful crossing.

Behind the wall, the First Battery of the Jordanian Ninth Field Artillery Regiment had its observation post under Lieutenant Kaman Jaradat. The battery's commander, Captain Shawkat Jawdat, had occupied this very OP himself ten years earlier and knew the scene intimately. Lieutenant Jaradat called in his battery's fire as the paratroopers attacked.

The city was pitch dark. The only light was from burning buildings. Everything was quiet except for the shelling. Even before the attack, paratroopers were being hit. Siema Hazan, the twenty-five-year-old professional ambulance driver, received a radio call that a soldier was badly wounded in a bunker on the line. Her white ambulance was shot at; she pulled off her white gown under heavy fire and crawled to the bunker. With her flashlight she located the unconscious, bleeding soldier. He seemed dead but she would not decide that. Another soldier helped her put him on a stretcher and carry him to the ambulance. By the time she brought him to Sha'are Zedek Hospital, he had died.

At exactly 2 A.M., huge searchlights, which the paratroopers had brought with them and installed on top of the Histadrut Building, were turned on. The night sky filled with light beamed at Jordanian Jerusalem. The Jordanian buildings behind Nablus Road were illuminated. No-man's-land, in a dip in the topography, lay in darkness. At the same time, special small trucks with Swiss S-11 wire-guided rockets and half-ton charges of TNT let go a single volley against the Jordanian line. This had been a secret weapon until then. Mortars, machine guns and bazookas started firing.

The Jordanians returned fire immediately; but their aim was high, at the buildings on the Israeli side and at the blinding searchlights. The Twenty-eighth Battalion, waiting back among the Pagi buildings, was heavily shelled and took casualties.

At the border, two Israeli tanks and three Jeeps with recoilless rifles suppressed the Jordanian machine guns. Major Moshe Stempel, Gur's deputy, started cutting the wire, opening the way to no-man's-land. At the final moment, the missing bus showed up and ten bangalore units advanced, one after the other, to clear successive sections of no-man's-land. At 2:15, the paratroopers of the Seventy-first Battalion swiftly opened a narrow path. The bangalore torpedoes destroyed the barbed wire and blew up mines.

B Company led the way across, with A and D in its wake. C Company was charged with clearing no-man's-land and B Company, the area in Nablus Road at the Jordanian end of the breakthrough point. A and D companies would pass B Company and strike deep into East Jerusalem.

One B Company platoon attacked the largest building in

this part of no-man's-land. The platoon commander threw a grenade that caught in an iron window grill. The grenade burst in his face. The rest of the platoon took the building, which was later used for the paratroop wounded. Under converging fire from three sides, B Company crossed no-man's-land to a small grove of olive trees and found the break in the stone wall shielding Nablus Road.

With the Israelis overrunning his forward observation post, Lieutenant Kaman Jaradat called for artillery fire on his own position. His vehicle was destroyed and he and his men were wounded. All of the Jordanian Ninth Field Artillery Regiment's eighteen guns fired ninety shells at his position. Jaradat and his small unit—Privates Mohammad Shafiq, Fayez Ahmed and Ali Mazari—were not heard from again. Later, there were mystical rumors among the Jordanian soldiers that the heroic Jaradat had been seen on the West Bank, but Captain Jawdat of the First Battery knew that Jaradat had not survived the bombardment.

The Seventy-first Battalion was on Nablus Road; Major Eilam radioed his progress to Gur. Gur shouted back over the radio, "You deserve a kiss!"

As his men attacked, Eilam moved up with B Company and then went back to help C Company and bring on the recoilless-rifle Jeeps, half-tracks and tanks that were having trouble maneuvering through the narrow breakthrough gap. Only one of his three Jerusalem Brigade tanks made it across. Then, Eilam rushed forward with his command group and set up a CP in a house in the American Colony section. A and D companies positioned machine guns on a small rise across Nablus Road from the border and pushed rapidly eastward through the American Colony.

The American Colony had been founded by a fundamentalist Protestant group from Chicago led by Horatio and Anna Spafford. Horatio Spafford was a lawyer greatly influenced by the evangelist Dwight L. Moody. In 1873, Anna Spafford and her four daughters were sailing across the Atlantic when their ship was struck by another vessel. All four daughters were drowned. Mrs. Spafford was saved but inconsolable, and in 1881 the Spaffords and their followers came to Jerusalem to start a new life. Joined in time by 115 Swedes from Chicago and Sweden, they founded a charitable nursing mission and, eventually, the Anna Spafford Nursing Home and the American Colony Hotel. The Spaffords' doors were open to all races and creeds. By 1967, the American Colony Hotel, in a charming former Turkish villa on the east side of Nablus Road, was directed by their widowed daughter, Mrs. Bertha Vester, and her oldest son, Horatio, a graduate of Columbia University.

While the paratroopers were attacking just to the north, the small group of UN officers in the MAC house tried to protect themselves. They were in no-man's-land between the two armies. Lt. Col. Stanaway notified both sides that he would keep on the lights in the MAC house; he figured this way the combatants might avoid hitting the building. About midnight, the electricity went out and the MAC house switched over to its own generator.

As the shelling increased, the MAC officers moved down from their second floor offices, where they had placed mattresses under the tables, to the crowded basement. Mortar and artillery rounds were trying to knock out their generator. The brightly lit building was threatening the safety of the paratroopers crossing no-man's-land in the dark. The gunners never found the generator, and Stanaway kept on his lights.

UN officers crawled upstairs several times to make radio contact with General Bull's radio vehicle in Israeli Jerusalem and to bring down the beer from their refrigerator. With daylight, some of the UN officers climbed to an unused room on the top floor and watched the paratroopers spread out through the northern sections of Jordanian Jerusalem.

Farther to the east on the top of Mount Scopus, the Israeli garrison watched every movement of the paratroopers' breakthrough, which was intended for its rescue. Major Sharfman in the Magnes tower followed the flash of weapons. The men at the radio listened to the paratroopers' orders and message traffic. Remembering the excitement of those hours, Sharfman says, "The war was a tremendous feeling. It is how Josephus Flavius describes the war as the soldiers going to their mistresses rather than the enemy."

Watching the paratroopers' assault, Sharfman realized the Jordanians had missed their opportunity to attempt to take Mount

Scopus. They had not attacked and the Israeli Air Force had forced away their armor. Now, it was too late.

Throughout the night, Sharfman was in constant touch with Ben-Ari and his Harel Brigade. Through his binoculars he watched the tank attack on the distant Nebi Samuel ridge and repeatedly talked personally with Ben-Ari. Ben-Ari, using the Mount Scopus calling code, "Menachem," radioed Sharfman to ask what was happening on the far side of French Hill, which Ben-Ari could not see from the Castel and Sharfman could see clearly. In contrast, Sharfman was never able to talk even once directly to Gur throughout the battle. All Sharfman will say is, "In this war Ben-Ari excelled himself."

When the paratroopers' Seventy-first Battalion reached Nablus Road, it had only three men killed and a few wounded. Surprise and the effective night attack had worked. Most of the casualties the Seventy-first and Twenty-eighth Battalions would suffer occurred after sunrise because the artillery and Air Force had not destroyed the Jordanian strongpoints along Nablus Road and in the areas behind it. At daybreak, the Seventy-first Battalion's A and D companies were advancing with B Company trailing them and C Company struggling to wipe out the defenders around the Green Line with the help of E Company's recoilless rifle and demolition platoon. C Company's commander, Uzi Eilat, was wounded.

The paratroopers in the lead followed a road through the American Colony sector above and parallel to the steep, roughly terraced, barren valley of Wadi el Joz just to the north. They moved in two columns on each side of the street, dashing from building to building and cover to cover. The Jordanians fired on them from the rise of Sheikh Jarrah north of Wadi el Joz. At one corner the paratroopers left three men with a machine gun to cover their advance.

A Jordanian vehicle loaded with ammunition sped out of a side street. The driver suddenly saw the Israelis and tried to escape. Paratroopers chased the car, firing; and it went up in a fireworks of exploding shells.

Suddenly, the paratroopers in the rear and at the machine-gun strongpoint, thinking the soldiers attacking the car were Jordanians, started to shoot at them. They fired back at their own men. One man in A Company was mortally wounded in the paratroopers-against-paratroopers fire fight before the commander of D Company could block the fight with his own body and shout, "Stop firing! Stop firing!"

After setting up a first-aid station for the wounded, they plunged forward on the road above the valley without serious resistance. They established a strongpoint in a corner house and ambushed Jordanian soldiers trying to flee the battle.

The mission of Captain Zamush's A Company was to capture low-lying Wadi el Joz and the heights south of it. A Company's men were to force open a route to Mount Scopus, which rose ahead of them on their left at the end of the wadi. They took house after house. One of Zamush's platoon leaders was wounded. Then, D-Company, commanded by Captain Moshe "Mussa" Gilboa, moved ahead. Zamush and his men went down into Wadi el Joz and advanced parallel to the road. There, they met fierce Jordanian fire and hard fighting. Men from B Company came up to help. By 8 A.M., they had cleared the way nearly to the rear or north side of the Rockefeller Museum and to the road leading to Mount Scopus.

The Jordanian soldiers behind Nablus Road in the Sheikh Jarrah quarter, named for the surgeon in Saladin's army, were soon caught between paratroopers at their front and the others who swept around and attacked them from the rear. They came on so fast that Brig. Gen. Hazzáa, in his underground command post, was convinced that they had leapt over his lines by helicopter.* Captain Jawdat of the First Battery says, "The paratroop attack was disastrous for our company as a whole in Sheikh Jarrah."

The paratroopers of D and A companies of the Seventy-first Battalion stayed on the heights and in Wadi el Joz the entire day. They were posted on the roofs of the Arab villas above the fire station and above the road to Augusta Victoria. Several Jordanian Jeeps speeding down the road were fired on and were destroyed near the produce market at the bottom of the hill.

A paratroop sergeant, a survivor of the concentration camps,

---

*Although Trevor N. Dupuy in his book *Elusive Victory*[1] states as fact that the paratroopers used helicopters, Major Achmon, the brigade intelligence officer, says it is "absolute nonsense."

and two of his buddies decided suddenly in the midst of battle that they needed a shower to cleanse them of the caked dirt and blood. They approached an Arab house; a couple and a child came to the door. The Arabs were obviously deeply frightened. But the Israelis only wanted to know where they could take a shower. The family trembled so in terror that through the sergeant's mind flashed the scene of when the Nazis came to the home of his father, a banker, and shot his family. He, then a child, was hiding behind a curtain, trembling like these people. The sergeant saw a curtain in the house behind the Arab family move. He thought it was a Jordanian soldier and he prepared to fire. Just before he did, another child stepped out from behind the curtain. Then, he said later, he understood what happens to someone who is conquered—and one who conquers.

— Chapter 15 —

"THE FIGHTING ROAD"

Lt. col. "yossi" fradkin's twenty-eighth battalion followed Eilam's Seventy-first Battalion across no-man's-land,
swung right and headed for the Rockefeller Museum just outside
the Old City wall. The Twenty-eighth, proud that it was the
Israeli army's oldest reserve paratroop battalion, was chosen
to stand ready to take the Old City if the order should come.

The man who led the Twenty-eighth was a modest thirty-
nine-year-old farmer, open faced, with the thin blue eyes of
a man who worked in the sun, dirt under his nails and a
practical, straight-ahead mind. He left his wife, Hannah, and
their three young sons at their small *moshav,* a farming village
called Tel Adashim (Hill of Lentils), where he had a nursery
of fruit trees. He had fought in the War of Independence and
with the paratroopers in the Sinai in 1956. He had commanded
the Twenty-eighth for three years and was Gur's senior battalion commander.

Fradkin hardly knew Israeli Jerusalem and the Arab section
not at all. He was given no aerial photographs, no coordinates.
The information gap between Narkiss' Central Command and
Gur's brigade was almost total and would prove deadly.

But Fradkin's orders were clear: Follow the Seventy-first
Battalion across the Green Line, take Nablus Road to the right
and branch off onto Salah ed Din Street toward the Rockefeller
Museum. As the battalion assembled in Shemu'el Hanavi Street,
the area was full of smoke and dust and the wounded of the
Seventy-first; the battle was already under way.

Waiting there, exposed, the Twenty-eighth was smashed by
twenty Jordanian 81-mm mortar shells. They hit every officer
in Fradkin's command group, except him and one other officer.
D Company, concentrated in the back of the street, was badly
mauled. The medical unit and the battalion surgeon, Dr. Eli

Raz, were struck down. Corpsman Shlomo Epstein, a native of Jerusalem, was dressing a man's wound when a mortar round came in. Epstein threw himself over the wounded man and was killed. In all, thirty-five men were killed or wounded before the battalion could even start. For the moment, the Twenty-eighth was shattered. Fradkin quickly reorganized and reported to Gur atop the house in Yoel Street. Then it was time to move; crossing no-man's-land, only one paratrooper in the Twenty-eighth was hit.

A Company, which considered itself the oldest and best in the brigade, had the point. Led by Captain Yossi Avidan, a kibbutznik from Ein Harod in the north, the men hurried through the break in the wall into Nablus Road. By the time they reached the gas station on the right side of the road, they began to take fire. It was now becoming light as night turned into day.

The battalion quickly ran into trouble. The road climbed steeply from the gas station. Two of A Company's platoons advanced on the right side of the road and one on the left. The houses along the road had been turned into Jordanian strongholds. Small units fought hand-to-hand in the street. The Jordanians jumped from their concrete bunkers to the road and fought the Israelis there. Major Achmon says, "They were excellent soldiers, excellent soldiers."

The fighting in Nablus Road was fierce. Achmon says, "We fought the enemy where they were. They were in the windows of the buildings and on the walls. We didn't know exactly. The fighting was very scattered, not even in squads. Everyone was fighting for his life."

One paratrooper took a bullet in his forehead; several more were wounded. Two hurled grenades into a house opposite the American Colony Hotel. The Jordanian firing positions faced no-man's-land and the Israelis attacked them from the rear. The Jordanians shot the advancing troops and then were wiped out. Daniel Artom, Captain Avidan's communications sergeant, says, "The Jordanians had many Bedouin soldiers. They didn't run. They stayed and they fought. They fought very bravely, very well. Between forty and fifty Jordanians were killed here."

The Israelis fought past the home of Anwar Nuseibeh, who had been the Jordanian ambassador to the Court of St. James's.

223

They crashed into his house, killed a Jordanian soldier in the street in front and another in the rear garden where a bunker faced no-man's-land. (Later, the Nuseibehs had the unknown soldier buried in their garden.)

Across the road, the Nuseibehs were in bed listening to the battle "getting nearer, nearer, nearer." Saqr, who was six, and the Egyptian consul general's wife were frightened. The war threatened to come right into the house. Israeli soldiers entered, weapons at the ready, looking for resistance. There was none. They checked out the house and then left. The Nuseibehs listened to the battle move past them up Nablus Road. Says Anwar Nuseibeh, "The soldiers who came through the first day were extremely well behaved. The best people either die or go to fight another war."

In front of Nuseibeh's house, the Twenty-eighth Battalion was supposed to veer to the left into Salah ed Din Street, the main street of Arab Jerusalem, where it forked off from Nablus Road. This would lead the paratroopers away from the concentration of Jordanian troops dug in on the Green Line and steer the Israelis directly to Herod's Gate and the Rockefeller Museum. But here Lt. Col. Fradkin and Captain Avidan, who had taken over A Company from Major Achmon only a few months earlier, made a disastrous error. They missed the intersection and charged straight ahead up Nablus Road along the fortified border where the Jordanians had massed their strength.

One A Company platoon leader recognized the mistake and started to direct his men into Salah ed Din Street. A Jeep filled with Jordanian soldiers and armed with a recoilless rifle came roaring down on them and killed one of the paratroopers. They knocked out the Jeep, and the platoon leader decided he had better stay with the main body in Nablus Road—mistake or not.

Lt. Col. Fradkin says they overlooked the fork in the road because his men "were pulled toward the fighting." In the plan he had been given, he was not told that the Jordanian soldiers were concentrated in Nablus Road and that it was fortified. He only recognized that this was "the fighting road." They could not leave it; they were drawn by the firing. That is where the battle was.

Suddenly, the paratroopers of A Company heard tanks approaching and took cover in the buildings along Nablus Road. When they saw the tanks were old Shermans, they knew they had to be Israeli.

They were Captain Yeshaya's. He had taken seven of his tanks across no-man's-land with Yaffe's Sixty-sixth Battalion at the Police Training School. Following the engineers' white tapes, the tanks passed through the minefield, exploding antipersonnel mines; knocked down a fence at the school, and moved east into the Sheikh Jarrah section. There, they waited a long time. As it became light at about 5 A.M. someone came shouting that there was a big fight on Ammunition Hill and asked for two tanks to come and help. Yeshaya sent the last two tanks in line to help the paratroopers there. He was rejoined by the three tanks that had crossed with the Seventy-first Battalion. They destroyed a pillbox in front of the Mount Scopus Hotel, and then Gur ordered them to move toward the Damascus Gate of the Old City.

In Nablus Road, they found the paratroopers of the Twenty-eighth Battalion heavily engaged and with many wounded. Past Nuseibeh's house, four tanks took the lead; and the paratroopers continued the attack down the street. As they moved forward against heavy fire, two men of A Company were killed and five wounded. The tank commanders had to fight with their bodies exposed in their turrets because the paratroopers were not trained to fight with tanks or to use the telephone outside each tank to communicate with the crew inside. Almost all of Yeshaya's tank commanders were wounded.

At the Mandelbaum Gate just west of Nablus Road, Lieutenant Ghazi Rababa suddenly heard tanks *behind* his Jordanian position. For a couple of hours, he had listened to heavy firing in the Sheikh Jarrah section to his right. All the action seemed to explode there. It had been quiet around the gate, but the huge Israeli searchlights lit up the area and blinded the Jordanians.

Now, hearing tanks behind him, Rababa sent Corporal Salim Dhabaan with four soldiers and two bazookas to attack them. The paratroopers killed the four bazookamen and wounded the corporal in the neck.

Lieutenant Rababa received a last telephone call from Captain Nabil Suheimat, his company commander. The captain

225

called, "Ghazi! Ghazi!" And then the line went dead. Rababa figured Suheimat's command post had been overrun. He now had no communications and no orders, and he was surrounded by the Israelis. At about 6 A.M., he told Cadet Melkawi to pull back his men from the gate and join him.

Lieutenant Rababa saw Israeli soldiers in the street. He took 1st Lt. Haikel al-Zaban, the commander of his reservists, and a corporal and tried to find a way out. "Suddenly, a tank which was concealed shot at us with its main gun," Rababa remembers. "The shell went just over our heads. After that we were no longer nervous. Life began to mean nothing. We did not hurry. We went with cold blood.

"Our problem was we had no defense to the east. All our positions were to the west. So it was very difficult. The morale of my soldiers began to go down more and more. We realized that we would die—but not in a good battle, because we didn't have a chance to do battle. It was a moment of death."

They had to get out of there. About fifty yards away was the United Nations MAC building. Outside was parked a white UN car. Says Rababa, "I concluded that if we go to that building we will be secure because the Israelis cannot attack a position of the United Nations. I told my soldiers to cross the street quickly in groups of five to that building. We all reached it with no casualties under fire. I tried to break in the door but it was iron. I heard them speaking inside; I called to them but nobody replied."

Lt. Col. Stanaway, the chairman of the MAC, and his party were in the basement. The building had once been an orphanage and next door was the home of its former Armenian director.

Rababa says, "I kicked in the wooden door of the building next door. It must have been a residence. There were three rooms; they were empty. I let all my soldiers go in." Unknown to Rababa, the family that lived in the building had been taken into the basement of the MAC building by Stanaway.

"At about 9 A.M., 1st Lt. al-Zaban went to find a way to withdraw. He told the corporal to cross the street; if there was no shooting, we could join our unit. When the corporal crossed the street, there was no shooting. But when 1st Lt. al-Zaban tried to cross, he was shot and killed.

"Israeli soldiers were surrounding the building. We saw them from the window. They were trying to clear the trench of the unit to our right. There were no curtains on the window, so we put the dresses of the lady who had been living in the house over the window. There were no communications and our soldiers were very tired, so I decided to wait until night.

"A strange thing happened with me and my soldiers. All of us thought we should sleep. I could not find one of my soldiers who could keep his eyes open. I tried to keep my eyes open; I felt responsible. But we were all exhausted. If any Israeli had entered he could have killed us all." Later, they put women's dresses over their uniforms and escaped.

While Lieutenant Rababa was trying to save his men, the Israeli paratroopers of A Company, Twenty-eighth Battalion, were fighting their way past the Anglican Cathedral of St. George and St. George's Close. Sergeant Daniel Artom, the twenty-seven-year-old kibbutznik and radio man, led a few soldiers into the schoolyard on the right side of Nablus Road. They met two Jordanian soldiers. Says Artom, "We were quicker and we killed them."

As the paratroopers felt their way forward, four or five more were wounded. The men in the van were followed by the tanks. Lt. Col. Fradkin was advancing with the lead company.

They started taking heavy fire from the YMCA building on the right side of the road. Jordanians were spotted on the roof and in the top floors. The paratroopers raced past the building, firing and taking fire from both sides, from the YMCA on their right and from the vicinity of the Jordanian governor's office farther off on their left. Two men were hit. Yeshaya's tanks fired at the YMCA's windows, and the Jordanian fire from that side stopped. Paratroopers from C Company, which was following A Company, went in and cleared the YMCA building and destroyed a Jordanian machine gun. Two more paratroopers were killed in front of the YMCA.

The commander of one Israeli tank, Sergeant Menachem Nietsan, a native of Jerusalem and a Ph.D. in biochemistry at Hebrew University, was killed by a machine-gun bullet in his head. He was the second Jerusalem Brigade tanker killed in the battle—the other, the loader in Sergeant Kantor's tank. All told, seventeen of Kamara's tankers were wounded. In a long-range fire fight with Jordanian Patton tanks, one Israeli tank at Government House was destroyed and five soldiers severely burned. Later, Prime Minister Eshkol visited the wounded in the hospital and asked if these five men were Arabs; they were unrecognizable.

By 6 A.M., the Twenty-eighth Battalion's A Company was in front of the American Consulate, where Nablus Road and Shemu'el Hanavi Street form a V. The fighting intensified. Sergeant Artom says, "We were fired on from the American Consulate. Somehow, the roof and yard were in Jordanian hands. Two more of our men were killed here and two wounded when they and a tank tried to penetrate into the consulate." Captain Yeshaya also insists Jordanian soldiers were firing from the consulate roof and yard.

There were no Jordanian soldiers in the American Consulate. Huddled in the first-floor rooms were twelve unarmed civilians. The consulate did not even have a Marine Security Guard since the Jordanians had banned the U.S. Marines in 1956. The ban followed a series of riots on December 20, 1955, and on January 7, when a stone-throwing mob of three hundred was repulsed by U.S. Marines with small arms and tear gas.

The thick-walled consulate building was under fire most of Monday and was hit by its first shell around 2:30 A.M. Tuesday. Consul Hall and those in his charge fled into the windowless downstairs kitchen, and Mrs. Hall picked slivers of broken window glass out of her hair. They spent the rest of the dark hours in the tiny, stifling kitchen, waiting for the next shell.

When it grew light, they shared some instant coffee; and Mrs. Hall went upstairs to search for Teddy and Daisy, the Halls' mother-and-daughter cats, the only occupants on the second floor. They had survived but the apartment was a shambles. The windows were blown out, the remaining steel shutters were pierced by bullet holes and shrapnel had riddled the walls and every one of Mac Hall's suits.

As the paratroopers' A Company, Twenty-eighth Battalion, approached down Nablus Road, the war got exciting enough even for old Mr. Amasa Holcombe. Fourteen Israeli tank shells hit the building. Hall had a large American flag flying, but it did not dissuade the Israelis in the heat of battle. Even Mrs. Hall's laundry hanging in the garden was shot away. Hall felt utter frustration: "We couldn't shoot back. They were firing at us and we had nothing to shoot back with. They shot up our house and would have killed us for no reason. We had the biggest American flag flying we could find. There was no excuse."

When the Israelis wanted to search the consulate, Hall stopped them and Mrs. Hall angrily ordered them to get out. Hall and Richard Ross went outside and prevented them from commandeering the consulate's cars. Hall escorted an Israeli captain and one of his men through the building and convinced them that there were no Jordanians and no machine-gun positions in the building. The Israelis were shocked at the damage to the second-floor living quarters.

Fortunately, although the building was badly damaged, none of its occupants was killed or wounded. Hall says, "It was a miracle. Twelve people in the building and nobody was even scratched. There were bodies of Jordanian and Israeli soldiers in the garden and in the streets outside."

That evening, Consul General Wilson called Hall over their unofficial intercom radio system and asked how everyone was. Hiding his exhaustion, Hall lightly said they were just sitting down to a candlelight dinner (there was no electricity) and could not decide whether to have red or white wine. Hall added later, "We had red, I think."

After A Company fought its way past the consulate, Sergeant Artom says, "We reached the junction and it was quite dangerous to cross it because there was no cover. The other road (Shemu'el Hanavi) led back to the Mandelbaum Gate. The firing was coming from the mosque in front, from the buildings and from the Mandelbaum area." One paratrooper dashed out down toward the Mandelbaum Gate and killed several Jordanians and captured five.

A Company fought through the open square in front of the American Consulate under heavy fire. Some of the men went into the mosque on the far side of the plaza. Others dashed across the square and took possession of the court of the Dominican Church and Monastery of St. Stephen, which was fronted by a high wall. Inside in a basement they found about thirty civilians. Captain Avidan and Sergeant Artom stood outside in a sheltered corner of the wall, from where Avidan directed his men's advance.

In the open square near the mosque, the paratroopers gathered their wounded. Captain Yeshaya in the turret of the lead tank saw that the wounded were being fired on from a concrete pillbox guarding the border. Firing his cannon directly over the wounded, he exploded the pillbox.

The paratroopers, on foot and vulnerable, hugged the line of tanks. With two tanks still on Ammunition Hill and Nietsan's tank out of action while its crew took away their dead commander, Yeshaya now had seven Shermans.

Ahead on the right side of Nablus Road, opposite the wall where Captain Avidan stood, was a hidden alley called Chaldean Street. Down the narrow alley, a hundred yards from Nablus Road and fifty yards from the border, the Jordanians had a strongpoint, part of their main line, with a bazooka and a machine gun facing no-man's-land.

As the Israelis approached, the Jordanians swung around. They killed the first paratrooper to try to cross the alley's mouth. The deputy company commander, Lieutenant Mordechai "Mordi" Friedman, a twenty-nine-year-old Sabra and father of two, jumped into the middle of the road, fired his weapon down the alley and carried back the dead sergeant. Two more paratroopers tried to cross and were shot dead. Another pair raced across and were also hit. Firing again, Friedman dragged a wounded private out of the line of fire. He called up Yeshaya's tank; and when it arrived, Friedman stood at the corner of the building and tried to throw a grenade. He was shot in the chest. As he sank slowly to his knees, the grenade in his hand exploded, killing him.

The advance stalled here for nearly twenty minutes. A paratrooper climbed a building and threw grenades without success. Yeshaya's tank was in position in front of the alley. He saw the paratroopers killed. He had a shell ready in his cannon; but before he could fire, the Jordanians shot an antitank rifle grenade, which bounced off the front of his tank and fell harmlessly in the street—a dud. Yeshaya fired one shell and saw three Jordanians at the end of the alley explode. They had stood and fought, Yeshaya thought; they were good soldiers.

The strongpoint was wiped out. The site of the bloody ambush became known as Death Alley.

Now, more than a half of A Company of the Twenty-eighth Battalion were casualties. The company was finished. The men made the St. George Hotel into a hospital for their wounded. C Company, commanded by Captain Alex Klein from Kibbutz Giv'at Haim, took over the point.

The Jordanians were firing at the Israelis from behind a fence near the street. Yeshaya could not spot the source of the fire, but the next tank crushed the Jordanian position.

The street bent slightly, and the tankers were now in full view of the Old City wall and the Damascus Gate. Yeshaya tried to back the rear of his tank into the courtyard of the Schmidt Girls School and out of the line of fire. He turned his gun to the left and fired at the top of the Old City wall. The tank commander now behind him saw that the Jordanians had a bazooka in a firing hole in the wall and with one perfect shot destroyed the bazooka.

The Jordanians were acting like the defenders of an ancient walled city—against modern armor. Yeshaya called up the second tank to a position parallel to him. The two tanks fired intensively at the wall. The commander of the second tank, Sergeant Eli Shlayin, took a machine-gun bullet through his arm and hand and fell back into his tank. Yeshaya was slightly wounded in the neck, back and hands. He continued to fire at the wall until he was fifty yards from it.

All the tanks took positions and fired at the wall. Although Yeshaya was not trained to fight in a built-up area, he stayed in his open, exposed turret. He did not know what Gur wanted him to do next; they stood and fought there while Yeshaya tried futilely to reach Gur on the radio. Yeshaya saw the C Company paratroopers take over the Schmidt Girls School, but they were not following his tanks into the open area before the Damascus Gate. He felt uneasy without infantry to help protect his tanks but knew that infantrymen would have been shot down by the defenders behind the wall.

Yeshaya stood exposed to Jordanian fire for more than an hour. "Just waiting—for nothing!" he says angrily. The tanks, firing at the gate and wall, began to run low on ammunition. Finally, Gur came on the radio and let Yeshaya take his tanks back to the Police Training School to refuel and rearm.

Meanwhile, the paratroopers' C Company and Lt. Col. Fradkin fought through the buildings and yards of St. Stephen's to avoid the Jordanians concentrated on the Old City wall near

231

the Damascus Gate. One unit zigzagged through an Arab cemetery and in heavy fighting advanced to the Rivoli Hotel on the west side of Salah ed Din Street in clear sight of Herod's Gate.

The fight for control of the hotel chewed up Salah ed Din Street, the main business street of Jordanian Jerusalem. All the shops were closed tight and their owners had fled the battle zone. Across from the Rivoli Hotel, the Universal Library, a superior bookstore owned by Hanna Sirhad, a Lutheran Arab who had been born in the Old City half a century before, was destroyed. The black marble front, the cases inside and hundreds of books were wrecked. Sirhad, a gentle and wise man, had stayed home in Beit Hanina. He says, "I hate wars. I studied theology and I don't think people who read theology love wars. We believe everybody must live together with his brother whether he is a Jew or Muslim or Christian. We are all humans. We must love each other." But this day his warm feeling of brotherhood had to give way to the cold steel of war.

It was eleven o'clock when Fradkin and Gur finally met at the Rockefeller Museum. Gur assumed that the Twenty-eighth Battalion had come down Salah ed Din Street according to plan and told Fradkin now to go back and fight his way down Nablus Road. Fradkin simply said, "We did it already."

It was an epitomic moment of this battle. Fradkin had gone into the fight not knowing what to expect, and Gur did not know where his men were fighting or had fought. The result was a battle plan botched and many men killed unnecessarily. Says Fradkin, "That's what happens in war."

By now the streets of Israeli Jerusalem were filled with vehicles rushing the wounded to the city's hospitals. At 5 A.M., Lieutenant Karni Kav had emerged from the basement shelter to breathe the fresh air of Jerusalem. At that moment, the Fifty-fifth Brigade's administrative officer, covered with the smoke and burns of battle, drove by in a Jeep. He mustered Kav and her tiny group to go to the hospitals and organize lists of brigade members who were dead and wounded so the commanders would have some count. Kav sent one woman soldier to Hadassah, the other to Biqqur Holim, and she raced off to Sha'are Zedek. She passed cars and station wagons filled with wounded, a horrible sight to the young Sabra who had never seen war before. She says, "I felt like everybody was a brother of mine."

At the hospital, she spotted men of the brigade by their red paratrooper's boots. She went through the pockets of the unconscious and the dead to identify them. Few men wore their identification discs. She was half interrogator, half nurse, helping the men in pain and thirst. The wounded lay very quietly. She found men she knew. "There were some bad sights—boys with just a hole in their foreheads. Hit by snipers. I lined myself with iron so these things would not get to me. Otherwise, I would not be able to do the job. With the first guy I knew, I would probably have collapsed."

She checked the other hospitals and at Hadassah found her good friend, First Sergeant Natan Malinov, a combat veteran and member of the brigade's intelligence unit. On the evening before the war started, he had asked her for a good luck charm and she had given him a ring. He wore it around his neck. Before the breakthrough began, someone in his unit left their maps in a vehicle on Zefanya Street. Sergeant Malinov went back for them. Near Gur's command post in Yoel Street, he was hit by a tiny piece of shrapnel from a Jordanian shell—probably the first paratrooper casualty of the war in Jerusalem. The sliver struck him in the chest, pierced his lung but narrowly missed the heart, diverted by something he wore. At Hadassah, the doctor who operated on him told Karni Kav that her ring had probably saved Malinov's life.

— Chapter 16 —

THE ANGEL

As the paratroopers' attack gained momentum, two soldiers appeared at the station of the Magen David Adom, the civilian emergency corps like the Red Cross. They needed ambulances. A tiny woman, sitting outside the station, jumped into her ambulance—the driver's seat had an extra cushion because she was so small. She drove the two soldiers to the brigade's first-aid station in a yeshiva in Shemu'el Hanavi Street near the Green Line. The station had been struck by Jordanian shells and the wounded lying on stretchers were hit again. Several corpsmen were also wounded.

The woman went to work giving the wounded morphine and plasma and extinguishing fires. Suddenly, Dr. Jacob "Jackie" King, the brigade doctor, spotted her, shouted at her that this wasn't a woman's place and told her to go back. While she answered him she kept working. She says, "I had a private war between Dr. King and myself." Finally, Dr. King agreed to let her stay but told her to put on a helmet. A mortally wounded soldier gave her his helmet, saying he did not need it anymore. The helmet, much too large for her, covered half her face.

This little woman was an exceptional character with a dramatic history. When Esther Arditi was five, the Germans had come to Florence, Italy, where she had been born; and her parents fled with her and her three brothers to the mountains. Her father and two brothers, who were considerably older than she, joined the partisans. Her mother hid on a farm with her and her two-and-a-half-year-old brother. In the village down the mountain from the farm was an SS headquarters, and the Germans learned that someone in the area was listening to the

234

BBC. A Fascist in the village told the SS that Jews were hidden on the farm and maybe they were listening to the BBC.

When the Germans came, the farmer, as they had planned, put the three Jews in the big oven used for baking bread and closed the iron door. It was dark but warm and the smell was delicious. Her mother held the baby in one arm and hugged the girl. They were very quiet. The little girl heard the German boots. A man's hand reached into the oven and grabbed the mother's sleeve. The Germans pulled them out and asked her mother who was listening to the BBC; she said she didn't know. The German officer asked her where her husband was; she said she didn't know. The officer grabbed the baby from her arms and threw it up into the air. The baby laughed. While the little boy was still in the air, the officer shot him. The mother grabbed the officer's shirt and shouted "Murderer!" He shot the mother too. As she was dying, her mother shouted to Esther to run. The entire scene took only seconds. The little girl ran into the woods.

She lived in the forest alone; she found a white sheep and befriended it and drank its milk to stay alive. The sheep kept her warm at night. She hid in a little cave in the day and went out at night and found food for the sheep.

One day she heard a shot outside her cave and ran out and saw her white sheep was dead. She lay over it crying. Suddenly, two bearded men appeared. They had been looking for food and killed the sheep to eat it. One of the men was her older brother. He took her to the partisans who put her in a convent for the rest of the war.

After the war, her father returned from Auschwitz with a number tattooed on his arm. A brother also survived. In 1948, she says, "I heard there was a state of Jews where you did not have to hide and where they even fought back. I decided to go there."

Her father was furious. Count Folke Bernadotte, the United Nations mediator, had just been assassinated in Jerusalem. "Jews can be murderers too," her father said. He would not let her go. She saved coins in a piggy bank and in 1949 left a note telling her father she was going to Israel. She was eleven. She took the train to Naples where she had heard a boat was going to Israel. Fortunately, her father found the note quickly and notified the police; they dragged her off the ship. It was sailing not for Israel but for Africa. When she was brought home, she threatened to keep running away; and her father promised her that when she finished school he would sign her permission to go to Israel. She graduated at the young age of sixteen and arrived in Israel in 1953.

She joined the army and was trained as a medical corpsman. Since she had no family in Israel and nowhere to go, she volunteered for nighttime and holiday duty. One night she was on duty in a military airport tower. A plane loaded with ammunition came in for a landing just as a violent storm broke. Lightning put out the airfield's electricity and hit the plane. The plane landed, flaming like a torch. She grabbed her first-aid kit and jumped on an ambulance racing toward the plane. The ambulance bogged down in deep mud; she walked toward the plane. Its ammunition began exploding. She heard someone in the plane calling "Mother!" Leaving her boots in the mud, she ran barefoot to the plane. Near its nose she found the navigator, Shlomo Artzman, unstrapped him from his parachute and rolled his burning body in the mud. She dragged him away from the plane. He told her the pilot was still trapped inside.

Fearing that the plane would explode at any moment, she ran toward it and by the smell of burning flesh located the pilot strapped in his burning seat. A bullet scratched her face and hit the pilot's forehead. He fell on her and the flames around him caught her long braids on fire. She managed to free the pilot, Yaacov Shalmon, and rolled him to where she had left the navigator. Then she collapsed. All three were rushed to the hospital. She and the pilot survived but the navigator died. Shalmon's parents adopted her and they became her family in Israel. Chief of Staff Moshe Dayan decorated her for "incredible and unusual courage." She was the only woman in the Israeli army with such a military decoration.

After the 1956 Sinai campaign, she married and, as Esther Arditi Bornstein, left the army, became a nurse, and worked part-time at Hadassah Hospital. Her husband was called into the army before the 1967 war.

On Monday morning she was seeing her two young children off to the school next door to their home in the Beit Ha-Kerem section when the sirens sounded. At first she thought it was the kettle whistling on the stove. Later, she stood with the children outside the school watching the tanks from the Jerusalem Brigade going down Herzl Boulevard. Her children asked her why she didn't go with them; their teacher, Carmela, would take care of them. Her six-year-old daughter said, "If you go with them, everybody will come back safely."

So she hitchhiked to the Magen David Adom station and found the ambulance she had driven earlier and spent the afternoon driving around Israeli Jerusalem, collecting wounded civilians and taking them to hospitals.

About midnight she came upon buses of paratroopers. She asked one of the soldiers where they were going. He said, "We're going to free the Old City." She thought it was just a soldier's joke.

Back at the Magen David Adom station, everything was quiet for a couple of hours and then she heard a heavy bombardment in the direction of eastern Jerusalem. For the first time she thought maybe the soldier had not been joking. When the two paratroopers came, she drove with them to Dr. King's first-aid station.

Toward dawn, the first-aid station started running out of supplies. The paratroopers did not know where to get more from a warehouse in Pagi a few hundred yards away, but Esther's adoptive parents lived nearby and she knew the area. They came to Pagi just after a frontline bunker was hit. She stayed to help the wounded and from there went with the paratroopers who attacked Ammunition Hill. With a soldier's khaki battle jacket thrown over her white nurse's robe, she helped the wounded as the soldiers advanced. She would give first aid, prepare the wounded to be evacuated and move on. Men around her were hit but somehow no harm came to her. She thought that she was going farther and farther away from her children into danger.

In time, Esther continued to Mount Scopus and joined the troops entering the Old City through the Lions Gate. There were still many snipers. The Israelis would push open a door with their Uzis and then throw in grenades. Not far from the Temple Mount, a young woman ran out of a house, screaming and carrying a year-old child. A piece of shrapnel from a grenade had cut an artery in the child's hip. Esther took the child from its mother and put a pad on the wound to stop the bleeding. Then she saw a white flag on a building. It was a church and she knew it would have a clinic. She knocked on the door and a priest came out and she gave him the baby.

She was alone and unarmed in the Old City. Her white gown was red with the blood of the wounded and dying. Her helmet was nicked by shrapnel marks. Snipers fired over her head. She didn't know where she was. She was terribly frightened. Suddenly, she heard someone running toward her. Terrified, she pressed against a wall and prayed it would swallow her up. She closed her eyes. "I could almost feel the taste of death in my mouth."

She opened her eyes and there stood an old Arab with a huge box of candy tied with a yellow ribbon. He gave her the box. He was the grandfather of the child she had just saved. Through her mind flashed the thought that the ribbon would go beautifully in her daughter's hair.

She continued to walk in the direction her instinct told her was right. She opened a gate and in a yard on the Temple Mount saw soldiers and Dr. King. This time, the doctor and the nurse hugged each other, and he said it was a miracle that they met again. She helped Dr. King care for the wounded. Many of the men gave her telephone numbers and asked her to call their families. After a while she heard the shofar blowing from the direction of the Western Wall. She had no more work to do so she went home to her children.

One of the soldiers in the hospital said he had dreamt that "a white angel" had come and taken care of him. Others remembered the angel in white. The newspapers started writing about the anonymous woman who had succored the wounded in battle. Colonel Gur gave a speech about the unknown woman who had joined the fighting and refused to leave and then had disappeared. The newspapers said there was now a second woman in the army who was a hero. Carmela, the teacher who had taken care of her children, told someone who the unknown woman was. The army had only one woman hero. Esther received a civilian medal from the President of Israel, Zalman Shazar, and became known as the Angel in White.

— Chapter 17 —

THE ROCKEFELLER MUSEUM

OF THE MORE THAN ONE HUNDRED PARATROOPERS OF A COMpany, Twenty-eighth Battalion, who had started down Nablus Road, only thirty were still able to fight. More than thirty had been killed. The remnant remained at the Monastery of St. Stephen and the able cleared the area westward as far as the Convent of Notre Dame de France. This is the section of the religious buildings around the Garden Tomb, which in Protestant tradition was the site of Jesus' burial outside the present-day Old City walls.

When C Company had taken the Rivoli Hotel in Salah ed Din Street on Tuesday, three buses of mortarmen attached to the Fifty-fifth Brigade from the Eightieth Brigade drove up the street. The bus drivers, trying to find their way to the Rockefeller Museum, missed the intersection where they were supposed to turn off Salah ed Din. Once past that intersection the street twists to the left, and the first two buses were immediately taken under heavy fire from the Old City wall at the head of the street. The soldiers fled from the buses. Some ran into the Rivoli and under the pillared archway in front of its shops. Others ran into a Muslim cemetery just north of the hotel. They were confused and panicked. Dead and wounded lay in the street. Men from Fradkin's C Company were killed helping the wounded. In the entry to the hotel lay a seriously wounded soldier. A corpsman warned that he could not be moved without a stretcher. The only stretchers were in the buses. Private Chaim Rossek, who had been born in Russia in 1938 and reached Palestine after World War II, volunteered to get one. The lean soldier leaped the exposed five yards from the archway into the bullet-riddled bus. He shouted that there were no wounded left in the bus and that he was bringing a stretcher. He stood in the doorway of the bus for an instant and pushed the stretcher toward the Rivoli. Then he jumped. This time the Jordanians were ready, and a machine-gun bullet killed him instantly.

In the midst of this one-sided fight, a staff car drove up with Major Achmon's deputy, Captain Mattan Gur; Sergeant Major Jacob Barnea, and three other soldiers. Colonel Gur's driver, Moshe Ben Tsur, was behind the wheel. They were returning to the Rockefeller Museum after taking a captured Jordanian officer to General Narkiss' headquarters in the Convention Hall. They too had missed their last turnoff. They drove around the bend in Salah ed Din Street and ahead of them loomed the Old City wall. Seeing the battle in the street in front of the Rivoli Hotel, Barnea grabbed the wheel and steered the staff car between the two buses. The men in the car leapt out. Captain Gur was severely wounded in the left leg by a machine-gun bullet. Four of the men went into the Rivoli. The stocky Barnea, although he had hurt his spine in a parachute jump a year before, ran, with the Uzi slung and his pipe clenched in his teeth, for the Muslim cemetery.

The others, not seeing Barnea, thought him dead. In the cemetery, Barnea found frightened, confused men from the buses. He tried to calm them and told them to lie down. He was high on a rise in the cemetery, and a machine gunner on the wall picked away at him. He hid among the tombstones, stuck his helmet out one side of a stone and then, when the shots came, jumped in the opposite direction. He finally ran to the rear of the cemetery out of sight of the wall and entered a house. He found himself in an Arab doctor's office. There were three Israeli soldiers already in the room, obviously in shock. In a bizarre moment he later could not explain, he picked up a rubber hammer with which the doctor tested reflexes, tapped each soldier sharply on the knee and assured him that he was okay.

Barnea walked out through the house into Salah ed Din Street. He was now behind the bend in the road out of sight of the Jordanians on the wall. Out from a side street came a large car, carrying General Shlomo Goren, the chief rabbi of the Israel Defense Forces, and his deputy. Rabbi Goren asked Barnea to direct him to Colonel Gur. Barnea firmly told the two rabbis to put on their helmets. Then, out of nowhere appeared a half-track. Barnea loaded the two rabbis in it; and as they drove near the Rivoli, Barnea had the half-track stop and pick up two wounded Israelis lying in the street. It was a dangerous moment; the half-track was open on top and the Jordanians on the wall were high above them. But they got away with it. And they rumbled on to the Rockefeller where Rabbi Goren and Colonel Gur hugged each other warmly. Goren said to Gur, "Do you remember the last time we met? I said if there will be a war in Jerusalem, you will be the commander who will free Jerusalem and I will go with you." The colonel said he remembered.

Barnea reported to Colonel Gur the disaster at the Rivoli and told Major Achmon that four of the eight men in his intelligence section were trapped in the hotel. It was already after 5 P.M., and they decided to wait until dark to try to rescue the wounded. Then, an intelligence unit Jeep was sent to the Rivoli. But someone forgot to disconnect the brake lights; and when the Jeep stopped in front of the Rivoli, the red lights lit up, and the Jordanians on the wall fired at them. Yehuda Ben Zeev of the intelligence section was killed on the spot.

Earlier that afternoon, the special mortar unit of which Sergeant Yuval Beham was a member fought its way down Salah ed Din Street. It attacked building after building, clearing them of Jordanian defenders. Halfway toward the post office building and Herod's Gate at the end of the street, the men climbed to a roof on the left side of the street to jump to the next building. Now they came in range of the Jordanian sharpshooters on the Old City wall. Several paratroopers were killed here. Young Beham was mortally wounded by a sniper's bullet and died on the way to the hospital.

Two paratroop companies moved into positions dominating the Damascus Gate, Herod's Gate and the Rockefeller Museum opposite the corner of the Old City wall. Gur wanted to take the gates of the Old City even though his men did not have permission to go into the Old City itself.

One of Fradkin's support units, commanded by Captain Michael Odem, reached the Rockefeller Museum and attacked it. This was the job of Fradkin's line companies but they were still fighting on Nablus Road. The support unit had come through

Wadi el Joz and met no heavy resistance. But several of its men were wounded assaulting the museum; there were still Jordanian soldiers inside.

The museum's ten acres were a Jordanian stronghold. The museum, an imposing gray building with an octagonal tower, had been built in 1929 with a $2 million grant from John D. Rockefeller, Jr., to house archaeological treasures. Captain Odem's small group of about a dozen paratroopers, feeling outnumbered and isolated, hid themselves in the museum until the main body of paratroopers arrived.

When Gur and Achmon and some paratroopers reached the corner of the Old City wall opposite the museum, they were shot at by Jordanian soldiers on top of the wall. Gur's driver threw the half-track into reverse and they got out of the line of fire fast.

Major Achmon found a rear gate, and the paratroopers blew the lock. Not knowing Captain Odem's small unit was ahead of them, they exchanged fire with those paratroopers. But then the crucially located museum was in Israeli hands. It was not yet 10:30 A.M.

Now, in still another mistake of war, Israeli artillery, reaching for the Old City wall, hit the museum. A member of Amnon Eshel's headquarters combat platoon was severely wounded by an Israeli shell. On the way to Sha'are Zedek Hospital another shell hit him; this time, not even his identification disc was found. Eshel's platoon suffered five of its seven casualties at the Rockefeller.

Some soldiers were sent onto the roof of the museum to suppress the fire from the Old City wall. Among them was Sergeant Gabai of the scout unit. He was now sorry he had left the bazooka in the Jeep back at Beit Ha-Kerem; his Uzi could not reach the Jordanians. Maybe, he thought, its bullets would scare them.

Tuesday at first light, about 4:30, Hassam al-Khalidi climbed to the fifth floor of the Ritz Hotel. Mortar shells had punctured the water tanks atop the hotel and the roof was flooded. Looking north through his binoculars, he saw two soldiers running communication wire. One had a wire-roller on his back. Suddenly, al-Khalidi realized that unlike the Jordanians who wore British-type helmets, the two men wore American-style helmets. He didn't want to believe what he saw. But then the soldiers raised an Israeli flag. There was no longer any doubt. The Israelis had broken through.

At 6:15 A.M., Brig. Gen. Hazzáa, who took pride in the fact that a brigade commander was so far forward, emerged from his underground command post and saw small units of Jordanian soldiers being pursued by Israelis and exchanging fire with them. A sergeant with four men came up to him and asked, "Sir, why are you standing here? You are surrounded by the Jews." The sergeant wanted to stay and protect the general, but he sent them to the Second Infantry Battalion's headquarters to try to help.

A few hours later, Captain Shawkat Jawdat, using a tourist map to locate his target, directed his Second Battery of the Jordanian Ninth Field Artillery to fire on the Israelis in the museum. The regiment's other two batteries, the First and Third, had already been ordered to withdraw seven miles to the east. Captain Jawdat had been covering their withdrawal until he aimed his fire at the museum. After he switched targets, Jawdat says, "I felt happy that none of the shells from my guns hit any Arab houses."

Major Mansaur Kreishan, commander of the Second Infantry Battalion headquartered in the Al-Rashidiya College just west of the Rockefeller Museum, told Captain Jawdat to engage three Israeli tanks at the Damascus Gate. Jawdat refused because he feared that he would endanger the Jordanian forces and the Arab civilians in the area of the gate and the city wall. Captain Jawdat says, "At this moment nothing was clear. There was no communication with my officers or with the infantry force in the Old City. My battery was now given orders to withdraw. It was very good luck that only the four men of the OP and two gunners of my battery were killed and one was wounded."

By now, Brig. Gen. Hazzáa's forward command post was surrounded and cut off. He had no communication with the West Bank Command. His intelligence officer climbed out of the bunker and watched the Israelis occupy the Rockefeller Museum. Hazzáa still had a telephone line to his Second Infantry Battalion's headquarters. He called Major Kreishan and told him the Israelis were behind his position and asked if he saw them. Kreishan said he did not. Hazzáa asked him if he had any antitank guns. He had one 106-mm antitank gun and said he would move it to engage the enemy.

Hazzáa saw Israeli armor assembling in Sheikh Jarrah. He turned to Major Salah, his artillery commander, standing next to him, and said, "You don't need any maps. There is the enemy. Start engaging him."

The major went to the radio to call his batteries. He came back and told Hazzáa, "Sir, it is all finished. I'm sorry. We have no guns functioning." Beyond Mount Scopus to the east, Brig. Gen. Hazzáa watched some fifteen Israeli fighters bombing the area around Anata. The Israeli pilots smashed and drove back Jordanian armor coming up the road from Jericho. The Israelis' General Yariv says, "If it wasn't for the Air Force, Gur would have been in bad shape."

Now, the Jordanians had no armor and no artillery support. The Second Infantry Battalion, from Sheikh Jarrah to the Damascus Gate, was overrun, with eighteen noncommissioned officers, sergeants and above, killed. The Fourth Battalion to the north and the Eighth Battalion inside the Old City and south of it were still intact. The Eighth Battalion's headquarters was in the Armenian Quarter, and the brigade commander ordered the battalion commander to engage the Israelis with his antitank weapons. He sent a group with bazookas up on the city wall opposite the Rockefeller Museum, but his 106-mm antitank gun had been destroyed by Israeli fire.

Brig. Gen. Hazzáa decided to withdraw into the walls of the Old City. He and Major Salah and Captain Jawdat groped through the heavy smoke of battle. "You couldn't see your own hands," Hazzáa remembers. They were fired on both by the Israelis and by the Jordanians on the wall.

Inside Herod's Gate, Hazzáa found Major Kreishan and his adjutant and about forty men of the Second Battalion. The soldiers from Al-Rashidiya College had burned their classified papers and fled through Herod's Gate. Hazzáa went up to Major Kreishan: "I asked him, 'Why did you leave your post?' He said his position was heavily bombed and he had several men wounded and left the doctor with them and felt it appropriate to withdraw into the Old City at Herod's Gate." Hazzáa put the battalion adjutant in charge of the defense of the gate and took Major Kreishan with him to the Eighth Battalion's headquarters.

From there, he telephoned Governor al-Khatib at the Ritz Hotel and insisted he come into the Old City. He did not want the governor captured. Although disgusted with the Jordanians' inability to defend Jerusalem, al-Khatib agreed. Al-Khalidi led the governor and his group toward the city walls. Al-Khalidi crawled across the open ground and dashed safely for the Damascus Gate. The second man was fired on. The governor was the fourth to make the attempt. Al-Khalidi could see tracers track him, but the governor made it to safety. The fifth man was killed.

Governor al-Khatib says, "I went there to continue resistance from the Old City. We thought we could manage to resist." At first, he insisted on going to the al-Aksa Mosque. He said he refused to be captured; he wanted to die in the mosque. But after some time, he went to the military headquarters and ate lunch with the officers there. They discussed the conditions under which soldiers surrender.

Governor al-Khatib tried to organize the Old City. Arms were passed out to civilians; there was plenty of ammunition stored in the Old City. The governor wanted to form a city government to hold out under siege. Mayor Rouhi al-Khatib refused to leave the safety of the Latin Patriarchate, even though twelve policemen were sent to escort him.

The governor and his party set up a headquarters in the Muslim Trust Building near the Temple Mount. Soldiers and policemen came there and turned in their arms. One army sergeant, who handed in his bazooka and six rounds, later returned and took back the bazooka and ammunition. He said he and his men had decided to die. The sergeant, who came from the village of Burin south of Nablus, and his team stationed themselves in the Muslim cemetery outside the Old City's eastern wall overlooking the Garden of Gethsemane. They were later credited with knocking out three Israeli tanks before they were killed by napalm.

At ten o'clock Tuesday morning, Brig. Gen. Hazzáa received a message from the Fourth Infantry Battalion commander at Shu'afat in the north, reporting that the Israelis were approaching in a three-pronged attack from Sheikh Jarrah and Nebi Samuel and the Ramallah road. "What shall I do?" he asked Hazzáa. Since his battalion was intact and entrenched,

245

Hazzáa says, "I said to him, 'This is your battle. Fight it to the last man.'"

Hazzáa called the West Bank Command to ask for help. He told Maj. Gen. Salim that his right wing was under heavy attack and he needed reinforcements. Hazzáa says, "They said, 'None is coming. Manage the situation in the best manner you can.' I told them I would be fighting with the Eighth Battalion in the Old City." Now two of his battalions were wiped out; he had only the Eighth left.

At noon, Hazzáa ordered two companies of the Eighth Battalion that were positioned outside of the Old City to the south, where there was no heavy Israeli attack as yet, to pull back inside the Old City walls and resist until reinforcements arrived. He had less than six hundred soldiers inside the Old City. He placed forty men at each gate and under an officer he appointed personally. "Their orders were: No withdrawal until the last man. This is your last battle."

According to Hazzáa, the Israelis began pushing their tanks toward the Damascus, Jaffa and Herod's gates. The Jordanians concentrated their antitank weapons at the three gates. One 106-mm antitank gun was carried up on the wall. Hazzáa says, "The momentum of the attack was stopped. They pulled back about three hundred yards and started firing the main guns of the tanks at the gates." After dark, in Hazzáa's view, the Israelis concentrated their attacks on the gates and especially the Lions Gate on the east side of the Old City.

At 5 P.M., Major Badi Awad, commanding the battalion that had attacked Jabal Mukaber, reported from Abu Dis that the Israelis were preparing to attack from the Government House area. Hazzáa told him to wait until dark and then withdraw to the east. At ten o'clock, Major Badi Awad started to lead his force east from Abu Dis.

During the evening, a Jordanian tank company arrived at Al-Azariyah (Bethany) to support Hazzáa's brigade in Jerusalem. Realizing it would be badly outnumbered and did not know the city, Hazzáa ordered it not to enter Jerusalem but to join Major Badi Awad's Ussamah Bin Zeid Battalion at Abu Dis. Hazzáa said, "They were coming for a massacre."

Chapter 18

AMMUNITION HILL

AMMUNITION HILL BECAME THE FIFTY-FIFTH BRIGADE'S ARMA-geddon in Jerusalem. At no other place did it fight more intensely; in no other single engagement did it take more casualties. The paratroopers attacked determined, entrenched Jordanians; and the fight was probably unnecessary. The hill could have been neutralized at less cost.

It was a classic attack, brutal and unexpected. C Company of the Sixty-sixth Battalion assaulted the eastern side of the hill. B Company headed for the western side. And when the going got tough, A Company tried to support them. The Bedouin defenders led by their Palestinian company commander stood and fought, virtually to the last man. Not a yard of the strongly fortified hill was surrendered easily; every one was paid for in blood and agony.

When the Seventy-first Battalion first entered no-man's-land, Major "Yossi" Yaffe's Sixty-sixth Battalion attacked the 150-yard-wide zone 800 yards farther north near the bottom of Bar Ilan Street.

Because of the haste to fight in the dark, Captain Nir Nitzan, the deputy commander of B Company, who was to command the point after the breakthrough, had five minutes to study an aerial photograph of Ammunition Hill. He quickly sketched a rough copy: "I had no time to learn and to assign forces for each task." Other officers had no maps or photographs at all. One private was shown a general map of Jerusalem; on it Ammunition Hill was smaller than a dime. The paratroopers' lack of intelligence information caused them to underestimate Ammunition Hill's strength.

But their esprit de corps was expressed by Nitzan's judgment of Major Yaffe and his own B Company commander, Captain David "Dodik" Rutenberg: "I don't know other commanders in my life who were so tough, so honest with themselves and especially with the mission as those two." Rutenberg, the cool, taciturn senior company commander in the battalion, was a powerful man, self-confident, who thought through every order calmly.

Half an hour before the assault, Major Yaffe ordered mortars and artillery to blanket no-man's-land. Then Captain Giora Ashkenazi, a kibbutznik from the Jezreel Valley, took forward D Company, the Sixty-sixth Battalion's lead company. Bangalore teams smashed a path through the mines and four barricades of barbed wire. The crouching, crawling men followed the narrow white-taped lanes cleared in the dark minefield and were covered by intense fire from four tanks and from machine guns on the roofs of the apartment houses in Pagi.

In the crossing, one officer in the lead company lost a foot to the mines. In later waves, eight more paratroopers had their legs blown off. The Israelis' 25-pounders hammered Ammunition Hill, but the Jordanians stayed unharmed in the ancient stone burial caves—which dated from the Second Temple period. When the covering bombardment finally lifted, the defenders reappeared to fight; and Jordanian artillery and 81-mm mortars pounded the attackers.

D Company crossed no-man's-land just south of the Police Training School to avoid the fire from Ammunition Hill rising on its left. The school dated from the days of the British Mandate. Although the Israelis still insisted on calling the building the Police Training School, since 1951 it had been the unarmed headquarters of the UNRWA in Jerusalem. It helped provide rations, health care and education for 1.8 million Arab refugees. But by Monday most of the UNRWA staff had left.

The grounds of this UNRWA headquarters, only 150 yards inside Jordanian territory, were surrounded by thirty-four Jordanian army bunkers. Jerusalem Brigade tanks fired at the UNRWA's windows as the paratroopers headed for a space between the building and a high concrete wall. In front of the building and the wall ran the main defensive trench; north of the UNRWA building, it curved to the rear. Beyond the trench were three concrete barracks that had once been used by the British police.

When the breakthrough had been made, D Company signaled Captain Rutenberg's B Company with flashlights. B Company started across. Since the Israelis expected the school building to be the main Jordanian strongpoint here, B Company's first job was to clear the bunkers around the school and then advance to the British barracks between the school and Ammunition Hill.

The men found resistance to be less than they feared. Unknown to the Israelis, Brig. Gen. Hazzáa had made Ammunition Hill, not the UNRWA building, his main position in this area. Some of the Fourth Platoon of the Second Company of his Second Battalion pulled back from the building to Ammunition Hill. But others stood and fought. Private Farid Abdul-latif Yousuf, already wounded, jumped from his trench, ran at the paratroopers and threw two grenades before he was killed by machine-gun fire. Near him, Private Ali Abdullah Munawar destroyed an Israeli machine gun with a grenade before he too was killed. The Jordanian platoon commander, Lieutenant Saleh Salim Nazal, ordered Private Ali Mustafa Jaber to take his machine gun and cover the break the paratroopers had opened in the wire. Lieutenant Nazal led a counterattack with bayonets. Private Jaber continued firing until he exhausted his ammunition. He picked up the rifle that Private Yousuf had dropped and fought until he was killed by Uzi fire. Corporal Abdul-Karim Mohammad Salim told his squad to cover him and he attacked with grenades until he was killed. Then the Fourth Platoon was destroyed.

Captain Rutenberg's B Company needed a half hour to dig out all thirty-four bunkers and make sure no one was left alive to attack the paratroopers from the rear. They killed or wounded more than twenty-five Jordanians.

Captain Gabriel "Gabi" Magal's A Company assaulted the two-story UNRWA building itself. Jordanian Private Etewi Mansour Mohammed lugged a box of thirty-six grenades to the upper floor and threw them, one after the other, at the attacking Israelis. Most of the remaining Arabs in and near the building fled to Ammunition Hill, just to the north; and A Company cleared the building. Israeli numbers and firepower were overwhelming.

Before first light, the paratroopers began reaching Ammunition Hill—called Jabal el Mudawware in Arabic and Givat

Ha-Tahmoshet in Hebrew. The hill was not high, but it dominated the Pagi area and the route to Mount Scopus. To the north, the higher, larger fortified Mivtar Hill loomed over Ammunition Hill.

Ammunition Hill was honeycombed with concrete-covered bunkers and a complex system of winding trenches. On it stood the three concrete military barracks and in a large ancient burial cave, the underground headquarters of the Jordanian unit defending the area. The defense of the hill was entrusted to the Second Company, Second Infantry Battalion of the King Talal Infantry Brigade—about ninety men commanded by Captain Sulamin Salayta, a Palestinian. His company sergeant major, Staff Sergeant Ahmed Hassan, had fought as a private with the same company when it had attacked the Police Training School in 1948.

The ferocious and slow-moving battle for Ammunition Hill raged for hours. It became a miniature war unto itself. The strength of the Arab resistance on the hill shocked the paratroopers and their commanders. They had not prepared for it. "Enemy fire was very strong. The Jordanian soldiers stayed inside the bunkers and fought until you came inside and killed them," says Lieutenant Amnon Eshel.

Maj. Gen. Ma'an Abu Nuwar, who built the defenses of Ammunition Hill when he commanded the brigade defending the Jordanian part of the city and who made an intensive study of the battle soon after the war, says, "The men were fighting for the honor of Jerusalem. They were fighting to die. Talking with these men as I did, I found that it was a religious honor; it was a nationalist honor; it was love of a city where they had been for a long time. They were defending their own city. I found men stayed in their trenches because they wanted to die there out of their religious belief and did not want to desert the wounded—men fought to the end really for what they believed in.

"The Israelis who fought the battle presumably fought it for religious feelings, for nationalist feelings, for something they wanted as a prize. Our chaps fought because it was worth fighting for the honor of Jerusalem and for their honor."

The Jordanians defending Ammunition Hill were surrounded. West of the hill was a minefield; from the north Israeli

250

tanks were closing in, and the paratroopers were attacking from the south and east. The Jordanians had to stand and fight. Captain Sulamin Salayta knew it.

Under fire, he checked his trenches. He was nicked by shrapnel but he hid his wound from his men. He told them: "Today is your day. Jerusalem is calling you. God is calling you. Listen and obey! Live long. But let's have Hell rather than shame."

A wounded soldier came to Captain Salayta from the police school and told him the enemy had penetrated to the left of the school with two companies and tanks. He reported that the Fourth Platoon commander, Lieutenant Nazal, said he was in control but had lost communications and asked for artillery fire. The captain relayed the message, and the Ninth Artillery Regiment concentrated its fire on that spot.

Captain Salayta ordered Sergeant Major Hassan and a group of men forward to help the Fourth Platoon. They zigzagged around the eastern side of the hill and ran into elements of the Sixty-sixth Battalion's C Company, led by Captain Oved "Dedi" Ya'akobi. He had been ordered to follow B Company into the main trench and then veer to the right and attack Ammunition Hill's eastern flank.

At a point named Iron 4 in the main trench leading to the hill, Captain Nitzan brought in preplanned mortar fire to help C Company reach its objective, and then he headed to the left and the hill's heavily defended western perimeter trench.

Sergeant Major Hassan reported C Company's advance to his captain, who sent him and his men back to prevent the Israelis from reaching his company command post on the hill's northeast side. Salayta called in artillery fire and sent two squads from Sergeant Dabaan Salman Suliman's Sixth Platoon, stationed at the rear of Ammunition Hill, to counterattack. Salayta ordered another squad from the Sixth Platoon to circle to the west and help protect the hill from that side.

The paratroopers' C Company immediately met catastrophe. Three platoons, advancing toward the east side of the hill, encountered bunkers and Jordanians who had fallen back from the Police Training School. Within minutes, a bullet killed Captain Ya'akobi's deputy commander, Yehuda Eshkol. The Second Platoon leader on the right flank, Lieutenant Yohanan Miller, was wounded by a grenade and evacuated.

At the foot of the hill, Lieutenant Yoram Eliashiv led his Third Platoon through a hole in a stone wall. He detached a four-man fireteam to attack the three concrete barracks. It was still dark. A bazookaman positioned himself in front of the wall and fired a rocket at one of the barracks. The backfire hurled stones from the wall and one struck the bazookaman in the head. Lieutenant Eliashiv, who was up ahead, called for the bazooka, his platoon's heaviest weapon. Private Jacob "Yakki" Chaimovitz, a tall, twenty-one-year-old Sabra and engineering student at the Technion in Haifa, ran back, took the bazooka and struggled to the front of the column until he was the third man behind Eliashiv.

Three trenches climbed the hill in front of C Company. Miller's Second Platoon advanced up the right trench. Eliashiv sent a four-man fireteam up the left trench. Two of its men, including the team leader, were quickly killed and a third wounded. Firing was heavy. The sky was filled with tracers. Branches from the pine trees on the hillside crashed to the ground. The Jordanians hurled grenades and hit a paratrooper carrying demolitions on his back. He exploded.

Taking fire from the Jordanian bunkers above his Third Platoon sector, which was very low, Eliashiv pulled his platoon toward the right. By mistake, Lieutenant Danny Ezrachi's First Platoon of C Company tried to advance behind the Third Platoon, leaving only a single fireteam in the center trench. The team was wiped out.

These moves left the area in C Company's center uncleared. Captain Nitzan says, "That started the confusion."

Eliashiv led his men single file in the trench, advancing slowly and carefully up the left side of the hill. He stayed in front and his men fed him more ammunition. He killed the defenders as he moved forward. Near the top of the hill, the trench ended. Eliashiv started down the back side of the hill. He was thrilled that he had fought that far forward. "We killed them. We succeeded," he shouted. A bullet through the chest wounded him fatally.

Two squad leaders were seriously wounded. C Company was stopped. With the daring Eliashiv out of action, the men in front called for Lieutenant Zvi Magen of the Fourth Platoon, the heavy weapons platoon. In the confusion they could not locate him. Some of the men took positions and hurled back

Jordanian grenades. They prevented the Jordanians from organizing a counterattack. Most of C Company's commanders were now killed or wounded. The men fought on almost without leadership. Of the eighty men in C Company, Captain Salayta's defenders had already killed seventeen and wounded forty-two.

The paratroopers reached within fifteen yards of Salayta's command post. Sergeant Major Hassan and three privates held them off in hand-to-hand fighting with bayonets and grenades. Two of the Jordanian privates were killed and the third, wounded. But they gave Salayta a few moments to reorganize. He called in artillery fire and led a grenade attack at a group of paratroopers near his command post. He fought his way to his Fifth Platoon's position on the west side of the hill and brought back two squads. Helped by a squad from the Sixth Platoon, they held off the Israeli attack. Many were killed and wounded. To Captain Salayta the situation now looked desperate.

With Captain Gabriel "Gabi" Magal in the lead, the paratroopers' A Company tried to come forward and help C Company. But the men were afraid to spread out; it was safer to follow the man in front.

A squad of Israelis approached the place where Captain Salayta was surveying the fight. One paratrooper fired an Uzi burst at him and missed. Salayta threw one of his two grenades and leapt over the communications trench and dived back into his command post. From there he reported that the enemy was advancing up the hill fighting from trench to trench. He asked for SOS ("Save Our Souls") artillery fire directly on his own position.

With the paratroopers up front now leaderless and Lieutenant Eliashiv mortally wounded, Private Jacob "Yakki" Chaimovitz, the Technion student, took charge. He handed the bazooka he had been carrying to another soldier and told the men to follow him. He led them through a trench down the north side of the hill. It had grown lighter in the dawn, and at the bottom of the hill Chaimovitz could see a Jordanian artillery piece and its crew. A head with a British-style flat helmet popped up, and Chaimovitz fired his FN rifle. The head disappeared.

Chaimovitz advanced across the back side of the hill, made a sweeping U-turn and entered a deep trench in which a man could stand up and still be protected. He could see nothing.

253

He heard shouts in Arabic. Then Lieutenant Zvi Magen from the heavy weapons platoon arrived and took a bazooka and knocked out the bypassed Jordanian artillery piece. It began to burn. No one fired on the Israelis from that position again.

Lieutenant Magen told them to continue with Chaimovitz in the lead. The Jordanians spotted them and began to fire and throw hand grenades. The Israelis threw back grenades until their supply was exhausted. Chaimovitz's magazine was empty; he stepped into a bunker to change magazines, and a number of soldiers passed him. Suddenly, he heard shouts, and the men came running back. They were wounded. They said ahead was a large bunker and no one could pass it.

Chaimovitz found himself alone out front. Looking ahead, he could see two figures in the trench; one seemed to be kneeling and the other lay on his face. He heard firing and the explosion of grenades above his imprisoning trench, which was now filled with dust. Out of the dimness a wounded Jordanian lunged at him with a bayonet on his rifle. Chaimovitz shot him. He reached the two men in the trench. They were dead; they were Private Michael Gertner and Lieutenant Zvi Magen.

Chaimovitz saw what appeared to be a black hole directly ahead of him. A concrete slab covered the trench at the entrance to a large bunker. He fired at the black hole and received fire in return. He moved cautiously. Here the trench was straight; there were no angles or corners to protect him. He made it past the big bunker safely. He was alone. He saw Israelis above the trench and asked them for grenades and warned them not to shoot at him. He tried to fire at the big bunker, but the walls were thick concrete. His bullets made no impression. Ahead, in the distance, he thought he saw Israelis coming up the trench firing at him. He shouted the paratroopers' code signal—a phrase from an old Palmach song—and in reply had grenades thrown at him. He shouted the code again as loud as he could. No one answered. So he shouted the only two Arabic words he knew, hoping to convince his unknown enemy to surrender.

Captain Rutenberg, B Company's commander, appeared and, seeing that the paratroopers' forward motion had been stopped, sent Private David Shalom down into the trench with Chaimovitz, who quickly explained the situation to him. Shalom, a dark, trim, Iraqi-born twenty-five-year-old, had no grenades left; and his attempts to fire his weapon at the big bunker were fruitless. An Israeli tank suddenly loomed above them on the peak of the hill. They showed the bunker to the tankers, but the tank's gun could not be lowered enough to reach it.

Lieutenant Danny Ezrachi, C Company's First Platoon commander, came up with grenades, which they hurled at the bunker; but still it held. Ezrachi was wounded and had to go back. A paratrooper arrived with a bazooka. Chaimovitz told him to fire a rocket against the bunker wall. He stood only ten yards from the wall but his missile made no impact. He tried with an antitank rocket; the heavy bunker wall still stood firm. Chaimovitz crept up and tried to fire into the bunker's entrance. The Jordanians fired back.

Private Yehuda Kandel said he would climb out of the trench, crawl to a spot above the bunker and drop grenades inside. Chaimovitz told him it would be suicide. But Kandel swiftly climbed the wall. He came under fire from Mivtar Hill, but he crawled to the bunker and hurled in a phosphorous grenade, which filled the trench and bunker with thick smoke and killed one Jordanian. Kandel jumped back into the trench and, followed by Chaimovitz and Shalom, started to advance again.

They were out of grenades so Chaimovitz went back to the big bunker, where he had seen Jordanian grenades. The bunker was filled with smoke from Kandel's grenade, but Chaimovitz saw that beyond the main room of the bunker was a second, smaller room. Out of the corner of his eye, he caught the shadow of a man in the little room. They were a yard apart. The Jordanian stuck his rifle in Chaimovitz's face; he jumped aside and the Jordanian's shot missed. Chaimovitz shot him in the stomach and he fell backwards.

Chaimovitz spotted four more Jordanians hidden in the smaller interior room; they had not been harmed by Kandel's grenade. In the smaller room was a heavy machine gun positioned to fire on the buildings of Pagi. Chaimovitz ran into a bunker. Kandel came forward to find out what had happened to Chaimovitz and to take full magazines from Magen's and Gertner's bodies. When Chaimovitz saw Kandel approaching, he shouted to him that the Jordanians in the big bunker were still alive. Kandel could not hear him over the noise of the battle. But he sensed that something was wrong. He started to run, and the Jordanians' bullets tore into the wall just behind him. Kandel made it safely to Chaimovitz's bunker. Only Shalom was beyond the big bunker. They motioned to him to stay there.

Lieutenant Ofer Feniger, a giant, twenty-four-year-old platoon leader in Captain Magal's A Company and a native of Kibbutz Giv'at Haim, now appeared and organized the final assault on Ammunition Hill.

While Eliashiv and then Chaimovitz led C Company up the east side of Ammunition Hill, Captain Rutenberg's B Company was fighting its own war on the hill's west side. After B Company cleared the bunkers at the Police Training School, Captain Nitzan led the company's point, a platoon with grenades and submachine guns, into the main trench on the west side. "The principle was to stay close to the enemy so that he becomes confused and afraid," says Nitzan. "Most of the fighting was inside the trenches and the bunkers. Men fired and threw grenades; and when their magazines were empty, they would fall to the ground and others would run over them while they changed magazines."

"Forward!" Nitzan cried and took his small group into the trenches. Suddenly, he ran into a barbed wire fence. He had no means to blow it up. D Company had an extra bangalore and in less than thirty seconds its men had breached the fence.

Nitzan sped on and cleared one section of the trench after another. An 81-mm mortar round fell among the paratroopers following the point and killed the sergeant and one squad leader of Lieutenant Yoav Tsuri's Second Platoon. Five or six were killed attacking the bunkers here. Other men came forward to replace them. A short, skinny, chain-smoking medical corpsman, Yigal Arad, dragged the wounded into a small depression. Arad, a Polish-born, twenty-five-year-old night-shift mechanic in a refrigeration plant, had come to Israel only in 1960. He was married and had two children. Under constant fire from the Jordanians higher up the hill, he left the relative safety of the trench to save the wounded. After it became light and the number of casualties grew, Arad was the only corpsman in B and C companies still alive and unwounded.

He was trying to care for eight wounded paratroopers in a shallow trench. "The sight was terrible. The guys were totally smashed. There was blood everywhere," he says. Arad felt weak himself and leaned against the side of the trench to regain his composure. "Then I turned to ice. From then on I worked like clockwork." He ran outside the trench to get more dressings and splints from a corpsman named Didier Guttel whose arm was severely wounded. Arad says with a wry sense of humor, "The bullets did not hit me because I'm so skinny."[1]

Nitzan and his men knew nothing of what was happening to the other units on the hill. When they reached their first objective, they stayed there for half an hour helping the wounded and listening to the firing. Dawn began to break. Nitzan had been struck above one eye by a grenade fragment. Blood streamed down his face and he was splattered by the blood of the Jordanians he had fought.

He tells what happened next: "It was like a butcher shop. Sometimes, a Jordanian came out with his hands up and another with his weapon hidden behind him. This was not a fight in which you aim and shoot. Someone would grab your legs and you had to deal with him. I was covered with blood and brains because I was in the front. Dodik [Rutenberg] always relaxed me: 'Are you okay? Okay. Do it slowly.' He was a few men behind me and he organized hand grenades and magazines to keep up the fire. When we stopped our first advance, we had three killed and seven or eight wounded. We didn't know where were the other [B Company] platoons. We thought they were killed and we had no time to look for them. We asked over the radio and Yossi [Yaffe] said he knew nothing about them.

"Dedi [Ya'akobi of C Company] called over the radio: 'I need help! Where are you?' We tried to locate each other. We didn't know where he was, and we were afraid that if we went forward we would get fire from our own people."

They moved forward in a shallow trench. The Jordanians shot at them. Captain Rutenberg ordered Nitzan to go back and get first aid for his wound and let Lieutenant Yoav Tsuri, the twenty-five-year-old leader of B Company's Second Platoon, take the lead. Tsuri and five or six men started to attack the bunkers. They received heavy fire from behind a wall and from two bunkers in front of the wall. Three or four men were killed here; the rest stayed in the trench.

Tsuri told Rutenberg it was impossible to continue. Rutenberg forced him: "Do it fast!" Tsuri said people were shooting from the left side, so Rutenberg sent Tsuri to the left and with seven men he himself took the lead against the fire from the wall.

Nitzan says, "I ran to Dodik [Rutenberg]. I was afraid he would get a bullet and I would be the commander; I didn't know the area and I would have to lead the men. When I reached him, he said, 'Dedi is in trouble. Let's go.' Suddenly, I heard Yoav, who had not entered the trench, say, 'I can't continue. It is impossible to continue.' I asked Dodik if I should go and help Yoav and he said, 'Okay, go! We'll meet at the top.'

"I started to crawl from the trench to the north and I saw Yoav and five or six others running back. They were under fire. One man was killed here. I was shocked. I saw my friends running away. I ordered them to stop and take positions. A few lay down and started to fire. I tried to organize people, but suddenly the fire came at me; I couldn't raise my head. Yoav and a few others were lying in the open, pretending to be dead. I didn't know they were alive. I thought the enemy killed them. I thought I was alone. I thought that everybody was killed. I shouted our password and nobody answered. I saw the MAG [machine gun] operator and called to him to help me. I put him behind a tree and ordered him to fire at the trenches. He laid down a covering fire. Three others came over to me. By now it was light in the east.

"Dodik ran up the hill with seven men to reach the crest trench, which dominated the area with heavy fire. He knew he had to reach it. He shouted, 'Let's go!' and ran fast and reached the wall. His men hesitated, but Dodik said anyone who wants to stay alive will run immediately. They ran.

"I must interrupt my story to tell you something. Just a few days before the war, two men in our company, a squad leader named Shlomo Magri and a corpsman in his squad named Didier [Guttel], a newcomer from France, had an argument. Magri ordered him to dig a hole for some garbage and Didier refused in front of the whole platoon. Dodik assigned me to settle the matter. I talked to both of them. Magri said there was no discipline in the company and Didier had refused his order. Didier said Magri didn't like him and was always choosing him for the dirty work. I told Didier to do the digging he had been ordered to do; and then I called them together and said, 'We are almost at war and you never know who you will be fighting with and when you will need each other. Be good to each other; you never know what will be in the future.'

"Now in the battle, Magri ran after Dodik; and the last man to pass the exposed place was Didier. He took three or four bullets in his right arm; it was barely hanging onto his body, just by threads. Magri crawled back to him under fire and gave him first aid. Didier showed him how to tie on the tourniquet and told Magri to go and save himself. Magri advanced and suddenly shouted that he saw where the fire was coming from. He raised himself, tried to fire his Uzi and got a bullet in his throat and he died.

"I lost any sense of time but I know that every minute was like one year. I was afraid to go on. We had to pass out ammunition from our bags. We were fighting with our packs on. Later, Yossi [Yaffe] said that was a mistake but he was afraid the war would go on and on and we would need our supplies. But it was difficult to run in the narrow trenches with the packs on.

"Dodik found Dedi in a trench on the right side of the hill. Dodik tried to encourage him. Dedi said, 'I lost almost all my company. Eshkol [his deputy] died.' Dodik brought up his group and was almost killed by a Jordanian sergeant who came out of a building and aimed his pistol at Dodik's back. But his radio operator had his finger on the trigger of his Uzi and killed the Jordanian.

"The morning started and I began to collect people. Dodik started to evacuate the people from Dedi's company. Dodik thought I was killed. He urged the men on. Yossi Yaffe and Gabi Magal ordered a platoon of Magal's company commanded by Lieutenant Ofer Feniger to go and reinforce the men on the left side of the hill.

"I was encouraged because I heard on the radio that people were continuing the fight. I organized people to defend the area. One Jordanian came close behind me. Yoav Tsuri killed him. A little later, the man guarding our rear shouted that the Jordanians were trying to get around our flank. I became afraid of attacks from all sides.

"I heard tanks. I didn't know that Yoav had come up with two of our tanks to coordinate an attack; I knew nothing about this. But, suddenly, I saw Yoav; I called 'Yoav, come to me, come to me.' I didn't know why Yoav and five or six others were coming across an open area. We were used to fighting in the trenches. Because I heard the tanks, I was afraid that Jordanian tanks were counterattacking. I told my people not to expose themselves and not to fire until the tanks were over them. My heart was down in my trousers.

"For the first time in my life, I had three people come close to me like baby birds and ask what they should do. I was afraid more than them. I pretended to be cool and quiet. I prayed— I don't know to whom. Then I saw the tanks were ours, and Yoav cried: 'Don't be afraid. The tanks will help us. Assault! Forward!' We reached the place where several trenches met between olive trees."

Captain Salayta watched the two tanks approach. He ordered rocket launchers fired at them and saw the tanks hit and pull back. The paratroopers advanced, hugging the walls and coming through the trenches in groups of seven to ten. The Israelis were getting closer and closer to his command post. The fighting was intense. Private Hamid Defula Mayshud fired his light machine gun until he was killed. Corporal Jessar Hamadi and Lance Corporal Hamad Feyard fired their medium machine guns, although they were wounded, and then fought with hand grenades until they were killed. They were ardent Bedouin soldiers, among the best of Salayta's men.

On the west side of the hill, Lieutenant Yoav Tsuri tried to throw a grenade and, leaping over a trench, took a bullet in his chest and fell dead.

When Captain Nitzan saw Tsuri fall, he cried, "Everyone down in the trench." In the deep trench the men could not see anything. Nitzan says, "I am not tall and I climbed outside to see what was going on. In two minutes I organized people with Uzis. If one got wounded, he would lie down and others would step over him. It took thirty minutes to clear forty or fifty yards; there were five Jordanians in each bunker."

Captain Salayta pulled back from his command post to his Sixth Platoon on the rear slope of the hill. From there he directed the efforts of the Fifth Platoon on the west side. It was obvious that the remnant of the Fourth Platoon could no longer resist as an organized unit. A few of its men still fought on, throwing grenades, firing, the wounded crawling to more protected positions and fighting until they were killed. The paratroopers were now attacking the Sixth Platoon's trenches. "It was a dogfight. There was no tactics in it," says Maj. Gen. Nuwar. "They defended every trench. It was a personal fight for every soldier." Corporal Ayyoub Elayan, out of ammunition, fought a paratroop officer with his bare hands. The officer had been trying to change his magazine and Elayan strangled him.

Captain Nitzan says, "Somebody threw a grenade in the trench perhaps half a yard from me. But it was not a fragment grenade. We advanced a little farther and I saw someone jump over the trench. He was stupid not to throw a grenade into the trench. I ordered a light machine-gun operator named Eitan Nave, a strong, good man, to climb up and kill everyone who was lying or moving outside. It was so dangerous to run in one narrow row with no cover outside.

"We heard heavy fire from Jordanians outside. One tank came up but could not depress its gun enough. Yossi's operations sergeant, First Sergeant Yorash Shina'ar, climbed the tank and started firing its machine gun. But it was difficult for him to support us because of the fire from Mivtar Hill. Eitan Nave killed five Jordanians outside and one who was waiting for me in the last bunker. We owed him our lives. He was a brave man." The blond, twenty-three-year-old Sabra was killed on the hill.

Meanwhile, Captain Salayta was able to get back to his command post at the top of the hill and reported to his superiors that his ammunition was almost exhausted. He had been wounded a second time and his uniform was covered with blood; a grenade had ripped his right leg and side. He said that he was going to the Fifth Platoon on the northwest side of the hill and would not communicate again. He called for fire on his position. His battalion commander replied: "Give the brothers my greetings. Death is better than shame. The name of the brigade is above all. God be with you." And he ordered the artillery to fire; in minutes, 180 shells poured down on the hill. This was repeated four times. The barrage seemed to halt the paratroop attack momentarily; the Jordanian Sixth Platoon on the rear slope cleared some of its trenches and the Fifth Platoon was able to hold on.

Captain Salayta reached the Sixth Platoon as it was being attacked by Lieutenant Ofer Feniger's A Company platoon.

Feniger was under fire from the Jordanians' Sixth Platoon and distant shelling from Mivtar Hill. Several of his men were killed. But Feniger's platoon managed to take half the trenches of the Sixth Platoon in hand-to-hand fighting.

The two Israeli tanks were on top of Captain Salayta's command post. One was damaged; the other was firing. His radio operator flung grenades at the tanks and at the paratroopers nearby. Two privates with Salayta were killed. The second one, Private Ali Mugbel Suliman, went out of the trench with his hands raised to the enemy. In one hand he held a grenade. When a paratrooper shot him, he threw the grenade, which exploded among the paratroopers. He was riddled with bullets.

Salayta was wounded a third time, again in the leg, and crawled to the Fifth Platoon's trenches on the west side of the hill. By now, Feniger's men had overwhelmed the Sixth Platoon on the north side and killed its last six fighters. The surviving wounded made their way to the Fifth Platoon, where Salayta gathered all the men still fit to fight. He ordered the wounded to supply covering fire while the able men counterattacked his Israeli-occupied command post. But the paratroopers stopped this attack, and the Jordanians fell back to the Fifth Platoon's position. The paratroopers advanced in force. Almost all of Salayta's company had been wounded or killed; only about twenty men, many of them wounded, could still fight. They were nearly surrounded. Privates Jemin Muhmad Mohammad and Salman Said Salman jumped from one trench to the next and lunged at the approaching paratroopers with grenades. The pair killed several paratroopers before they themselves were killed.

Now the paratroopers controlled most of the trenches on Ammunition Hill. Their final battle was with the Jordanian Fifth Platoon. The Jordanians' machine guns on the peak of the hill were still firing down on the attackers. The paratroopers overran every one of the machine guns. The gunners fought until they were killed. Jordanian Lance Corporal Said Hamid Salada, an expert sniper, picked off Israeli Headers from the Fifth Platoon's position until he too was killed.

The paratroopers fought through the Fifth Platoon's trenches, killing at least five Jordanians and wounding others in close combat. The Jordanians put their most seriously wounded men in the center of the platoon and Captain Salayta gave them water. He remembered that they asked him about his own wounds just before they died. As he counted the dead and wounded around him, it went through his mind that the men's green brigade flashes were red with their blood. He saw that ammunition was running out and knew there were no alternatives to capture or death.

The last Jordanian strongpoint on Ammunition Hill was the large two-room bunker that Privates Chaimovitz, Kandel and Shalom had risked their lives to destroy. It had withstood grenades and rifle and bazooka fire. It seemed impervious.

As the battle approached its climax, Chaimovitz and Kandel were in the trench on the north side of the bunker and David Shalom was alone just south of it. At battalion's orders, Lieutenant Feniger of A Company arrived with his men and checked the scene with Chaimovitz and Kandel. Feniger brought with him a bag of ten pounds of explosive material. Originally, each paratrooper had such a bag with which the brigade intended to destroy the Egyptian guns guarding the city of El Arish. The men of C Company, who were assigned to fight in the trenches on Ammunition Hill, left their bags on the buses that brought them up to Jerusalem; but A Company's men carried theirs into battle.

Feniger collected five bags of explosives and two blocks of dynamite. The men pitched them one after another to Shalom on the far side of the bunker and told him to pile them against the bunker wall. Kandel had a detonator and flipped it to Shalom. Chaimovitz, who had been trained to handle demolitions, shouted instructions to Shalom for using the explosives.

All the time, the desperate Jordanians in the smaller inner room of the bunker tried to shoot the Israelis in the trench; but their angle of fire was too limited. Feniger, Chaimovitz and Kandel fired at the bunker's entrance to keep the Jordanians inside.

Captain Nitzan remembers: "At that moment I came up and Ofer raised his head and signaled me not to move. We got down in the trench. Then I heard a tremendous explosion. Chaimovitz and Shalom had blown up the biggest bunker. Everybody who had been exposed to it had been wounded or killed!"

The explosion bowled over David Shalom, the nearest Israeli. Chaimovitz, in a bunker ten yards away, planned to run forward and shoot the Jordanians through the hole blasted by the explosion. But it knocked him over; and when he recovered, he saw that both the concrete slab over the trench and the entire bunker wall had disappeared.

It was five minutes before 7 A.M. The explosion smashed Chaimovitz's watch at that moment.

The Jordanians were still firing from the bunker. "It was unbelievable," says Chaimovitz. "They were very good Bedouin soldiers—professional." He shouted to Nitzan and his men to come up and finish them off. They had to go in and kill the four Jordanians still alive inside the bunker.

This was the end of the battle for Ammunition Hill. The paratroopers had lost thirty-five killed and more than seventy wounded on this knoll.

Jordanian soldiers, alone and in small groups, ran from the bunkers and were shot and killed. The paratroopers on Ammunition Hill were now under fire from Mivtar Hill just to the north. Lieutenant Feniger organized his platoon facing that hill. He raised his head to shoot the fleeing Jordanians and was wounded by a machine-gun bullet from Mivtar Hill. The powerful young kibbutznik was a respected man and leader, an artist and teacher who had spent the summer of 1965 as a counselor in a Zionist youth camp in the United States. Now, groaning with pain, he was carried to a Land Rover and driven to an aid station where he was treated and sent on to a hospital. He died there and was buried in Jerusalem.

At the end of the struggle on Ammunition Hill, Captain Salayta had eight soldiers with him; four of them were wounded. He decided to try to break out through the paratroop squad north of them. They crawled through the trenches, fought their way through the paratroop squad; and he and three of the men escaped to Mivtar Hill.

The Jordanian brigade commander, Brig. Gen. Hazzáa, believes that the last Jordanian fighting on Ammunition Hill was Staff Sergeant Ahmed al-Yamani, a native of Yemen. Hazzáa says, "He was alone. When he was surrounded by the paratroopers, he started firing all around him. He fought hand-to-hand outside the trenches. He killed about twelve Israelis before he was killed. He was the last Jordanian alive on Ammunition Hill."

* * *

As soon as it was light, Colonel Gur sent Major Moshe Stempel forward to check on the battle for the hill. Stempel picked a small group of men, and they crossed the border at the Police Training School at about 5:30 in two open command cars. Near Ammunition Hill they came under fire. Sergeant Major Jacob Barnea in the second car saw some of the paratroopers walking off Ammunition Hill: "I never saw such a look as I saw on their faces. They looked right through you."

The two Jordanian strongholds in Jerusalem had been Mivtar Hill and Ammunition Hill. Mivtar had been conquered relatively easily by Ben-Ari with tanks and artillery. But Ammunition Hill had been attacked man against man.

Afterwards, Colonel Ben-Ari was highly critical of the costly battle for Ammunition Hill: "When the paratroopers attacked, I was still busy at Biddu and Nebi Samuel. But after four hours, I was at Tel el-Ful; and they should have told the paratroopers to stop. I could have done the job easily from the Mivtar Hill. Tank fire could have finished the battle of Ammunition Hill in a minute. That was the mistake, to tell them to continue and continue and continue. You have to change your plans when the battlefield develops differently than you thought. That was a mistake. The paratroopers paid dearly for what I could have done just like that. Somebody didn't think. Sometimes you are trapped in your own plans."

Colonel Amitai of the Jerusalem Brigade says only, "We usually don't like to attack strongpoints, but this was the shortest route to Mount Scopus."

While some paratroopers were advancing beyond Ammunition Hill, they spotted tanks approaching down the Ramallah road from the north. Thinking they were Jordanians, the paratroopers called on the Jerusalem Brigade's Shermans that were with them to engage the oncoming tanks. Other paratroopers on Ammunition Hill carried the heavy machine guns from the big bunker to the foot of the hill where the Jordanian artillery piece had stood and where they could intercept the tanks if they came nearer. Before the tanks were close enough to hit, the paratroopers recognized them as Israeli; but Israeli jets and the Jerusalem Brigade's Shermans attacked. They were battling Ben-Ari's lead tanks.

*   *   *

In Chaimovitz's C Company platoon of twenty-five men, six were dead and fourteen wounded; only five escaped unscathed. Chaimovitz helped with the wounded.

Captain Nitzan walked wearily to a high school near Ammunition Hill. All the men there were finally catching some sleep. Nitzan spotted Captain Rutenberg. He tapped Rutenberg gently on the shoulder three times. Rutenberg awoke and at first thought he was dreaming. "We thought each other was dead," says Nitzan. Then the two battle-worn veterans kissed each other.

During the fight on Ammunition Hill, the rest of the Sixty-sixth Battalion moved directly to the Sheikh Jarrah quarter just south of the hill and on into Wadi el Joz. The battalion commander, Yossi Yaffe, led them between Ammunition Hill and the Spanish Consulate and had no idea of the intensity of the struggle on the hill.

A paratrooper came back to Ammunition Hill the next day and made a sign from a cardboard carton which he left behind: "Here lie 18 Jordanian soldiers who fought bravely like heroes."

When General Narkiss, in his command post at the Convention Center, heard that the way to Mount Scopus was clear, he drove his Jeep through the Mandelbaum Gate with Dayan sitting next to him and Weizman and "Gandhi" in the back. The group from General Headquarters had just flown up from Tel Aviv. At the Ambassador Hotel they picked up envelopes and signed and exchanged them as souvenirs. There was still shooting. They passed bodies in the street and a burned-out tank. A soldier obviously in shock was wandering about, vaguely looking for something.

On Mount Scopus, one of Major Sharfman's men told him that Dayan was waiting for him. Sharfman thought he meant on the telephone; but the messenger said, no, he is here. Sharfman was amazed. He and Dayan had fought the Arabs together in 1938 on the Lebanese border. And now Mount Scopus— the vulnerable, the endangered, the symbol—was relieved not by hard-charging, bullet-spewing Israeli paratroopers but by the resplendent military VIPs. Sharfman believed Ben-Ari could have reached Mount Scopus; he said, "It is a funny war."

Sharfman, whose cook had been in the British army and insisted on serving the men hot meals in their positions on Mount Scopus, now proudly gave the visiting brass a hot lunch. They signed the guest book of the Hebrew University, and Narkiss described how he wanted to assault the Old City through the Lions Gate. But the Israeli government had not yet decided to attack the Old City.

That afternoon most of the Sixty-sixth Battalion moved on through Wadi el Joz nearly to Mount Scopus. The isolated height, which had worried the commanding Israeli officers from the beginning, was now safe.

Shortly afterwards, Narkiss returned to Mount Scopus with Mayor Kollek. Accompanying Kollek, Danny Bloch had a scoop. He was the first journalist on Mount Scopus since 1948. He wrote the story for his paper and for the *Jerusalem Post*, but the military censor held up his articles until late that night. They finally made the second editions.

As Narkiss and Kollek returned to Israeli Jerusalem, paratroopers being relieved drove out through the Mandelbaum Gate. Large crowds of excited residents clapped and cheered. The soldiers, dog tired, just smiled.

One soldier spotted Mayor Kollek and shouted: "We've made your city bigger."

Kollek, in his usual style, replied, "A bigger headache, you mean."

— Chapter 19 —
ABU TOR

BEFORE DAWN ON TUESDAY MORNING, WHILE THE PARA-troopers were pounding across no-man's-land and fighting for a foothold in Jordanian Jerusalem and while Ben-Ari's tanks were struggling toward Tel el-Ful, President Nasser called King Hussein in Amman by radio telephone. Nasser wanted Hussein's cooperation in announcing that British and American forces were participating in the war on the side of Israel.

The conversation ended this way:

Nasser: In the life of Allah, I say I will publish the announcement and you will publish the announcement and we will make the Syrians publish the announcement to the effect that the American and English airplanes participate in the war against us from the aircraft carriers.

Hussein: Okay. Very well.

Nasser: A thousand thanks. Keep the faith. We are with you with all our heart. Our airplanes are over Israel today and they are hitting the Israeli airfields since this morning.

Hussein: A thousand thanks. Be well.

The conversation was intercepted and recorded by Israeli Intelligence at 4:30 A.M. Three hours later, Radio Cairo began broadcasting the false story of British and American participation. The Israelis played the taped conversation over the radio. Anwar Nuseibeh, who heard the tape, says, "You couldn't mistake the voices. President Nasser was telling the king not to worry, not only that the Egyptian Air Force had not been destroyed but that it was on the offensive. The tape was never denied, at least I never heard it denied." The U.S. government called Nasser's announcement of U.S. intervention a "gross falsification" and cabled its embassy in Amman to "call upon

[King Hussein] now to give evidence [of] his good faith by puncturing Nasser's lie."

Most civilians of Israeli Jerusalem stayed in their shelters on Tuesday. They were surrounded by war and the Jordanians were still shelling their homes. While President Shazar and his wife were in the basement shelter of their residence, where he had planned the reception the evening before, the building was hit, part of the wall blown out, all the windows broken and the furniture splintered. The danger to civilians was by no means finished.

But they felt a subtle difference. Monday's fears had peaked. Ben-Ari, Gur and Amitai were carrying the war to the enemy. Men and tanks and guns were fighting right across town and it was fierce, but the battle was clearly sweeping away from the Israeli sector. To some significant degree, anxiety moved aside and was replaced by a growing confidence.

Early Tuesday, Dr. Yosef Burg, the former Berlin rabbi who was now Israel's minister of social welfare, lay on his bed in his house in Ben Maimon Street fully dressed even to his shoes: "In case something happens, if we get shelled or I get a call from the government, I would be ready."

At five o'clock his telephone rang. It was another member of the Cabinet. The conversation:

"Are you asleep?"

"No."

"Are you in bed?"

"No."

"Where are you?"

"I am on the bed."

When it was time to get up from the sleepless night, he went to rouse his daughter. She was lying on her bed reciting Psalms to herself. Dr. Burg says wryly, "According to Jewish custom it helps."

He continues: "Tuesday morning I did not go to the office. All the war-making was concentrated in the Greater Tel Aviv Metropolitan Opera and I had nothing much to do in Jerusalem. I got a telephone call from Tirat Tzevi, one of our religious kibbutzim in the north:

"'Yosel (that's me), it's true?'

"'It's not true. You are asking if Jerusalem is in our hands?'

"'Yes.'

"'It's not true.'

"'Last night they told us in Bnei Berak [a city of Orthodox Jews] that we have it.'

"'In Bnei Berak they are more pious so maybe they know more than I do. It is not true.'"

While the Harel and paratroop brigades were fighting north of the Old City Tuesday morning, the Jerusalem Brigade received orders from Central Command to put pressure on the Jordanians on the south side of the city and attack the hill of Abu Tor. This steep, populated hill rose immediately south of the Old City, separated from it by the deep, narrow Hinnom Valley, where human sacrifices had been made to the Ammonite god Moloch before David's time. The valley's ancient name means Hell.

The Green Line ran up and over Abu Tor, and Arabs and Jews lived near each other on either side of the line, sharing a magnificent view of the Old City below. At places, Israeli and Jordanian fortifications were not more than twenty yards apart.

Amitai sent against Abu Tor Lt. Col. Michael Peikas' 163rd Battalion, which had helped Ben-Ari seize the Radar position north of Jerusalem the previous night. The battalion would be supported by a mortar company down in the German Colony and by fire from five of Major Aaron Kamara's tanks.

On top of Abu Tor, the Jordanians had converted four border buildings into blockhouses with concrete and sandbags. Peikas planned to send a company against each of these strongpoints. Although Peikas was an experienced and courageous leader, it was a bad plan. If he had attacked from the flank, he could have concentrated his power on the four blockhouses one at a time and rolled them up—"crossed their T," in naval terminology. Captain Eli Kedar, one of his company commanders, objected to Peikas' plan. He pointed out that the hill was densely built up and deeply terraced, and it would be difficult to coordinate Peikas' attack. But Peikas felt that opposition would be light and speed was essential to overwhelm the defenders before they could get set.

About three o'clock—a beautiful blue-sky afternoon—Peikas' attack got off to a calamitous start. His lead company, commanded by Lieutenant Uzi Yalovsky, a tough, able biochemist, was marching up a street to its jumping-off point and was clobbered by Jordanian shells. Three men were killed and nearly twenty more were badly wounded. Under fire, Dr. Uri Freund, the battalion doctor, and some of the soldiers carried the wounded on their backs to a collecting point. It took nearly an hour to bring up ambulances and send the wounded to the hospitals in the city.

Yalovsky's assignment had been to take the blockhouse on the left flank, which the Israelis nicknamed the "Yellow Shuttered House." The bombardment delayed and weakened his attack. This exposed Major Yacov Even's company on Yalovsky's right to fire from Jordanians on Mount Zion just across the Hinnom Valley from Abu Tor.

Even's mission was to seize the Jordanians' strongest fortification, called the "Platoon House." Following a 120-mm mortar barrage, Even blasted his way with bangalores through a stone and concrete wall topped by barbed wire. Even, his runner, radioman and three more soldiers dashed through the hole in the wall. One man fell into a deep trench behind the wall and broke his leg.

Even led the way swiftly across an open area into a small empty house. The Jordanians fired on them. The major saw that the rest of his company was not following him. He was furious: "I didn't know what's going on." He sent back a man to find out. What was happening was that the Jordanians with precise fire picked off the next twelve men through the gap in the wall. Even plunged on into the next building, a two-story house in front of the Platoon House. This building was not empty; Even and his handful of men wiped out its defenders. Even stepped out on a second-floor balcony to survey the Platoon House. He was immediately hit twice in the left shoulder and hand by a Jordanian sharpshooter on Mount Zion. A cement pillar deflected some of the shots, but Even was hurled off the balcony to the steps below.

Recovering from the shock of the fall and under cover of smoke from grenades and mortars, Even and his men stormed the Platoon House. They met no opposition. By now, Yalovsky's remaining soldiers were attacking the Yellow Shuttered

House and Even's men helped them dislodge a Jordanian platoon.

Meanwhile, on Even's right, Captain Kedar's company attacked the next blockhouse—the two-story, stone "Lion House"—and killed four Jordanians inside. Once it was taken and the area nearby cleared, Kedar reported to Lt. Col. Peikas, who had come forward to direct the battle. Four Jordanians fleeing from the houses on the left ran toward them. The Israelis killed two, but the others dove into the trench where Peikas was standing. One of them shot him in the back. Captain Johnny Heyman, the battalion intelligence officer, grappled with the Jordanian who had shot Peikas. Heyman fought hand-to-hand and with a knife until he could get to his Uzi and kill him. The fourth Jordanian was mortally wounded.

Kedar, the first to reach the badly wounded Peikas, tried to bandage him. He called frantically for Dr. Freund to come up. The doctor had established an aid station just on the Israeli side of the Green Line near Major Moshe "Shvung" Rosenblatt, Peikas' second in command and a lawyer in civilian life. Freund faced a dilemma: Should he leave the wounded? Should he have Peikas brought to him? Should he jeopardize himself, the only doctor on the battlefield? He decided quickly that if he radioed for Peikas to be brought to him, it would be regarded as cowardice. He says, "The morale of the battalion would suffer. It was clear to me that I had to go there. I would never forgive myself if I didn't go for any reason."

To reach Peikas, Dr. Freund had to cross a street covered by Jordanian machine guns. Everyone who had attempted to pass that spot had been killed or wounded. Freund and a medical corpsman tried to advance. They tried to fool the machine gunners by throwing stones, hoping for a pause in the fire. In the end, Freund just went. He made it across; the corpsman did not. Freund dashed on alone from trench to trench, trying to locate the trench where Peikas lay. By the time he reached it, Peikas was obviously dead. He had died in several minutes. "There was nothing to do."

They carried Peikas out on a stretcher and Freund returned to his aid station, where many casualties were gathered. He and his five corpsmen worked hard, stopping bleeding and fixing broken bones.

By now, Lieutenant Moshe Haviv's company had taken the

fourth blockhouse—the "Lulav Position"—on the right flank. Before Peikas was shot, he had ordered Haviv forward to take "Banana Hill." His advance was to be preceded by a mortar barrage. But because the battalion was short of walkie-talkies, a runner had to be sent back with the message for the mortars to open fire. This took time; and when the mortars started firing, Haviv's company was already on Banana Hill. The Israeli mortar fire killed and wounded about forty in the company.

Both Eli Kedar and Aaron Kamara, the tank commander who had joined the battle in his Jeep, saw the mortar fire plowing into the Israeli company. For a moment, both officers thought it was extremely accurate Jordanian fire; but suddenly each one realized it might be Israeli fire. Swiftly, Kamara radioed and was told that the Israeli mortars were indeed firing on Abu Tor. He shouted, "Stop the bombing. You are shelling our own soldiers." Kedar also radioed Major Rosenblatt to halt the fire. It was too late. The barrage was already over with disastrous results.

The battle went on all afternoon. Plunging through the Arab part of Abu Tor, the Israelis bypassed Jordanian soldiers in some of the buildings. They came out of the houses behind the Israelis, and hand-to-hand street fighting broke out. The Israelis had to battle their way back through the area to clear it.

Major Even was sure he could go down into the valley, break into the Old City and take the Western Wall. He says, "My soldiers were trigger-happy at the moment because we had so many casualties. We caught an Arab soldier and discovered that they were putting on women's clothes over their uniforms and running away as women. Some soldiers wanted to fire indiscriminately at running Arabs, but I was very severe about this and the fire stopped immediately."

Even radioed that he wanted to go into the valley toward the Old City. He was ordered to hold his position. "I didn't understand it. As a soldier, one of the first principles of battle is to exploit your success. To my surprise, I was not allowed to do it. I wanted to talk to Peikas personally because I knew he would send me farther. He was a very capable officer. Everybody told me, 'Wait, wait, he can't talk to you just now. He's delayed. He has problems in some other place. Just wait and don't move.' So I stayed in my place. Of course, Peikas was dead by that time and they were all under heavy shock. I think we could have taken the Wailing Wall that afternoon and saved the paratroopers very many casualties."

Captain Kedar's company had only one soldier killed. He had been sent back for ammunition after the fighting and ran into a Jordanian soldier and they killed each other. Kedar's men evacuated the wounded from the terraces of Banana Hill. It was exhausting work and took from 6 P.M. until 1 A.M., when a second-line battalion relieved the remnant of the 163rd Battalion. Of the two hundred Israelis actually in the fighting for Abu Tor, seventeen were dead and fifty-four wounded badly enough to be evacuated. Most of the casualties were in Yalovsky's and Haviv's companies and the majority were caused by Israeli fire.

It was the Jerusalem Brigade's hardest fight of the war. Although it had attacked in daylight with minimal support, it had been punished heavily by long-range fire, both Jordanian and its own. But by now, Kamara says, "The Arabs had lost the will to fight."

A number of the Israelis who fought on Abu Tor remember vividly a beautiful seven-year-old Arab girl who was wounded by a bullet in the chest and was found by men of Even's company. They brought her and her mother to Dr. Freund; the girl was dying and Freund was deeply touched by the sight. He had children of the same age. He removed blood and air from her chest, gave her an intravenous injection and rushed her to Sha'are Zedek Hospital. In the emergency room her heart stopped, but she was revived. Freund visited her when he came to see his wounded after the war; she was lying among the soldiers. She stayed in the hospital for many months and later died.

While the battle drove north and south of the Old City, the noncombatants stuck in the UN's MAC house in no-man's-land remained in danger. General Bull had left the decision of evacuating the MAC house to Lt. Col. Stanaway, and the New Zealander said he would stay unless he were ordered out.

At 2:30 P.M. Tuesday, Stanaway decided it was safe to evacuate all nonessential personnel. Eight of his vehicles had been destroyed, but another dozen were still operable; and Stanaway sent most everyone west to Ein Karem.

While they were outside evacuating most of the UN personnel, they heard cries from a Jordanian pillbox near the MAC house. Two officers went over to see where the cry was coming from and found two dead bodies and a man with a broken arm. Apparently, a paratrooper had lobbed in a grenade during the night. The wounded man was sent to Hadassah Hospital and recovered.

Five volunteers remained in the MAC house: Stanaway, two Australian and one Canadian officer and a Filipino male secretary who was also a superb cook. One of the Australians left a few hours later, and the remaining four were busy keeping in contact with their outstations and writing up reports of the battle. Most important from their point of view, they kept the building occupied and the UN flag flying.

Mohammad Koshour, his wife, Amenah, and their six young children lived on the Arab side of the line on Abu Tor. Koshour, who was twenty-nine and wore a neat small mustache, had worked for ten years as an inspector of services for the Municipality of Jordanian Jerusalem. On Monday, the family had collected in their home and watched the battle begin. They had no shelters, and about sixty people from seven or eight families huddled in a cave through that long, embattled night.

On Tuesday, when the Israelis attacked Abu Tor, Koshour says, "I saw one tank come at my house and crush two rooms. Houses of my neighbors were also damaged. I saw the Jordan soldiers escape and running. I saw the Jewish soldiers kill the young people and take the girls. It seemed like a dream. It happened so quickly.

"I told my people they should not run away. It is our city. They take us or not take us. We know from '48 that nothing happens. We must stay in our homes.

"But the women and small children started crying. So about four in the afternoon we moved to the east, walking through the Kidron Valley and six or seven kilometers. We found a cave and slept in it. There were more than twenty families in this big cave.

"Wednesday morning, we continued walking through the valleys and mountains. We saw airplanes and heard the guns. Everybody was frightened. Most of us were without shoes; we had no arms. We had six children and no water, no milk. My youngest son was five and a half months old. We got to the old road between Jerusalem and Bethlehem. We saw buses and trucks escaping from Hebron to the east. One driver asked if we wanted to go to Jordan. But I thought it is better to go to my parents in the village of Dura, which is fifteen kilometers southwest of Hebron. We walked south to Hebron. From a mountaintop we saw the fire in the Augusta Victoria Hospital on the Mount of Olives. We had nothing to eat. That night, very tired, we slept in a cave with many other families. We found water there but no milk, and my wife wouldn't give the children milk directly from the goats. One man had a little sugar so we put sugar in a cloth and put it in the water and put it in the baby's mouth."

Tuesday evening, Colonel Amitai took out his assault troops to rest and reorganize and put a second-line battalion on Abu Tor. The Jerusalem Brigade had secured the whole southern side of Jerusalem. The brigade was now in position either to circle the city from the south and cut the Jericho road or to strike out to the south.

At dusk, the Jordanian infantry brigade in Jerusalem received orders to withdraw. Its officers were told that Jerusalem had fallen. As the troops moved eastward, Israeli flares lit up the area between Jerusalem and Jericho. The Jordanians had to escape before Ben-Ari's armor in the north and Amitai in the south could pinch off the West Bank of the Jordan Valley and trap them. Whoever could, got out Tuesday night and Wednesday morning. By 5 A.M., the Jordanians moved back north of Jerusalem and arrived at Jericho at midmorning. They tried to reorganize the units that assembled there, but Israeli air attacks drove them back across the Jordan River.

In Jerusalem, the city outside the walls was in Israeli hands.

Meanwhile, inside the Old City, Governor al-Khatib, exhausted, had gone to rest at the Islamic Council Center near the Temple Mount. The Jordanian brigade commander could no longer communicate with his units.

At midnight, the governor sent Brig. Gen. Hazzáa a note, addressing him as the father of his eldest son as a sign of respect:

My brother Abu Abdullah:

History will record this heroic deed of you and your men.
You have done more than a usual soldier would do and
beyond your capacities as human beings. I sincerely hope
reinforcements will arrive soon. Would you mind in-
quiring about the situation at Beit Hanina because Um
Hashim [his wife] and Hind [his daughter] and Hashim
[his son] are alone there? With a thousand thanks.

Sincerely yours,
Anwar
June 6, 1967

In the morning, the Israelis occupied Governor al-Khatib's
house in Beit Hanina, but no harm came to his family.

The fighting at the Old City's gates continued until about
1 A.M. Wednesday. The Jordanians had one company at Zion
Gate on the southern side of the Old City, but the Israelis did
not attack in that area. Hazzáa recalls thinking, "The Israelis
may have left it open to let the men get out. All the other gates
were heavily attacked.

"At 1:30, the Israelis started using loudspeakers advising
the civilians and the army to lay down their arms. A delegation
headed by the mayor of Jerusalem came to me requesting that
we lay down our arms. But I would not give in. I said, 'After
we are finished, gentlemen, you can do what you like, but I
have a duty to do.'"

But the Jordanian resistance began to dwindle. Hazzáa says,
"The soldiers had been fighting nonstop for forty-eight hours
and were exhausted. About 2:30, reviewing the situation again
and knowing that the army had withdrawn to the east, I came
to the conclusion that it was no use spilling the blood of exhausted soldiers. I discussed the situation with Governor al-
Khatib and Hassam al-Khalidi and put before them three
proposals: continuing resistance to the last man or to withdraw
or to surrender.

"The governor gave me a kiss on the forehead and said,
'Abu Abdullah, whenever the subject of Jerusalem is men-
tioned, I will bow my head to the ground in honor of what you
and the Jordanian armed forces have done in Jerusalem. This
is in appreciation for what you and your men have done with

the limited resources you had. My advice is that you withdraw with your men."

As for himself, Governor al-Khatib says, "I preferred to remain here among my people. Whatever happened, I wanted to share their fate."

Hazzáa was deeply moved by al-Khatib's statement. The general had tried to defend Jordanian Jerusalem with one brigade against three Israeli brigades. The promised reinforcements of Jordanian and Iraqi troops had never arrived. Of the loss of the city, he says, "It wasn't our mistake. It was the Arab mistake."

Around 3 A.M., Brig. Gen. Hazzáa left the Old City on foot through Dung Gate. "With me were my intelligence officer, my Second Battalion commander and two men—my driver without a car and a bodyguard, a private. The next evening we found Jewish tanks in Jericho so we went to the right toward the Dead Sea and crossed the [Abdullah] bridge."

In the Old City, there remained at the gates about forty soldiers from the Second Battalion and about one hundred men of the Eighth Battalion. Some soldiers changed into civilian clothes and stole out of the Old City. By the time the Israelis finally entered the Old City, there was no organized resistance. Soldiers fought in small units and alone.

Major Salah, the artillery commander, and others of the command group spent Tuesday night in the streets of the Old City near the Temple Mount. Early Wednesday morning, Salah decided to leave the Old City and try to reorganize his units. He and Captain Jawdat and a driver took a Land Rover, opened the wooden doors of the Lions Gate and sped down the road past Gethsemane on the road to Jericho south of the Mount of Olives. An Israeli machine gun fired on them as they fled, and a bullet hit the Land Rover's radiator. They made it to Al-Azariyah, raced on to Jericho, crossed the Jordan River and met up with Captain Jawdat's Second Battery near the Allenby Bridge east of the river.

Chaim Herzog, who was assigned to be the military governor for the Israeli Central Command, had organized his staff at Ramla on Monday and told them to be ready to move up to Jerusalem the next day. He drove ahead to Jerusalem in his private Peugeot; and on Tuesday at 2 P.M., he broadcast from the radio studio in the Russian Compound: "I am broadcasting from Jerusalem to the sound of heavy shelling. A strange form of quiet and anticipation has fallen along the front line, a quiet that may foretell great tidings . . . These hours may yet be among the greatest in the history of our people for thousands of years. Every man and child will retell the story of these times until his dying day. For we have been privileged to live to see the Armies of Israel with the Lord of the Hosts of Israel at their head poised before the Gates of the Eternal City."[1]

— Chapter 20 —

THE RIDGE

IN THE MIDDLE OF TUESDAY AFTERNOON, CAPTAIN YORAM Zamush, the religious young commander of A Company of the paratroopers' Seventy-first Battalion, walked from his command post, which was on the balcony of an Arab villa almost directly above the fire station and overlooking Wadi el Joz, to battalion headquarters in a house near the open square facing the Rockefeller Museum and the corner of the Old City wall.

Outside the headquarters building, he saw piles of weapons and ammunition collected from the paratroopers who had been killed and wounded. For the first time, Zamush had an idea of what had happened to his fellow paratroopers. He says, "It was quite frightening."

By now Gur's brigade had more than eighty men dead and hundreds wounded. The unsupported night attack, the headlong dash down Nablus Road and the fight on Ammunition Hill had cost dearly in lives.

But Ben-Ari's tank brigade commanded the northern approaches to Jerusalem; the Jerusalem Brigade held Government House and Abu Tor south of the Old City, and Gur's paratroopers had swept over the Arab quarters north of the Old City walls.

During the late morning, Gur had moved his headquarters from the apartment house in Yoel Street to the Rockefeller Museum to command the next phase of the battle.

The first job was to clear the high ridge east of the city, from Mount Scopus south through Augusta Victoria to the Mount of Olives. At the Rockefeller Museum, Major Moshe Stempel, Gur's deputy, worked out a plan for the afternoon. The Seventy-first Battalion, which had been battered less than the other two, would attack the eastern ridge as soon as possible. Major Sharfman on Mount Scopus reported that Augusta Victoria was empty of Jordanian troops.

Until now, the paratroopers had been asked to accomplish their mission at all costs. But they found that, despite their expectations, the Jordanians had fought well. The paratroop commanders decided the next stage would be more carefully prepared, more cautious, slower, more massive—and with tanks. They had been taught a lesson.

That's when the call went out for Major Eytan Arieli's tanks from the Harel Brigade to report to the Rockefeller Museum. They were delayed en route, and the afternoon was gone before four of Arieli's tanks arrived at the museum.

And Captain Yeshaya was summoned back from the Police Training School where his Jerusalem Brigade tankers had been refueling and rearming. Ben-Ari's supply column was passing through the police school area and there was great confusion. The people bringing Yeshaya more machine-gun ammunition could not find him. It was evening before Yeshaya's tanks reached the museum.

Because of all the delays, Gur's attack on the ridge was becoming another night operation. Israeli aircraft worked over the ridge and set fire to the Victoria Augusta Hospital. Gur told Yeshaya to have two tanks fire toward Augusta Victoria "just to annoy them"; a shell was shot at the ridge every ten minutes or so. The staff and patients were safely in the hospital's basement shelter.

At about 5 P.M., attracted to the expectation of climactic battle, a special scout unit showed up at the Rockefeller Museum, looking for a share of the fighting. It was commanded by Major Micha Kapusta, a veteran guerrilla fighter; and he was accompanied by the legendary Meir Har-Zion, whom Dayan had called "the best soldier Israel ever had."

The two old war dogs had fought together with Unit 101, a small commando force that had been organized in 1953 with never more than forty carefully selected men under Major Ariel Sharon to execute reprisal raids against Arab guerrillas—without arousing American and other outside objections. In those days, Har-Zion had been Kapusta's commander; in 1967, their roles were reversed—but it really didn't matter.

Kapusta, whose assignment with the Eightieth Brigade had been washed out, like Gur's, by the rapid progress on the

Egyptian front, was known throughout the Israeli army. He was a cool, blue-eyed, muscular man of thirty-three who had been wounded in action four times and was now a farmer north of Haifa and the father of two small children. Today, Gur had work for Kapusta and his men.

Under the attack plan, Captain Yeshaya's tanks would go first. Arieli's tanks would provide covering fire against the ridge. Major Eilam's Seventy-first Battalion would attack on foot across the Kidron Valley and up the long road exposed to Jordanian shellfire to the ridge. While the Sixty-sixth Battalion held Sheikh Jarrah, the Twenty-eighth Battalion, which had been so badly chewed up in Nablus Road, would clear the area short of the ridge and, if the order ever came, would attack the Old City from the Rockefeller Museum.

The operation started with still another disaster. About 7 P.M., the brigade organized an assault unit of ten tanks followed by seven of Kapusta's Jeeps, armed with machine guns and recoilless rifles, to lead the way to Augusta Victoria. Major Achmon tried to show Major Eilam, Major Kapusta and Captain Yeshaya how they were to go. Because of sniper fire, they could not actually see the road itself. There was little time to study maps; Gur was pressing to get started.

Between the front of the Rockefeller Museum and the northeast corner of the Old City wall, the open square, where five roads converged, was under heavy fire from the Jordanians on the wall. The assault unit was to dash through this square and make a very sharp left, go down the steep hill between Sammy Mustaklem's fire station and the city produce market and rush up the hill road at the end of Wadi el Joz, pass the Palace Hotel and on the ridgetop turn left to the Augusta Victoria.

When the assault unit started out at 7:30, Captain Yeshaya in the turret of the lead tank missed the sharp left turn into the valley. He says, "It was very dark; you saw nothing. I continued without knowing that I passed the turn. I could not see it. The turn to Augusta Victoria was a U-turn; if you missed the entrance, you didn't know it."

In single file, the tanks groped blindly forward under fire from the Jordanians high above them on the Old City wall. From his turret, Yeshaya could barely see the road; part of the time he thought his tank was on the sidewalk. For a stretch the road sweeps away from the city wall and is protected by a low retaining wall of a Muslim cemetery between the road and the city wall. Then, it drops quickly into the Kidron Valley between the Old City and the Mount of Olives on the eastern ridge. The tanks drove down the hill as far as the bridge where the road turns abruptly left by the Garden of Gethsemane. Jesus had spent his last night there outside the city walls, and now the Franciscans kept the place immaculate with flowers and ancient gnarled olive trees.

As he passed the Lions Gate and approached the bridge, Yeshaya called Gur on the radio and said he thought he was on the wrong road. Gur told him to put on his lights and see where he was. The tank lights had been shot out so Gur ordered a searchlight turned on. There, on the bridge—almost directly below the blocked-up twin Golden Gate of the Old City through which Jesus had passed on the first Palm Sunday and through which, Jewish tradition has it, the Messiah will enter the Old City directly to the Temple Mount—the Israeli assault force was caught and pounded by Jordanian fire from the Old City wall and a machine gun in the cemetery of the onion-domed Russian Orthodox Church. The city wall dominates the exposed bridge, and the Jordanians had zeroed in on it in advance. The Israelis plunged into the trap.

"It was something horrible," says Yeshaya. "I saw that I was trapped and I gave my tanks orders to return. All my tanks turned and climbed back toward the museum. Mine was standing on the bridge, shooting toward the wall giving covering fire. I started to turn and the Jordanians started shooting flares. They caught me there like in daylight. I was wounded above the eye and the blood started and I could see hardly anything. I told my radioman to take command."

Yeshaya's tank had already started to turn and was standing crosswise on the bridge with its cannon pointed right toward the Old City wall. When the radioman got out of the tank, he thought mistakenly that the tank was facing the same way as its guns. He told the driver to go straight ahead. The move happened too fast for Yeshaya in the turret to stop it. The tank bulled across the bridge, crashed over the side, fell more than twenty feet and landed upside down. Yeshaya was knocked unconscious.

The entire episode happened very quickly; distances were short. Gur realized that something was terribly wrong. He thought that Yeshaya turned left too soon and had headed north rather than east down into the valley. He sent Kapusta's waiting recon unit to see what was happening.

Back in the square, one tank received a bazooka round; its camouflage netting burst into flames. Its commander got out to extinguish the fire. He was hit. Trying to get around the tanks in the square, Kapusta's spearhead platoon commander repeated Yeshaya's mistake and headed down the hill parallel to the city wall. The Jeeps overtook Yeshaya's tanks and were caught in the Jordanian fire.

The driver of the lead Jeep kept his head and swung his vehicle around. The spearhead platoon commander sitting beside him and the two men in the rear were wounded, but the driver brought the damaged Jeep back to the first-aid station at the Rockefeller. One of the men died there.

The rest of the column was brought to a bloody halt. The driver of the second Jeep, Uri Arbell, tried to turn but the next vehicle struck him from behind. Bullets hit Arbell's fuel tank, turning his Jeep into a torch. Uri Koton from Kibbutz Dafna and Yoav Gross were killed. Reuven Cohen, shot in the legs, found himself thrown into the road facing the sky. The fourth Jeep, with its driver, Reuven Schacham, shot, slid against Cohen's body and stopped.

Bullets tore off a toe and smashed into the thigh and abdomen of the fourth Jeep's commander, Uri Levitan. He lay on his Jeep's hood, swung its machine gun around and fired at the city wall until another bullet struck his shoulder and mortar fragments ripped his face. He struggled to reach the wall of the bridge, fell over it and was badly hurt again. But he climbed back up the hill to safety.

Three Jeeps stood on the bridge; their occupants, easy targets. Arie Golan was sitting next to Sergeant Gabai in the back of Arbell's Jeep when its gas tank was hit. Golan's uniform was set on fire. Arbell grabbed an Uzi and tried to cover Golan while he fought the flames. Arbell was wounded. Gabai jumped out and tried to help Levitan and his men. Both Jeeps were burning. Shrapnel wounded Gabai badly in the foot. He lay down on the bridge; and when there was a break in the fire, he found Reuven Cohen. Holding hands, they staggered up the road, helping each other. Near the Lions Gate, they reached the protected part of the column. Gabai tried to go back and help bring out the wounded, but he lost consciousness.

Inside the Old City, Brig. Gen. Hazzáa recalls, "I could easily hear the Israeli soldiers crying from destroyed tanks and armored personnel carriers."

Major Kapusta in the fifth Jeep sent soldiers forward to rescue the wounded near the bridge, and recon men from the rear of the column started to run down the hill to help. Captain Ya'acov "Hubi" Eilam rushed from the seventh Jeep, still shielded by the cemetery wall. A big man and an athletic champion, Eilam had been born thirty years before in Hadassah Hospital on Mount Scopus across the valley and was now an honor student in medicine at the new Hadassah Hospital in Ein Karem. He was also an oboist and had recently been accepted to play with the Jerusalem Symphony. Eilam repeatedly made his way to the bridge under fire and carried out five men to the sheltered Jeeps.

Sergeant Israel Shindler hurried forward from the last command car. Born in Hungary in 1940, Shindler was a religious man with a full beard, glasses and a yarmulke. In 1959, he had been severely wounded with shrapnel in his liver, but he had fought his way back into the recon unit. He and Eilam and several others tried to cross the road from the cemetery wall to the bridge. A Jordanian flare threw them into brilliant light. They drew fire immediately and jumped back against the wall. Shindler told Eilam he thought they had no chance to get out alive. Eilam didn't answer. When the flare died, Shindler and another soldier raced out and dragged back a wounded soldier. Shindler returned to the bridge and found Arie Golan with his uniform in flames. His hands were burned badly and he could not extinguish the fire. Golan screamed at Shindler to shoot him and end his pain. But Shindler cut off Golan's jacket and shirt with his commando knife and lifted him onto his shoulders. At that instant, the wounded man took a bullet in his head. Shindler vaulted over the wall of the bridge and hung there by his now severely burned hands.

Captain Eilam called for tanks to protect the remaining men; then, as the firing increased, he too hung from the bridge out of the line of fire. In the darkness, Eilam and Shindler did not know how far was the drop off the wall if they let go. Finally,

Shindler's burned hands could hold no longer. He fell some twenty feet, injuring his leg and back. But he managed to crawl up the hill until he reached Dr. Hadas' recon aid station. The doctor examined him by the light of a flashlight and found that his hands were burned to red flesh and that he had two bullet wounds. But Shindler, seeing more seriously wounded come in, shrugged off the offer of a morphine shot and dragged himself back to Dr. King's brigade aid station.

Two of Arieli's tanks arrived at the bridge. Captain Eilam hoisted himself from the bridge back onto the road and helped the wounded. The second tank was hit by a bazooka shell. The crew escaped; "Hubi" Eilam was killed.

The assault unit's radios were now knocked out. Gur sent Major Achmon forward. He had to cross the open square under intense fire. He took a bazooka team and tried to silence the shooting from the wall. The bazooka's backblast hurled Achmon into the air. He ordered a machine gun set up; and under its covering fire, he and his small group ran downhill to the trapped men. They brought back some of the wounded and left the Jeeps and the dead—Koton, Gross, Eilam and Golan—by the road.

Meanwhile, Captain Yeshaya and his crew were in their upside-down tank at the bottom of the ravine next to the bridge. Jordanian lights still held the tank in their grip; so many bullets hit the tank that virtually all the paint was scraped from its shell. When Yeshaya regained consciousness he was just able to squeeze out of the turret. The tank's main gun was almost buried in the ground. The crewmen escaped through other hatches. Yeshaya could not find his glasses; without them, everything seemed a blurred nightmare. He was being fired at and fired back. He says, "I didn't know what was going on. I thought the bridge was covered with Jordanians. I took my pistol and waited for them to catch me. I didn't know where my people were. I moved two hundred yards from the tank and lay under an olive tree in the garden.

"I heard steps and I took out my pistol to shoot. I heard they were speaking Hebrew. I shouted at them and they shouted back and found me. It was my crew. Now we were five. Only the driver was unhurt. I told him to go back to the tank and bring the Uzis and the maps. I was afraid the maps would fall into the hands of the Arabs. When he came back with the Uzis and maps, we hid under the bridge for more than two hours." Then, they started up the hill toward the museum and met the crew of the Harel Brigade tank that was burning on the bridge. Although they had to climb only a few hundred yards, it took them nearly until dawn to reach the Rockefeller Museum and to report to Gur. Yeshaya was taken to Hadassah Hospital to have his wounds treated and new glasses made. It was mid-afternoon before he rejoined his unit.

"All battles are full of mistakes," Yeshaya says philosophically. But he cannot understand why his tanks were sent out first without infantry protection in the night attack. He adds, "Infantry people think a tank can solve every problem."

Hours after the tragedy at the bridge, when the survivors had returned up the hill, Major Kapusta saw that he was still missing six men. Hoping they were alive, he was determined to find them. His men located two wounded; the fate of the last four haunted Kapusta. Crawling as silently as an old guerrilla fighter could and followed by Har-Zion, Kapusta led a single file of a platoon of his men down the hill in the wadi east of the road out of sight of the defenders on the city wall. At the bottom, they could find no one alive. Kapusta in desperation called out the names of the missing men. He shimmied up a water pipe to the edge of the bridge and saw the four bodies.

High above them on the city wall, an Arab soldier started chanting in the darkness. To the Israelis, it sounded not like a song of joy or victory but a dirge of mourning. Kapusta said quietly, "There is nothing more to do." They crawled silently back to the Rockefeller. It was 2 A.M. Kapusta's elite unit, which never had a chance to face the enemy, now had five men dead and fourteen wounded. Before the battle was over, nine would be dead and thirty-one wounded.

During the deadly night battle on the bridge, across town Lieutenant Karni Kav was taking her lists of dead and wounded to the headquarters at the Evelina de Rothschild School. Driving through the blackout, she says, "The horizon was all on fire because they were attacking Augusta Victoria. It was all red and you could hear the bombs and shells in the distance."

Although the hospitals in Tel Aviv were almost empty, those

in Jerusalem were overflowing with an estimated 500 casualties. By Tuesday evening, Sha'are Zedek Hospital had received seventy-five civilian casualties and five had died of their wounds. Biqqur Holim Hospital in Nathan Strauss Street had nine civilian casualties of whom two had died. And Hadassah Hospital had admitted 250 wounded.[1]

The paratroopers of the Seventy-first Battalion, who were supposed to follow the tanks across the valley to the ridge, waited in the streets. They napped and talked. They heard rumors that the Jordanians were mounting a massive counter-attack from Jericho and about the assault unit's bitter fight on the bridge. A few were sent to help with the wounded.

At 8 P.M., the tanks of the assault unit that had returned to the Rockefeller Museum and seven or eight more that had now joined them set out again with two paratroop companies of the Seventy-first on the correct road past the produce market. One of Yeshaya's tanks broke down there and turned over.

When the Israeli force advanced only halfway up the hill to Augusta Victoria, brigade headquarters radioed that some forty Patton tanks of the Jordanian Sixtieth Armored Brigade were roaring up from Jericho toward Jerusalem. From Mount Scopus, Major Sharfman said the report was false—there were no Jordanian tanks. He asked to speak to Gur directly but could not reach him. Gur and his staff had no desire to meet the expected Jordanian tanks in the dark. Achmon says, "We decided that we didn't want to fight tanks in the night in a place we didn't know and we called them back." Major Uzi Eilam, the Seventy-first Battalion commander, spread out bazookas and small antitank missiles to stop them. At 10 P.M., the attack on Augusta Victoria was put off until 11:30 P.M. The paratroopers' commanders had reason to grow more cautious.

About 3 A.M., Major Eilam went to his battalion CP in an Arab house down the street from the museum. The lady of the house fed him a lavish chicken dinner and he slept for an hour.

Meanwhile, as the battle swirled around them, Sammy Mustaklem and his men were enduring their second day hidden in the firehouse without food or water. As Mustaklem says, "We were in the cellar of the battle."

They listened to the Israeli tanks clamoring outside the build-

288

ing, and evil-smelling black smoke from their exhausts filled their hiding place. They sat quietly, hoping not to be discovered. They heard the tanks exchanging fire with artillery on the Mount of Olives. They heard winches trying to rescue the tank that had broken down in front of the market. Their storeroom was loaded with kerosene, naphtha and benzine and with stacks of hay for donkeys and mules of days long past. Mustaklem feared that a spark would incinerate them all. He thought of putting something on his body, perhaps a key, so it would be identified if they all died.

Toward dawn, the man with the heart attack grew worse. He begged constantly for help they could not give. Says Mustaklem, "I decided the best thing would be to open the door and ask for help. Later, I heard the Israelis had announced that whoever went outside with a white flag wouldn't be hurt. But we didn't know this. I opened the door. I looked and I could see the hospital on Augusta Victoria burning. I couldn't see any houses on the Mount of Olives because of the black clouds from the shelling. I thought all the houses on the Mount of Olives were destroyed." Mustaklem closed the door.

About 4 A.M., General Narkiss began pressing Gur to prepare to attack. Narkiss feared that the Great Powers would intervene. Achmon says, "Motta tried to tell him to relax. We didn't want to be in a hurry a second time. The first day we had a lot of casualties and we didn't want to hurry again." At 5:30, Narkiss informed Gur that at 8:30 A.M. aircraft would attack Augusta Victoria and the paratroopers should start their assault.

Brigade headquarters moved from the museum to a nearby roof where the officers could overlook the whole field of battle. They found seven Jordanian soldiers hiding in the attic. At 6 A.M., Gur called the commanders of the Twenty-eighth and Seventy-first Battalions to the roof. He talked on the radio with Yossi Yaffe, the commander of the Sixty-sixth Battalion, and ordered him on to Mount Scopus, and sent his operations officer to brief him. This time, the Sixty-Sixth would join the attack on the ridge. This time, they would have air support.

"Our order was to capture the ridge," says Achmon. "The plan was very simple. Yossi Yaffe was to go from Mount Scopus to Augusta Victoria, and Uzi Eilam would cross the valley and climb Augusta Victoria and take the Arab village of Et Tur on the Mount of Olives. The tanks and the reconnaissance unit would go by road to the Inter-Continental Hotel on the top of the Mount of Olives. The brigade headquarters in two half-tracks and a few command cars would follow the Seventy-first to Augusta Victoria." The Twenty-eighth, the hard-hit old-timers, would wait in case they could take the Old City. Gur ordered the artillery to fire at the Old City wall to drive away its defenders. Two rounds hit the paratroopers in the museum courtyard, killing at least eight.

Early that morning, Dr. Farah, the director of the Augusta Victoria Hospital, told his people that he could no longer protect them. He gave them each five dinars, and some, including the last two soldiers, left the bomb-wracked hospital to try to reach Jericho or even Amman.

Mrs. Zumurod Kawas, a Greek Orthodox senior staff nurse who had been born in the Old City, was responsible for twelve maternity and gynecological patients. When Dr. Farah dismissed the staff, Mrs. Kawas went quickly among the pine and olive trees to the Ascension Church in Bet Faji before Bethany. Planes were bombing and she stayed in the church. That afternoon, she went to the Russian Convent in Gethsemane. On the way, an old man near her was killed. But she reached the convent safely and remained there until the fighting was over.

The Israelis attacked exactly at 8:30 A.M. with aircraft and artillery softening the area in front of the paratroopers. They advanced. Four Super-Mystères attacked from Mount Scopus toward Augusta Victoria with napalm and then strafed.

The ground attack led by nine tanks commanded by Arieli went smoothly because during the night the Jordanians, broken by Tuesday's battles, had pulled back to the east. The garrison on Mount Scopus watched them go. And the Israeli Air Force had destroyed any Jordanian tanks that might have come up from the Jordan Valley.

Rabin says, "General Riad issued a withdrawal order to all the Jordanian forces west of the Jordan. King Hussein interfered and that night the order was changed. In the evening, the Egyptian forces were ordered to withdraw behind the [Sinai] passes; and therefore, Nasser couldn't tell King Hussein, 'You continue to fight!' To get an order to withdraw and five or eight hours later to get an order, 'No, you shouldn't; you have to continue to fight'—is not very healthy."

The morning attack on the ridge flushed no resistance. Seeing the paratroopers advancing far below his post in the Magnes tower on Mount Scopus, Major Sharfman radioed that Augusta Victoria was empty. Nevertheless, with the tanks leading and with air support and engineers clearing the mines near Mount Scopus, the two paratroop battalions attacked the ridge. B and D companies led the Seventy-first Battalion's assault. The Sixty-sixth came across from Mount Scopus supported by machine guns it placed on the hill. The commander of the Sixty-sixth's attacking task force, Captain Giora Ashkenazi, D Company's commander who had led the battalion across no-man's-land thirty hours before, was killed by machine-gun fire while climbing the road from Mount Scopus to Augusta Victoria. Standing high above the attack force, Sharfman raced down and ordered the machine gunners to stop firing. The pointless assault was soon over, and Colonel Gur notified Central Command headquarters that Augusta Victoria "is ours."

Inside the Augusta Victoria Hospital, a guard spotted tanks approaching up the ridge from Jerusalem and rushed to tell Dr. Farah that the Iraqis had come at last. "Where are they?" Dr. Farah asked excitedly.

Carrying two white sheets, a small party led by Donald Scott, the head of the Lutheran World Federation in Jordan who had come up from the Old City on Monday, went out to meet the tanks. The Israeli officer in charge asked where the Jordanian soldiers were. Scott assured them this was a hospital. The Israeli asked for the medical director and Dr. Farah came outside. The Israelis inspected the building thoroughly. No one moved while they searched for the soldiers they believed to be hidden there. They ordered the staff, and the forty local residents who had come to the hospital Tuesday night for safety, to come outside with their hands on their heads and to bring out the patients. Several could not be moved. The Israelis could not tell if any of the seeming civilians had been soldiers a few hours earlier. They told all of them to face the wall, empty their pockets and lay everything on the ground in front of them. The Israelis searched each one. Says Dr. Majaj, "Everyone was scared stiff. The impression was they would machine-gun everyone."

After an hour, while the staff and patients sat on the ground with their hands on their heads, the Israelis allowed everyone to return to the basement and the staff to make lunch. A schedule was arranged by which a doctor and two nurses were on duty in two-hour shifts. No one in the hospital was wounded or killed in the battle. The Israelis took down the UN flag and raised their own.

Achmon says, "I was in charge of communications with headquarters and Motta was on the radio nets with the units. Just as we were on our way, we received permission to go into the Old City. So we raced to the Inter-Continental Hotel and reached it at about half past nine. In the square in front of the hotel, overlooking the entire Old City, we made the last plan and formed the last order of how we would enter the Old City."

Chapter 21

THE OLD CITY

EVEN WHEN THE ISRAELIS INVADED JORDANIAN JERUSALEM, they had still not decided to retake the Old City. At the Cabinet meeting in the Knesset basement Monday evening, the ministers favored taking the Old City but delayed a decision and Dayan recommended surrounding it and letting the Arabs hang out white flags. On Tuesday, while the Israelis advanced into East Jerusalem, the Defense Committee of the Cabinet discussed whether to take the Old City. Yigael Yadin says, "That Tuesday, Dayan was against taking it by storm. He said it is a tough job to take the whole city. Let's not hurry. The commander in Jerusalem, Uzi Narkiss, and Motta Gur both pressed all the time to go and take the Old City. The one who was hesitating at that time was Dayan. His point was that it would be a costly operation and they are surrounded anyhow."

That evening, the Cabinet met in Eshkol's office in the Tel Aviv suburb of Sharona. The ministers were getting nervous. There was argument. Eshkol wanted to seize the moment. Menachem Begin and the National Religious Party members no longer trusted the idea of waiting for the Arabs to surrender the Old City. There might not be time. But Moshe Chaim Shapiro, the Interior Minister, still had doubts. The head of the Religious Party warned that if the Old City were taken it could never again be given up; maybe it was better to keep praying for it. They all worried about the safety of the Holy Places. "It became like a holy meeting," Aviad Yaffe thought. "Begin, 'the Polish Baron,' said it was a historic moment. Each one of us felt it."

Mrs. Uzay, the Cabinet Secretary, remembers, "They all said if this war has any sense, it is to unify Jerusalem again."

The ministers decided they could no longer wait for Dayan's

white flags. Yadin says, "The final decision was taken. Dayan's hesitations were overruled, because we saw the war may be finished soon [by a UN cease-fire], and it was inconceivable that the Old City would not be conquered."

On Wednesday morning, the *Jerusalem Post* published a front-page editorial entitled simply: "Jerusalem." "The battle for Jerusalem has been won," the *Post* said. "Israel cannot permit itself to be locked out of the Old City again or to rely on the uncertain services of the UN for its right of access."

At 5 A.M., Eshkol called an emergency Cabinet meeting in Tel Aviv to confirm the plan of attack on the Old City. A rump group gathered and agreed. Eshkol said, "First of all, we have to take the Old City and the eastern part of the city so that the bombarding and shelling will stop, because this may harm the Holy Places of all nations and creeds." Miriam Eshkol remembers her husband's feelings: "He always wanted Jerusalem back. There was no Jew in the world who wouldn't like it back. He always said that Jerusalem meant for him from childhood the drive to come back to Israel. He was a boy of eighteen when he came here by himself."

Chief of Staff Rabin says, "Only on the morning of the seventh, after we had Mount Scopus with a combination of Motta's brigade and Ben-Ari's brigade, a Cabinet decision was made to take the Old City. Only then were we first allowed and then instructed to take the Old City. There was fear that the Arabs would ask for a cease-fire."

The order traveled down the chain of command. Barlev telephoned Narkiss and told him to take the Old City: "Get it and get it fast!" And Narkiss ordered Gur, who would do the job. Eshkol recessed the Cabinet until one o'clock.

About 7 A.M., Deputy Chief of Staff Haim Barlev flew up to Jerusalem in a small plane and landed at the tiny airstrip in the Valley of the Cross. He wanted to be on the scene to make absolutely sure that the Holy Places were not damaged; he knew that a worldwide outcry would arise if the Jews injured the Christian sites. He says, "It was a delicate question."

Barlev went to the Central Command's headquarters, where Lt. Col. Arik Regev, Narkiss' brilliant operations officer, was on the telephone to Gur. Then Barlev went to see Gur at the Rockefeller Museum. This Wednesday morning the streets were almost deserted. Shops were shut tight. There was no electricity. The few cars moved at high speed as though to avoid being targets. At odd intervals a bread truck would appear and a crowd would gather since no groceries were open. This was a city embattled; and even though the Jordanian army had been thrown back, the people still sensed danger and knew that final victory had not yet come.

The command group of Gur's Fifty-fifth Brigade stood in front of the Inter-Continental Hotel atop the Mount of Olives. From this hill, in Christian belief, Jesus had ascended to heaven after His Resurrection. Immediately below the paratroopers sprawled the vast old Jewish cemetery from which, pious Jews believed, the first dead would rise when God sat in the Valley of Jehoshaphat on the Day of Judgment.[1] The cemetery was now a shambles; the Jordanians had looted the rectangular tombs and the gravestones for building stones. The Israelis were appalled by the devastation.

In front of the Israeli commanders, the golden-roofed, blue Dome of the Rock and the silver-topped al-Aksa Mosque on the Temple Mount flashed in the early morning sun. Beyond and above the walled Old City rose the jumble of buildings and towers of the new Jewish section. The sight was stirring. History and modernity melded in an unparalleled panorama, which, since the Jordanians had captured the ridge nineteen years before, no Israeli had seen.

At the Temple Mount, several hundred men, many of them armed, gathered to defend the Old City. They saw jet fighter planes overhead; and, mistaking the Israeli Mystères for Iraqi aircraft coming to the rescue, the crowd shouted with joy.

The planes started bombing Augusta Victoria. Says one Jordanian official who was in the crowd, "We thought they were bombing the Hebrew University while, in fact, they were bombing the Augusta Victoria Hospital. With the dust coming up from the explosions, we couldn't see that. Then, Israeli tanks started to descend the Mount of Olives road and everybody disappeared. Suddenly, the place was empty."

That morning, while Mrs. Hall and the others tried to clean up the chaos in the consulate on Nablus Road, U.S. Consul

Pierson Hall, carrying an American flag, went out with his driver to check on Americans living in the area. He visited Mrs. Bertha Vester, now nearly ninety years old, at the American Colony Hotel, and Mrs. Alice Johnson, the Marine lieutenant colonel's wife, in the apartment off Nablus Road. He was able to tell her that her husband was alive.

As soon as Hall returned to the consulate, heavy shelling started again. A large shell destroyed the balcony outside the upstairs dining room. A water pipe broke and the office floor flooded. Thoroughly frightened, Mrs. Hall said to her husband, "This is the end, darling."

Shortly afterwards, Vice Consul M. David Bowe drove over from the consulate on the Israeli side and took Mrs. Hall and her parents to Agron Street. The Holcombes left for Rome as soon as possible.

Later, Alice Johnson was also brought across, and her husband met her at the consulate. He says, "I walked there, and there was Alice. I hadn't had any word from her." It was an emotional reunion.

The paratroopers planned to enter the Old City through the Lions or St. Stephen's Gate. Its former name comes from the pair of stone lions in relief on each side of the gate above the entrance. The lions face each other with their tails curved up over their backs. Above them are slits for snipers. Its Christian name memorializes the belief that St. Stephen, the first Christian martyr, was stoned to death nearby. The gate had been built in 1538 by Suleiman the Magnificent, who, it is said, dreamt that unless he rebuilt the Old City walls he would be eaten by lions.

The Lions Gate was the only opening on the eastern side of the Old City—the most vulnerable side, as Titus and the Crusaders had long ago proved. The Golden Gate, directly opposite the Mount of Olives, had been sealed since A.D. 1530.

The Israeli paratroopers launched their attack. General Barlev had Dayan's approval to support the paratroopers with ten mortar rounds fired into the Muslim Quarter of the Old City.

"There was no time to collect the commanders. Motta gave the order by radio," says Major Achmon. "We started by shelling the Muslim Quarter in the northeast section of the Old City for about twenty minutes. We thought the Jordanian Legion was there. We avoided hitting any of the Holy Places." But the lovely Crusader Church of St. Anne, dedicated in Romanesque style to the Mother of Mary, was damaged.

Gur's headquarters echelon of armored cars and tanks, with two half-tracks from the Jerusalem Brigade, drove down the Mount of Olives and approached the Lions Gate from the south. The Twenty-eighth Battalion at the Rockefeller Museum went by foot around the corner of the city wall to the gate; and the Seventy-first Battalion, from Augusta Victoria.

Although the main thrust was to be through the Lions Gate, one small unit was sent around to the Jaffa Gate in the far western wall of the Old City. Two others raced for the Zion Gate and the Dung Gate on the southern side of the Old City. Another headed for the Damascus Gate in the northern wall. The reconnaissance units and half of the tanks were ordered to Abu Dis to set up a block against any Jordanian armor that might try to come up from Jericho. Achmon says, "They were very angry that they had to do that rather than go into the Old City.

"Then we raced for the Lions Gate in the half-tracks. We were very eager." They drove past the onion-domed Russian Orthodox Church of St. Mary Magdalene built by Czar Alexander III. "At the bridge we passed the five Jeeps and friends who had been killed in the night battle and lay there on the ground."

"Meanwhile, Captain Yoram Zamush and his A Company were bringing up the rear of the Seventy-first Battalion's advance across the valley toward Augusta Victoria, because Gur had promised him he could be the first to take the Temple Mount and the Western Wall. When A Company reached the Palace Hotel in the valley, Major Eilam, already on Augusta Victoria, sent Zamush word that the Old City was to be entered. Two half-tracks came to him; some of his men rode them and the rest ran all the way to the Lions Gate.

As the paratroopers ran past the firehouse, where Mustaklem and his men were still hidden, the fire chief opened the door and called to a soldier. He walked over and put his rifle into Mustaklem's chest and asked, "What do you want?" Mustaklem said, "I have a man who is dying inside. I need an ambulance." The paratrooper said, "There's no time for an ambulance now.

We are going to conquer the Old City. If I am alive, I'll bring an ambulance." He left.

Two more soldiers approached, and Mustaklem asked them for help and an ambulance. One of them pointed to a Volvo parked by the firehouse and ordered Mustaklem to start the car. He told him he didn't know how without the key. The paratrooper said, "If you don't start it, I'll kill you." Mustaklem brought out another fireman and they opened the hood but did not start the car. The soldier stood the two Arabs against the wall of the firehouse and pointed his Uzi at them. Mustaklem shouted, "Wait! I have children. Why do you want to kill me? I don't have a gun. This is a cold-blood killing." The paratrooper didn't say a word, but Mustaklem saw his eyes glittering and he was shivering. Mustaklem said to his companion, "This is our end. Finished!" The second paratrooper shouted angrily to the first in Hebrew that Mustaklem could not understand and pushed his Uzi aside. Mustaklem and the fireman ran into the firehouse.

The two soldiers ordered Mustaklem outside. The soldiers told him to get a taxi parked across the road by the produce market started in two minutes or they would kill them all. Mustaklem had two mechanics inside. He persuaded one, frightened that he would be killed if he could not start the taxi, to go out and try. As soon as the mechanic touched the ignition, the taxi started. The two paratroopers drove off.

The stone Lions Gate stood at the top of a narrow uphill road defined on both sides by walls higher than a man. The walls supported cemeteries, Muslim on the right, Jewish on the left. The road was almost a wide trench. If there had been serious opposition, this could have been a death trap. But resistance was light. Zamush arrived at the entrance to the road just as Gur did. "Motta succeeded in jumping in front of me by a millimeter," says Zamush. "I was stupid enough to wait in my half-track for my men who were coming up on foot."

From the entrance to the road, one of Major Arieli's Harel Brigade tanks shelled the wooden doors of the gate. Part of the stone arch crumbled. The left door fell. Shells from the tank set a deserted Arab bus near the gate on fire. Gur shouted to his big, bearded driver, Moshe Ben Tsur: "Ben Tsur, Sa! Sa!" Go! Go! The two brigade half-tracks with Gur's in the lead, avoiding the burning bus, crashed through the Lions Gate and entered the Via Dolorosa.

"We were the first because we had the half-tracks and because we were very ambitious to go first," Achmon says. Gur jumped out first and Achmon covered him. The third man out was an Israeli reporter named Eli Landau. A half dozen officers and a bevy of communications men followed them. Straight ahead was Al-Mujahideen Road and the Via Dolorosa. To their left, the flat, open square of El-Ghazali, which was once the site of a reservoir that supplied water to the Temple, led to the Temple Mount. The square was empty, but there was sniper fire. The command group from the two half-tracks crossed the square for the Temple Mount.

Following Gur on foot, Zamush entered the Lions Gate and sent a sergeant with a squad to protect the flank. Lieutenant Amnon Eshel's brigade headquarters combat platoon fought Arab soldiers on several nearby rooftops and in a minaret to the right of the square. By now Eshel's platoon had one man killed and six wounded. Eilam's C and D companies came up behind them.

At 9:50 A.M., the paratroopers passed through the Bab el Asbat Gate in a stone wall running at right angle to the city wall. It was quiet on the Temple Mount. The Jordanians had left a field camp there. Tents were pitched and cars parked under the arches on the right. Gur's half-track had smashed a motorcycle. A field kitchen was still set up against the wall on the left. They saw few Jordanian soldiers and captured one very fat Arab who could not run away.

Next to the Dome of the Rock, Gur gave the order over the radio to cease fire on the holy Temple Mount. At 10 A.M., he radioed Central Command and laconically, dramatically announced: "Temple Mount is in our hands. Temple Mount is ours. Temple Mount is ours."

Narkiss replied emotionally: "Message received. Great show. Great show."[2]

On the steps of the Dome of the Rock, Captain Zamush caught up with Colonel Gur. They hugged each other. Neither could speak.

Achmon and the brigade communications officer ran to the Dome of the Rock. Achmon remembers, "I blasted the lock of the front door of the Dome with my Uzi and found a staircase inside the east wall that took us up to the bottom of the Dome. At the beginning of the gold dome, there was a little plate that you could open and go between the gold roof and the stone dome beneath it. And there was a ladder leading directly to the top of the dome, where there was another wooden plate. I opened it with a stick and went out on the dome. When we came out, everyone—Arabs and Jews—started shooting at us. It was hell. I had a flag with me. Very quickly we hung the flag above the dome and dived down like hell.

"Motta in his famous broadcast told how we put up the flag, but it was only broadcast once before it was censored out of his talk. A friend of mine was at home and taped it. But that flag is gone from history. It was a strange thing."

Actually, there was nothing strange about it. When Dayan and Rabin and their entourage entered the Lions Gate a couple of hours later, Dayan saw the flag and said, "Who the hell did that? Let's get it down right away. I don't want any political problems." Achmon remembers, "I told one of my sergeants to go up and take the flag down. I didn't want to do it." The Israeli flag on the Dome of the Rock was photographed and the Arabs used it as propaganda to stir up opposition against Israeli control over one of the holiest places of Islam.

Achmon spotted Sergeant Major Barnea of his intelligence group and shouted to him, "Don't leave this place. You are the guard of the Dome!" Achmon ran off to look for the Western Wall. Barnea stayed on the empty Temple Mount, on guard duty. Peering into the Dome of the Rock, he was awed by its holiness and silence.

On the Temple Mount, Zamush suddenly thought of two people who he felt should be there that day: the venerable Rabbi Zvi Yehuda Kook and the so-called "monk rabbi" who had been in the Jewish Quarter in 1948 and afterwards had vowed that he would never again leave his house until the Old City was freed. He never did. Zamush told one of his men to take a Jordanian Jeep from the Temple Mount and find the two rabbis and bring them to the Western Wall. He did.

Four Arab civilians ran into the Dome of the Rock, and Zamush sent in men to capture them. Then, Stempel, Gur's second in command, and Zamush ran from the Dome of the Rock to clear the area toward the Western Wall and find the way to the Wall. For nearly two thousand years, the Western Wall had been for Jews the cherished symbol of their destroyed Temple. The Wall was not actually part of the Temple but part of the gigantic containing wall of the Temple enclosure built of huge limestone blocks about 20 B.C. by Herod the Great. Zamush left soldiers at key spots along the way to the Wall. Finding a very old Arab, they asked him the way. He said in Hebrew that he would show them. With a huge key, he opened the Mughrabi Gate to the old stone stairs leading down to the Wall.

On the way down the stairs, they saw a Jordanian truck with an antitank gun. Several soldiers hid behind it and started shooting at them. When the paratroopers fired back, the Jordanians dove under the truck, which immediately blew up and killed them. One of Zamush's men was wounded slightly.

While Stempel and a group of paratroopers stood guard on the stairs, Zamush, a sergeant and two soldiers went down to the path in front of the Western Wall. The area was so narrow they had to raise their heads to see the Wall. Zamush remembered the time he had last seen the Wall, when he was four years old. "I thought—if my father knew where I was at that moment. We had closed the open account we had with Titus." On a building near the Wall he saw freshly written in Hebrew: "If I forget thee, O Jerusalem." Perhaps, he thought, a Jewish tourist had written it. They found two Arabs and Zamush left the two soldiers to guard them.

He reclimbed the stairs and with Stempel and Landau and about ten paratroopers walked over to a fence above the north side of the Wall and tied there the flag from 1948 that the Cohens had given him on Monday evening.

Zamush returned to the bottom of the Wall and had about fifteen minutes alone there with a half dozen of his soldiers. They put on tefillin, which are worn by observant Jews during morning prayers as a reminder of the presence of God—and prayed.

At this time, Deputy Chief of Staff Barlev was making his way in a Jeep from the Rockefeller Museum to the Lions Gate. The Jeep took fire from the area of the gas station across the road. Suddenly, Barlev saw the white-bearded Rabbi Shlomo Goren, the military chief rabbi, approaching, followed by a chain of about ten aides. Because the tank blocked the road leading to the Lions Gate, Barlev dismounted and went the rest of the way on foot. He found Colonel Gur and reminded him that the war was not yet over; this was not just a celebration. He warned him to be careful and to keep his troops in hand.

Barlev and Rabbi Goren arrived together at the Western Wall. The general was impressed by the rabbi and his attendants walking through the smoke and fire of battle to the Wall. Barlev touched the Wall. "My feeling was that this was a historic moment. After it happened, it was clear that it was inevitable."

Major Eilam was at the Wall with Zamush and the soldiers. When Rabbi Goren arrived, Eilam went up to meet him and bring him down. Eilam says, "He was very emotional and trying to blow the shofar [ram's horn], and it wasn't going well. I said, 'Rabbi, give me the shofar. I'm a trumpet player. I can do it.' And I blew it."

Rabbi Goren stood at the Wall and said: "I, General Shlomo Goren, Chief Rabbi of the Israel Defense Forces, have come to this place never to leave again."

While the paratroopers were preparing to attack the Old City from the east, the Jerusalem Brigade was making similar preparations on the western side. The 163rd Battalion, which had taken Abu Tor the day before, was ordered to take Mount Zion up against the southwest corner of the Old City wall. Lt. Col. Yosef Brosh was now in command in place of the dead Peikas.

Brosh took his company commanders out from the university grounds on a reconnaissance tour and chose the First Company, which had not fought on Abu Tor, to seize Mount Zion. But Captain Eli Kedar, figuring that they would go on from there into the Old City itself, had a special reason for wanting to be first on Mount Zion.

Kedar was a rough-hewn, mustached carpenter with tousled hair. He and his seven brothers and sisters had been born in the Jewish Quarter of the Old City. In 1948 as a fifteen-year-old, he and his Kurdistan-born father had been among the last Jews the Jordanians removed from the Jewish Quarter; the Jordanians imprisoned them for nine months. Over the years, Kedar came to say it very positively: He was the last Jew to leave the Quarter.

Now his urge to be the first one back resembled that of

Yoram Zamush, the paratrooper captain who had won Gur's promise to let him lead the way to the Western Wall. But Zamush's fervor was religious; his goal was the Wall. Kedar's desire was to return to the Jewish Quarter, his boyhood home.

On the recon tour with Lt. Col. Brosh, Kedar radioed his company to move up to Mishkenot Sha'ananim, the long building that Sir Moses Montefiore of London and Judah Touro of New Orleans had built west of Mount Zion. Jordanian recoilless guns fired on Kedar's men from Mount Zion but without effect. From Mishkenot, Kedar moved his company through an old tunnel just north of the bridge across the narrow valley to Mount Zion. The Jerusalem Brigade had cleared the tunnel prior to the war. Before the attack on Mount Zion could begin, Kedar told Lt. Col. Brosh that his men were already in position to take the hill.

Jay Bushinsky of the *Chicago Daily News* was watching the battle from a fourth-floor balcony of the King David Hotel, west of the Old City. As the Jerusalem Brigade stormed Mount Zion, he saw the Dormition Abbey engulfed in flames, its dome a hollow shell, and wrote: "Clusters of orange lights flashed from its belfry set by the machine-gun and artillery fire that has raged in this city for the last two days. Judging from the Jordanian antiaircraft tracer shells and the yellow Israeli flares, it looked as if the Jews and Arabs were engaging in mortal battle for control of all of Jerusalem—old and new."

The Jordanians on Mount Zion fled from the Israelis. They advanced along the Old City's southern wall to the Dung Gate. Its two heavy metal doors were closed but not locked and there was a hatch through which a man could enter. Kedar was the first. He believes it was about 7:30 A.M., long before the paratroopers assaulted the Lions Gate. He looked around for Jordanian defenders. There was no shooting; and hanging from doors, windows and roofs he saw hundreds of white flags.

About fifty of his men followed him in, and they would long argue with the paratroopers about who, in fact, had been the first inside the Old City. There was little fighting; only a few Israelis were wounded. Dr. Uri Freund says, "It was like a ghost town."

Lt. Col. Brosh ordered Kedar to move to the Western Wall, but Kedar convinced him to let his men take the high ground of the Jewish Quarter first. Other companies of the battalion entered the Dung Gate and secured the area. The soldiers cautiously worked their way through the narrow, winding streets. Kedar knew them by heart; nothing had changed in the devastated Quarter he remembered.

They advanced toward the Jaffa Gate, where Kedar first met the paratroopers. Because he felt an overwhelming desire to share his experience, Kedar raced to his father's home in the German Colony just west of the Old City and brought him back. They went to the house in the Jewish Quarter where they had lived. His father met some of his former Arab neighbors. Then, father and son went together to the Western Wall. It all seemed so familiar.

Meanwhile, the paratroopers of the Twenty-eighth Battalion from the Rockefeller Museum snaked along the stone wall of the Muslim cemetery outside the Old City toward the Lions Gate. They had trouble crossing the open square in front of the museum. The Jordanians still had machine guns on top of the corner of the Old City wall. Their fire was not heavy but deadly.

Once the paratroopers crossed the square, the path dropped steeply, and under sniper fire they hugged the retaining wall of the cemetery. Near the bottom was the path that led upwards toward the Lions Gate.

Private Israel Harel, a journalist in civilian life, was one of the first paratroopers to cross the square in front of the Rockefeller Museum and live. He says, "The Jordanians had several machine guns on the corner of the wall and everyone who put out his nose was hit. It was like rain. We hesitated but we ran. I was in the first group that did it. We ran like mad. Everyone who went before me was hit, killed or wounded. If you're a soldier, you do what you have to do. Then, I knew it was my turn.

"Just before I had to run, I heard: 'Stop!' I pulled back. It was Uzi Narkiss. He had arrived with Chief Rabbi Goren. Narkiss said, 'Why are you running? Are you crazy? First, you have to deal with them.' There were already several dead and wounded in the square. Narkiss shouted, 'All those with bazookas to me!' He took two or three bazookas up to the hill near the museum and had them all fire at once to knock the Jordanians off balance. And then I ran. They shot but they didn't hit me. I made it. The bazookas shot a second time and blew up one of the machine guns. Several other men ran across. We took the dead and wounded and pulled them out of the line of fire. And then hundreds of us went very slowly, one after another, toward the Lions Gate. Snipers shot at us. We exchanged fire with them but we could not see them.

"It wasn't as it is sometimes told with the paratroopers shouting 'To the Wall!' 'To the Wall!' What you heard was: 'Idiot, put your head down!' 'Where is the radio man?' 'Where is the medic?'

"One of the men I knew, Guterman, got a bullet in his neck and fell like a stone. He was right in front of me. This is how war is. After a day and a half of fighting and losing friends, I was not shocked. I was numb. I felt nothing could touch me anymore. You come to a moment when you are so exhausted and have so many emotions and you have seen so much, you survived so much, that you don't react."

Once the paratroopers turned the corner and started up the narrow road to the Lions Gate, they moved carefully toward the Old City wall. Half an hour after Gur entered the Old City, the Twenty-eighth reached the gate. The battalion commander, Lt. Col. Fradkin, remembers it was less like going to war than—with Rabbi Goren along—going to a wedding. "It was like a vacuum pulling us up the hill toward the Lions Gate," says Harel. "It was like a mob moving forward. We lost all discipline. I tried to yell to my soldiers to get down, to take care, but I myself didn't. It was very exciting—like you fly a little bit. I didn't know where the Wailing Wall was exactly. I just knew I was going to the Old City. Once we were inside, we didn't know where to go."

Snipers fired on them as they dashed for the inner Bab el Asbat Gate leading to the Temple Mount. "I fired two clips from my Uzi but it was better for close fighting. Inside the gate, we found Jordanian mortars. We saw Jordanian soldiers running away. It was very quiet. It was like a dream; for nineteen years we never thought such a day would come.

"Rabbi Goren was with us and he asked several officers if he could blow the shofar. We said it would be an exaggeration; let's wait until we go to the Wailing Wall.

"We were posted to defend the Temple Mount against reinforcements; others reached the Wailing Wall at eleven o'clock. An hour later, they came back excited and shaking. We wanted to go there, but we had to go toward the Damascus Gate and had to fight there."

Fradkin met Gur on the Temple Mount and was ordered to take the Damascus Gate from the inside because Prime Minister Eshkol was expected to enter the Old City there. Most of the battalion concentrated around the Damascus Gate. Israel Harel says, "We lost two officers there, and several men were wounded by ambushes in the narrow alleys. Only the next morning could we, who were the first of the battalion on the Temple Mount, make our way to the Wailing Wall." Lt. Col. Fradkin did not get to the Western Wall at all; from the Damascus Gate he was ordered to the Golan Heights.

Harel continues, "When the first soldiers came to the Wailing Wall, an Arab who spoke Hebrew came to them and asked for a doctor. There was a doctor there, Dr. Uri Frand, and the Arab said my wife is going to give birth, maybe you can help us. He went over and helped her and everything was okay. Later we learned her story. She had been a very young Jewish girl from Jerusalem who fell in love with an Arab and she married him and converted to Islam."

The paratroopers had taken the Temple Mount and the Western Wall. As soldiers they had achieved their target; as Jews they had reached the ancient symbols of their religion and their heritage. The failure of 1948 had been redeemed. And at the same time, their very presence beamed a spotlight of world attention on the city of Jerusalem. It stirred age-old questions to which there would be no easy answers.

— Chapter 22 —

REACTIONS

Each Israeli had strong reactions on reaching the small crowded space in front of the Western Wall of the ancient Temple enclosure. One paratrooper, Moshe Mirav, said, "When we came to the Wailing Wall, we felt like messengers of all the generations from the Diaspora who always prayed and could never make it. I am not religious and I don't know why I was chosen. I prayed but I could not say 'Amen.' I put my hands on the stones and started to cry."

Colonel Gur leaned against the Wall and felt he had come home. Historical names flew through his mind: The Temple Mount. The Mount of Moriah. Abraham. Isaac. The Temple. Maccabees. Bar Kochba. The Romans. The Greeks.

Ilan Engel, a paratrooper, said: "When we came in the Lions Gate, we felt we were running in an athletic race. We had a flag with us that was carried by those who fought in 1948 and didn't make it into the Old City. When we came to the Wailing Wall, we saw Rabbi Goren. He was praying. But I felt something was not normal. Here people were still shooting and people were already praying. I couldn't."

Someone took out a bottle and passed it around, and they drank "L'chaim!" Each one felt this was a historic moment, but their feelings were mixed.

Abraham Schechter, another paratrooper, said: "Before the war, I came with my family and looked at the Old City from far away. We couldn't see the Wailing Wall; I didn't believe I would ever come there. When we were there at last, I lay down and couldn't move. My commander asked me if I were wounded. Then I got up and started to pray. All those words which I said every morning were today so different. They had a meaning that I had never felt so deeply."

Michael Elkins, the broadcast journalist, put a handkerchief on his head and leaned against the Wall. "I'm not religious. I'm a Jew," he says. He wrote on a cigarette pack and stuck it in a crevice in the Wall. It said: "May my son Jonathan and all his generation find peace."

A paratrooper, an artist in civilian life, represented another, more pragmatic kind of Israeli. He says, "I felt removed. For me this was an artistic scene, not an emotional one. One of the men who had come with me to the Wailing Wall was shot between the eyes. For me, this was more important. If even one of us is killed, it wasn't worth it."

Siema Hazan, the young ambulance driver, was also one of the first to reach the Wall; and like the artist-paratrooper she felt it was not worth all the lives and the wounded, the blood and the pain. She had driven the dead and wounded away from outside the Lions Gate, as twenty-four hours before she had carried them off Ammunition Hill. And now she, with a girl friend sitting beside her, drove her empty ambulance near to the Wall just as the shofar was blown. When they reached the Wall, her girl friend was so excited she fainted in Hazan's arms. Siema could only think of the dead children she had carried in her arms. She suddenly felt terribly tired and depressed.

While these first Israelis were reaching the Western Wall, the hard-hit paratroopers of the Twenty-eighth Battalion's A Company—"the oldest and the best"—who had led the attack up Nablus Road and spent the night in the grounds of St. Stephen's Monastery, met new trouble. At midmorning, a heavy mortar bombardment killed four more men. Israelis still argue today over whose mortars they were. Sergeant Artom's life was saved when the radio on his back was destroyed by shrapnel.

A Company had suffered grievously. Eleven of the company were dead of the battalion's 26 killed, and the company had nearly a third of the battalion's 140 wounded. Of the 100 or so men who had started the battle with A Company, only 32 were still able to fight.

This remnant crossed over the Temple Mount to the Western Wall. The area in front of the Wall was crowded. Artom says, "To be honest with you, we didn't care much about the Wailing

Wall after the bombardment had killed four more people. Only a few were crying. That picture grew later. We didn't really pay attention to the Wall."

The apparently ever-present Yehuda Arbell, a man experienced in battle, joined the long chain of paratroopers, trucks and tanks moving slowly toward the Lions Gate. There was still sniping, and a heavy machine gun peppered from the direction of the Russian Orthodox Church above the Garden of Gethsemane. The tanks fired at the machine gun, and then the scene was much quieter. Arbell descended to the front of the Wall. "Some soldiers were praying. Some were just sitting there. Most of them looked exhausted. I am not religious, but I felt something in my throat." Then he went back to his office and telephoned everyone he knew. "I told them I had come back from the Western Wall. I felt much more emotional. I realized what had happened."

In Israeli Jerusalem, Lieutenant Karni Kav, the woman officer of the paratroop brigade who had been keeping track of the dead and wounded, heard soon after ten o'clock that the Old City had been entered. She burst into tears, releasing the feelings she had bottled up. She ran to a telephone booth and called her father in Tel Aviv; she knew the news would thrill him. She screamed over the telephone: "The boys are in the Old City!"

Her father, while in a British jail as a young man, had become very close to the elderly Rabbi Arie Levin, who was the beloved rabbi of the imprisoned Jews. The closeness had endured over the years. Now, Karni Kav's father told her to go to the rabbi's home in Jerusalem and ask his blessing before she went into the Old City.

She stopped the first Jeep she could find and persuaded the driver to go to the rabbi's home in the Mishkenot section. When they arrived, Shmuel Tamir was already there. He had been imprisoned in Latrun and was now a member of the Knesset and the leader of the Free Center Party. He also had come to Rabbi Levin's home before going to the Old City; with him were his wife, Ruth, and other members of his family. The old rabbi embraced Tamir and cried and said to him, "We have to pray now for a lot of compassion." Tamir, mystified, said, "Rabbi, what is the trouble? Everything is great. This is a wonderful day." Rabbi Levin said simply in Yiddish, "The Gentiles will not let us enjoy it."

Then the rabbi put his hands on the heads of the young Jeep driver and Lieutenant Kav and blessed them. He said, "Bless the boys and tell them they are heroes."

The Jeep driver and Karni Kav drove through the Pagi section and up to Mount Scopus. Below them, she remembers vividly, "It was a golden Jerusalem and everything was shining and beautiful." Entering the Old City through the Lions Gate, she met paratroopers she knew and everyone was hugging and kissing her. They wanted to know from her who was alive and who was dead. "It was a very mixed feeling of happiness and sadness."

If those in uniform and in the fighting reacted in such varied ways to the Old City and the Western Wall, this was even truer for the city's civilians. Erwin Frenkel, news editor of the *Post*, says, "I never expected, even after the war with Jordan started, to take the Old City and make it part of Israel. That came to me as a surprise. It wasn't part of my life. That city over there was another place."

When Frenkel finally reached the Wall, he saw soldiers kissing the Wall and praying. "The emotion of others gripped me more than the Wall itself. It confirmed for me that this was part of the Jewish experience, of which these people were a part."

Although he had been a rabbinical student before he came to Israel, he says, "Religiously, the Wall means nothing to me. It is a pile of stones. As a monument in Jewish experience, it means something to me. The Wall for me is idolatry. For the Orthodox it is not idolatry. As far as I'm concerned, it is an aberration of Judaism. I couldn't bring myself to kiss the Wall; I couldn't bring myself to pray at the Wall. It did bring tears to my eyes. But it wasn't the Wall; it was the interaction of the people who were at the Wall. It is a monument to a certain kind of human experience. I was part of that."

Frenkel's colleague on the *Post*, Charles Weiss, had gone to the King David Hotel Wednesday morning to meet David Weber, whom the National Broadcasting Company had sent in from London. Weiss remembers being startled by the long line of soldiers in the hotel lobby waiting to use the pay telephone to call their families. Then, he and Abraham Rabinovich, who had come to report the war for *Newsday* of Long Island, New York, entered the Old City through the Lions Gate. On the Temple Mount, Rabinovich interviewed soldiers, and the reporters were separated. Weiss went to the Wall alone. He spotted Alvin Rosenfeld of NBC sitting at the Wall with a typewriter on his knees, banging out a story. Weiss shot a roll of film and started back to the newspaper office.

A man stopped him and asked his help. He said that he was Ted Yates' cameraman and he wanted to know how to recover Yates' body that had been taken to the Austrian Hospice in the Via Dolorosa. Weiss took him to Weber, who, with Meron Medzini, a government press official, had Yates' body released.

Yehuda Avner, the Foreign Office official who had been ordered to go to the Israeli Consulate in New York, was still in Jerusalem. "My flight for New York would be leaving that afternoon. I was not leaving until I had seen the Wall. I was taken up in this living crowd of soldiers moving toward the Wall. Some were still fighting. Suddenly, I found myself there. I remember bursting into tears. Then, I realized I was smelling something. I was smelling the authentic aroma of what my forefathers thousands of years ago had smelled when they placed their hand against the Wall. Time and erosion of the elements had done their will with that Wall, but the smell remains in its absolute authenticity.

"We fought our way back and went to my home. I still hadn't packed, but I took my beloved tropical fish from my aquarium and flushed them down the toilet. I asked my secretary, Rivka Sofer, to supervise the packing, and I made my plane for New York. On the flight most of the people were singing."

Years later, when he was the Prime Minister of Israel, Menachem Begin thought back on his feelings during the battle and wrote the author:

"On that day, unique in the annals of the Jewish people, I could hear the echo of the voices of the Roman Legionnaires shouting 'Hep, Hep'—'Hierosolyma est perdita'—meaning, 'Jerusalem is lost, Jerusalem is lost.' . . . I remember thinking to myself: . . . Where are the cohorts of Vespasian and Titus?

They had all disappeared behind the cloud of history, whereas the Jewish people are back here, alive, having made their rendezvous with their destiny where we started our national life and the building of our civilization.

"Yes, indeed, we are back home, we survived all the holocausts, every persecution and found strength enough to rise again and fight for our liberation and for the defense of our independence. Upon pondering this unprecedented metamorphosis one cannot but stand in awe before the moral greatness of an ancient people and young nation reborn."

When he heard the news in New York, Consul General Michael Arnon was swept by "a tremendous feeling of elation on the one hand and the question: Can this really be true? Because I was not in Jerusalem but in New York, the thought immediately arose—knowing the attitude of the Vatican and some of the churches in Jerusalem—that we had to really get cracking and explain what Jerusalem means to us.

"The thought of leaving Jerusalem never occurred to me. What did occur to me was how long it would take before the world at large reconciled itself to the fact that Jerusalem was in Israeli hands. After all, the American Embassy was still in Tel Aviv. Would our enemies who were certainly many—would not the Catholic Church, for instance—now go into battle fully against us? 'The Jewish infidels are controlling the whole of Jerusalem!' They were still calling for the internationalization of Jerusalem."

Arnon anticipated "a Christian onslaught against Israeli control of all Jerusalem." To his surprise, no Christian backlash developed. The Vatican stopped talking seriously about internationalization. When he tried to analyze the reasons, he decided that the Vatican authorities were realists and knew that Israel would not give up Jerusalem; also they had found that under Jordanian rule the city had been dominated not by Christian Arabs but by Muslims, and Christian interests fared poorly; and finally by 1967 they realized that internationalization would give the Soviet Union a political presence in Jerusalem.

After the Old City had been taken, the soldier who had promised Sammy Mustaklem that he would bring an ambulance if he survived showed up at the firehouse at the bottom of the hill. He spoke with Mustaklem in English and went over to the tap at the produce market and brought back water for the sick man inside the firehouse. They had had no water or food for two days, and the chief sent firemen with the soldier across the road to the market and they carried back boxes of tomatoes and apples and peaches. The men ate. One said they had no cigarettes; the soldier, who turned out to be a fourth-year medical student, tossed them their first package of Israeli cigarettes. The soldier examined the man with the heart condition and went off to seek an ambulance. Mustaklem then found the Jordanian soldier who had been injured in the Land Rover lying in the garden. Also sitting there was an Arab civil engineer who had been shot in the leg. When the Israeli soldier returned with an ambulance, the three were loaded in it and driven to a hospital.

While the Israeli paratroopers were entering the Old City, Jordanian Governor Anwar al-Khatib was in the deserted Muslim Trust Building near the Temple Mount with Hassam al-Khalidi; the Muslim Qadi, the chief religious judge of Jerusalem, and a courageous old attendant who refused to leave them. Al-Khatib and al-Khalidi shaved for the coming confrontation with the Israelis.

The governor and the judge waited inside, and al-Khalidi stood at the top of the long staircase outside. When the first Israeli soldier appeared, al-Khalidi raised his hands above his head. The paratrooper sergeant spoke English, and al-Khalidi told him of the two dignitaries inside the building. The sergeant searched him and they were escorted to the Temple Mount to meet Colonel Gur. Gur asked the governor if he had the authority to stop the resistance. Al-Khatib told him he was not in communication with anyone; there was no organized government or resistance in the Old City.

Governor al-Khatib remembers: "I had a little chat in English with Mordechai Gur. He said he was sorry he had to kill people and asked me how many people I thought were injured in the Old City. I said I had no idea. He said that if anything happened to us he would make hell out of it. I told him frankly that the Jordanian army had left the city and the civilians had no weapons."

The governor and about twelve Jordanian officials were

placed under armed guard in the basement of the building of the Supreme Muslim Council. After about six hours without food or water, they were released. Al-Khalidi went to stay with cousins in the Old City. Al-Khatib spent the night at a hospice, and the next day he walked to his home in Beit Hanina.

Israeli soldiers searched the houses around the Lions Gate and herded all the Arab men they could find to the Temple Mount. Salah Jarallah, the town clerk, was taken from his home near the Lions Gate and says, "We were very scared that the Israeli soldiers would kill us all, but no one was hurt and after an hour we were allowed to go home."

An Israeli shell had penetrated and killed twenty people in the basement of a house near the Lions Gate, and shells severely damaged the Indian Hospice near Herod's Gate. The al-Aksa Mosque on the Temple Mount was damaged; Jordanian snipers had been firing from its roof. Governor al-Khatib later accused the Israelis of bombing and shelling the Old City. He says, "Unfortunately, they used their airplanes and bombed some quarters. A few civilians including one whole family were killed. I never thought the Israelis would use any heavy guns or airplanes to raid the Old City. They disappointed me. In my opinion, they wanted to smash any attempt by the civilians to defend the city and they wanted to show that they meant business: If you try to defend yourself, this is the answer. Shelling and bombing and they did it. I have proof." The Israelis admit firing mortar rounds into the Muslim Quarter of the Old City and using small arms against Arab snipers, but they emphatically deny using either heavy artillery or aircraft against the Old City.

Hassam al-Khalidi speaks for many Arabs when he remembers his feelings on the fall of the Old City: "Like most Muslims, I felt resignation. We were certainly embittered and disappointed and angry, but we were very calm. I think the best came out of us. We accepted our fate, whatever our fate was to be. We did not panic. We felt let down by the whole Arab world, not just by Amman.

"Naturally, we were aware that fables and lies don't save you. We started off with the lie that we had five brigades in Jerusalem, when we only had a very weak garrison brigade. We realized the whole stake was built on illusion. Everybody, locally and worldwide, was made to think that the Arab Legion was a very strong army. It was a well drilled army. It was a good internal security army, a very repressive force, but not a fighting force.

"I think we all regard ourselves as Arabs, as members of a greater nation. But we certainly have our local identity. We realize that colonialism succeeded in parceling the Arab world off into states for their own purposes. Like all people, we have our weaknesses, because we are not fully developed to see ourselves as one nation. So far we have not been acting as one nation. A lot of people would still like to be a big fish in a small pond. We will outgrow it."

A fifteen-year-old Arab boy, who lived inside the city wall near Herod's Gate and whose father was a hotel waiter, says, "We wanted to be soldiers to fight the Jewish, but by Tuesday there were no Jordanian soldiers to hold the gates of the city. There were Jewish soldiers outside all the gates. My family and I slept in a house near the Dome of the Rock.

"On Wednesday, we saw the Jewish soldiers come down from the Inter-Continental Hotel. We thought they were Iraqis coming to help. After about two hours, we found Jewish soldiers in the Temple Mount with machine guns, shooting. There was not much shooting in the Old City because the Arabs were not fighting. The Jewish soldiers came inside the Dome of the Rock and put their flag on top.

"I was so afraid. I heard the Jewish would kill the young boys and the men. But when they came in, they said, 'Don't be afraid. You stay here, be quiet. Put out something white.' I had a radio and a soldier took it. Nobody shot at us."

The clergy in the Greek Orthodox Patriarchate were exposed to little of the war. Says the Metropolitan Vassilios, "At our Patriarchate we were happy to see that nothing happened to us. I saw the soldiers in the Old City from my window. I was astonished that they were just marching as though they were going to a procession. I saw the soldiers coming one after the other, taking precautions, but they gave us the impression of a procession.

"The Holy Sepulcher fortunately was untouched. No place was hit or bombarded or attacked, especially the churches and the holy shrines." Of the Christian shrines, only St. Anne's Church in the Old City and the Dormition on Mount Zion outside the walls were damaged. For the Christian clergy in the Old City the battle seemed over quickly.

At 10:40 Wednesday morning in Tel Aviv, Aviad Yaffe, Eshkol's secretary, received a telephone call from General Narkiss that the Western Wall was in Israeli hands. Twenty minutes later came a call from General Hod, the Air Force commander, that they had taken Sharm el-Sheikh at the southern tip of the Sinai Peninsula; the Red Sea was once again open to Israeli shipping. "It was a fantastic moment," Yaffe said. "The good news came flowing over us. It was almost too much to take."

Dayan reported to the Cabinet: "The Old City fell into our hands. I gave instructions to let a tank go through the Lions Gate. The Jordanians were shelling the Temple Mount. I gave instructions to open all the gates of the Old City. Our soldiers came up to the square between the two mosques. Instructions were given not to touch the mosques or the Holy Sepulcher. There were very strict instructions to preserve all the Holy Places."

The Eshkols and Yaffe and Colonel Le'or, the prime minister's military aide, drove for two hours in an armored Buick over the back roads to Jerusalem. Tired, hot and unshaven, Eshkol and Yaffe went to their respective homes to clean up and put on appropriate dark suits. It was the first time Yaffe had been home in ten days.

"I dressed and got ready to go with my husband to the Old City," says Miriam Eshkol. "Suddenly, I said, 'Look, do you mind if I don't go with you?' He asked, 'Why?' I said, 'I won't go with you and that's it.' For religious Jews it was no place for a woman. I am anything but religious, but I didn't want to mar his moment. He said he understood, and he said, 'You'll regret it all your life.' I said, 'I already regret it but I can't do it.'"

Eshkol's bulky armored car could not squeeze into the narrow streets of the Old City. Jordanians were still sniping. Accompanied by Israel's two chief rabbis, Eshkol reached the Western Wall about 2 P.M. Among the dirty, exhausted paratroopers, Aviad Yaffe says, "We looked like two crows."

The soldiers cheered the prime minister, who so recently had been bitterly criticized by his people. As the *Jerusalem Post* said the next morning, "He was the first leader of a Jewish

Government to visit the site of the Temple since its loss 1,897 years ago.... [The soldiers sang 'Jerusalem of Gold'] which the mayor had commissioned 23 eons—or was it just days?—ago."

At the Wall, Eshkol stuck between the great stones a written wish that Miriam had given him and Yaffe brought a bottle of oil from his wife, Ora.

Those who were responsible for the prime minister's safety began to grow nervous, fearing a sniper might take a final shot. They tried to hurry the official party back to the now safe Israeli sector. But there was too much to see, too much to feel. White flags hung from many houses. Soldiers herded Jordanian prisoners to collecting points. Captured snipers lay face down on the streets. Burned-out vehicles were scattered in the streets, and Israeli soldiers drove around in Jordanian Jeeps; one had a large picture of King Hussein on its radiator. Eshkol and his group lingered, absorbing the moment.

Dayan had already stolen Eshkol's triumphant moment. Because the prime minister had stopped to change before going to the Western Wall, Dayan and Rabin and Narkiss had already been there and had a picture taken that was sent out around the world.

Rabin tells how it happened: "Dayan decided to have some sort of formal, emotional ceremony; and he initiated that he, myself and Narkiss would make an entrance to the city. He said I have this in mind and I want you to join me. We went to Jerusalem by helicopter and landed at Uzi's headquarters at the Convention Hall. And from there we went by command car and entered through the Lions Gate and walked all the way up to the Temple Mount." Dayan, wearing a helmet with camouflage netting and a chin strap, was accompanied by his special assistant, Moshe Pearlman, the Israeli writer, and a host of photographers. Dayan, with a sense of the historical moment, called Rabin and Narkiss over to him for the picture.

It was approaching 2 P.M. when the party crossed the Temple Mount and walked down the stairs to the Wall. As Dayan, Rabin, "Gandhi," Narkiss and Raphael Levi stood in the narrow passage in front of the Wall, Dayan pulled out a notebook and wrote something on a page, tore it out and jammed it between the huge stones. Pearlman says, "It astonished me that he was

317

moved to do this. Jews for generations had put their pleas into the crevices of the Wall. I asked him what he had written. He didn't say but he took out his notebook again and wrote what he had written. What he had written was: 'Would that peace would descend on the whole house of Israel.'

"Then he found some flowers growing out of the crevices of the wall. They were cyclamens. I asked him what he was doing and he said, 'These are flowers sprouting from the Western Wall.'"

Rabin says, "I was very much excited but I didn't pray and I didn't put a paper in the Wall. Later on, we were interviewed. I said I felt this was the height of my life. I said for me, as one who was born in Jerusalem and fought in '48 in the besieged Jerusalem—trying to take the Old City and not succeeding—and now as chief of staff to bring about the unification of the city and visiting the Western Wall, I said it's a fulfillment of a dream. After all, a Jewish boy who was born and grew up in Israel could not have dreamt something beyond that."

The commanders went back to Narkiss' headquarters in the Convention Hall and held a meeting in a small basement room with no windows and lit by batteries. There was a field telephone on a table and a cot and on the floor a radio. It was very close and quiet.

Rabin asked, "How do we control a million Arabs?"

"Gandhi" said, "A million and a quarter."

Nobody had an answer.

Rabin said, "We have to open the roads for supply." He asked, "Who is going to Hebron?"

Narkiss replied, "The Jerusalem Brigade started to move to Bethlehem an hour ago."

Kol Yisrael, the public broadcasting authority, arrived to tape an announcement from Dayan about taking the Old City. Dayan shooed everyone out of the room; only "Gandhi" stayed to hold the lights. Dayan gave a formal statement to the press: "This morning the Israel Defense Forces liberated Jerusalem. We have united Jerusalem, the divided capital of Israel. We have returned to the holiest of our holy places, never to part from it again."

A reporter asked Dayan if he wanted territorial negotiations. He replied in his regal style: "I am ready to give peace and take peace."

The other government officials also dashed up from Tel Aviv. In the excitement, the elderly Minister of Education, Zalman Aranne, and Mrs. Uzay failed to get the word. When Mrs. Uzay returned to Eshkol's office at one o'clock for the now-forgotten Cabinet meeting, she found it deserted. She went back to her room in the Dan Hotel and listened to the radio, feeling forgotten and neglected. She wept.

Yigael Yadin finally reached Jerusalem from Tel Aviv: "This was the most emotional nonprivate feeling I have had in my life, even more than the War of Independence when we declared the State and I was Chief of Operations. I wouldn't say I was responsible for losing the Jewish Quarter in 1948, but obviously I couldn't do much at the time to retain it. To come back was uncanny. They say when you are in danger or about to die everything comes back to you. This was in reverse. The whole history—my history—came back in a second when I touched the Wailing Wall.

"The '48 war should have ended, from our point of view, with the Old City in our hands. That was the biggest objective that was not achieved. Without the Old City in our hands, we are always in danger, as we were on the eve of '67.

"The last time Jerusalem was under Jewish control was in A.D. 134 with Bar Kochba. After about eighteen hundred years, Jerusalem came again under Jewish sovereignty. I had discovered the dispatches and letters of this semilegendary Bar Kochba in 1960 and '61 in the caves of the Judean desert. He was really the last Jew who was in control in Jerusalem. From both a military and historical point of view, I think this was the greatest day of the whole Six Day War."

When Prime Minister Eshkol came home from the Wall, Miriam Eshkol says: "He was rather white and I asked him what happened. So he said, 'I have had such a palpitation of the heart. I cannot remember anything like it for years—maybe once when I cheated and I was afraid my father would find out.' He described the streets of the Old City and the people coming out of their homes like mice, not knowing exactly what the reaction would be. Some of them were servile, some with pride, some hateful. He described all that. He was very quiet. He could hardly breathe. Whenever he was excited, he would sing a sort of Hassidic song that was no song whatsoever; and he went around the room singing it and telling me to write down what he told me. Then he was called to the office to meet with the representatives of the various religions."

At 3:30, Eshkol met with the two rabbis in his Jerusalem office. He promised them the Western Wall would be placed under the authority of the Ministry of Religious Affairs—a decision that would create problems. Yaffe said later, "That was a mistake."

At 4 P.M., Eshkol met with the Christian leaders from the Old City. They came with mixed feelings and fears for the future. Dr. Yaacov Herzog, the director of Eshkol's office, had prepared a statement for him to read. It said that their rights would be observed and there would be complete freedom of religion and worship. He said the Israelis did not come as conquerors. Religious authorities would retain control of the Holy Places. Eshkol wanted to assure the various religious leaders that Israel would respect and protect the Holy Places. He wanted to forestall opposition to the realization that the Jewish state now controlled Jerusalem.

Patriarch Benedictos of the Greek Orthodox Church, as the representative of the oldest Christian community in Jerusalem, spoke for the dignitaries. He said he was pleased that nothing had happened to the shrines and churches and monasteries; they were prepared to render unto Caesar and not to interfere in politics. It was a sober but ecumenical moment.

Vassilios felt less confident. He says, "It was a sudden change, and we couldn't immediately appreciate the change. We were uncertain. We didn't know what would follow. The military were military, no doubt, although I remember below the Rockefeller Museum my car stopped. I don't know what happened to it. General Herzog was passing. When he saw me standing outside, immediately he stopped. 'Anything wrong? Do you want any help?' I was impressed with his kindness, with his interest. He didn't know me. He just saw that I was clergy and stopped his military car."

Back home, Eshkol was upset. He asked his wife, "Were the Jews, when we had to meet with all sorts of Gentiles who were oppressing us, who were conquering us, as miserable as they were when they had to face me?" He said he sensed not a feeling of hatred, but that the church leaders could not believe that they, "the lords of two thousand years," were now required to come to the Jews. Miriam Eshkol adds, "My husband was not hysterical. He was a very straight, earthly sort of person. Don't mix him up with Begin. For him this was Israel, this was another era. He was an Israeli; he chose to be what he was. To him Jerusalem meant a lot of things, but it didn't mean to him to drive away the Arabs. Whenever he won a battle, he was magnanimous enough not to behave like a conqueror."

Afterwards, Eshkol and his entourage went back to the Wall. Justice Minister Shapira was with him. "I felt the greatness of the moment," he remembers. "This is the day when the Jews again regain Jerusalem after nearly two thousand years. There, one feels happy that the Jews are so stubborn. You want to belong to people on whom you can rely in matters of paramount importance. In great matters, it is not only an honor, it's a comfort to be a Jew."

About 4 P.M., Dr. Yosef Burg's nephew came to visit his uncle. The young man was assigned to an army burial company made up of religious youths, because, as Dr. Burg says, "It is not a very nice task. You need a bit of idealism and love of life and the living in order to deal with the dead." Burg decided he wanted to go with his nephew to the Western Wall. "When we arrived there was still shooting. Eshkol was there wearing a steel helmet. [President Zalman] Shazar was there. It was about 5:30. Sons of friends of mine were laying tefillin. It is something that should be done in the morning, but they had no time. They were fighting. So I was saying my afternoon prayer and they were laying tefillin of the morning. But I am sure that God loved them more than me.

"What was promised by Hussein in 1949—that Jews should have free access to the Wailing Wall—was not kept. So for nearly twenty years there was something between us and this Holy Place. Now it had a moral impact even on people who had no religious tradition."

Efforts to resurrect normal life in the Arab sector of the city started immediately. Maj. Gen. Herzog commanded the military government unit that would govern the West Bank, and Shlomo "Chich" Lahat was his military governor for Jordanian Jerusalem. On Wednesday morning, Herzog was ordered to be at army headquarters in Tel Aviv at 7 A.M. He was supposed to see Ezer Weizman, the Chief of Operations; but Weizman had run down to Sharm el-Sheikh. Dayan gave Herzog a bite of breakfast and then Rabin called him in. "He was in euphoria," Herzog remembers. He called in Meir Shamgar, the judge advocate general, and had him draft Herzog's appointment as commander of forces in the West Bank as there was no official position of "governor." It was typed out on a plain piece of white paper: "Appointment of commander of Israeli forces in the West Bank. I hearby appoint General Chaim Herzog to be commander of forces in the West Bank held by the Israel Defense Forces. This appointment is effective from the seventh of June 1967." Rabin signed it.

After Herzog gave his ten o'clock broadcast, which he had been writing while he waited to see Rabin, he drove himself to Jerusalem and told his military government staff to assemble at the Ambassador Hotel on a high point on the Nablus Road in the Sheikh Jarrah Quarter just north of the road to Mount Scopus. When he had been the commander of the Jerusalem District during the 1956 Sinai campaign, he had picked out the Ambassador for exactly this purpose; but that time the Jordanians had stayed out of the fight.

Herzog joined the convoy of commanding officers heading for the Old City with Dayan. "We drove through Me'a She'arim and everyone stood and waved. Dayan was sitting in the front thoroughly enjoying himself. I remember saying to Shamgar who was in the car with me, 'If we have sense, the Arabs are in shock and we will call in their leaders today and give them immediate home rule under Israeli sovereignty.' We walked through the Lions Gate to the Temple Mount; there was shooting still going on. This was the famous picture of Dayan and Rabin and Narkiss entering the Old City.

"Rabbi Goren was at the Wailing Wall, and he kissed us and Dayan put his little piece of paper in the Wall. I had been to the Wall very often before '48 with my father. I was very moved." His father had been the Chief Rabbi of Ireland and in 1936 had been inaugurated Chief Rabbi of Palestine in the Old City's Hurva Synagogue, which had now been destroyed by the Jordanians. Herzog says, "As we walked out, Dayan sort of said to me, 'It's your baby, now you take over.'"

At the Ambassador Hotel, Herzog put men in charge of economics and transportation and appointed governors for the various areas of the West Bank. In the beginning, the West

Bank and Jerusalem were treated as one. Herzog says, "I gave instructions to get life back to normal. We had dead people lying all over the place. No food, no milk, no water. Teddy [Kollek] got to work. He was fantastic. Raphael Levi, the district officer, brought all the heads of the Christian communities and I addressed them in the bar of the hotel. They thanked me for our behavior and our attitude and because we hadn't fired at the Holy Places.

"The Anglicans were unpleasant; at that time they were terribly moved by what had happened. However, the Anglican bishop got up and said he wanted to place on the historical record the fact that the Israel Defense Forces endangered their soldiers in order not to affect the Holy Places.

"I told him that as the son of the Chief Rabbi I knew them all and they had been to my home and it was a great privilege for me to be able to announce that from now on there would be complete freedom of religion. We handed out champagne and they all drank to the President of Israel.

"It took us ten days to get out all the ammunition and explosives from the area of the Temple Mount. It could have blown the whole place sky high. The governor of Jerusalem, Anwar al-Khatib, told me he had begged the Jordanian Legion not to put it there. They used the whole area as a weapons and arms base. He told me he had phoned the king; it didn't do any good."

Captain David Farhi, a thirty-one-year-old university teacher with a command of Arabic and Turkish and a deep interest in Islamic history, was sent to find the mayor of Arab Jerusalem. He knew only that the man's name was Khatib, and there were two Khatibs, one the governor and one the mayor; Farhi did not even know the mayor's first name. At the Ambassador Hotel, an Arab waiter told him the mayor was called Rouhi al-Khatib and he lived in Beit Hanina on the way to Ramallah. Taking the frightened waiter with him, Farhi drove to Beit Hanina. He was armed with an American carbine he had taken that morning from the body of a Jordanian soldier at the Mandelbaum Gate.

The mayor's wife said she did not know where her husband was. As Farhi left the house he noticed a man peeking out of the window of the neighboring house. He told Farhi the mayor

323

was hiding in one of the Catholic monasteries in the Old City, but he did not know which one.

"As I drove back," Farhi says, "it dawned on me that the Greek Catholic Bishop of the Galilee was very friendly to the State of Israel. I would take greetings from him to the Greek Catholic Bishop in the Old City and find Rouhi al-Khatib." Farhi used a hotel tourist map of the Old City to locate the Greek Catholic monastery just inside the Jaffa Gate. Knowing that gate was blocked by barriers and no-man's-land, he drove to the Lions Gate and asked the platoon commander of the paratroopers at the gate for an escort through the Old City. He and three paratroopers started walking up the steep, narrow Via Dolorosa. Near the Third Station of the Cross, they were fired on. They hit the ground and returned the fire. Farhi had only one clip for his carbine. They ducked into an alley. One of the paratroopers stuck out a hand and drew another shot. They spotted the soldier on a balcony and killed him. They continued up the Via Dolorosa hugging the walls.

At the Greek Catholic Patriarchate, Farhi banged on the door, which was opened by Father Hilarion Capucci. Farhi said later he came to know him to be "very cunning, very suave, very slippery—an Arab nationalist. I told him, 'Father, I am not a regular officer. I teach at the university and I am a friend of the Bishop of the Galilee. He sends you his regards. He told us that you are his friend, and we want to look after your safety. We know the mayor is hiding in one of the monasteries. We don't care where. But we want to activate the municipality and to convene the Municipal Council.' Father Capucci said he knew where the mayor was. I said, 'If you find your way to pass him the word, we will come back tomorrow.'"

Farhi relocated the military government headquarters in the governor's building, which had offices and telephones and the Ritz Hotel nearby to house their personnel. Then, he took two border policemen and a Lebanese airline clerk who was in the lobby of the Ritz Hotel and brought back to headquarters the deputy mayor, Dr. Ibrahim Tlil, a Christian and a doctor at the Augusta Victoria Hospital. "He was not very cooperative." But after they shouted at him, he gave them the names of the Arab officials who were responsible for water and electricity and other municipal services. People were sent out to bring in these officials to start organizing the Arab section of the city.

The next day, Father Capucci told Farhi that he had been in touch with the mayor and the Municipal Council would meet the following morning at 9 A.M. at the Arab city hall.

Meanwhile, the Israeli army continued securing the Old City. In scattered fighting with the remaining Jordanian regulars and with Arab Jerusalemites who picked up abandoned army weapons, three Israelis were killed.

Captain Zamush took his paratroop company from the Wall to clear out the market and the Citadel and David's Tower near the Jaffa Gate. The men helped themselves to food in the Arab shops. At the Citadel, Zamush's paratroopers met Captain Kedar's company of the Jerusalem Brigade. Kedar wanted to seize the Citadel and David's Tower, but the paratroopers insisted it was their job and Kedar acquiesced.

Not knowing that the Jordanians had boobytrapped the bridge leading into the Citadel, Zamush and another paratrooper crossed the bridge. Nothing happened. But when the next pair crossed, the bridge blew up, burying both paratroopers under a pile of rubble. Soldiers pulled away the rubble and rescued the injured men.

In the Citadel, the paratroopers found Jordanian soldiers who did not resist. A Jordanian sergeant asked Zamush whether they were Kuwaitis or Iraqis; and when he was told that they were Israelis, he collapsed on the spot.

At the jail called the Kishle behind the Citadel, the imprisoned criminals had gotten hold of weapons and were shooting crazily at everyone in sight. Zamush pushed the Jordanian sergeant in front of them with his hands raised, using him as a shield. It worked. The paratroopers took the Jordanian flag off the Kishle, and Zamush kept it as a souvenir.

By now Zamush was shirtless. He had discarded his uniform top, which had been covered by the blood of a paratrooper wounded while they were fighting through Wadi el Joz. A paratrooper found well-pressed uniforms of the Arab commander of the Kishle and brought one and the commander's silver pistol to Zamush. From the Citadel, Zamush and his men walked along the rampart of the city wall and cleared it from the Jaffa Gate to Mount Zion.

One of the paratroopers, a powerfully built American named Hopstadter, climbed to the top of David's Tower and found a

325

Jordanian drum there. He pounded the drum and waved his arms joyously for half an hour, as though to tell the people of Israeli Jerusalem that the battle was over and the Old City had been captured. Civilians in the King David Hotel and other buildings along the border came out on balconies and roofs when they heard the drumming from the top of the Tower. Zamush says, "It was a wonderful moment."

The final battle in the Old City was fought inside the northern wall near the New Gate, where a stubborn and determined squad of Jordanian soldiers were holed up in a small two-story hotel. Major Eilam and his deputy battalion commander, Major Dan Ziv, and a handful of Israeli soldiers, all dreading to be killed when the war was actually over in Jerusalem, tackled them.

The paratroopers killed one and wounded another of the defenders, but the Jordanians held the second floor of the hotel. Eilam says, "They were very tough people with lots of guns and ammunition. They didn't know the war was over."

The hotel had only one entrance and the Jordanians controlled it by firing shots and rolling grenades down the single staircase. Eilam rushed a team to the top of the city wall behind the hotel, but it could not reach the Jordanians.

Major Ziv tried to lead a group into the building across the narrow street in front of the hotel. Ziv was shot in the leg and arm. Once in the building, his men climbed to the roof and tried to take the Jordanians from there without success. Someone would have to get inside the hotel.

Eilam and two men went around to the side of the hotel and climbed up the outside to the second floor. By now, the Jordanians had retreated to the roof for a last stand. The Israeli platoon commander, Lieutenant David Baron, dashed up the hotel staircase, followed by a paratrooper with a light machine gun. They passed Eilam and climbed carefully up the stairs to the roof. Baron shot through the wooden door leading to the roof, heard someone scream in pain and kicked open the door.

Facing Baron were two Jordanians with their rifles aimed directly at him. For a split second, Baron thought he would be killed; but the Jordanians hesitated. The shot Baron expected never came. He fired and killed both of them. Looking to his left, he saw two more Jordanians hiding on that side of the roof. He killed them. He thought the fight was finished. Suddenly, there was another Jordanian. Baron shot him. Just as Major Eilam reached the roof, Baron spotted still another Jordanian behind the roof's water tank. He shouted a warning to Eilam. The Jordanian hurled a grenade, and fragments wounded Eilam in the left hand and leg. Then, Baron killed the sixth and last Jordanian on the roof—singlehandedly. It was 2:30 P.M.—the final organized action in Jerusalem.

Eilam put Captain Moshe "Mussa" Gilboa, his D Company commander, in charge of the battalion; and he and Major Ziv headed for Hadassah Hospital to have their wounds tended. Eilam took along Dr. Yigal Genat to make sure they could get out of the hospital again. Dr. Genat, a medical school classmate of Dr. Uri Freund, was the Seventy-first Battalion's doctor and had also covered for Dr. Eli Raz, the Twenty-eighth Battalion's doctor who had been wounded on Monday night. By nightfall, Eilam, Ziv and Genat were back with the battalion.

The paratroop brigade suffered by far the most casualties of the Israeli units fighting in Jerusalem. It had 92 killed, of whom 12 were officers and 80 enlisted men, and 407 wounded, of whom 34 were officers and 373 enlisted men. It was a high price.

The war for the Holy City was over. Damage inside the Old City walls was minimal. The only Holy Place that had been seriously hurt was the Church of St. Anne inside the Lions Gate. The church had been consecrated in A.D. 1140, and after the Crimean War it was restored under the care of the White Fathers. In 1956 when some old buildings were demolished, the twin Pools of Bethesda, dating to the Second Temple period, were uncovered on the grounds of the handsome church. Early Christians believed that in these pools Jesus performed his miracle of healing the paralytic.[1]

Although the Old City had been saved, the battle had cost many lives on both sides. Because of their energetic preparations, only about a dozen Israeli civilians had been killed. But the tragedy went beyond numbers. Paratrooper-journalist Israel Harel says, "I met people who lost their entire family in the Holocaust, came here and built a new family, usually at an age when they could have one child and not more, and they lost him in this war. I knew one couple—he had lost his whole

327

family; she had lost hers—they married and had one son and lost him."

Most Israelis wanted eagerly to visit the Western Wall, which had been out of reach and sight for nineteen years. But for the moment this was a privilege reserved for the soldiers who had fought their way there and for the VIPs. Uzi Narkiss took Mayor Teddy Kollek there. Kollek says, "We walked through Lions Gate and through the little gate that is called the Gate of the Tribes. On the Temple Mount there were hundreds, maybe thousands, of boxes of ammunition and hand grenades with British army markings. The thing that astonished me was the risk they had taken with the nearby mosque. If a shell had hit all this, it would have been terrible. On the contrary, we were so conscious of the danger to the mosques and the churches. It was almost unbelievable."

Of seeing the Western Wall, Kollek says, "I felt it was a historic moment. It was tremendous. But I was pretty calm. I don't get excited over big things. I get excited over little things."

Kollek went back a few hours later, bringing Danny Bloch with him. Bloch touched the Wall and saw the mayor do the same thing. Even nonreligious Israelis felt a need to confirm that after nearly two decades they were able to touch the Wall once again.

While they stood there, Dov Joseph, who had governed Jerusalem during the battle and siege in 1948, and General David Shaltiel, who commanded the Haganah in Jerusalem during those days (a veteran of the French Foreign Legion and a survivor of Dachau), both arrived. Narkiss said to them happily that the task they had not been able to complete in 1948 had now been achieved.

Late on Wednesday afternoon, HKJIMAC formed a convoy to bring out the families of the United Nations and the consulates from East Jerusalem and Shu'afat. Yehuda Arbell had acquired the Land Rover which belonged to Colonel Mohammad Daoud, the Jordanian liaison officer with the Mixed Armistice Commission, and helped form up the convoy of private cars and vehicles. A veteran of World War II and the 1948 war, Arbell always seemed to be where the action was. The first cars of the convoy carried many children. Suddenly, the entire convoy stopped and Arbell drove forward to inspect the trouble. Dead Jordanian soldiers still lay in the road. Arbell did not want the children to see the bodies. He got out of the Land Rover and covered them with paper boxes.

At his headquarters in the Russian Compound, Shaul Rosolio, the chief of police, was receiving Arab consuls and diplomats who were being dumped on the police by the army. They included representatives from many countries, but the PLO people had escaped. Five Arab consuls—three Egyptians, one Syrian and one Iraqi—had been taken prisoner in the Old City and, after being held overnight at the Ambassador Hotel, were brought to the police station. Rosolio had dealt with the Arabs since his days in joint British-Jewish police units during the Arab revolts in 1936. He said of his new charges: "They were terrified like I have never seen in my life. They were certain that they would be shot to death on the spot. It was a very unpleasant sight." Although he could speak Arabic fluently, he reassured them in English. The army took them and their families to a camp and soon let them return home. Rosolio adds, "At that time we were still optimistic."

That night after the radio news, Maj. Gen. Herzog broadcast his final commentary of the war. He said: "On the altar of the Temple Mount and Mount Moriah, the people of Israel offered up today priceless sacrifices which swell the toll of sacrifice by earlier generations. Our victory was not lightly achieved and at this moment it is well that we remember those who offered up their lives for the glory of the Almighty and the nation.

"Jews for generations to come will recount the tale of this day, of these people, of its army and its commanders, and will remember us, the privileged ones, who united as one people, who suddenly discovered that there are more important things than day-to-day dissension, who rose to the call of the hour and turned their backs on that internecine strife which had brought about the destruction of the Temple, and who lived to see this great moment. And in the words that Shakespeare put in the mouth of Henry V on the eve of battle: 'And gentlemen in England now a-bed/Shall think themselves accurs'd they were not here.'"

* * *

In Amman, people were equally moved by the suddenness and decisiveness of the battle. Maj. Gen. Ma'an Abu Nuwar said later, "It was certainly one of the most dramatic battles of the century." In an era of historic battles from Belleau Wood to Stalingrad to Iwo Jima, the battle for Jerusalem took its special place.

— Chapter 23 —

A DOCTOR'S STORY

Dr. AMIN AL-KHATIB WAS THE ONLY ARAB MEDICAL DOCTOR, or one of the very few, working in the streets of Jordanian Jerusalem during the battle. Most Arab doctors worked in the hospitals; but Dr. al-Khatib was out in a neighborhood where the war was being fought.

Dr. al-Khatib was the brother of Mayor Rouhi al-Khatib. They were members of a Muslim family that traced its roots in Jerusalem back for nine centuries. A religious family, it held the hereditary honor and responsibility for being in charge of the main prayers in the Old City on Friday, the Muslim Sabbath. The family's religious power was intertwined with political power.

Dr. al-Khatib had been born in the Old City, studied medicine in Damascus and practiced in Amman and Jericho and for UNRWA. But under Jordanian rule, he was not permitted to serve in the army. In 1958, he opened his own clinic at the Second Station of the Cross on the Via Dolorosa. He became a member of the Council of the Jordanian Red Crescent Society in Jerusalem with special responsibilities for first aid and for relations between the Red Crescent and the International Red Cross. In 1967, he was forty-one years old, a bright, astute, quiet-spoken but forceful man. He thought of himself as a Muslim, an Arab and a Palestinian. This is his story:

"We were expecting the war and we created subcommittees in each quarter outside the walls of the Old City. Because my house was located near the American Colony in Wadi el Joz, I was responsible for the whole area there. We formed emergency teams to help people if they needed food or water or if a house were blown up. It was well organized in our area; we were ready.

331

"We were disappointed because the government was not ready. The people were not allowed to have weapons at home like the Israelis who have a soldier in every house and everyone knows how to use a rifle and grenades. The Jordanians were afraid that if we had a weapon we would use it against them.

"The Jordanian government was not prepared for a war at all. When war took place we found nothing was ready. There were no soldiers in the middle of our area. On the border it was something else. It was our decision not to fight in our homes. If they come, let them come. A few rifles cannot defend against an army.

"Two weeks before the war I began to give first-aid lessons to the people in our quarter. It was the most crowded area. Every night we gathered together and discussed what we could do for our people. We told families, if you want to leave the quarter, leave now before war takes place. If not, you will not be allowed to go. We didn't want the others to panic and leave. During the war, many people from other quarters fled; but none from our quarter, none at all. We had some casualties, but we had the least casualties in our area.

"In the south, when one family left, the others followed. And so many died on the route between Jerusalem, Jericho and Amman. They died from heat and hunger or from airplanes. But nothing happened to those who remained, especially in the Old City and our quarter. We didn't want war, but we were obliged to endure it.

"I was worried about my mother, old and bedridden; my aunt who was also about ninety years old and bedridden, and my sister who was sick and bedridden. We couldn't move the three of them at all. My wife was with them and one of my sons who was ten years old had to bring them food and take care of them. My little children were moved to our neighbor's house, which had underground rooms. But the rest of us had to stay in our apartment, which was on the second floor.

"Monday night was hell for us and Tuesday morning we saw the Israeli soldiers around. The war went right through our quarter. We were the first to face it, but none of our people left their homes. We had underground rooms and our families were hidden there.

"The emergency team was collecting the dead and wounded people. I was there all the time. My headquarters was in a school; there we arranged about twenty-four beds for wounded people. We were well organized and had lamps because we expected the electricity to be stopped.

"One doctor, who came on the second day after things settled down, took care of the dead. He tried to take information about them, collect their properties and bury them in cemeteries and some of them in gardens around houses. In certain places they dug a big hole and buried them as a group. It was war and thank God there was no disease, although it was summertime.

"I was the only one who was hovering around treating the wounded people. My colleague was the only one who was taking care of the dead.

"In the Old City were many doctors and hospitals. They remained. There were doctors in Augusta Victoria Hospital, but not around that area. Patients had to come to the hospital to be treated. There were two young doctors in Wadi el Joz, but one had an accident to his ankle and couldn't move. People who went to his house were treated. Other doctors, such as those in Beit Hanina, found it very difficult to come to this area. We don't blame them at all.

"I tried to carry the wounded to the government hospital in the Old City and to the Augusta Victoria Hospital. At first I could not bring people to the Old City because the Israeli army was coming through and all the roads were full of soldiers, tanks and cars.

"I was the only one in that area who moved without any permit. I was wearing a white coat with a Red Crescent, and the driver, the same thing, and the mistress of the school was helping us. She was carrying a white banner. We had a station wagon. Our ambulance was ruined.

"The wounded soldiers were on the border and it was very difficult for us to go there. I reached Mr. Nuseibeh's house [in Nablus Road], but I could not reach the area toward Mount Scopus. From around Mr. Nuseibeh's house I gave wounded people first aid and moved the serious cases to the Old City and to Augusta Victoria. It was rather dangerous to move but we couldn't stay still. Being a doctor I had to do it.

"None of the Jews interfered with my work. None of them. They knew I was a first-aid man. If they stopped me, I said, I am a doctor and I want to pass; I have wounded people. They allowed me to pass.

"Early Wednesday morning, I saw some tanks. Believe me, we thought they were Iraqis. But I heard some of them speaking Hebrew and I said to my people, 'They are Jews! Take care!' I went to my house, and two bullets came through the window into the ceiling. The daughter of the owner of an Arab newspaper was there and was wounded. I took the bullet from her. I stopped the bleeding, stitched the wound and gave her some antibiotic. Thank God, she did not need surgery. Her father also had two bullets in him. I removed one from his shoulder and the other was removed a few days later in the hospital. This happened in my house because they saw a crowd of people there and they shot.

"Later, I went to the Israelis' headquarters near St. George's Cathedral, opposite the Alhambra cinema, and was given permission to go and help the children in the Spafford hospital in the Old City. I went to the Spafford hospital and helped the patients there. For the first three days I did not sleep at all. After the third day I went to sleep and slept for twenty-four hours.

"My brother [the mayor] was in one of the convents in the Old City. When the city was occupied and the gates were reopened, he came to my house and I took him to his house in Beit Hanina.

"There were between thirty-five and forty civilians wounded in my area. Altogether, around four hundred civilians were buried the first three days. We saw three hundred wounded.

"The soldiers who died were not ready to follow the orders given to them by their officers [to withdraw]. They were real Arabs. When they faced the Jews, they fought to the last bullet or until they were killed. Although their officers asked them to withdraw, they did not. Those who did not withdraw were killed. A few of them stopped the Israeli soldiers for a time, especially those who were near Nuseibeh's house and up in Sheikh Jarrah. To the last they would not give up. They did not surrender at all. We were proud of them. Most of them were Bedouins from Jordan. Very few Jerusalemites died while fighting, even in the army. These Bedouins were really good fighters and died for Jerusalem."

Chapter 24

THE TEMPLE SCROLL

A PECULIAR AND DRAMATIC ACHIEVEMENT OF THE WAR IN Jerusalem began at about four o'clock on Tuesday morning. Yigael Yadin, asleep in the Dan Hotel in Tel Aviv, was awakened by a telephone call from Maj. Gen. Rechavam "Gandhi" Zeevy at General Command headquarters. "Gandhi" recalls, "When you are down in the headquarters, you forget about sleeping and rest. It's like Las Vegas."

"Gandhi," who, like Yadin, cared ardently about archaeology, told Yadin that the paratroopers would soon seize the Rockefeller Museum, where thousands of fragments of Dead Sea Scrolls were deposited. They were in the care of an international team of archaeologists, headed by a Frenchman Ronald de Vaux and including French, American and British experts. The Jordanians allowed no Jews among them.

"Gandhi" said the army would make a headquarters of the Rockefeller Museum and he was worried about what would happen to the Scroll fragments. He told Yadin to send someone to the Rockefeller and make certain that the Scrolls and other antiquities were protected.

Yadin and his father, the late Professor Eleazar L. Sukenik, were both professors of archaeology and had been involved with the Scrolls since they had been spotted in caves above the Dead Sea by a Bedouin boy twenty years before. The Scrolls dated from the end of the Second Temple period and the lifetime of Jesus; they are the oldest known Hebrew texts. Those owned by Israel were displayed and studied in the Shrine of the Book, the uniquely beautiful building of the Israel Museum.

As soon as he received "Gandhi's" predawn call, Yadin telephoned his wife in Jerusalem and asked her to get in touch with Dr. Abraham Biran, Director of Antiquities for Israel;

Professor Nahman Avigad, Yadin's father's successor as Director of the Hebrew University Department of Archaeology; and Yosef Aviram, Secretary of the Israel Exploration Society. Carmella Yadin called Biran, the government official, and he telephoned the others.

In the middle of the morning, the three archaeologists, dressed in civilian clothes and without helmets, set out for the Rockefeller Museum in a half-track with Narkiss and Gur. At the museum, Jordanian fire from the Old City wall forced them back. They swung around to the rear of the building and dashed inside.

The museum was full of Israeli soldiers, many of them sleeping after a hard night's fight. Outside, the shooting was still going on. The archaeologists found that the Scroll fragments and other treasures were safe in locked rooms. Professor Avigad says, "Professionally, it was extraordinary. Suddenly, new horizons were open for us to excavate in Jerusalem. It was a very important date for archaeology."

In the middle of the next night, after eastern Jerusalem had been overrun, Yadin suddenly awoke again. He remembered that six years earlier, while on sabbatical leave in London, he had been approached by an American who said he represented a man who had other ancient scrolls to sell. "He wanted millions of dollars. He brought a little scrap of a scroll; I saw it was from an unknown book. It was in Hebrew but I couldn't identify it as a Biblical book. I mailed the piece back to him with my appreciation. He came back again and we negotiated. We agreed finally on $100,000. He was given $10,000 in advance, collected through friends. He left the little fragment with me and then disappeared. We corresponded for a year or two. Then, slowly, I forgot about it."

Now Yadin realized that the war had brought the dealer of the scroll within reach, either in eastern Jerusalem or in Bethlehem. "In the morning, I went immediately to Mr. Eshkol and said I would like the General Staff to second an officer of Intelligence to locate that dealer immediately. I knew it was an important scroll. Aharon Yariv, the chief of Intelligence, seconded a colonel, and I briefed him exactly and warned him that this chap might deny the whole thing.

"The colonel found the dealer in his shop in eastern Jerusalem. He denied it, of course, but when they told him they came on my behalf, he said he was waiting for ten years for me to come. He took them to his house in Bethlehem. There, under the tiles of his floor was hidden the scroll, which he was holding illegally also from the Jordanians. After that, the Temple Scroll was in our hands."

The dealer was arrested and the Temple Scroll confiscated. He was then severely interrogated for several days to find out whether he had more hidden materials. There was heated discussion at the highest level, especially between Dayan, Yadin and Raphael Levi, Dayan's advisor on Arab affairs, over whether the dealer should be paid for the Temple Scroll. Whether he was eventually paid is still classified information because if he had been paid, he would be in trouble with the tax authorities and with the Arabs for making a deal with the Israelis.

The whole incident is clouded in Middle Eastern smoke. Clearly, the Israelis strong-armed the dealer and then either paid him or claimed to have paid him for what they had taken. One story is that he received $130,000 for the Temple Scroll. And an official close to the affair says that today Israel would not take $10 million for the Scroll. The story is one that the Israelis involved prefer to keep classified.

— Chapter 25 —

"A RETURN TO ORIGINS"

THE APPROACH AND ADVENT OF WAR INSPIRED PEOPLE AROUND the world to rush to Israel and help. Most of them were Israelis desperate to join their families or military units; others were foreigners drawn to the flame of danger. Three of their stories are of special interest.

Zubin Mehta was conducting at the Pablo Casals Festival in San Juan, Puerto Rico, when the crisis heated up in the Middle East. He had become professionally involved with Israel in 1961 as a leader of the Israel Philharmonic and returned repeatedly. He says, "As my relationship with the orchestra grew, my relationship with the country grew also. I don't feel *for* them; I feel *out of* there. When I talk of Israel, I am talking from within."

In 1967, Mehta, now thirty-one, was the music director of the Los Angeles Philharmonic Orchestra and the Montreal Symphony Orchestra. He was a Parsee from Bombay, India; and his father was a violinist and a founder and conductor of the Bombay Symphony Orchestra.

On his way to Puerto Rico, Zubin Mehta had cabled the Israel Philharmonic from the Los Angeles airport: "If you need me, I'll come." He had heard that Erich Leinsdorf, the music director of the Boston Symphony Orchestra who was leading the Israeli orchestra at the time, had packed up and left the country.

When Mehta reached San Juan, he told his friend Isaac Stern, the world-famous violinist and a staunch supporter of Israel, "I have to go. Those people are without a conductor." Mehta canceled his planned tour as a guest conductor in Europe and flew to New York's Kennedy International Airport, where Stern arranged to have an Israeli visa waiting for him.

Sunday night, June 4, Mehta boarded a TWA plane for Tel Aviv. Approaching Rome the next morning, the pilot announced that war had broken out and he could not fly to Israel. At his hotel in Rome, Mehta found fellow conductor Leonard Bernstein and tried to persuade him to go on to Israel with him; but Bernstein had a commitment in Vienna he could not ignore.

Mehta lunched with the Israeli ambassador and told him emphatically, "You must send me!" Tuesday, the Rome airport was jammed with Israelis trying to get home, but he was whisked through the mob and onto the last El Al plane to Israel: "It was full of boxes that said 'USA' and the name of an army base in Georgia. We had two other passengers: David Horowitz, Governor of the Bank of Israel, and the *Newsweek* correspondent Curtis 'Bill' Pepper. Mr. Horowitz told me not to say anything to the man from *Newsweek* about the ammunition on this plane. As though he couldn't figure it out. We sat on the boxes and landed around ten o'clock Tuesday night. The airport was completely darkened, just the runway lights were on.

"In the dark at the airport, they were all shaking my hands. I was a symbol that one friend had arrived. I telephoned the concertmaster of the Israel Philharmonic in Tel Aviv, Zvi Haftel. He couldn't believe I was there. A Jeep brought me to the Dan Hotel; there Haftel met me and drove me to the orchestra's house where artists stay. I slept with them and the next morning telephoned Teddy Kollek in Jerusalem. Teddy said, 'Well, if you can, come.'

"I rented a car and drove alone the long way through the mountains. I picked up a couple of soldiers. They asked me, 'Who are you? You don't even speak Hebrew.' I knew the Hebrew word for 'conductor.' They had heard on the radio that I was there.

"In Jerusalem, I could hardly drive; the streets were full of troop carriers and tanks. I reached the King David Hotel and dropped my bag and went straight to Teddy's office. Ben-Gurion was sitting there. Teddy had things to do; he suddenly was the mayor of another city.

"So I was talking to Ben-Gurion. The news that the Western Wall was taken had just come, and he was elated. He told me *'This* we will never give back.' The Old Man was already

339

thinking that something will have to be given back. Then he said, 'Who wants the whole Sinai? What will we do with it? We don't even have Jews to fill our own country.' I said to myself that I wish the Arabs could hear this. He told me how the French mistreated Ho Chi Minh after World War II. He knew a lot about Zoroaster. I am a Zoroastrian. He told me about the Book of Esther. Esther married a Zoroastrian king, Ahasuerus, and saved the Jews.

"That Wednesday night I slept in the King David. My room faced the Old City. During the night I heard a terrific bang. But I was very tired and kept on sleeping. When I woke in the morning, a picture on the wall in front of the bed had a bullet through it.

Around six o'clock, I went with [Meir] 'Memi' de Shalit [of the Ministry of Tourism] through the Mandelbaum Gate to see Mount Scopus. It was his idea that a victory concert should be played in the amphitheater there on Saturday. Every step in the amphitheater was covered by tall grass. The whole amphitheater was just a grassy slope. But we decided we will do it. We'll get the army to clean it up. But the army told us the entire area was mined. No way were they going to let the public in. So on Saturday night we played the concert at the Convention Hall."

Narkiss' wartime Central Command headquarters became a concert hall of peace. Mehta conducted the "Hatikva," Israel's national anthem, and the overflow audience joined in singing what the *Jerusalem Post* called "one of the most enthusiastic renditions of 'Hatikva' ever heard." Pianist Daniel Barenboim and cellist Jacqueline du Pré, who had flown together into Israel a week before the war, played with the Israel Philharmonic. After Beethoven's Fifth Symphony, Mehta remembers, "When Teddy came on the stage at the end of the concert, that was just phenomenal. Teddy was the hero of Jerusalem. It was an adoration from the public." The following week, Daniel Barenboim and Jacqueline du Pré were married in Jerusalem.

Dr. Louis Miller, a tall, handsome, South African-born psychiatrist who was Director of National Mental Health Services in Israel's Ministry of Health, learned of the war while lecturing at Expo 67 in Montreal. Miller had served in the South African and British armies in World War II and came to Israel and stablished psychiatric services in the Air Force when the State was founded.

In 1967, on a year's sabbatical, he was setting up community centers on the Near West Side of Chicago for the State of Illinois. He had been invited to Montreal to lecture on the issues of urbanization. He says, "As I was lecturing, a Jewish social worker tiptoed up to me and whispered in my ear that the war had broken out. I finished my lecture; and then I arranged to get out of Montreal immediately, which was very difficult because of Expo. But someone found a seat for me to Toronto and then to Chicago. I informed Joyce [his wife] that I was on my way back and to try to get a *proteczia* [through personal connections] seat for me across the Atlantic from New York. She did. I got as far as Rome, but I couldn't get out of Rome to Tel Aviv.

"Of course, it was a tremendous blow to my ego. I wasn't seen as someone of quality. My impulse was to get back to Jerusalem and my work. I got out of Rome on the first El Al plane that took civilians. When we arrived, it was already dark and everything was blacked out.

"In Jerusalem, there was a tremendous sense of relief and elation. One felt one had to say some hymn of praise. The feeling was that you had come through the shades of hell, gone through the underworld, and come back, as it were, from the dead—that you might have gone under and you didn't go under. It wasn't so much a sense of triumph but of survival. This was admixed by the attitude of being back in the Old City and going to the Western Wall and by an outburst of historical, if not religious, identification. There was an atmosphere of a return to origins."

Jacobo Timerman, the editor of an Argentine weekly news-magazine, tells his story: "When the Six Day War started, I presented myself to the Israeli Embassy in Buenos Aires and asked to go to the war. I was then forty-four and had three children. The Israeli ambassador said, 'Relax, you are *meshuga*, crazy.' I said, 'I want to go to the war because I missed the '48 war, so this war is my war and I want to go and fight.' He said he would arrange my flight and prepare my papers.

"It was a tragedy at home. I had made my will with the lawyer, and my children were crying that their father is going

341

to the war. My wife, Risha, said, 'But you have three children.' I said, 'This is a spiritual problem; I must be in that war.'

"So I went to the police department to ask for a renewal of my passport. In Argentina, you must have it validated every six months. They said, 'We cannot give you a new passport because the mayor of Buenos Aires is suing you over one of your articles denouncing that he made some arrangement with the taxi drivers. You need permission of the judge who is in charge.'

"It was late to go to the judge, so the second day I went to the judge. He asked, 'What if you are killed?' I said, 'If I am killed it is my problem.' But the judge said, 'If you lose the case and you are killed, who is going to pay the mayor his indemnification?' He said, 'If you deposit the maximum amount of money in the name of this court, I can give you permission. If you do not lose the case and you are killed, your widow will get back the money.'

"So I must go to the bank. The bank was closed. The third day of the war I went to the bank and deposited the money, about one thousand dollars, and went back to the judge. The judge was closed. So the fourth day of the war I went back to the judge and he gave me the permission. I went to the police and they were closed. The fifth day of the war I went to the police. They gave me the passport, and I went to the Israeli Embassy and they said, 'Come back tomorrow and we will have everything arranged now that you have the passport.'

"The sixth day the war was finished. So it was six days of applications and applications. For six days I fought the war with applications."

Chapter 26

"THE END OF THE WARS"

AT 10 A.M. ON WEDNESDAY, COLONEL AMITAI FINALLY RE-
ceived approval to attack to the south. Shortly after noon, his
Jerusalem Brigade advanced toward Bethlehem with Major
Langotsky's recon unit in the lead. Near Ramat Rachel the
brigade suffered four more casualties from Israeli mines. In
the battle for Jerusalem, the Sixteenth Brigade, the hometown
unit, had forty-six killed, five officers and forty-one enlisted
men, and 244 wounded, twenty-four officers and 220 enlisted
men.

After the first echelon of the brigade had passed heading
south, Dr. Lichtenstein, still with his crutches and still prowling
around trying to help, drove to Ramat Rachel and saw a car
on the Bethlehem road. The doctor who lived on Bethlehem
Street and had never been to Bethlehem turned his car around
and raced back home. He told his wife, Hannah, the road to
Bethlehem was open and they had to go. With their two children
they drove immediately to Bethlehem. Dr. Lichtenstein remembers they had coffee with a friendly Arab named Nasser
and started to drive home again.

Near the monastery of Mar Elias, where the day before pilot
Dan Givon had bombed the Jordanian artillery position and
been shot down, the Lichtensteins met the headquarters company of the Jerusalem Brigade stopped in the road. The road
was too narrow for Dr. Lichtenstein's car to pass and he started
to drive to the shoulder. Someone yelled, "Mines!" and Lichtenstein stopped.

The army column had halted because the commander had
discovered Givon's crashed plane on the hillside beside the
road. Sergeant Major Mishael Yitzhakov, a lean, athletic dem-

olitions expert with a trim Genghis Khan mustache, was ordered to go in and see if he could rescue Givon, who lay on the hillside about one hundred yards from the road. Yitzhakov, whose parents came from Tashkent thirty years before, was a former paratrooper and member of the Knesset Guard. He was an ardent soccer goalie and had received eleven medallions for completing the famous Israeli Annual Four Day March to Jerusalem.

The hillside was thickly mined, and Yitzhakov could see the wreckage of the plane. Tense but confident in dangerous work he had survived many times before, he took with him a folding stretcher and a special knife for locating mines. He says, "I got down from my Jeep and walked slowly, slowly. I found five or six mines and I lay down a white tape to know how to come out the same way. When I came to the pilot, he was dead. He seemed serene—a young boy." Yitzhakov read the pilot's name on a knife he carried. He opened the stretcher and carefully lifted Givon's body. It slipped off the far side of the stretcher. As Yitzhakov pulled the body back, he stepped forward, and a mine blew off his right leg above the ankle.

He shouted to the soldiers on the road not to come in. He yelled that the pilot was dead and he was going to die also. He called out the pilot's name. He shouted to a close friend to take care of his parents and his wife and his two young daughters. Then he lost consciousness. The blood flowed from his severed leg.

Another soldier, following Yitzhakov's tape, reached him and brought in a wooden board and dragged him out. They had to leave the pilot's body.

Hearing the explosion of the mine that wounded Yitzhakov, Dr. Lichtenstein had tried to enter the minefield to help him but had been restrained. He treated the unconscious demolitions man by the side of the road. He stopped the blood and bound his leg stump with a large abdominal pad he had in his car. Hannah and the two boys sat in the car watching. Dr. Lichtenstein says, "It was a crazy, dangerous scene."

The army rushed Yitzhakov to Jerusalem and Biqqur Holim Hospital, where he had been born twenty-eight years before. He survived.

Wednesday evening, David Ben-Gurion came to Mayor

Kollek's office. They had a long history together. Kollek spread out a large map of the city, and he and his aides explained to Ben-Gurion how the Jordanian sector of the city had been conquered. They talked a very long time. Ben-Gurion was thrilled.

It was 8:40 Wednesday evening in Jerusalem when the UN Security Council in New York finally passed unanimously a resolution calling for a cease-fire in the Middle East war beginning at 10 P.M. Israeli time. The Soviet Union, which had at last reversed itself and proposed the simple cease-fire resolution, threatened to break diplomatic relations with Israel if it did not obey the UN resolution immediately. Foreign Minister Abba Eban said Israel would observe the cease-fire if the Arab nations would also. At first, Egypt, Syria and Iraq refused; but after a final belligerent blast from King Hussein, Jordan agreed. The U.S. Embassy in Amman cabled Secretary Rusk late Wednesday: "Israel's delay in honoring cease fire has cost Jordan any semblance of an army." Egypt took another day to join the cease-fire. Meanwhile, the fighting continued. The last element of the cease-fire went into effect on the Syrian front on Saturday evening.

For all the people of Jerusalem, Wednesday's end of the battle for the city brought overwhelming relief. For the Arab population, it meant deep disappointment; for the Israelis, it carried the excitement of triumph. The job of restoring life in the battered city began with small steps.

"When the curfew was lifted for an hour or two, I decided to return home to get at least my toothbrush," says Anwar Nuseibeh. "When we had left, we never expected to be away for long. We said there will be a battle and we will win and that will be that. The house was now a shambles. Terrible. One of our soldiers had been killed in front, another soldier behind. I felt numbness beyond anger."

There was no water, no electricity. He collected a few things and went back across the street until the curfew was lifted again. Then, they returned to their home. For the Nuseibehs, the war was scarring and intimate. As for so many others on both sides in Jerusalem the battle had been fought in their streets and their homes.

345

Wednesday night, Sammy Mustaklem heard on a radio that all municipal employees should report to the city hall near the Jaffa Gate in East Jerusalem. Mustaklem went and found a group of officials gathered, including Mayor Kollek, several military officers and members of the City Council. They said the priority was to remove the bodies from the streets. Mustaklem and his men were assigned the job. The firemen, inspectors and several civilians drove around and collected about 120 bodies and buried them in the Muslim cemeteries next to the Old City wall. Before the job was done, more than 650 bodies were buried.

There were also ordered to remove all meat and fish from refrigerators, because there had been no electricity, and to distribute milk and bread in the Arab quarters. No groceries or bakeries were open. Mustaklem organized a number of stations where people could come and get milk and bread for their families. Now that the fighting was done, efforts were made immediately to prevent disease, clean the streets, feed the population and restore the battle-torn city to some semblance of normal life.

Wednesday night, the paratroopers remained on duty in the Old City and along the entire border between Arab and Jewish Jerusalem to protect the Holy Places and prevent looting. Part of their job was to keep Israeli civilians from entering the Jordanian sector. Says Sergeant Artom who spent the night in the Old City, "Many of those civilians along the border had suffered a lot for nineteen years and said 'Let's get something.'"

Looting was a problem. "Some Jews acted in a reprehensible manner and we locked them up," Maj. Gen. Herzog says. The Spanish consul was not in his house near the spot where the paratroopers had crossed into Jordanian territory in Sheikh Jarrah. U.S. Deputy Consul General Hall says, "He had a great collection of silver. He lost everything. The Israelis took it all—just denuded the house."

Wednesday night, Hall moved his staff out of the severely damaged consulate to the house of the director of the American School of Oriental Research in Salah ed Din Street. That night, some Israelis, thinking the consulate deserted, backed up a large truck and prepared to move out the furniture. The young

American vice-consul on duty surprised them and chased them off.

Late Wednesday afternoon, after the Old City had been occupied, Lieutenant Mohammad Ali Khreisat, the young observer for the First Battery of the Jordanian Ninth Artillery Regiment, was still at his post at the monastery south of Jerusalem. The regiment had already retreated. Finally, Captain Mohammad Fayyadh, his battery commander, ordered the lieutenant to withdraw and join him at Abu Dis village.

Khreisat and his small observer group left the post they so long and loyally held, under covering fire from the Jordanian First Tank Company commanded by Captain Mamud Salim. Salim fired all his ammunition. In the darkness, they withdrew to the east and safety. "If we had had our heavier guns, the 155-mm howitzers, the results may have been different," Khreisat says, "but we fired all the ammunition we received during the war. We fired more than six thousand shells in those two days."

The Jerusalem Brigade moved easily through Bethlehem and by evening reached the hilltop at Kfar Etzion, where the Jordanian Arab Legion had wiped out or imprisoned three hundred Jewish settlers in May 1948. Now it was deserted.

The troops were exhausted, and Kamara's tanks and the vehicles had to be refueled. At 4 A.M. on Thursday, Amitai started south for Hebron. Along the way, the brigade captured twenty-five British-built Centurion tanks deserted by their Jordanian crews. Hebron was silent; no one fired at the Israeli column. The tired Kamara said, "It is really dirty work, and I have had so many experiences at this dirty work."

Also on Wednesday, while the paratroopers were entering the Old City, Colonel Ben-Ari's Ninety-fifth and 106th Battalions were finally ordered down into Jericho. They captured Jordanian 155-mm guns and more than twenty tanks stuck in deep mud. The men had with them trumpets they found in a Ramallah hotel and blew them in Jericho. The 104th Battalion advanced north almost to Nablus.

Ben-Ari, exhausted but still full of drive, sent his recon unit across the Jordan River. "The Americans were mad, and Dayan ordered me to retreat immediately and to blow up the bridges—

not so the Jordanians should not cross into Israel but so I should not cross the river and take Amman." He figured he could have occupied Amman in twenty minutes; there was no one to stop him. As Dayan wrote, "This will demonstrate our intention to cut ourselves off from the East Bank."[1] Ben-Ari says of Dayan's order, "That's how silly you can get." His engineers blew up the three Jordan River bridges.

On Thursday morning, Mohammad Koshour and his wife, Amenah, and their six children left the cave somewhere south of Jerusalem. Koshour says, "We started walking again. I would carry one of the youngest children a hundred meters and then go back and get the other. After we walked about two more hours, we met a man from our neighborhood who was coming back from his village near Hebron. He said it is better to go back; in Hebron there is nothing. So we turned back to Jerusalem.

"In the evening we met soldiers in the Kidron Valley. But they saw us with a white flag and saw that we were tired and without shoes and with children, and they said go home and stay there. At our home on Abu Tor everything was damaged. We found some dry milk and made milk for the children and slept outside that night. Most of my neighbors came back from Jordan and the mountains."

Koshour helped to clear the streets of bodies and remove the decaying perishables from damaged shops and houses. He remembers, "It was a terrible time." They located bodies in all the sections of the city where fighting had taken place. Most of those in uniform were near the Police Training School and the Sheikh Jarrah quarter, but they also found about forty inside the Old City and seven in the woods near the Government House. They buried them in mass graves in the cemetery outside the walls near the Lions Gate. Most of the soldiers, they found, were from the East Bank of the Jordan; the civilians were from Jerusalem.

The battle for Jerusalem cost an estimated 840 dead, including 14 Israeli civilians and 249 Arab civilians. Hundreds more lay wounded. Six hundred Israeli houses had been damaged and 250 Arab.[2] To grasp the unexpected ferocity of the battle for Jerusalem, it is only necessary to compare the figure for Israeli military dead in the entire Six Day War—777—

with the total Israeli military dead in Jerusalem and vicinity—186. Israeli military casualties in the battle for Jerusalem included 812 wounded (sixty-seven officers and 745 enlisted men) and twenty-four officers and 162 enlisted men killed. The official figure in Amman for Jordanian military dead in Jerusalem is 120, including three officers. Another source cites 396 Arab military dead in the battle.

In recognition of their courage and, in four cases, their sacrifice, Israel's highest military award, the Chief of Staff's Commendation, was given to ten men who fought in Jerusalem—two from the Jerusalem Brigade and the rest from the Fifty-fifth Brigade. They were Asher Driezin and Zerach Epstein of the Jerusalem Brigade and Yigal Arad, Jacob Chaimovitz, Eitan Nave and David Shalom at Ammunition Hill; Mordechai Friedman at Death Alley; Israel Shindler at the bridge by the Garden of Gethsemane; Shlomo Epstein in the bombardment in Pagi, and Chaim Rossek at the Rivoli Hotel. The awards to Nave, Friedman, Shlomo Epstein and Rossek were posthumous.[3]

The battle that Jordan had started with artillery and aircraft and at Government House ended with the loss of all Jerusalem and the entire West Bank of the Jordan River. Territory lived in by hundreds of thousands of Arabs was in Israeli hands.

Thursday's *Jerusalem Post* led the paper with an article that read:

After 60 hours of battle, Israel's forces yesterday controlled most of the West Bank of Jordan including the Old City of Jerusalem, Nablus, Ramallah, Jericho and Bethlehem; in Sinai they cut through the approaches of the Suez Canal and captured Sharm el-Sheikh, the chief of staff of Israel, Rav Aluf [General] Yitzhak Rabin, said yesterday.

After accepting the cease-fire in the early hours of Thursday, King Hussein held a hastily convened press conference at his military headquarters. Tired, unshaven, still in battle dress, and obviously depressed, the king said that the loss of Jordanian troops had been "tremendous" and that his country had been "almost left alone...by our many friends" in the battle for

Jerusalem. If the battle resumed, he said, Jordan "once again will fight to the last man."

Hussein made a public broadcast and said he had been deserted by President Nasser. "At least after my meeting with Nasser I thought we would now be ready for the battle of liberation," Hussein said. "But I was again let down."[4]

He took upon himself none of the blame for the decision to do battle against the Israeli forces or for the failure to prepare adequately the defenses of the section of Jerusalem he had ruled since 1948. He told his people over Radio Amman, in a voice cracking with emotion, "If in the end you were not rewarded with glory, it was not because you lacked courage but because it was the will of Allah."[5]

The victory opened a second era in the brief history of the State of Israel. She had pushed her borders away from her main population centers and taken control over the responsibility for great numbers of non-Jews. Since 1948, these West Bank Arabs had lived under the Jordanian flag but had steadily strengthened their sense of identity as Palestinians. They were not content to live indefinitely under Israeli rule guarded by Israeli guns. Many of them demanded a nation of their own; others preferred to return again to Jordanian sovereignty. Some Israelis called the 1967 war the War of Palestinian Liberation.

As the militants among the Palestinians sought to change the postwar status quo through violence, some Israelis wanted to tighten the screws of military occupation while others wished to return a demilitarized West Bank to Jordan. Few Israelis perceived any safety in the creation of a separate Palestinian state between Jordan and Israel. One prominent Israeli looks back at the 1967 war and says, "Maybe Hussein was relieved when he got rid of the West Bank. He's a very clever man. The Palestinians were always very militant. There was always a danger for him in the West Bank." That thinking gives the Hashemite king too much credit, but it expresses the dilemma of what would be the place of the Palestinian Arabs in a Middle East at peace.

The paratroop brigade command spent Wednesday night on the Temple Mount and Thursday morning set up headquarters in a building called the Verandah on the Mount of Olives.

Major Arik Achmon says, "We could see the Dead Sea and knew that Uri Ben-Ari's brigade was in Jericho. In the afternoon, Uzi Narkiss called a meeting for all the brigade commanders in his headquarters in the Convention Hall. We saw a small Piper flying from the Jordan Valley to Jerusalem, and Motta told me, 'I am sure this is old Uri Ben-Ari flying from the Dead Sea to the meeting in Jerusalem.' From the Verandah we could see the Dead Sea and the Old City and Ben-Ari flying to the meeting. It was unbelievable because it was so swift. Two days before we were in another world.

"We were so tired. When we finished the war, the main feeling was sadness. We knew many men had been killed. We heard constantly of friends who had been killed. We knew each one.

"Motta joked with me that he would come to work with me in civilian life because there would be no work in the army now. The wars are over. After two or three weeks we understood that the situation was more complicated. But then everything had been so swift that we felt that this was the end of the wars."

On Thursday, Dr. Uri Khassis, the medical officer in charge of Israeli Jerusalem, came up and visited Augusta Victoria Hospital. Despite the denials of Dr. Farah, the medical director, Dr. Khassis was convinced that some of the hospital's patients were Jordanian soldiers; he says, "There was no doubt that this was a stronghold of the Arab Legion." That same morning, a party came from the Knesset to apologize for the bombing of the hospital, and Dr. Farah received Israeli army doctors and doctors from Hadassah Hospital. They sent blood and serums and two suction pumps run by foot, because the hospital had no electricity.

Dr. Farah says he never could understand why the Israelis bombed the hospital. He admits he could only vouch for the absence of Jordanian troops until he and his people went into the basement Monday evening. If army units came into the area later, he saw nothing.

Dr. Majaj was outspoken about his feelings at the time. He compared 1948 and 1967: "The difference between '48 and '67 was that we had no water or electricity in 1948, but we had parties and dancing and singing. But after 1967, we had water

351

and food and electricity and nothing to celebrate. We were very depressed."

When the Israelis lifted the curfew for two hours at 1 P.M. on Thursday, Antonique Bakerjian was able to leave his house on the edge of the Armenian Quarter of the Old City. He inspected the UNRWA food depot near the Lions Gate and the medical supplies stored near Herod's Gate. At the medical supply center, he found windows shattered and cupboards of medicines overturned; but, he says, "I kissed the ground when I saw that our eight hundred tons of foodstuffs were intact."

Bakerjian walked out of the Damascus Gate to the American Consulate in Nablus Road and asked Mac Hall to report the situation to UNRWA headquarters in Amman and Beirut. He saw the damage to the YMCA and in Saleh ed Din Street saw destroyed shops, burned vehicles and dead bodies. Then he went home. Like so many Arabs, he was stunned by the totality of the defeat.

And yet as the city was opened up, Bakerjian shared in the spirit of warmth and friendship that swept over Jerusalem. Jewish friends and Jewish former classmates at the Terra Sancta School came to inquire for his safety. A man came all the way from Haifa to find him after all those years. Bakerjian remembers, "On both sides, people were looking for each other. These simple humans—who were not in the hands of the politicians and had no political aims—made it their business to go out and look for each other."

Hadassah Hospital's exhausted chief surgeon, Dr. Nathan Saltz, finally went home on Thursday evening. His wife and their two children were safe; the only damage was a broken milk bottle on the porch, shattered by a piece of shrapnel. "I thought I would sleep for a week, but after a few hours I woke up and went back to the hospital. I couldn't stay away. We had won the war and it was a great and glorious victory, but in the hospital you were there with results and it was not so glorious. You saw the permanently damaged people and they were very young. That sort of glory doesn't exist for the doctor who is working on the casualties, especially when you are there with the young soldier's parents or his wife or his girl friend.

"I was especially struck with the way the Sephardi [in this

case, Jews from Arab countries] relatives reacted, with a great deal of dignity and restraint. Many of them had come from Arab countries not very long before. This was the first time they had been engaged in a fight for *their* country; and they reacted with a great deal of pride.

"We all were fighting here for our own country in a very difficult situation in which we were surrounded on three sides. No one in the world thought we would come out of this—except us. It was a very special war, a very special situation, and it may sound corny but all of us were proud to be part of it."

Captain David Farhi of the military government of Jerusalem concentrated his attention on the Muslim leaders and Holy Places. He thought, "Everyone will be messing around with the Christian Holy Places. I will see what is happening with the Muslim Holy Places." He met with Muslim religious leaders in their homes, using his Arabic and knowledge of Islam to gain their confidence. But when he tried to enter the Temple Mount, he was stopped by Israeli soldiers. So he wrote a formal letter, which he signed himself, asking the commander of the military unit on the Temple Mount to permit him to enter; and he was allowed in: "You don't argue; you have to find a way."

Farhi was told to gather all the Muslim religious leaders in Jerusalem to meet with Dayan. They met at the entrance to the al-Aksa Mosque on the Temple Mount and went inside and sat down. Dayan assured them that the Israelis regarded the Temple Mount as belonging to the Muslims. He said he had only one demand: that Israelis be allowed to visit—not to pray on but to visit—the Temple Mount. That was agreed.

Anwar Nuseibeh came and asked Maj. Gen. Herzog to recover his wife's car, which had been taken by Israeli soldiers. The car was located and returned. Governor Anwar al-Khatib also called on Herzog and told him that Israeli troops had entered his village. Herzog says, "I was worried and asked him what they had done to him. He said, 'Nothing,' I asked, 'You expected them to behave as you would have behaved to us?' And he said, 'Yes.' And he broke down and cried. The shock."

At the Western Wall, Herzog had his own shock. "When we came there, we found the Arabs had built a public latrine against the Wailing Wall. It's not generally known. I gave instructions to knock it down immediately."

Herzog took time to search for his grandparents' graves on the Mount of Olives. His father's father had been a rabbi in Paris; and when he died, the teenaged Chaim Herzog had come with his father to bring his grandfather's body to Jerusalem.

Now, when he located the graves, he found that the stones had been smashed. He says, "Like the other graves, they had been desecrated by the Jordanians. I had the stones replaced; and on my grandfather's it says that it was replaced by his grandson, the first military governor of the West Bank."

On Thursday morning, the sniper fire in the Old City had been suppressed enough to risk bringing Ben-Gurion to the Western Wall. They put a helmet on his head. At the Wall, Ben-Gurion advised Mayor Kollek that if the city was to be truly reunited, the walls of the Old City should be torn down. Kollek protested that they were of historic significance. Ben-Gurion said they were built in Turkish times; they were not from Biblical days and were not holy. In his view, if Israel was to unite the city and prevent world pressure from trying to divide it again or internationalize it, the walls should be demolished. Ben-Gurion single-mindedly ignored history and archaeology and proposed a dramatic and drastic stroke that he believed would help keep all Jerusalem in Jewish hands.

To the Wall with Ben-Gurion and Kollek came Baron Edmond de Rothschild and a party from France and a group from England. Axel Springer, the West German publisher, and his right-hand man, Ernst Cramer, had also reached Jerusalem.

After the visit to the Wall, they all went back to the Kolleks' home for lunch. Tamar Kollek remembers, "Everyone was so exhilarated, despite the losses, that they felt that all the wars were over, that this was the end. Somebody asked Ben-Gurion what he thought, and he shocked us all by saying right away, 'No, this is not the end of the war. The Arabs cannot take such a defeat and such humiliation. They will never accept it.' We believed in his wisdom."

Mayor Kollek saw his first task was to bulldoze the Arab buildings of the Mughrabi Quarter clustered about the Western Wall and open a plaza to accommodate the two hundred thousand Jews who, he expected, would throng to the Wall for the holiday of Shavuot, the Feast of Pentecost, the following Wednesday. The minister of religious affairs protested to Maj. Gen. Herzog, but the job was quickly done and a spacious plaza created. The ministry and the municipal authorities argued over who would control this area. Herzog says, "I maintained that unless it went to the municipality we would regret it over the years because the only one who had any imagination was Teddy."

Some Jews were upset by the destruction of the Arab neighborhood in front of the Western Wall. Charles Weiss, the American-born night editor of the *Jerusalem Post*, watched the bulldozers tear open a room. On its exposed wall hung pictures of the Arab family who had been removed from the house the night before. Weiss wrote a story of what he had seen; and Ted Lurie, the newspaper's editor, killed it. Instead, the paper ran a story of how Moses Montefiore had tried to buy the area a century earlier and been refused; that, Weiss said, was supposed to legitimize the Israeli action.

Weiss reacted strongly: "The Wall became for me a symbol of how Israel was losing an opportunity for a breakthrough. All that happened was we ended up with all these territories. It could have been parlayed into something magnificent. Then, in Jerusalem people would have been ready to accept you. Instead, it was important to find room for thousands of people to come to the Wall. The real breakthrough for peace didn't occur.

"What happened at the Wall was, for me in any case, the first indication that Israel was not interested in peace as much as it was in consolidating a misconception of the Zionist dream, which was that the land, the territory, was the important thing and not the ability to blend into the area. I think the Zionist dream means living together. At that time, the Arabs were completely flattened out. Israel could have achieved what it ostensibly sought for twenty years—which was acceptance. It had an opportunity for initiative and instead it went in the wrong direction."

A meeting was held on the patio behind the King David Hotel. Minister of Defense Dayan, Mayor Kollek, General Narkiss, Police Chief Rosolio and Meron Benvenisti, whom Kollek had assigned to administer the former Jordanian sector

355

of the city, were among those present. Kollek pressed to start restoring municipal services, especially in the devastated eastern part of the city and in the Old City. Dayan raised the question of opening up the city. Rosolio said: "I regard this not as a technical problem but a political decision—as long as you know it is a risk."

Dayan wanted the immediate destruction of the barriers along the Green Line that had divided the city. Kollek was more cautious, but, as he said later, "Dayan thought the Arabs would accept facts once created. And the quicker you created the facts, the better. Why wait?

"In tearing down the buildings next to the Western Wall and tearing down the buildings between New Gate and Jaffa Gate, I had similar feelings. And tearing down buildings in no-man's-land occupied by squatters. From in front of the Western Wall, we moved 106 Arab families, people from Algeria. I felt people would accept in war what they wouldn't accept afterwards and we could get the whole thing done.

"But on demolishing the wall dividing the city, I was scared. I was concerned about violence if the two people met while they were still armed. Obviously, I was wrong. Dayan had a better insight. We adopted this idea and it worked."

Police Chief Rosolio organized law and order swiftly in East Jerusalem. The sector had no administration, no services, no water, milk, garbage collection. "There was complete chaos," he says. "I did not make the mistake of policing the east side with Israeli personnel. They would have had to concentrate on staying alive. And I had to have people who knew the city and who people were." He was able to convince former Jordanian policemen to stay on the job by warning them that if there were violence, burglary, rape and looting on their side, it would be their responsibility.

The Green Line was eradicated, and Arabs and Jews moved freely in each other's sector, and there was no violence.

Israel annexed East Jerusalem on June 28 and reunified the city after nineteen years of division.

Looking back at the events of those brief days in the spring of 1967, Yehuda Avner says, "What happened in 1967 is a very important contribution to understanding the Israeli psyche of our times. I am a citizen of Israel and will not permit a situation in which my children's children, my grandchildren, will have to face a Jerusalem cut in two; that ridiculous nine-mile narrow waist; those totally vulnerable, indefensible boundaries. I will not allow that to happen. The lesson of 1967 is that territory is important."

Yitzhak Rabin says, "I believe that out of the four major wars two really changed the situation. Of course, the most important war that we have ever fought was the War of Independence for the establishment of Israel. Then the Six Day War because it was the first war that gave Israel the kind of areas which you can exchange to get peace. It changed Israel's security situation. The Yom Kippur War proved it."

Haim Barlev saw another reason for the Six Day War's importance: "My generation, those who fought the War of Independence, had the feeling that that war had not accomplished everything that rightly should have been accomplished. And the main object was eastern Jerusalem. Jews lived there then. Attempts to hold the Old City were made and we lost it.

"When Jordan did not stand up to her commitments that we could go to the Wailing Wall and to Mount Scopus, we felt cheated. Therefore, when the Old City and Mount Scopus were captured—or freed, if you want—we felt a big relief and an accomplishment that went back twenty years. Divided Jerusalem during those years had been a focus of a kind of guilt complex. When we finally completed the job, it was like paying off an old debt."

The decision to take Jerusalem, said the poet-soldier Chaim Guri, "was something mysterious, fateful, inevitable. It was something spiritual that nobody could control."

And Aviad Yaffe said, "It was not only unexpected. It was involuntary. We wouldn't have started a war for it; but once the war showed us that we were insecure even in Jerusalem, it was forced on us.

"A religious leader said Jerusalem was often taken away from us by force, but never did we give up voluntarily what God had given us. It was a factor in the Jewish heart."

A Christian leader in the city, a man who lived in Jerusalem the greatest part of his life, who loves the city deeply, also speaks of what happened in those three days in the spring of 1967 as part of a long pattern. The Greek Orthodox Metropolitan of Caesarea Vassilios says of the Israeli conquest: "It was an important landmark in the long history of Jerusalem. It was another change. We know that Jerusalem has undergone many changes. This is one of so many.

"The various administrations have gone and the Church of Jerusalem remains. This is what strikes everybody: Romans, Byzantine, the Arabs, the Crusaders, the Turks, the British, the Jordanians, the Israelis . . .

"The Gates of Hell won't prevail over the Church. Whatever may happen, the Church *has* to remain because the Church is founded by Christ and Christ is eternal. His mystical body which is the Church must be eternal. It is not a human institution; it is divine, certainly governed by men, but behind man is God who reigns all over the world.

"Jerusalem is the unique center of the three monotheistic religions. Without fanaticism, we can live together harmoniously. But fanaticism hasn't any room in religion. There are fanatic Jews. When they meet us, they spit on us. I respect them because they have their own religion. I demand and I want them also to respect mine. Why does he spit on me? It has happened to me many times. He does it because of fanaticism. That's why he cannot live together with me.

"I say the Orthodox Church has the truth in its faith. I don't try to convert others. I keep it to myself. Let the Jew who feels his religion is the only true religion keep it for himself. I don't want him to be a Christian, an Orthodox. Let him also not try to convert me. So we may still live together. If they are tolerant, then we can live together.

"You have good people everywhere. We have good and bad people. In every family. Even the fingers are not equal."

Some time after the war, a paratrooper who had lost several of his closest friends on Ammunition Hill came back to visit the site of that battle. As he walked around for hours over the ground where he had fought, he saw a veiled woman dressed all in black sitting silently. She sat there a long time. Finally, she asked him in English, "Did you fight here?"

"Yes," he said.

She asked him, "How were the Jordanians? How did they fight?"

He said, "They were very brave." And he told her about

them and how bravely they had fought. He told her that he had been wounded and his friends killed.

She said, "My husband was a captain and the commander of the hill."

The long hostility between Jews and Arabs in Palestine climaxed not only in the war of 1948, which the new State of Israel fought to assure its existence, but also in the spring of 1967, when the two nationalisms met not with reason and compromise and goodwill but with threats and guns and conquest. In 1967, nearly two thousand people were killed and wounded in the city of Jerusalem.

Years before, Albert Einstein, a Zionist as well as a physicist and philosopher, had foreseen this harsh course of the conflict. In 1915 he had written: "It would seem to me that men always need some . . . fiction in the name of which they can hate one another. Once it was religion. Now it is the state . . ." At the same time, ". . . a rational relationship between countries, a sane union and understanding between nations, mutual advancement without interference with the particular customs of any nation . . ." were what he devoutly wished for. He believed: ". . . We, that is to say the Arabs and ourselves, have to agree on the main outlines of an advantageous partnership which shall satisfy the needs of both nations. A just solution of this problem . . . is an end no less important . . . than the promotion of the work of construction itself . . ."

The 1967 battle between Jews and Arabs for the city of Jerusalem was a sad milestone in the history of mankind. When the fighting was over, the people from both sides mingled in the streets of the reunited city with joy and relief. But the drum of history kept rolling to the war of October 1973, to more acts of terrorism and reprisal, to the invasion of Lebanon in 1982, to fears and tension. And the question lingered in the minds of all peoples: Can modern Jerusalem ever find tranquility, "a sane union and understanding?" Can Jerusalem—the place of David and Jesus and Mohammad—ever truly become the symbol and the city of peace?

Appendices

— Appendix A —

THE FUTURES OF PEOPLE IN THIS BOOK

IN MANY CASES, WHAT HAPPENED LATER TO PEOPLE WHO fought or were otherwise involved in the battle for Jerusalem in 1967 may be of interest. Here are the situations of some of them at the time of this writing.

Arie "Arik" Achmon, in 1967 the intelligence officer of the paratroopers' Fifty-fifth Brigade, is now the director general of an inland charter airplane company called Kanaf and also a sports parachutist.

Captain Taysir Mohammad Ali, adjutant of the Ninth Artillery Regiment, became a colonel and an artillery instructor in the Jordanian Command and Staff College.

Yigal Allon was deputy prime minister and foreign minister in the Cabinet of Prime Minister Yitzhak Rabin until 1977 and died after a heart attack on February 29, 1980, at the age of sixty-one.

Colonel Eliezar Amitai, commander of the Sixteenth Infantry Brigade which included the Jerusalem Brigade, is now director general of Attarim, the company developing the waterfront of Tel Aviv.

Corpsman Yigal Arad, decorated for his role on Ammunition Hill, was killed at the Suez Canal in 1973.

Yehuda Arbell now works for the Canadian Pacific, which runs the Jerusalem Plaza Hotel.

Michael Arnon, the consul general in New York, was the Secretary to the government during the 1973 war and is now the chairman of the executive committee of the Israel Museum and chairman of the Israel Securities Authority.

Lt. Col. Eldad Avidar, deputy commander of the Tenth Brigade, the Harel Mechanized Brigade, is now in the Israeli Ministry of Education.

Yehuda Avner, who worked in the prime minister's office in 1967, served as counselor to the Israel Embassy in Washington when Yitzhak Rabin was ambassador and later as an advisor to prime ministers Rabin and Begin. Avner's secretary, Rivka Sofer, and her husband were killed by a terrorist bomb in Jerusalem's Zion Square.

Nahman Avigad, the director of the Department of Archaeology at the Hebrew University, devoted ten years to excavating the Jewish Quarter of the Old City, including houses that had been burned by the Romans in A.D. 70 and the Nea Church built by the Byzantine emperor Justinian.

Yosef Aviram, the archaeologist for the Israel Exploration Society, became the director of the Archaeological Institute of the Hebrew University.

Dr. Uriel Bachrach, the microbiologist who was the deputy commander of civil defense for the northern part of the city in 1967, was in charge of civil defense in the Old City in the 1973 war. He now heads the molecular biology department in the Hadassah Medical School.

Sergeant Doron Bar-Adon, who fought with the Jerusalem Brigade's recon unit, lives in Hofit on the sea north of Netanya, teaches drawing and painting and works as a sculptor and environmental artist.

Menachem Begin became the prime minister of Israel in 1977.

Yohanan Beham, acting director of the Israel Museum, represents the Hebrew University in the New England area of the United States.

Colonel Uri Ben-Ari, commander of the Harel Mechanized Brigade, was the deputy commander of the Southern Front under Haim Barlev in the 1973 war and later Israel's consul general in New York.

Benedictos, the Greek Orthodox Bishop of Jerusalem and Patriarch of Palestine, died in the Hadassah Hospital on December 10, 1980, at the age of eighty-eight.

Major Uri Berez, commander of Tank Company P of the Harel Mechanized Brigade, is now a police officer in Beersheva.

Daniel Bloch, who assisted Mayor Kollek, is a senior journalist with *Davar*, the Mapai Party newspaper, and a member of the board of the Israel Broadcasting Authority. His mother was killed at Entebbe.

Dr. Yosef Burg, the minister of social welfare in 1967, became the minister of the interior in the Cabinet of Prime Minister Menachem Begin.

Hilarion Capucci became the head of the Greek Catholic Church in Jerusalem and active with the Arab nationalists against Israel. In August 1974 he was arrested when the Israeli police found arms and explosives in his car. He was sentenced to twelve years in prison but was later released and exiled.

Colonel Mohammad Daoud, Jordan's liaison officer with HKJIMAC, became a general and was briefly the prime minister of Jordan. When he died, he was buried in the Muslim cemetery between the Lions Gate and the corner of the Old City wall in Jerusalem.

Moshe Dayan was the defense minister during the 1973 war and was blamed for Israel's initial defeats. He served in Menachem Begin's Cabinet as foreign minister and resigned in October 1979. On October 16, 1981, he died in Tel Aviv at the age of sixty-six.

Shlomo Doron has retired as the principal of the Ge'ulim School and lives in Beit Ha-Kerem. The school honored Dan Givon, the pilot who was killed protecting the school. A monument has been erected for Givon across the road from Mar Elias.

Lt. Col. Asher Driezin, commander of the 161st Battalion of the Jerusalem Brigade and leader of the battle for Government House, changed his name to Asher Dar. He served in the army twenty-seven years and became the director general of the Magen David Adom. He is now the chairman of the Town Council of Kiriyat Ono near Tel Aviv.

Major Uzi Eilam, commander of the paratroopers' Seventy-first Battalion of the Fifty-fifth Brigade, became a brigadier general in the reserves and director general of the Israel Atomic Energy Commission.

Avi Ella, the student on Abu Tor in 1967, is now the manager of the Caesar Hotel in Elat, which was built and owned by his family.

Zerach Epstein of the reconnaissance unit of the Jerusalem Brigade died of cancer in Jerusalem in 1977 at the age of forty-three.

Major Amnon Eshkol, who commanded the reconnaissance company of the Harel Mechanized Brigade, now is the commander of a brigade in the Israeli army.

Major Yacov Even, company commander in the 163rd Battalion of the Jerusalem Brigade, later became the commander of the brigade.

Dr. George Farah, the medical director of the Augusta Victoria Hospital, created and became the director of the Princess Basma Jerusalem Crippled Children Center, which is on the Mount of Olives and helps Arab children of the West Bank, Gaza and Jerusalem.

Captain David Farhi became a colonel and advisor on Arab affairs for the military governor of the West Bank. He died in 1977 while swimming off the beach near Netanya, Israel.

Captain Mohammad Fayyadh, commander of the First Battery of Jordan's Ninth Artillery Regiment, was killed fighting the Palestinians in 1971.

Dr. Uri Frand, the doctor of the paratroopers' Fifty-fifth Brigade, was shot down in a helicopter over Suez in the 1973 war and killed.

Lt. Col. Yosef Fradkin, commander of the paratroopers' Twenty-eighth Battalion, still lives in Tel Adashim, nurturing his five acres of nursery fruit trees as he has done for thirty years with wartime interruptions.

Dr. Uri Freund, who was decorated for his work on Abu Tor, is a surgeon at Hadassah Hospital. When he was serving in a field hospital near the Suez Canal during the 1973 war, a call came in for a doctor and Dr. Uri Frand volunteered. Uri Freund waved him good luck. The helicopter was shot down by an Egyptian missile.

Dr. Yigal Genat, doctor of the paratroopers' Seventy-first Battalion, is a psychiatrist in Jerusalem.

Colonel Mordechai Gur, commander of the Fifty-fifth Brigade of paratroopers, was given charge of the Northern Command and later became Israel's chief of staff.

Siema Hazan, the young ambulance driver, after the war rejoined the national police with whom she had worked before joining the Magen David Adom.

Brig. Gen. Atta Ali Hazzáa, commander of the King Talal Brigade, is now retired from the Jordanian army.

Maj. Gen. Chaim Herzog, the military governor of the West Bank and the former Jordanian sector of Jerusalem immediately after the war, served as Israel's ambassador to the United Nations from 1975 until 1978.

Captain Johnny Heyman, intelligence officer of the 163rd Battalion of the Jerusalem Brigade who fought on Abu Tor, became a lawyer and was killed in the 1973 war.

Dennis Holland, the chief administrative officer at Government House, retired from the United Nations in 1980 after serving as chief of communications services of the UN.

Lt. Col. Floyd M. Johnson, Jr., retired as a colonel of the U.S. Marine Corps in 1968 after twenty-nine years of service and became an archaeologist.

Major Aaron Kamara, commander of D Company of tanks attached to the Jerusalem Brigade, is the chief license supervisor of Jerusalem.

Lieutenant Karni Kav, who was in charge of the women soldiers in the paratroopers' brigade, is now a lieutenant colonel in the Israeli army.

Captain Eli Kedar, who fought on Abu Tor and led the Jerusalem Brigade into the Old City, became the military governor of Hebron and after the 1973 war rose to the rank of lieutenant colonel. He now owns a restaurant in Jerusalem.

Dr. Uri Khassis, the medical director in Jerusalem during the war, is the administrator of Hadassah University Hospital on Mount Scopus.

Dr. Amin al-Khatib still runs his medical clinic at the Second Station of the Cross on the Via Dolorosa in the Old City.

Rouhi al-Khatib, mayor of Jordanian Jerusalem in 1967, lives in Amman and still regards himself as the mayor of East Jerusalem.

Mohammad Koshour, who with his family hiked south from Abu Tor toward Hebron, worked for the Jerusalem city hall after the war in charge of Muslim projects in the Old City. Each year on the identical days in June he walks the same route alone.

Major Mansaur Kreishan, commander of the Second Battalion of the King Talal Brigade in Jerusalem, was killed by mortar fire in 1969.

Shlomo "Chich" Lahat, the Israeli military governor of the former Jordanian sector of Jerusalem, became the mayor of Tel Aviv.

Major Yosef Langotsky, commander of the Jerusalem Brigade's reconnaissance unit, became a colonel and an Israeli military attaché in Washington, D.C. Later, he headed the government company that searches for oil in Israel. He married Ruth Eilam, the widow of Ya'acov Eilam, the paratroop captain killed at the bridge near the Garden of Gethsemane.

Dr. Israel Lichtenstein, who tended the wounded on crutches, is now the chief director of the French Hospital, which treats patients with chronic diseases and advanced cancer.

F. T. Liu, the principal political advisor to the United Nations Truce Supervision Organization in Jerusalem during the war, is now director and deputy to the under secretaries general for special political affairs at United Nations headquarters in New York.

Arthur Lourie of the Foreign Ministry served as Israel's ambassador to Canada and to the United Kingdom and died in Jerusalem on October 4, 1978, at the age of seventy-five.

Dr. Amin S. Majaj became the director of the Augusta Victoria Hospital.

Zubin Mehta became the music director of the New York Philharmonic in 1978.

Dr. Louis Miller became the chief national psychiatrist of Israel in the Ministry of Health and established mental health services throughout the country.

Lieutenant Yohanan Miller, platoon leader in C Company on Ammunition Hill, was killed in the 1973 war.

Sammy S. Mustaklem, the fire chief, is now a lieutenant colonel in the Jerusalem Fire Brigade and still commands the fire station where he served in 1967.

Captain Nir Nitzan and Captain David Rutenberg, who fought together on Ammunition Hill, served together again in the 1973 war, when the Fifty-fifth Brigade was badly mauled. Rutenberg was seriously wounded and Nitzan saved his life. Nitzan is now a lieutenant colonel in the Israeli army.

Major General Ma'an Abu Nuwar, who commanded the Jordanian brigade in Jerusalem before the war and made a detailed study of the battle afterwards, served as Jordan's assistant chief of staff and later as its ambassador to the Court of St. James's. In 1976, he became the mayor of Amman.

Lt. Col. Zvika Opher, commander of the Sixty-eighth Battalion of the Jerusalem Brigade, was killed tracking terrorists in 1969.

Shimon Peres rejoined the Labor Party and served as minister of defense following the 1973 war. He became chairman of the Labor Party in 1977 and was its candidate for prime minister in 1981.

Meira Perry became the curator of prints of the Israel Museum.

General Yitzhak Rabin, the chief of staff of the Israel Defense Forces in 1967, was the prime minister of Israel from 1974 to 1977.

Lt. Col. Arik Regev, operations officer of the Central Command, was killed in the Jordan Valley on July 27, 1968, while pursuing a group that had infiltrated into the West Bank.

General Abdel Moneim Riad, the Egyptian officer who commanded the Jordanian front from Amman, later became the chief of staff of the Egyptian army and was killed in 1969 by an Israeli shell near the Suez Canal.

Major Moshe Rosenblatt, deputy commander of the 163rd Battalion of the Jerusalem Brigade, died a few years after the war of a heart attack.

Meir Samgar, the Israeli judge advocate general, became a justice of the Israel Supreme Court.

Colonel Zaid bin Shaker, commander of Jordan's Sixtieth Armored Brigade, fought the Syrians in 1970 and as a lieutenant general became commander-in-chief of the Jordanian armed forces.

Minister of Justice Ya'acov Shimshon Shapira after the war became chairman of the Cabinet committee on Jerusalem and drafted the law reuniting the city.

Major Menachem Sharfman, commander of the garrison on Mount Scopus, spent a year as commander of the Israeli garrison in Hebron and then became governor of the southern Sinai from 1968 until 1973. He fought in Lebanon before retiring from the army in 1978 as a lieutenant colonel.

First Sergeant Yorash Shina'ar, Major Yosef Yaffe's operations sergeant who fought on Ammunition Hill, was killed in the 1973 war.

Israel Shindler, a sergeant badly burned on the bridge at the Garden of Gethsemane, was killed in the Sinai in the 1973 war.

Ahmed Shukairy, first head of the Palestine Liberation Organization, was dismissed from his post after the Six Day War and died of a brain tumor in Amman University Hospital at the age of seventy-two on February 26, 1980.

Major Moshe Stempel, deputy commander of the paratroopers' Fifty-fifth Brigade, was later killed fighting in the Jericho Valley.

Shmuel Tamir served as minister of justice in the Cabinet of Prime Minister Menachem Begin.

Yosef Tekoah was Israel's ambassador to the United Nations during the 1973 war and later served as the president of the Ben-Gurion University.

Jacobo Timerman became the publisher of the daily *La Opinion* of Buenos Aires, spent thirty-three months in jail and under house arrest, and in September 1979 was permitted to emigrate to Israel, where he joined the staff of the daily newspaper *Ma'ariv*.

Charles Weiss, the night editor of the *Jerusalem Post*, remained on its staff until 1974 and later became the Pentagon correspondent of the Voice of America.

Martin Weyl became the director of the Israel Museum.

Yigael Yadin studied the Temple Scroll for a decade and published three scholarly volumes on it. He served as deputy prime minister in the government of Prime Minister Menachem Begin.

Aviad "Adi" Yaffe, Secretary to Prime Minister Eshkol, became a member of the Knesset and died on May 19, 1977.

Major Yosef "Yossi" Yaffe, commander of the Sixty-sixth Battalion of the Fifty-fifth Brigade, was killed in 1975 when his Jeep hit a mine at Nitzana in the Negev desert.

Lieutenant Uzi Yalovsky, company commander in the 163rd Battalion of the Jerusalem Brigade on Abu Tor, was killed in the Sinai in the war of 1973.

Aharon Yariv called a Court of Inquiry after the war to investigate why the paratroop Fifty-fifth Brigade had attacked without adequate intelligence information. He held the post of director of military intelligence until 1972 and then became advisor to Prime Minister Golda Meir on problems of terrorism. He served in her Cabinet as minister of transport and in Yitzhak Rabin's Cabinet as minister of information. He created and now heads the Center of Strategic Studies at Tel Aviv University.

Captain Raphael Yeshaya, deputy tank commander in the Jerusalem Brigade, is a lawyer in Ashdod.

Sergeant Major Mishael Yitzhakov, the demolition expert who lost his right foot trying to rescue pilot Dan Givon, survived four operations. He served in the 1973 war, visiting the families who lost men in battle. He owns a gift and book shop in the Diplomat Hotel in Jerusalem.

Dr. G. Douglas Young, founder of the Institute of Holy Land Studies on Mount Zion, died in 1980.

Captain Yoram Zamush of the Fifty-fifth Brigade was one of the first Israeli soldiers to cross the Suez Canal in 1973 and was badly wounded.

Maj. Gen. Rechavam "Gandhi" Zeevy was the commander of the Central Command from July 1968 until the 1973 war. Always colorful, he kept three lions as living symbols of his Command and of Jerusalem. He retired from the army in 1973.

— Appendix B —

ACKOWLEDGMENTS

WRITING A BOOK OF A TRUE STORY IS BOTH A SINGULARLY lonely task and also a collaboration over many months with a surprising number of people. Many have helped me with this book, but the accuracy of the facts and the validity of the judgments presented here are totally my own responsibility.

This book was conceived with Marc Jaffe, then editor at Bantam Books and now editor-in-chief of Ballantine Books, over lunch in New York in 1977. By the end of that talk, we had agreed on the concept—the story—sixty hours long and four thousand years deep—of the battle for the City of Jerusalem in June 1967; and we both were excited by the vision of an idea worth doing.

Since then, I have made a half dozen trips to Jerusalem and others to Amman, Jordan; throughout Israel from Elat in the south to Kibbutz Cabri in the north; to the United Nations, Washington, London, Boston and even Gaza—wherever I could locate survivors of those sixty hours in Jerusalem. This book is based virtually entirely on my personal interviews with those participants. Documents, newspapers and books were used for background information or to check a fact or confirm a memory. With few exceptions, I taped these interviews and accumulated in the process ninety-seven 90-minute tapes. Approximately 150 interviews are the ore of this book.

I thank each of those who made the effort and took the time to answer my questions. Most of them are represented in the book itself, and I cannot list them all here. Only two participants whom I wanted to interview refused me. King Hussein did not make himself available; and Moshe Dayan, whom I had known well for nearly twenty years, repeatedly declined to talk about his role in this war.

373

There are a number of people without whose help this book could not have been written or at the very least it would have been less thorough, accurate and interesting. Mayor Teddy Kollek, whom I met on my first trip to Israel for *Look* magazine in 1961, seduced me to the beauty and fascination of Jerusalem over the subsequent years during which we became friends. In that meaningful sense, he inspired this book. He is a unique, vital figure on the world scene; and his love for Jerusalem and his conviction that Arabs and Jews can live together in peace in the city hold hope and promise for the future. Jerusalem since 1967 would have been a poorer place without him. Teddy opened doors for me, pointed me in fruitful directions and enabled me to base my work repeatedly at the lovely Mishkenot Sha'ananim guesthouse in Jerusalem.

Crucially important to this project has been Leora Nir, a most able researcher, interpreter, locater of missing people and a good friend. She did much to organize and make effective my visits to Israel.

I want to thank especially in Israel for their assistance and guidance Shula Eisner, Jacob and Edna Barnea, Israel Harel, Abraham Rabinovich, Yohanan Beham, Dr. Louis Miller, Ephraim Poran, Yehiel Shemi, Judith and the late David Farhi, Amnon Cohen, Jay Bushinsky, Joseph Abboudi of the Israel Air Force and U.S. Consul General Michael H. Newlin.

U.S. Ambassador Alfred L. Atherton, Jr., made possible the cordiality and trust on which my visit to Amman was based. There, Lt. Gen. Zaid bin Shaker, the commander-in-chief of the Jordanian army, offered to be my personal host and arranged a highly efficient and useful series of interviews with Jordanian military personnel who fought in the battle. Unlike the highly bureaucratic Israel Defense Forces, the Jordanian army leadership was cooperative and effective in arranging interviews for the book. The Israeli military headquarters staff was most useful by not interfering with my work and for giving active duty personnel permission to talk with me about the battle.

In Amman, U.S. Ambassador Thomas Pickering and Chief of Mission Roscoe Suddarth were most helpful, as was Amer Khammash, who was the Jordanian chief of staff in 1967 and the Court Minister to King Hussein when we talked. Amman's Mayor Ma'an Abu Nuwar generously shared with me his study and knowledge of the battle. And a personal word of thanks to Major Ahmed Shangiti, for his help, skill and attentiveness in overseeing my work schedule in Amman. Access to and the cooperation of officers and men who fought for Jordan in Jerusalem have given this book an important and unique dimension.

In the United States, I would express my appreciation to, among others, Marc Jaffe, Gail Russell, Bernard Lewis, Vera Stern, William A. Johnson, Brian Urquhart, Floyd and Alice Johnson, Peter Brunswick, Lynn Goldberg, Hamilton Whyte, Robert N. Ginsburgh, David C. Humphrey of The Lyndon Baines Johnson Library and especially over many years to the late Paula Mattlin for her wisdom and encouragement, her spirit and love. An able writer and a respected book and magazine editor in her own right, she shared with me much of the research and travel to Jerusalem involved in this book while fighting a long, courageous battle against cancer, which finally ended on June 10, 1981, at the cruelly young age of forty-seven. Mark, David and Nancy Moskin helped in many ways. Mrs. Phyllis Jackson, my literary agent for twenty years, saw this book started before her untimely death. Don Congdon took over those responsibilities with enthusiasm and judgment, and I have constantly found I could depend on him for guidance and patience. Those whose good sense and typing skill helped make order out of the various stages of this manuscript include especially Vivien Lyons and Gail Russell, and also Dell Green Martin, Erna Helwig, Cecelia Hobbs and Nancy Moskin. George Buctel created the original maps with skill and care, and Benis M. Frank prepared the index.

— Appendix C —

THE USE OF LANGUAGE

THE EXPANSE OF TIME AND THE CONFINES OF SPACE IN THIS story make inevitable problems for the writer. Over the centuries, various names have been used to identify a particular place. In the use of place names and the transliteration of Arabic and Hebrew place and personal names, I have tried to select the forms that are most familiar, most comprehensible in English and offer no offense. The solution of such problems is often not satisfactory to everyone.

For example, I have used the Lions Gate, the name in most common use today; but it is called St. Stephen's Gate in Christian tradition and Bab Sitty Miriam in Arabic.

In Arabic, I have tried to handle the many problems of transliteration in the most respectful and acceptable manner. For example, "al" or "el" before a family name is often an honorary article, and I have used the "al" form for consistency wherever I knew it was applicable. Whenever possible, I have used an Arabic personal name in the Anglicized form the individual prefers.

Similarly, the use of Hebrew names in English requires either the choice of the name's holder or of a commonly used and acceptable version. Secondary sources are useless. For example, in their books Abba Eban and Moshe Dayan use General Chaim Bar-Lev; Yitzhak Rabin's memoirs uses Chaim Barlev; a respected history of the Israel Defense Forces uses Haim Bar Lev, and in Yigal Allon's history of the Israeli army it is Haim Bar-Lev. I have used Haim Barlev because it is the general's preference.

— Appendix D —

BIBLIOGRAPHY

ALTHOUGH THIS STORY WAS WRITTEN PRIMARILY BY INTER-
views with participants in the battle and residents of Jerusalem,
this bibliography of many of the books related to the city and
the war may prove useful to others. Some of these volumes
were used as supplementary sources for understanding the background, events and ramifications of the battle.

Allon, Yigal, *Shield of David—The Story of Israel's Armed
Forces*. New York: Random House, 1970.

Antonius, George, *The Arab Awakening*. New York: Capricorn
Books, 1946.

Bahat, Dan, *Carta's Historical Atlas of Jerusalem—A Brief
Illustrated Survey*. Jerusalem: Carta, The Israel Map & Publishing Co. Ltd., 1973.

Barkai, Mordekhay, ed., *Written in Battle—The Six Day War
as Told by the Fighters Themselves*. Tel Aviv: Le'Dory Publishing House.

Ben-Sasson, H. H., ed., *A History of the Jewish People*. Cambridge: Harvard University Press, 1969.

Bethell, Nicholas, *The Palestine Triangle*. New York: G.P.
Putnam's Sons, 1979.

Benvenisti, Meron, *Jerusalem: The Torn City*. Minneapolis:
The University of Minnesota Press, 1976.

Bondy, Ruth, *Mission Survival*. New York: Sabra Books, 1961.

Bondy, Ruth; Smora, Ohad; and Bashan, Raphael, eds., *Mission Survival*. New York: Sabra Books, 1968.

377

Brecher, Michael, *Decisions in Israel's Foreign Policy*. London: Oxford University Press, 1974.

Bull, General Odd, *War and Peace in the Middle East*. London: Leo Cooper, Ltd., 1973.

Churchill, Randolph S. and Churchill, Winston S., *The Six Day War*. London: William Heinemann Ltd., 1967.

Collins, Larry and Lapierre, Dominique, *O Jerusalem!* New York: Simon and Schuster, 1972.

Comay, Joan, *Israel—An Uncommon Guide*. New York: Random House, 1969.

Dayan, Moshe, *Moshe Dayan: Story of My Life*. New York: William Morrow & Company, Inc., 1976.

Dupuy, Trevor N., *Elusive Victory: The Arab-Israeli Wars, 1947–1974*. New York: Harper and Row, 1978.

Eban, Abba, *Abba Eban—An Autobiography*. New York: Random House, 1977.

Eisenberg, Azriel, *The Great Discovery—The Story of the Dead Sea Scrolls*. London and New York: Abelard-Schuman Limited, 1956.

Elon, Amos, *The Israelis—Founders and Sons*. New York, Chicago, San Francisco: Holt, Rinehart and Winston, 1971.

Eshel, Lt. Colonel; Jacobson, Jay; and Eshel, Tamir, eds., Number 6. *Born in Battle—The Six-Day War*. Israel: Eshel-Dramit Ltd., 1979.

Feniger, Ofer; prepared by Feniger, Yael and Shapiro, Abraham, *The World Lived Within Me*. Jerusalem: Academic Press, 1978.

Fifty-one Commendations by the Chief of Staff. Tel Aviv: Chief Education Officer, Ministry of Defense Publishing House (in Hebrew).

Gilbert, Martin, ed., *Winston S. Churchill*. London: William Heinemann Ltd., 1975.

Gilbert, Martin, *Jerusalem—Illustrated History Atlas*. Jerusalem: Steimatzky's Agency Limited, 1977.

Gur, Lt. Gen. Mordechai; translated by Gillon, Phillip, *The Battle for Jerusalem*. New York: Popular Library, 1978.

Harel, Israel, ed., *Lions Gate: The Battle in Jerusalem as Experienced by the Fighters of the Paratroopers' Brigade*. Tel Aviv: Ma'arachot Publishing House, Israel Defense Forces Ministry of Defense Publications, 1977 (in Hebrew).

Hashavia, Arieh. *A History of the Six-Day War*. Tel Aviv: Ledory Publishing House.

Hashavia, Arieh, *The Reconnaissance Company; The Story of Micha Kapusta Ben-Ari*. Heroic Tales of the Six Day War. Tel Aviv: Staff Headquarters Publications, Chief Education Officer, Ministry of Defense Publishing House (in Hebrew).

Herzog, General C., *Israel's Finest Hour*. Radio Commentaries. Israel: Maariv Book Guild, 1967.

Herzog, Chaim, *The Arab-Israeli Wars*. New York: Random House, 1982.

Hussein of Jordan: My "War" With Israel as told to Vick Vance and Pierre Lauer. New York: William Morrow and Co. Inc., 1969.

Jiryis, Sabri, *The Arabs in Israel*. New York and London: Monthly Review Press, 1976.

Josephus, *The Jewish War*. Harmondsworth, England: Penguin Books, 1970.

Kraemer, Joel L., ed., *Jerusalem—Problems and Prospects*. New York: Praeger Publishers, 1980.

Kollek, Teddy and Pearlman, Moshe, *Jerusalem: A History of Forty Centuries*. New York: Random House, 1968.

Kollek, Teddy and Kollek, Amos, *For Jerusalem: A Life*. Tel Aviv: Steimatzky's Agency Ltd., 1978.

Landau, Eli, *Jerusalem the Eternal—The Paratroopers' Battle for the City of David*. Tel Aviv: OTPAZ Ltd., 1968.

Lewis, Bernard, *Islam in History*. London: Alcove Press Ltd., 1973.

Lewis, Bernard, ed., *Islam and the Arab World*. New York Alfred A. Knopf, 1976.

Luttwak, Edward and Horowitz, Dan, *The Israeli Army*. New York: Harper & Row, 1975.

Mansfield, Peter, *The Arabs*. London: Allen Lane Penguin Books Ltd., 1976.

Marshall, Brig. Gen. S.L.A. and the Editors of American Heritage Magazine and United Press International, *Swift Sword— The Historical Record of Israel's Victory, June, 1967*. New York: American Heritage Publishing Co., Inc., 1967.

Moskin, J. Robert, *Report from Jerusalem*. New York: Institute of Human Relations Press, 1977.

Natan, Moshe, *The War on Jerusalem*. Tel Aviv: OTPAZ Ltd., 1968 (in Hebrew).

Near, Henry (editor of English edition), *The Seventh Day— Soldiers' Talk About The Six-Day War*. Harmondsworth, England: Penguin Books, 1971.

Nuwar, General Ma'an Abu, *In the Path of Jerusalem*. Royal Jordanian Army: Courtesy of the author (in Arabic).

Nyrop, Richard et al, *Area Handbook for the Hashemite Kingdom of Jordan*. Washington, D.C.: U.S. Government Printing Office, 1974.

Pearlman, Moshe and Yannai, Yaacov, *Historical Sites in Israel*. Tel Aviv: Massadah-P.E.C. Press Ltd., 1964.

Peres, Shimon, *From These Men—Seven Portraits*. London: Weidenfeld and Nicolson, 1979.

Prittie, Terence, *Eshkol: The Man and the Nation*. New York: Pitman Publishing Corp., 1969.

Rabin, Yitzhak, *The Rabin Memoirs*. New York: Little, Brown and Co., 1979.

Rabinovich, Abraham, *The Battle for Jerusalem, June 5–7, 1967*. Philadelphia: The Jewish Publication Society of America, 1972.

Runciman, Steven, *A History of the Crusades*. Volume 1, 3 volumes. Cambridge: Cambridge University Press, 1951–54.

Said, Edward W., *The Question of Palestine*. New York: Times Books, 1979.

Setton, Kenneth M., ed., *A History of the Crusades*. Volume I. Philadelphia: University of Pennsylvania Press, 1955.

Shamis, Giora and Shalem, Diane, *The Jerusalem Guide*. London and Jerusalem: Abraham Marcus Ltd., 1973.

Taylor, A.J.P., *How Wars Begin*. New York: Atheneum, 1979.

Thompson, James Westfall and Johnson, Edgar Nathaniel, *An Introduction to Medieval Europe 300–1500*. New York: W.W. Norton & Company Inc., 1937.

Vester, Bertha Spafford and introduction by Thomas, Lowell, *Our Jerusalem—An American Family in the Holy City 1881–1949*. Lebanon: Middle East Export Press, Inc.

Wilson, Evan M., *Jerusalem, Key to Peace*. Washington, D.C.: The Middle East Institute, 1970.

Yadin, Y. ed., *Jerusalem Revealed—Archaeology in The Holy City 1968–1974*. Jerusalem: The Israel Exploration Society in cooperation with "Shikmona" Publishing Company, 1975.

— Appendix E —

SOURCE NOTES

THESE NOTES INDICATE THE SOURCES OF VARIOUS STATEMENTS and quotations in this book. Other direct quotations came from interviews.

Chapter I   The Dreams of Men/pages 3–11.
1. Joel L. Kraemer, ed., *Jerusalem—Problems and Prospects* (New York: Praeger Publishers, 1980), p. 132.
2. Bertha Spafford Vester, *Our Jerusalem—An American Family in the Holy City 1881–1949* (Lebanon: Middle East Export Press, Inc.), p. 280.
3. Kraemer, *Jerusalem—Problems and Prospects*, pp. 164–5.
4. Vester, *Our Jerusalem*, p. vii.
5. Kraemer, *Jerusalem—Problems and Prospects*, p.112.
6. Meron Benvenisti, *Jerusalem: The Torn City* (Minneapolis: The University of Minnesota Press, 1976), p. 31.
7. Ibid., p. 35.
8. Richard Nyrop, *Area Handbook for the Hashemite Kingdom of Jordan* (Washington, D.C.: U.S. Government Printing Office, 1974), p. 25.

Chapter II   "We'll Have to Take It Back"/pages 12–36.
1. *The Jerusalem Post,* 12 May 1967.
2. *The New York Times,* by James Feron, 16 May 1967.
3. Yitzhak Rabin, *The Rabin Memoirs* (New York: Little, Brown and Co., 1979), p. 68.
4. Gideon Rafael, *The Diplomatic History of the Six Day War,* (London: The Anglo-Israel Association, 1975), p. 5.
5. *The Jerusalem Post,* Reuters dispatch, 16 May 1967.
6. Ibid., 18 May 1967.

7. Ibid., 24 May 1967.

8. Martin Gilbert, ed., *Winston Churchill* (London: William Heinemann Ltd., 1975), pp. 558–579.; Nyrop, *Area Handbook for the Hashemite Kingdom of Jordan*, p. 19.

9. *The Jerusalem Post*, UPI, 24 May 1967.

10. Abba Eban, *Abba Eban—An Autobiography* (New York: Random House, 1977), p. 363.

11. C. Herzog, *Israel's Finest Hour* (Israel: Maariv Book Guild, 1967), p. 6.

12. *Hussein of Jordan: My "War" With Israel* (New York: William Morrow and Co. Inc., 1969), p. 46.

13. Nyrop, *Area Handbook for the Hashemite Kingdom of Jordan*, p. 34.

14. *The New York Times*, 27 February 1980.

15. Herzog, *Israel's Finest Hour*, pp. 10–11.

16. Shimon Peres, *From These Men—Seven Portraits* (London: Weidenfeld and Nicolson, 1979), p. 51.

17. Randolph S. Churchill and Winston S. Churchill, *The Six Day War* (London: William Heinemann Ltd., 1967), p. 58.

Chapter III   Monday Morning—Israeli Jerusalem/pages 37–55.

1. Rabin, *The Rabin Memoirs*, p. 30.

2. Israel Ministry of Foreign Affairs

3. *Hussein of Jordan*, p. 64; Odd Bull, *War and Peace in the Middle East* (London: Leo Cooper, Ltd., 1973), p. 113; Interview with F. T. Liu, United Nations.

4. *Hussein of Jordan*, p. 65.

5. Herzog, *Israel's Finest Hour*, p. 24.

Chapter IV   "Thus, Yehuda, The War Begins"/pages 56–79.

1. *The Jerusalem Post* by Charles Weiss, 6 June 1967.

2. J. Robert Moskin, *Report from Jerusalem* (New York: Institute of Human Relations Press, 1977), p. 34.

3. Teddy Kollek and Amos Kollek, *For Jerusalem: A Life* (Tel Aviv: Steimatzky's Agency Ltd., 1978), p. 192.

Chapter V   Monday—Jordanian Jerusalem/pages 80–102.

1. Kraemer, *Jerusalem—Problems and Prospects*, p. 89–90.

2. *Hussein of Jordan*, p. 61.

3. Larry Collins and Dominique Lapierre, *O Jerusalem!* (New York: Simon and Schuster, 1972). p. 455.

Chapter VI   Ten Rubles in His Pocket/pages 103–107.
1. *The Jerusalem Post,* 6 June 1967.

Chapter VII   "The Omen of Good Luck"/pages 108–123.
1. Vester, *Our Jerusalem,* p. 85.
2. Moshe Pearlman and Yaacov Yannai, *Historical Sites in Israel* (Tel Aviv: Massadah-P.E.C. Press Ltd., 1964), p. 23; St. Matthews 27.
3. Martin Gilbert, *Jerusalem—Illustrated History Atlas* (Jerusalem: Steinmatzky's Agency Ltd. 1977), p. 105.
4. Bull, *War and Peace in the Middle East,* p. 114.
5. Ibid., p. 115; Interview with F. T. Liu, United Nations.
6. Abraham Rabinovich, *The Battle for Jerusalem* (Philadelphia: The Jewish Publication Society of America, 1972), p. 117.
7. Kraemer, *Jerusalem—Problems and Prospects,* p. 167.
8. Rabinovich, *The Battle for Jerusalem,* p. 124.

Chapter VIII   Counterattack at Government House/pages 124–138.
1. Pearlman and Yannai, *Historical Sites in Israel,* p. 24.

Chapter IX   Advance into Jordan/pages 139–148.
1. Herzog, *Israel's Finest Hour,* p. 26.

Chapter X   "Do We Dare Do It?"/pages 149–159.
1. Peres, *From These Men—Seven Portraits,* p. 164.
2. Gilbert, *Winston S. Churchill,* pp. 558–561.

Chapter XI   Contingencies/pages 163–165.
1. Jeremiah 6:1.

Chapter XII   The Tanks—The Crucial Battle/pages 166–194.
1. Collins and Lapierre, *O Jerusalem!* p. 302.
2. Rabinovich, *The Battle for Jerusalem,* p. 157.
3. Ibid., p. 337.
4. All cables quoted are from Volume IV of the Middle East Crisis File, Country File, National Security File declassified at The Lyndon Baines Johnson Library in Austin, Texas.

Chapter XIV   The Breakthrough/pages 214–221.
1. Trevor N. Dupuy, *Elusive Victory: The Arab-Israeli Wars, 1947–1974* (New York: Harper & Row, 1978), p. 298.

Chapter XVIII   Ammunition Hill/pages 247–267.
1. *Fifty-one Commendations by the Chief of Staff* (Tel Aviv: Chief Education Officer, Ministry of Defense Publishing House) in Hebrew, p. 130.

Chapter XIX   Abu Tor/pages 268–279.
1. Herzog, *Israel's Finest Hour*, pp. 30–31.

Chapter XX   The Ridge/pages 280–292.
1. *The Jerusalem Post* by Malka Rabinowitz, 7 June 1967.

Chapter XXI   The Old City/pages 293–306.
1. Joel 3:12.
2. Mordechai Gur, *The Battle for Jerusalem* (New York: Popular Library, 1978), p. 362.

Chapter XXII   Reactions/pages 307–330.
1. Kraemer, *Jerusalem—Problems and Prospects*, p. 165; and Giora Shamis and Diane Shalem, *The Jerusalem Guide* (London and Jerusalem: Abraham Marcus Ltd., 1973), pp. 94–96.

Chapter XXVI   "The End of the Wars"/pages 343–359.
1. Moshe Dayan, *Moshe Dayan: Story of My Life* (New York: William Morrow & Company, Inc., 1976), p. 370.
2. Benvenisti, *Jerusalem: The Torn City*, p. 81.
3. *Fifty-one Commendations by the Chief of Staff*.
4. *The Jerusalem Post*, UPI report, 9 June 1967.
5. *Hussein of Jordan*, p. 97.

INDEX

ABOUT THE AUTHOR

J. ROBERT MOSKIN, AN HISTORIAN AND AN AWARD-WIN-
ning journalist, has reported from Jerusalem many times since
1961, when the city was still divided between Jordan and Israel.
Formerly the foreign editor and member of the editorial board
of *Look* magazine, he has been an editor-at-large for the *Saturday Review* and is now the senior editor of *World Press
Review* magazine. He served for five years as the editorial
director of the Aspen Institute for Humanistic Studies. His
reporting has received awards from the Overseas Press Club,
the National Headliners Club, the Newspaper Guild of New
York and the Sidney Hillman Foundation. A contributor to
many magazines, he has written several books, including *Mo-
rality in America, Turncoat, The Decline of the American Male*
(co-author), *Report from Jerusalem* and most recently *The U.S.
Marine Corps Story*, which received the Distinguished Service
Award from the Marine Corps Combat Correspondents Association. Mr. Moskin holds degrees in American history from
Harvard and Columbia Universities and during World War II
served with the U.S. Army in the Southwest Pacific. He has
been a member of the Boards of Directors of the U.S. Marine
Corps Historical Foundation and of The Jerusalem Foundation,
Inc.